D1520975

Radical Pragmatics

Radical Pragmatics

EDITED BY

Peter Cole

Department of Linguistics
University of Illinois at Urbana–Champaign
Urbana, Illinois

ACADEMIC PRESS

A Subsidiary of Harcourt Brace Jovanovich, Publishers

New York   London   Toronto   Sydney   San Francisco

P99.4.P72R3

ACADEMIC PRESS, INC.
111 Fifth Avenue, New York, New York 10003

United Kingdom Edition published by
ACADEMIC PRESS, INC. (LONDON) LTD.
24/28 Oval Road, London NW1 7DX

Library of Congress Cataloging in Publication Data
Main entry under title:

Radical pragmatics.

    Includes bibliographies and index.
    1. Pragmatics--Addresses, essays, lectures.
2. Languages--Philosophy--Addresses, essays, lectures.
3. Language and logic--Addresses, essays, lectures.
I. Cole, Peter, Date.
P99.4.P72R3   410   80-68551
ISBN 0-12-179660-4

PRINTED IN THE UNITED STATES OF AMERICA

81 82 83 84   9 8 7 6 5 4 3 2 1

Contents

On Time, Tense, and Aspect: An Essay in English Metaphysics 63

Emmon Bach

Stalnaker on Pragmatic Presupposition 83

Charles E. Caton

Syntactic and Semantic Indeterminacy Resolved: A Mostly Pragmatic Analysis for the Hindi Conjunctive Participle 101

Alice Davison

Intuitions and Presuppositions 129

Keith S. Donnellan

Contents

List of Contributors

Numbers in parentheses indicate the pages on which the authors' contributions begin.

Jay David Atlas* (1), Department of Philosophy, and Intercollegiate Linguistics Program, Pomona College, Claremont, California 91711

Emmon Bach (63), Department of Linguistics, University of Massachusetts, Amherst, Massachusetts 01003

Charles E. Caton (83), Department of Philosophy, University of Illinois at Urbana-Champaign, Urbana, Illinois 61801

Alice Davison (101), Department of Linguistics, University of Illinois at Urbana-Champaign, Urbana, Illinois 61801

Keith S. Donnellan (129), Department of Philosophy, University of California, Los Angeles, Los Angeles, California 90024

Charles J. Fillmore (143), Department of Linguistics, University of California, Berkeley, Berkeley, California 94720

Georgia M. Green (167), Department of Linguistics, University of Illinois at Urbana-Champaign, Urbana, Illinois 61801

Paul Grice (183), Department of Philosophy, University of California, Berkeley, Berkeley, California 94720

Stephen C. Levinson (1), Department of Linguistics, University of Cambridge, Cambridge, CB2 9DA, England

Jerry L. Morgan (167), Department of Linguistics, University of Illinois at Urbana-Champaign, Urbana, Illinois 61801

* PRESENT ADDRESS: Wolfson College, Oxford OX2 6UD, England

Geoffrey Nunberg (199), Department of Linguistics, Stanford University, Stanford, California 94305

Ellen F. Prince (223), Department of Linguistics, University of Pennsylvania, Philadelphia, Pennsylvania 19104

Jerrold M. Sadock (257), Department of Linguistics, University of Chicago, Chicago, Illinois 60637

Ivan A. Sag (273), Department of Linguistics, Stanford University, Stanford, California 94305

Dan Sperber (295), 33 rue Croulebarbe, Paris 75103 France

Deirdre Wilson (295), Department of Phonetics and Linguistics, University College London, London, WC1E 6BT, England

Preface

A pervasive question in generative grammar since *Syntactic Structures* (Chomsky, 1957) has been whether the relationship between meaning and pronunciation is best captured by a single set of principles, or whether the facts of natural language are best explained in terms of "the interplay of a number of relatively simple and autonomous subsystems [Bach, this volume, p. 64]." Some of these subsystems may be nonlinguistic in the sense that they deal with aspects of language use (performance) rather than with the principles involved in knowledge of the language per se (competence).

The purpose of this volume is to explore the consequences of viewing language as a number of relatively autonomous subsystems. The division of linguistic data in this way raises two immediate questions: (*a*) What are the subsystems? (*b*) Which data are to be accounted for by which subsystems?

Radical pragmatics concerns itself with two possible subsystems: semantics, that system involved in the determination of conventional (or literal) meaning; and pragmatics, that system involved in the determination of nonconventional (or nonliteral) meaning.[1] Radical pragmatics is the hypothesis that many linguistic phenomena, which had previously been viewed as belonging to the semantic subsystem, in fact belong to the pragmatic subsystem. The examination of the degree to which such a view can be supported is the question that relates to many of the chapters in this volume.

---

[1] I use these terms vaguely. As will be seen, the domains of semantics and pragmatics differ considerably from author to author.

Among the chapters that deal directly with this question are those by Davison, Grice, and Sadock. Grice's earlier essays on conversational implicature (1975 and 1978) have constituted the basis for much of the current work in pragmatics. In his contribution to this volume, Grice argues that the notion of conversational implicature may make it possible to defend Russell's (1905) theory of descriptions in the face of Strawson's (1950) apparently conclusive counterexamples.

Davison shows that the Hindi conjunctive participle -*kar* is not ambiguous, as might be thought from the wide variety of uses of the construction, but rather has a single, rather vague meaning which is "filled in" in particular cases by pragmatic principles of the sort described in Grice (1975). In a similar vein, Sadock argues that a sentence of the form *almost P,* though used as if it meant, among other things, 'not P', does not literally mean 'not P'. Rather, 'not P' is conversationally implicated by *almost P.*

The chapters by Davison, Grice, and Sadock, when viewed collectively, constitute classic instances of radical pragmatic argumentation. They show (or attempt to show) that aspects of meaning previously taken as integral to the literal meaning of a construction are in fact due to the application of principles of conversational implicature to a more restricted literal meaning.

The contributions by Atlas and Levinson and Sperber and Wilson have a similar goal to those of Davidson, Grice, and Sadock. Atlas and Levinson argue that given a rather enriched view of logical form (one that does not require that two sentences have the same truth conditions to have the same logical form), Gricean principles allow the reduction of many (if not, eventually, all) instances of presupposition to entailment and conversational implicature. Thus, the goal of Atlas and Levinson's contribution is essentially identical to that of Grice. The chapter deals primarily with the logic and pragmatics of *it* clefts.

Sperber and Wilson consider whether irony has a Gricean explanation. They conclude that it does, but not according to the explanation proposed by Grice (1975, 1978). According to Sperber and Wilson, a crucial step in the inference that something has been said ironically is the realization that the speaker has mentioned (rather than used) the proposition in question. This raises (in the mind of the hearer) the issue of what the speaker's attitude is to the mentioned propositions, and leads to the inference, in appropriate cases, that the attitude is one of irony.

Whereas there is general agreement that principles of conversational implicature play a major role in language, other pragmatic systems also are argued to play a part. Bach contends that the use of tense and time expressions is not strictly grammatical in nature, but rather is the reflection of certain metaphysical assumptions about the nature of the universe. Bach explores how these assumptions interact to determine the use of English tense and time expressions.

Prince explores the role of given versus new information in discourse. She argues that there are several degrees of "assumed familiarity," and that different roles in discourse are associated with each.

Green and Morgan's chapter is also concerned with discourse. They raise the issue of whether discourse should be described on the basis of the same sorts of principles used to describe the syntax of sentences. They conclude that the structure of discourse is primarily determined by pragmatic factors, and that any attempt to construct a discourse grammar (modeled on sentence grammar) is doomed to failure.

Fillmore's contribution also deals with discourse. Fillmore argues that, although syntax, semantics, and pragmatics are essentially independent, some syntactic facts require semantic and pragmatic explanations, and some semantic facts require pragmatic explanations. Fillmore examines instances of discourse that differ in significant pragmatic ways, and finds that they are structured according to different sets of syntactic and semantic principles.

Several of the chapters deal with presupposition. Those by Atlas and Levinson, and Grice were discussed previously. Caton considers Stalnaker's account of pragmatic presupposition. According to Stalnaker, whether something is pragmatically presupposed is determined by whether a speaker and addressee share certain beliefs, and whether the speaker believes the addressee recognizes that the speaker has these beliefs. Caton argues that this definition of pragmatic presupposition is inadequate because it does not take into account the degree of certainty (epistemic qualification) with which the beliefs are held. Caton proposes a revision of Stalnaker's account incorporating epistemic qualifications.

Donnellan reviews the logical intuitions on which Strawson's refutation of Russells' theory of descriptions is based. He contends that these intuitions are not at all straightforward.

The two remaining chapters deal with questions of methodology. Nunberg considers whether any straightforward tests can be constructed to distinguish literal meaning from conversational implicature. He argues that such tests are not possible in principle.

Sag raises the issue of whether semantics is really autonomous from pragmatics. Whereas the principles of composition (the heart of model-theoretic semantics) remain free of pragmatics, the meaning of the terms combined is taken to be essentially pragmatic. Thus, Sag's chapter would seem to be the most radical in the volume. In the view that he sketches, semantics is reduced to nothing more than the combinatorial principle by means of which various pragmatically determined "meanings" are combined.

In reviewing the chapters in this volume, one area of agreement is apparent. There is a tendency to attribute much more of "meaning" to pragmatics rather than to semantics. The degree to which semantics is reduced, however, remains in dispute.

An issue raised by a number of the chapters is whether pragmatics constitutes a unified subsystem. It is not at all clear that the pragmatic principles discussed by Grice, Bach, and Prince constitute a single system. Furthermore, is the pragmatics of indexicals (and similar matters raised by Sag) the same field as that of Grice? Gazdar (1979:2) inter alia has explicitly contended that it is not. A question very much left open by this collection is whether there is in fact a single field of pragmatics. This volume has, I believe, done a service to the study of language by raising this question.

I would like to conclude this preface by acknowledging the contributions of Elaine Degenhart and Elizabeth Pearce to this volume. Elaine assisted me in editing the chapters and Liz prepared the excellent index. They deserve public thanks for their efforts.

REFERENCES

Chomsky, N. Syntactic structures. In C. H. von Schooneveld (Ed.), *Janua linguarum 4*. Mouton: 'S-Gravenhage, 1957.

Gazdar, G. *Pragmatics: Implicature, presupposition, and logical form*. Academic Press: New York, 1979.

Grice, H. P. Logic and conversation. In P. Cole and J. L. Morgan (Eds.), *Syntax and semantics 3: Speech acts*. Academic Press: New York, 1975. Pp. 107–142.

Grice, H. Paul. Further notes on logic and conversation. In P. Cole (Ed.), *Syntax and semantics 9: Pragmatics*. Academic Press: New York, 1978.

Russell, B. On denoting. *Mind, 1905, 14*, 479–499.

Strawson, P. F. On referring. *Mind, 1950, 59*, 320–344.

It-Clefts, Informativeness, and Logical Form: Radical Pragmatics (Revised Standard Version)

Jay David Atlas and Stephen C. Levinson

For Nicholas Levinson and Robert Evren

1. THE STANDARD VERSION OF RADICAL PRAGMATICS AND THE STANDARD OBJECTIONS

The following is an elementary fact: Sentences with the same truth conditions, as in (1), can have different logical forms, as in (2).

(1) a. *It's done.*
     b. *It's done, and if it's done it's done.*

(2) a. p
     b. $p \, \& \, (p \to p)$

Obviously, in a broad sense, (1a) and (1b) differ in meaning. Sentence (1a) could be an answer to the question (3a) in a way that (1b) could not, whereas (1b) would be a natural response to (3b), though (1a) would not.

1

RADICAL PRAGMATICS

(3) a. *Have you done it yet?*
     b. *Oh dear, I wish I hadn't done that.*

The redundancies of (1b) that are due to its logical form (2b) create distinct conversational implicatures (Grice, 1975, p. 52). Conversational implicatures, we shall argue, are defined on the level of semantic representation (logical form).

Grice's program in "Logic and Conversation" is conservative with respect to semantic representation and with respect to the postulation of different senses for expressions. For example, the divergence between the "meanings" of the logical connectives and the words *not, and, or, if . . . then, all, some* was held to be a difference in their USE rather than in their contributions to the TRUTH CONDITIONS of the sentences containing them. Semantics turns truth-conditional and wears a comfortingly familiar face—first-order quantification theory and extensions thereof.

A Standard Radical Pragmatics view might have argued that "what is said (asserted)" in (4a) is the same as in (4b); their truth conditions would be said to be the same.

(4) a. *It was John that Mary kissed.*
     b. *Mary kissed John.*
     c. *Mary kissed someone.*
     d. *It wasn't John that Mary kissed.*

But (4a) exhibits presuppositional behavior that (4b) does not, namely, the preservation of the inference to (4c) under denial and questioning of (4a). Standard Radical Pragmatics would claim that (4a) entails (4c), but its negation (4d) does not. Sentence (4d) would be said to be an external negation (Allwood, 1972; Atlas, 1975a; Gazdar, 1976, 1977, 1979; Kempson, 1975, 1977; for qualifications see Atlas, 1975b, 1977, 1978). An internal negation understanding would be a GENERALIZED CONVERSATIONAL IMPLICATUM of a use of (4d). What Allwood (1972), Atlas (1975a, 1975b), Fogelin (1967), Grice (1961), Harnish (1976), Kempson (1975), and O'Hair (1969) intended was a conversational implicatum that in this chapter we will derive from a Principle of Informativeness. In a sense to be explained, the implicatum is the product of an INFERENCE TO THE pragmatically BEST INTERPRETATION. From the relevant internal negation understanding of (4d), it follows that Mary kissed someone, that is, (4c) follows.

The general hypothesis for presupposition is the obvious generalization. Whenever "presuppositions" occur—for example, those associated with proper names and descriptions, clefts, aspectual verbs, pseudo-clefts, iteratives, quantifiers, etc.—the propositions should be considered an entailment of the affirmative sentence and part of or entailed by a generalized conversational implicatum of saying the negative sentence. Sentences that give rise to presuppositions should on this analysis differ from their corresponding presuppositionless sentences at least in logical form if not also in truth conditions.

There are different sorts of objections to this kind of pragmatic theory. The first has been to challenge the division of labor in the theory: Affirmative sentences normally have entailments; external negations have generalized conversational implicata. It seems to us that the data do indicate a difference in behavior between affirmative and negative sentences. As an example, Gazdar (1979, pp. 199–213) has noted the cancelation behavior in (5).

(5) $John \begin{Bmatrix} ? \ has \\ hasn't \end{Bmatrix} stopped beating his wife because, in fact, he never beat her at all.$

Of this difference between affirmative and negative sentences Gazdar writes that it had "not been discussed by proponents of pragmatic theories of presupposition, because they had had no way to explain [it] [1979, p. 120]." And he goes on to say, correctly, that it "can be readily explained if we allow the factive to entail its complement [p. 121]." At the time that Gazdar originally wrote those lines a pragmatic theory appeared that met his demands. It was argued by Atlas (1975a, pp. 42–44) that affirmative factive sentences entail their complements and that the negative sentence does not entail, but its use does implicate, the complement. Gazdar (1976, 1977, pp. 126–127) expresses skepticism that such a Gricean explanation could be adequate.

Gazdar (1977, p. 127) complains that the negative sentence *John hasn't stopped beating his wife* is said to "presuppose" *John has been beating his wife* and to deny *John is no longer beating his wife* but that no Gricean argument EXPLAINS why those two sentences play just those pragmatic roles. (The sentences "seem, a priori [*sic*], equally informative, newsworthy, relevant, etc. to whatever discourse . . . might be contributed to [p. 127].") The analogous complaint for *know* would be that *John doesn't know that Caesar crossed the Rubicon in 44 B.C.* is said to presuppose *Caesar crossed the Rubicon in 44 B.C.* and to deny *John warrantedly believes that Caesar crossed the Rubicon in 44 B.C.* but that no Gricean argument EXPLAINS why those two sentences play just those pragmatic roles.

The reply, to abbreviate the account in Atlas 1975a, is that the negative sentence, whose logical form is taken to be an external negation, is relatively uninformative. To "presuppose" the truth of *Caesar crossed the Rubicon in 44 B.C.* is to understand a stronger claim by the negative sen-

tence, one that asserts John's ignorance. The stronger claim is a COM-
PETING INTERPRETATION of the negative sentence, as (independently of a
special context) no other English sentence both literally and more per-
spicuously can be used to express that claim (see the maxim of Manner in
Grice, 1975, p. 46). If the conversation is ABOUT John's epistemic state,
our Principle of Informativeness will lead the hearer to understand the
speaker's utterance in the expected way. Thus the negative sentence is understood as a particular internal negation, an instance of what is a generalized implicature from external to an internal negation. Which internal negation is implicated, when there is a choice to make, obviously depends
on what the sentence is understood to be "about," that is, on what the
sentence is understood to "presuppose," and on what the sentence is understood to be saying about it—on considerations, vaguely, of relevance.
A lovely piece of verbal play illustrating the way in which background can
shift focus and presupposition is discussed by Atlas 1975b. The datum is
taken from Tom Stoppard's play *Jumpers,* Act II.

(6)   Archie: *Ah!—I knew there was something!—McFee's dead.*
      George: *What?!!*
      Archie: *Shot himself this morning, in the park, in a plastic bag.*
      George: *My God! Why?*
      Archie: *It's hard to say. He was always tidy.*
      George: *But to shoot himself. . . .*
      Archie: *Oh, he could be very violent, you know. . . .*

The second problem is the projection problem, the problem of how the
presuppositions of a sentence depend upon the presuppositions of its
parts. If presuppositions have projectional behavior distinct from that of
conversational implicata, then prima facie they are different. On the other
hand, if we can show that their behavior is the same, this obstacle to the
reduction of presupposition to generalized conversational implicature can
be removed.

Sentence (7a) scalar-implicates (7b):

(7)   a. *John has three children.*
      b. *John has no more than three children.*

But when a speaker asserts the conjunction of (7b) and (7a), as in (8), he
does not implicate (7b).

(8)   *John has no more than three children, and in fact he has three.*

The same behavior is observed in the traditional cases of presupposition
in conjunctions, as is well known (see Karttunen, 1973).

Sentence (9a) implicates (9b):

(9)　a. *Some of the boys went to the party.*
　　　b. *Not all of the boys went to the party.*

When a speaker asserts a conditional sentence (10), he does not implicate (9b).

(10)　*Some of the boys went to the party, if not all.*

The same behavior is observed in the traditional cases of presuppositions in conditional sentences.

　Finally, when a speaker asserts a disjunction such as

(11)　*All of the boys went or some did.*

in which saying the second disjunct alone implicates *Not all of the boys went* and the negation of the first disjunct entails the implicatum, we observe that the speaker does not implicate *Not all of the boys went*. The same behavior is observed in the traditional cases of presuppositions in disjunctions.

　The "filtering" of implicata seems to occur in compound sentences in the same way that filtering of presupposition occurs. In these cases at least the projection properties are no bar to the pragmatic reduction of presupposition to generalized conversational implicature. On the other hand we do not want to deny that there may be some conventional element in presupposition. It is relevant that we reduce presuppositions to GENERALIZED conversational implicature, not to particularized ones. The generalized implicature is "conventional" in the sense that it is not calculated at each occasion of use of a sentence. There is a (defeasible) shared assumption that the implicata obtain in the context unless they are explicitly suspended or canceled (see Harnish, 1976, p. 353). Conversational inferences may well have degrees of conventionalization. (For a philosophical analysis, see Lewis, 1969; for linguistic discussion, see Brown and Levinson, 1978).

　Obviously we do not believe that these few remarks dispose of the projection problem. Gazdar (1979) uses his distinctions between potential clausal implicatures, scalar implicatures, and presuppositions to state conditions under which one ranks above the other: Potential presuppositions are not actual presuppositions unless they are consistent with actual scalar implicata; potential scalar implicata are not actual scalar implicata unless they are consistent with actual clausal implicata; and potential clausal implicata are not actual unless they are consistent with the propositions representing the context in which the sentence is uttered and (roughly) the proposition representing the sentence itself. To say whether potential generalized conversational implicata can be substituted for potential presuppositions in Gazdar's projection rules, and with what restrictions on the class of implicata and with what modifications of the rules, requires an exhaustive investigation, which we shall certainly not attempt here.

If projection properties will not distinguish presupposition from implicature, perhaps cancelation will. Karttunen and Peters (1977) note that the apparently factive "judgment" verbs like *criticize* and *forgive* allow overt denial of their associated suppositions in a way that factives like *realize* do not. Compare (12) and (13) and (14).

(12)   *John criticized Rick for farting, although he was in fact quite innocent.*

(13)   *John forgave Rick for farting, although in fact it was Mart who farted.*

(14)   *?John realized that Rick had farted, although in fact he hadn't.*

Karttunen and Peters claim that the suppositions associated with "judgment" verbs are not presuppositions ("conventional implicatures" in their unfortunate terminology) but generalized conversational implicata. However, given that in general "judgment" verbs and factives have identical projection properties and in so many ways behave alike (e.g., under negation, questioning, and in conditionals), the claim is tantamount to an admission that the devices of conversational implicature can account for all the characteristic features of presuppositional phenomena (see Rogers, 1978; Rogers and Gazdar, 1978).

It may well be that cancelation facts like these will in the long run turn out to be the crucial tests for the adequacy of presuppositional theories. The implicatural reductionist will have to find a motivated way of claiming that "judgment" verbs do not entail their complements in affirmative sentences, unlike true factives. An obvious starting point is to note that such verbs are in fact verbs of saying (Rogers, 1978) and that such verbs do not entail their complements.

The data for clefts, factives, and definite descriptions commit the implicatural reductionist to the claim that the affirmative sentences entail "presuppositions" and that saying the negative sentences implicates them. It is worth observing that a Radical Pragmatics theory is not commited to entailment. It may well be that uses of affirmative sentences themselves implicate the propositions. Gazdar (1976; 1977, p. 124) notes two examples where the "presuppositions" are not entailed. Sentences (15a) and (16a) "presuppose" (15b) and (16b); they do not entail them.

(15)   a. *Golda Meir will sack Moshe Dayan before she goes to Cuba.*
        b. *Golda Meir will go to Cuba.*

(16)   a. *Perseus is more of a hero than Bellerophon.*
        b. *Bellerophon is a hero.*

We shall not attempt an analysis of *before* or of comparative constructions. We merely mention one example (17) where affirmative and negative sentences both have implicata.

(17)   a. *The day is warm.*
        b. *The day isn't warm.*
        c. *The day is not hot.*

We must briefly mention lexical items, for example, *again, too, even, only,* whose SOLE content is taken by Wilson (1975) to be presuppositional. If these items have the properties Wilson attributes to them, our Radical Pragmatics program is in difficulty. For if an item has no conventional semantic content, it is difficult to see from what one would derive conversational implicata. However, in (18) we would argue that (18a) entails (18c) whereas saying (18b) implicates it.

(18)   a. *John went to church again.*
        b. *John didn't go to church again.*
        c. *John went to church before.*

This analysis explains the data in (19) and (20).

(19)   *?John went to church again and in fact he never went before.*

(20)   *John didn't go to church again, and in fact he never went before.*

But one might argue instead that the contents of *again, etc.* are CONVENTIONALLY (in Grice's sense) rather than conversationally implicated.

In the case of a word like *but* (see Wilson 1975), it is difficult to see how any other account of the difference between *and* and *but* might be given. Nonetheless, the choice between conventional and conversational implicata is a significant one. Levinson (1978) has argued that conventional implicatures form a distinct category with specific projection properties and other defining characteristics, so the reanalysis of some putative presuppositions as conventional implicata is a substantive, and not merely a terminological, issue.

Current views, as, for example, in Gazdar 1979 and Karttunen and Peters 1979, suggest that presuppositions are attached in a conventional way to aspects of surface structure. This intuition is attributable in part (see Grice, 1975, 1978; Horn, 1973) to the difficulty in distinguishing conventional from generalized conversational implicatures and in part to the fact that sentences with identical truth conditions can have quite distinct logical forms, which serve to trigger distinct conversational implicata.

The examples and arguments normally offered against a Radical Pragmatic theory do not seem to us to be as destructive as some have thought.

2. TRUTH AND LOGICAL FORM

When Paul Grice introduces implicating, he does so by contrast with saying or asserting. A speaker S implicates that q to a hearer H if (a) S says that p; (b) S does not say that q; and (c) S implies, suggests, means, *etc.* that q by saying that p (Grice, 1975, p. 43). And Grice adds, "In the sense in which I am using the word *say,* I intend what someone has said to be closely related to the conventional meaning of the words (the sentence) he has uttered [1975, p. 44]." What is implicated is not part of what is said, nor is it entailed by what is said, but the hearer's knowledge of what is said, which includes the SENSE of the sentence, is necessary for the hearer's coming to know what the speaker implicated. Since Frege first proposed it, philosophers have found it natural to identify the SENSE of a declarative sentence with its TRUTH CONDITIONS. Linguists recently have followed suit, taking the SEMANTIC REPRESENTATIONS to be LOGICAL FORMS (see Kempson, 1977, Chapter 3). As some seemingly plausible arguments against Radical Pragmatics in recent discussions rest on a curious view of the roles of logical form and truth conditions, we shall first assemble some "philosophical reminders" about the notions of truth and logical form.

Our interest in the logical form of a sentence of a natural language is foremost an interest in the entailment (or logical consequence) relation into which the sentence enters. We want to know what is a logical consequence of it and what it is a logical consequence of. But more, we want to know why these entailments hold, and a logical theory is an answer to that question. Typically we think of a logical form as a formula in first-order quantification theory, but this is not our only logical theory. So what logical form a sentence has depends on what logical theory is chosen. The theory has a formal language (a syntax) into which we paraphrase our sentence; it also has a particular interpretation (a semantics). The logical form of an English sentence is relative to the formal language of the theory and to its interpretation.

Logical theories being what they are, they may be used to give the truth conditions of an English sentence in a perspicuous manner. Logical theory isolates very general features of sentences upon which entailments can be seen to depend—their semantically significant structure—and represents them in a canonical notation, for example, by the logical constants, predicates, and variables of quantification theory. To the extent that one's linguistic competence consists in one's grasp of deductive relations among sentences, paraphrase into the canonical notation represents the content of that competence in a perspicuous fashion. Likewise, to the extent that one's knowledge of the meaning of a sentence consists in one's grasp of its sense (its truth conditions), paraphrase into the canonical notation represents the meaning of the sentence in a perspicuous fashion (see Strawson, 1974; Quine, 1977).

It is an elementary but sometimes curiously ignored fact that two sentences that are logically equivalent can have different logical forms. To take a trivial example, let the logical form of A be $p \& q$ and the logical form of B be $q \& p$. These are different, provably equivalent logical forms that individually represent the truth conditions of A and B. The logical equivalence shows us that necessarily A is true if and only if B is true.

But it is only when we INTERPRET the language of our logical theory that it can even begin to make sense to say that A and B have the SAME truth conditions. For example, let V be a "universal" set of elements and interpret the formula p as a subset $P \subseteq V$, the set of elements in V for which p holds, and likewise for q. Interpret $p \& q$ as $P \cap Q$, and $q \& p$ as $Q \cap P$, the set-theoretical intersections of P and Q and of Q and P. Elementary set theory shows that $P \cap Q = Q \cap P$. So the "meanings" of $p \& q$ and $q \& p$ UNDER THIS INTERPRETATION are the same. We can stipulate that sentences X and Y in language L have the "same" truth conditions if and only if the representations of their truth conditions in the semantical metalanguage ML have the same interpretation. Relative to the interpretation of our example, A and B will have the "same" truth conditions. But it is ONLY with respect to an interpretation of our metalanguage that the claim that object-language sentences have the "same" truth conditions can make sense. The mere fact that $\models p \& q \leftrightarrow q \& p$ does not itself imply any such claim. So much for "philosophical reminders." Clarity about such matters will help locate fallacies in arguments that we must now discuss (see Dana Scott, 1970b).

3. CLEFTS AND A CRITICISM OF RADICAL PRAGMATICS

It has been asserted by Deirdre Wilson and Dan Sperber that Sentences (21a) and (22a) convey the same information in different ways.

(21) a. *It is Peter who is married to Sarah.*
     b. *It is not Peter who is married to Sarah.*
     c. *Is it Peter who is married to Sarah?*

(22)   a. *It is Sarah that Peter is married to.*
       b. *It is not Sarah that Peter is married to.*
       c. *Is it Sarah that Peter is married to?*

In particular they claim that the classes of logical consequences of (21a) and (22a) are identical, and so those who adopt standard truth-conditional semantics must take the sentences to be "semantically identical" (Wilson and Sperber, 1979, p. 300). Of course (21a) and (22a) differ in an important respect. Whether the content of (21a) is asserted in (21a), denied in (21b), or questioned in (21c), in each case (23) but not (24) would be assented to.

(23)   *Someone is married to Sarah.*

(24)   *Peter is married to someone.*

Mutatis mutandis, whether the content of (22a) is asserted in (22a), denied in (22b), or questioned in (22c), in each case (24) but not (23) would be assented to. And this difference obtains despite the fact that (21a) and (22a) each entail (23) and (24), and in general, despite the "semantical identity" of (21a) and (22a) in truth-conditional semantics.

Anyone who takes this line, argue Wilson and Sperber, must take the observed differences between (21) and (22) to be purely pragmatic. It is then natural to seek an account modeled on Paul Grice's analysis of rational cooperation in conversation. Given that in "saying" (21a), (21b), or (21c) a speaker does not "say" but implies, suggests, or means (23), the "presupposition" of (23) by (21) might be best explained as an "implicatum." Wilson and Sperber argue:

> Someone who believes that presuppositions can be identified with Gricean conversational implicatures would have to show that [21a] and denials of [21a] . . . conversationally implicate [23] and not [24], whereas [22a] and denials of [22a] implicate [24] and not [23]. A conversational implicature in turn depends on the prima facie violation of one of Grice's conversational maxims concerning relevance, informativeness, brevity, and ease of comprehension. As long as [21a] and [22a] are treated as semantically identical, it is hard to see how they could bring about different violations of the maxims of relevance and informativeness. Indeed, for Grice, two semantically identical sentences must always give rise to identical conversational implicatures unless they differ rather dramatically in length or ease of comprehension, so that they differ in their violations of the two other maxims concerning brevity and perspicuity. There is no such difference between [21a] and [22a], which are not only truth-functional equivalents, but are also built on the same syntactic pattern, and contain the same lexical items. It seems, then, that the obvious pragmatic differences between [21a] and [22a] can never be attributed to Gricean conversational implicatures [pp. 300–301].

Although the argument that we have just quoted seems sensible and plausible, it suffers several defects. First, in Grice's view it is a necessary condition on conversational implicature (generalized or particular) that it be cancelable without anomaly. Because (23) is ENTAILED by (21a), (23) is not cancelable. A Gricean reduction of presupposition to implicature ought NOT to claim that saying (21a) implicates (23). One representative such theory (Atlas, 1975a, 1975b) makes no such claim. It claims only that (21a) entails (23). Such theories can and do claim that saying (21b) implicates (23) but not (24), that saying (22b) implicates (24) but not (23). If such implicatures were Gricean conversational implicatures in a narrow sense, they would arise solely from the FLOUTING of Grice's maxims. Implicatures that turn on infringements of Grice's maxims and perhaps on additional, similar principles can be termed *conversational implicatures* in a broad sense. Gricean theories need not and do not restrict their resources to Grice's formulations. One of the aims of this chapter is to formulate a pragmatic principle of informativeness distinct from the maxims of Grice's theory (see Section 10). Versions of such a principle have been employed by Grice (1961), Harnish (1972, 1976), and Atlas (1975a, 1975b) to explain the use of disjunctions, conjunction reduced sentences, and negations respectively. It was thought that the principle was a component, a combination, or a consequence of the maxims and argument forms canonized by Grice (1961, 1967, 1975, 1978). It is our contention that the practice, but not, regrettably, the theory, in these accounts points toward a different conclusion. Our principle of informativeness will be incompatible with standard applications of Grice's first maxim of Quantity ("Make your contribution as informative as is required for the current purposes of the exchange"). Thus we hold that, contrary to Wilson and Sperber's account of Gricean Radical Pragmatics, a pragmatic theory claims neither that saying (21a) implicates (23) nor that conversational implicature, broadly conceived, relies solely on the maxims described by Grice, or even on pragmatic arguments compatible with the standard inferences employing those maxims.

The third defect in the Wilson–Sperber criticism rests upon their understanding of the role of truth conditions in a Radical Pragmatics. Because Wilson and Sperber claim that (21a) and (22a) are the same logically, the same lexically, and the same syntactically, it seems to them that the NONDETACHABILITY of conversational implicature implies that (21a) and (22a) should be the same pragmatically. Because the sentences are not pragmatically the same, Wilson and Sperber conclude that a Gricean account cannot be correct. Of course it is true that (21a) and (22a) are provably equivalent if it is assumed that each spouse is monogamous. It is true that the sentences contain the same lexical items. It is even true that they have the same surface syntactic form: *It is N that S*. But a Radical Pragmatics rejects the claims that logical equivalence implies semantical identity and that surface grammar alone determines implicatures.

Wilson and Sperber refer to the pragmatic theory of Gazdar (1979) as a typical example. It is therefore worth recalling his discussion of the appropriate level of analysis for implicatures. The examples in question are Horn's (1972) scalar implicatures (e.g., *It's not the case that John possibly won the poetry prize* implicates *John probably won the poetry prize*). Gazdar (1979) writes

> It is both in the spirit of Grice's program and in the interests of economy to read these non-conventional inferences from the semantic representation. Presumably, at such a level a set of expressions such as {*perhaps, maybe, possibly*} will be represented by just one item for the reading they have in common. To read off [potential] conversational [implicatures] from the actual LEXICAL ITEMS given in the surface structure would be tantamount to treating them as conventional implicatures, besides which the [Horn] scales would require redundant listing of synonymous items. To read off [potential implicatures] from the semantic interpretation (i.e. the proposition it expresses) [N.B. not the semantic representation] would be impossible, since many different sentences can express a given proposition and many of these will not contain the scalar item and thus not carry the [potential implicature]. . . . Two disjunctive sentences having the same truth-conditions (i.e. expressing the same proposition) carry different [potential implicatures]. [The sentences are *John did it or Mary did it* and *John did it or Mary did it or both of them did it.*] In what follows I shall assume that [potential implicatures] derive from the sentences of a semantic representation. . . . The notion of semantic representation necessary (e.g. to cope with the disjunctive examples just mentioned) is a bit more "surfacey," or less abstract, than that hypothesized by generative semanticists. Logically equivalent sentences are not required to have the same semantic representation, but only the same semantic interpretation [pp.56-57].

To amplify Gazdar's last comment: The formulae in the language of semantic representation are given an interpretation. In his case a set of possible worlds, that is, a proposition in the sense of modal logic, is assigned to each closed formula. Because logically equivalent formulae are true in just the same possible worlds, they are interpreted as the same proposition. Gazdar properly distinguishes among English sentences, semantic representations of English sentences, and semantic interpretations of semantic representations of English sentences.

The relevant level of analysis for explaining implicature is the level of semantic representation. If two English sentences have logically equivalent semantic representations, they do NOT necessarily have the SAME semantic representations; by the convention we discussed in Section 2 they may be said to have the same semantic interpretation, but what is relevant to the calculation of implicature is the semantic representation. Although it may be acceptable to call the proposition associated with a sentence its INTENSION (Carnap), it is just a mistake to treat the proposition as its SENSE (Frege) (see Dana Scott, 1970a). Logically equivalent sentences have the same intension; they do not necessarily have the same sense.

The nondetachability of implicature is a matter of sense, not a matter of intension. If by "semantical identity" Wilson and Sperber mean SAMENESS OF INTENSION, what they say about (21a) and (22a) is true but irrelevant; if by "semantical identity" they mean SAMENESS OF SENSE, what they say is relevant but false.

It is one thing to show that a particular Radical Pragmatics account makes claims contrary to the ones Wilson and Sperber impute to it. It is another to provide a principled defense of the claims of the account. There are, of course, reasons why implicatures are understood as dependent on the SENSES of sentences.

4. IMPLICATURES AND LOGICAL FORMS

First, there are the evident problems in explaining the implicatures deriving from ambiguous sentences. For example the sentence *All of the arrows didn't hit the target* will have two senses, one given by (25) and the other by (26).

(25) $\neg \forall x (Arrow(x) \to Hit(x, \ the \ target))$

(26) $\forall x (Arrow(x) \to \neg Hit(x, \ the \ target))$

We may paraphrase (25) by *Not all of the arrows hit the target*. Saying a sentence with the truth conditions of (25) will implicate *Some of the arrows hit the target,* but the use of a sentence with the truth conditions of (26) will not have this implicatum. If implicata were derived from surface structure alone, no sense could be made of these data.

Second, there are the problems in explaining the implicata from different but related sentences. The use of Sentences (27) and (28) will implicate (29).

(27)   *Mart or Adam signed up for ceramics.*

(28)   *Mart signed up for ceramics or Adam signed up for ceramics.*

(29)   a. *Mart may have signed up for ceramics.*
       b. *Mart may not have signed up for ceramics.*
       c. *Adam may have signed up for ceramics.*
       d. *Adam may not have signed up for ceramics.*

Similarly, the use of Sentences (30) and (31) will implicate (32).

(30)   *Rick believes that John studied philosophy.*

(31)   *Rick believes John to have studied philosophy.*

(32)   a. *John may have studied philosophy.*
       b. *John may not have studied philosophy.*

It would seem ad hoc and redundant for a theory separately to explain the implicata derived from the pairs (27)–(28) and (30)–(31). An explanation employing a single semantic representation for each pair would be more satisfactory (see Gazdar, 1979, pp. 57–61).

Third, as Gazdar mentions in the passage quoted earlier, implicata dependent upon lexical meaning are derivable from classes of (more or less) synonymous items. For example, the uses of the sentences *Perhaps A, Maybe A,* and one sense of *Possibly A* will all implicate a sentence *Possibly not A.* A unified explanation would appeal to one underlying representation for the various sentences. In addition, if implicata were associated with the individual words in the surface structures by some linguistic rule, the difference between an explanation through CONVERSATIONAL implicature and through CONVENTIONAL implicature would be difficult to make out.

Wilson and Sperber assume that the proper object is the proposition, a reification of truth conditions as a class of logically equivalent formulae or as a set of possible worlds—what Gazdar calls "semantic interpretation." This indelicate view is supported by the incautious formulations of some philosophers and logicians. For example, Max Cresswell (1978) has written that language "becomes a rule-governed device for putting into the mind of another a representation of the same set of possible worlds which is in the mind of the speaker [p. 26]." (Unfortunately it is never clear just what representation it is.) The sentences (33) and (34) will be interpreted as the same proposition.

(33)   *A square has four sides.*

(34)   *Boys are boys.*

Though patently they have different implicata in various contexts, it would seem difficult to explain in what this difference consists if the sentences express the same proposition and the implicata depend on the proposition rather than the sense or meaning. Of course the same difficulty arises for necessarily false sentences such as the following:

(35)   *In class Ingrid is always there and not there.*

(36)   *Caesar both won the war and lost it.*

Gazdar (1979, p. 136) has pointed out that (37) has the same truth conditions as (38), yet only saying the former implicates an exclusive disjunction understanding of an utterance of the sentence.

(37)   *John did it or Mary did it.*

(38)   *John did it or Mary did it or both of them did it.*

He has also suggested that (39) and (40) have the same truth conditions.

(39)   *Some of the students were there.*

(40)   *Some, if not all, of the students were there.*

His suggestion relies on an analysis of the latter sentence as

(41)   *If not all of the students were there, some of the students were there,*

on the identification of *If A then B* with $p \rightarrow q$, and on the ENTAILMENT of (39) by (42):

(42)   *All of the students were there.*

because of the presence of the definite description *the students*. He properly observes that saying Sentence (39) implicates (43):

(43)   *Not all of the students were there,*

an implicatum suspended in Sentence (40).

Our examples have been maxim of Quantity implicatures. Quality implicatures for metaphorical sentences offer the familiar difficulties if the implicata are to derive from propositions. Sentences (44) and (45) are necessarily false, and so have the null intension, but obviously will yield different implicata.

(44)   *You are the cream in my coffee.*

(45)   *Carter is a fox.*

In Grice's example of a flout of the maxim of Relation (relevance), given in (46), McY is understood to implicate that McX's remark should not be discussed and that McX has committed a faux pas.

(46)   McX: *Mrs. Z is an old bag.*
            McY: *The weather has been quite delightful this summer, hasn't it?*

Unless McX's remark contains an idiom, it might be seen to require a Quality implicature prior to the Relation implicature, for McX's remark is like (45).

An intermediate case would be (47):

(47)   McX: *If Mrs. Z is not a harridan, then I'm a monkey's uncle.*
            McY: *The weather. . . .*

and the out-and-out insult might be (48):

(48)   McX: *Mrs. Z is an old vixen.*
       McY: *The weather. . . .*

As these flouts are only loosely tied to linguistic forms, such examples can hardly settle the dispute whether implicata depend on sense rather than on propositions.

Flouts of the submaxims of Manner "Be brief" and "Be orderly" at least seem to present no special difficulties for the "sense" view. Flouts of the submaxims "Avoid obscurity" and "Avoid ambiguity" obviously in different ways do, or at least could, depend upon surface structure. This is absolutely no surprise, and we are willing to let the matter rest there.

5. THE SEMANTICS AND PRAGMATICS OF CLEFTS: A UNIFIED THEORY?

Linguists who recognize that sentences may have the same truth conditions but different semantic representations have suggested that the semantic representations of (49a), (49b), and (49c) are (50a), (50b), and (50c), respectively (see, e.g., Gazdar, 1979, pp. 124–125).[1]

(49)   a. *Sam wants Fido.*
       b. *What Sam wants is Fido.*
       c. *It is Sam who wants Fido.*

(50)   a. *Wants (Sam,Fido)*
       b. $\lambda x(Wants(Sam,x))(Fido)$
       c. $\lambda x(Wants(x,Fido))(Sam)$

But with normal sentence stress on the last word of (49a), *Fido* has UN-MARKED INFORMATION FOCUS (Halliday, 1967), which is consistent with the general convention that old information precedes new information. Similarly the pseudo-cleft (49b) conforms to this convention. The "focus" (Chomsky, 1972) of (49b) is *Fido;* its "presupposition" is *Sam wants something.* The same analysis would give for (49c) the "focus" *Sam* and the "presupposition" *Something wants Fido.* In other words the cleft rhetorically parallel to the pseudo-cleft and the simple sentence is not (49c), as Gazdar and the order of items in surface structure seem to suggest, but (51), which contravenes the convention that old information precede new information. Gazdar's logical form for (51) would be (52).

---

[1] For a discussion of λ-abstraction, see Rudolf Carnap, *Introduction to Symbolic Logic and Its Applications,* W. H. Meyer and J. Wilkinson (trans.), New York: Dover, 1958, pp. 129–131.

(51)   *It is Fido that Sam wants.*

(52) $\lambda x(Wants(Sam,x))(Fido)$

The "focus" of (49b) and of (51) is *Fido;* the "presupposition" of (49b) and of (51) is *Sam wants something.* In Gazdar's logical forms for clefts and pseudo-clefts, the "focus" corresponds to the logical subject; the "presupposition" corresponds to the logical predicate. And the logical form of the pseudo-cleft *What Sam wants is Fido* is identical to that of the cleft *It is Fido that Sam wants,* that is, (50b) = (52).

We take it that a sentence with contrastive stress **Sam** *wants Fido* has *Sam* as "focus" and *Something wants Fido* as "presupposition." So the contrastively stressed (53) rhetorically parallels (49c) and (54). The Gazdar logical form for the latter two is (50c).

(53)   **Sam** *wants Fido.*

(50a)   *Wants(Sam,Fido)*

(49c)   *It is Sam who wants Fido.*

(54)   *Who wants Fido is Sam.*

(50c) $\lambda x(Wants(x,Fido))(Sam)$

Similarly the normally stressed sentence (49a) and the contrastively stressed (55) parallel (51) and (49b). The Gazdar logical form for the latter two is (50b).

(49a)   *Sam wants Fido.*

(55)   *Sam wants* **Fido.**

(50a)   *Wants(Sam,Fido)*

(51)   *It is Fido that Sam wants.*

(49b)   *What Sam wants is Fido.*

(50b) $\lambda x(Wants(Sam,x))(Fido)$

If one were to assume that (56) parallels (57), one might also assume that (49c) parallels (49a).

(56)   *It was John who went.*

(57)   *John went.*

(49c)   *It is Sam who wants Fido.*

(50c) $\lambda x(Wants(x,Fido))(Sam)$

(49a)   *Sam wants Fido.*

(50a)   *Wants(Sam,Fido)*

But as we have just seen, Sentences (49a) and (49c) are not parallel at all. The order of items in the surface structures of (49c) and (49a) is misleading. Misled by surface structure one might assume that the "logical subject" of both sentences is *Sam*. On this assumption, in (49c) the "focus" corresponds to the logical subject. But in the normally stressed simple sentence (49a) the normal "focus" is *Fido;* the "focus" there does NOT correspond to the logical subject. We shall be guided by "focus" rather than by surface order. We reject the suggestion that Sentence (56) pairs with the normally stressed (57); it pairs with the contrastively stressed (58).[2]

(58)   *John went.*

We believe that the identification of logical subject and "focus" in (49c) is just as mistaken as the same identification in the normally stressed (49a) would be. It seems to us that the semantic representations offered by Gazdar and others fail to make the semantic and pragmatic data COHERE. One of our aims in this chapter is to sketch an account that will unify the semantics and pragmatics, in a way to be expounded in what follows. But before proceeding with that discussion, we must consider another account of the semantics of clefts. (For discussion of the pragmatics of clefts, see Prince, 1978.)

6. A RECENT DESCRIPTION OF CLEFTS

On Halvorsen's (1978) view clefts differ from their corresponding simple sentences in their "conventional implicatures." Sentence (59b) has the same truth conditions as (59a), and so make the same assertion or express the same proposition, but, unlike (59a), (59b) "conventionally implicates" (59c) and something approximating (59d).

(59)   a. *Mary kissed John.*
        b. *It was John that Mary kissed.*
        c. *Mary kissed someone.*
        d. *There is only one person Mary kissed.*

---

[2] Independently Halvorsen (1978, p. 6) has argued against Akmajian (1970) that *It was himself that John wanted Mary to describe* pairs with *John wanted Mary to describe **himself**,* not with **John wanted Mary to describe himself.*

Sentence (60b) has the same truth conditions as (60a), but (60b) ''conventionally implicates'' (60c) and (60d).

(60) a. *Mary didn't kiss John.*
 b. *It wasn't John that Mary kissed.*
 c. *Mary kissed someone.*
 d. *There is only one person Mary kissed.*

And, analogously, the content of (61b) is the same as (61a), but (61b) ''conventionally implicates'' (61c) and (61d).

(61) a. *Did Mary kiss John?*
 b. *Was it John that Mary kissed?*
 c. *Mary kissed someone.*
 d. *There is only one person Mary kissed.*

The ''conventional implicata'' of a sentence, for example of (59b), are preserved under negation, as in (60b), and under questioning, as in (61b). This distinguishes ''conventional implicata'' from entailment. Halvorsen remarks that (59b) entails (59c), but obviously (60b) does not entail (60c) [= (59c)]. He also claims that (62b) has the same truth conditions as (62a) but ''conventionally implicates'' (62c) and (62d), and that (63b) has the same truth conditions as (63a) but ''conventionally implicates'' (63c) and (63d).

(62) a. *Mary didn't kiss John.*
 b. *It was John that Mary didn't kiss.*
 c. *There is someone that Mary didn't kiss.*
 d. *There is only one person Mary didn't kiss.*

(63) a. *Mary kissed John.*
 b. *It wasn't John that Mary didn't kiss.*
 c. *There is someone that Mary didn't kiss.*
 d. *There is only one person Mary didn't kiss.*

Obviously this implies that (59b) *It was John that Mary kissed* is logically equivalent to (63b) *It wasn't John that Mary didn't kiss,* both asserting *Mary kissed John,* and that (60b) *It wasn't John that Mary kissed* is logically equivalent to (62b) *It was John that Mary didn't kiss,* both asserting *Mary didn't kiss John.*

This review is incomplete unless something is said about Halvorsen's, actually Karttunen and Peters's (1979), notion of ''conventional implicature.'' Halvorsen's paradigm is *manage:* Sentence (64a) ''conventionally implicates'' (64b) and asserts (64c).

(64) a. *John managed to write a paper.*
     b. *It is difficult (for John) to write a paper.*
     c. *John wrote a paper.*

The CONVENTIONAL MEANING of an utterance depends on both the assertion made and the "conventional implicatum" conveyed. As noted earlier, the "conventional implicatum," like an old-fashioned presupposition and unlike an entailment, is preserved under negation and questioning.

As "conventional implicata" are part of the meaning of the sentence uttered, an assertion having a "conventional implicatum" conjoined with an explicit denial of the implicatum is contradictory (Halvorsen, 1978, p. 12), or logically contradictory and/or "internally infelicitous" (Sadock, 1978, pp. 290, 292). It is standardly necessary for felicitous utterance that "conventional implicata" constitute part of the common ground between speaker and hearer (Halvorsen 1978, pp. 16–17; Sadock, 1978, p. 292).

This conception of "conventional implicata" derives largely from Karttunen and Peters (1979). It must be remarked that this conception departs from Grice's original one, which was intended to be distinct from presupposition. Grice's (1961) paradigm *She was poor but she was honest* implied some contrast between (her) poverty and (her) honesty, but nothing that was asserted (said—in Grice's sense) carried that implicatum. By contrast Grice took it that presuppositions were carried by what was said. Because Grice's discussion of conventional implicature has been so sketchy, his other examples being *therefore* and *moreover* (Grice, 1968), philosophers have been tentative in their treatment of his idea. Linguists have been less cautious, and, we believe, often incorrect in their interpretation of Grice.

For example, Grice (1961) described the implicatum in *She was poor but she was honest* as detachable (from what is asserted) by uttering *She is poor and she is honest,* and as (in some sense) cancelable, in that *She is poor but she is honest, though of course I do not mean to imply that there is any contrast between poverty and honesty* is a peculiar but nonetheless noncontradictory and intelligible way of conveying that she was poor and honest. In the same essay Grice thought that presuppositions were nondetachable and noncancelable (not negated without contradicting the original assertion). Conversational implicata were nondetachable but cancelable.

Despite the recognition, originally by Grice, that nondetachability will not distinguish entailment from conversational implicature, there seems to have been no parallel recognition that noncancelability will not distinguish entailment from what linguists are currently calling "conventional implicature." On this LINGUISTIC conception of a "conventional implicature," "conventional implicata" are detachable (from what is asserted) and noncancelable. But noncancelability is NOT a SUFFICIENT test for "conventional implicature." (For an apparent use of the sufficiency test, see Sadock, 1978, p. 292.)

For example, Halvorsen notes that (59b) entails (59c) but claims that (59b) also "conventionally implicates" (59c).

(59b)   *It was John that Mary kissed.*

(59c)   *Mary kissed someone.*

The grounds for that claim cannot be just the unacceptability of (65); entailment suffices to explain that.

(65)   *?It was John that Mary kissed—and Mary kissed no one.*

Halvorsen (1978, p. 14) offers the following argument. In his paradigm for "conventional implicature," *John managed to write a paper,* he observes that (66b) follows from (66a), but (66c) does not.

(66)   a. *I just discovered that John managed to write a paper.*
        b. *I just discovered that John wrote a paper.*
        c. *I just discovered that it is difficult (for John) to write a paper.*

He asserts that (67c) does not follow from (67a).

(67)   a. *I just discovered that it was John that Mary kissed.*
        b. *I just discovered that Mary kissed John.*
        c. *I just discovered that Mary kissed someone.*

So he concludes that (59c) is "conventionally implicated" by (59b). Contrary to Halvorsen's assertion, it seems to us that (67c) does follow from (67a) in the same way that (67b) does. Halvorsen's argument is unsound.

Halvorsen offers two further observations. Relying on the invariance of "conventional implicature" under negation and questioning, he finds Sentences (68) and (69) unacceptable.

(68)   *?It wasn't John that Mary kissed—she didn't kiss anybody.*

(69)   *?I know that Mary didn't kiss anybody, but was it John that Mary kissed?*

In the case of the question, once again the test does not distinguish between "conventional implicature" and entailments of semantic content. In the case of the negative sentence, there is a critical worry and a controversy over the adequacy of the test.

Suppose *It wasn't John that Mary kissed* were AMBIGUOUS between a sentence (exclusion) and a predicate (choice) negation. On the predicate negation reading the sentence in (68) is contradictory and unacceptable; on the sentence negation reading it is consistent and acceptable. But on a predicate negation reading, it would appear that *It wasn't John that Mary kissed* ENTAILS *Mary kissed someone.* (If the latter is not true, neither is the former. But if the former is not true, this does not mean that *It was John that Mary kissed* is true if Mary kissed no one. These readings are contraries, not contradictories.) The entailment explains the unacceptability.

If this counterargument is to be defeated, some defense of the univocality of the sentence must be undertaken and some proposal as to its semantic representation be made. Halvorsen claims that its propositional content is *Mary didn't kiss John.* But on Halvorsen's view meaning is split between propositional content and "conventional implicature," and as Sentence (70) is acceptable, the propositional content will not yield the unacceptable (68).

(70)   *Mary didn't kiss John—she didn't kiss anybody.*

Obviously, the existential sentence *Mary kissed someone* will yield the unacceptable contradiction. But what we want to know is whether that sentence is "conventionally implicated" or entailed by *It wasn't John that Mary kissed.* What Halvorsen needs to prove is that the choice is just between "conventional implicature" and entailment and that there is no entailment.

The mere unacceptability of (68) does not make that case unless it is ASSUMED that noncancelability is a sufficient test for "conventional implicature". Alternatively, the case may be made if it is ASSUMED that, as the truth-conditional component of the meaning of *It wasn't John that Mary kissed* IS *Mary didn't kiss John,* and that cannot account for the unacceptability of Sentence (68), it must be the non-truth-conditional component of the meaning that does. That component must be, or entail, some proposition that contradicts *Mary didn't kiss anybody.* The simplest solution would be that the component is *Mary kissed someone.* And BY DEFINITION "conventional implicata" are non-truth-conditional components of literal meaning. Thus *Mary kissed someone,* it would be concluded, is a "conventional implicatum" of *It wasn't John that Mary kissed.*

In defense of the view that the truth-conditional components of *It wasn't John that Mary kissed* and *It was John that Mary kissed* are *Mary didn't kiss John* and *Mary kissed John,* Halvorsen (1978) claims that "it cannot be true that *It was John that Mary kissed* [sic] unless it is also true that *Mary kissed John* [sic], and vice versa [p. 14]" which is to say that necessarily one is true if and only if the other is true, that is, $\Box(Tr(A) \leftrightarrow Tr(B))$. If our language is bivalent (i.e., every statement is either true or false), this formula is equivalent to $\ulcorner\Box(A \leftrightarrow B)\urcorner$; A and B are necessarily equivalent. But if the language is not bivalent, there will be some sentences at which some valuation is not defined. Even if A and B are both true for all the same valuations, and so have the same TRUTH conditions, they need not be false for all the same valuations, and so need not have the same FALSITY conditions. If expressing the same proposition means that $\Box(A \leftrightarrow B)$, that is, $\ulcorner(A \leftrightarrow B)\urcorner$ is true for every valuation, and if $\ulcorner(A \leftrightarrow B)\urcorner$ is true in a valuation if and only if either A and B have values in $\{0,1\}$ and their values are equal or neither has a value, then in a nonbivalent language where $\Box(Tr(A) \leftrightarrow Tr(B))$ it is possible that there is a valuation at which B is false and at which A has no value. In that case A and B do not express the same proposition.

In a language in which semantically anomalous utterances have no truth-value, Halvorsen's claim about the TRUTH conditions, even if it were correct, would not show that the sentences express the same proposition. He has not shown that in such a language (e.g., ours?) the sentence *It was John that Mary kissed* is necessarily equivalent to *Mary kissed John*. But even if he had succeeded in showing this, there are difficulties.

Suppose it is common ground and true that Mary kissed no one. Then *Mary didn't kiss John* is true. Thus what according to Halvorsen is asserted in *It wasn't John that Mary kissed* is true. However, what is "conventionally implicated" is *Mary kissed someone,* and this "conventional implicatum" is not compatible with this context. As the felicitousness of an utterance in a context requires the compatibility of its "conventional implicata" with the context, the sentence *It wasn't John that Mary kissed* is in this context used to assert a truth, but its use is necessarily infelicitous.

The sentence *Mary kissed no one and it wasn't John that Mary kissed* would be even more peculiar. It would be true but "internally infelicitous" (which is the term Sadock [1978, p. 292] uses for contradictions arising from the "non-truth-conditional" component of meaning). Now a sense of reality is as useful in logic as it is in zoology. The suggestion that a sentence is self-contradictory because of features of its meaning and yet still true is sufficiently grotesque that one ought to ask whether a better theory can be found. The argument leading to this grotesquerie requires that *Mary didn't kiss John* ENTAIL *It wasn't John that Mary kissed*. This is a premise well worth doubting. In fact, we shall reject it. No cogent argument or convincing datum has been offered in its favor. (The view is popular nonetheless; cf. Halvorsen, 1978; Prince, 1978; Wilson and Sperber, 1979.)

It was once remarked of Herbert Spencer that his idea of tragedy was the murder of a beautiful theory by an ugly fact. Halvorsen's defense of

his claim that *It was John that Mary kissed* "conventionally implicates"
Mary kissed someone relies heavily on the unacceptability of *It wasn't
John that Mary kissed—she didn't kiss anybody.* Consider the variant *It
certainly wasn't John that Mary kissed—in fact Mary didn't kiss anyone.*
Here is the ugly fact: There is nothing wrong with these sentences. The
existential "implicatum" (presupposition) is cancelable, which shows
that it is not a "conventional implicatum" and not a direct consequence of
the meanings of the words or the sentence. We do not need to argue that
cancelability proves that the "implicatum" is conversational to see that it
cannot be "conventional."

Sadock (1978, pp. 292–293) may well be right that cancelability does
not discriminate between cases of privative ambiguity and cases of univocality plus conversational implicature.[3] Although discussions of the Radical Pragmatics position (e.g., Allwood, 1972; Atlas, 1975a, 1975b; Kempson, 1975; Sadock, 1975; Thomason, 1973, 1977; Wilson, 1975) have
focused on the univocality of negative presuppositional sentences and the
utility of appeals to conversational implicature, Radical Pragmatics has
not relied upon the cancelability test to prove DIRECTLY its account of
negative presuppositional sentences. It has used it to refute the alternatives: entailment, semantical presupposition, and "conventional implicature," and to refute the claim that the negative SENTENCE is univocally a
choice negation. It then offers itself as the best remaining account. Classical versions of Radical Pragmatics adopt the view that *not* is univocal and
identifies it with exclusion negation (e.g., Allwood, 1972; Kempson, 1975;
Gazdar, 1976, 1979) or with a nonclassical, nonspecific negation (e.g.,
Atlas, 1975a, 1975b, 1977).[4]

The other "conventional implicature" of clefts that Halvorsen discusses, namely, the exhaustiveness implicature, is for Halvorsen an admittedly troublesome feature. Whereas Sentence (71a) is acceptable,
(71b) is unhappy. The suggestion that (71c) "conventionally implicates"
(71d) confronts two difficulties, the first pointed out by Halvorsen.

(71)   a. *Mary kissed John, among others.*
       b. *?It was John that Mary kissed, among others.*
       c. *It was John that Mary kissed.*
       d. *John was the only person that Mary kissed.*
       e. *Mary kissed only one person.*

---

[3] Privative ambiguities have also created controversy over some tests discriminating between ambiguity and generality/nonspecificity. See Zwicky and Sadock (1975) and Atlas
(1977).

[4] For an important survey of negation, see Horn (1978a, 1978b).

"Conventional implicature" would require that (72) "conventionally im-plicate" (71d).

(72)   *Was it John that Mary kissed?*

But that would mean that the question "conventionally implicates" that its answer is *yes*. An analogous difficulty arises in the negative sentence (73) "conventionally implicating" (71d).

(73)   *It wasn't John that Mary kissed.*

For what it asserts, on Halvorsen's view, namely, *Mary didn't kiss John,* and what it "conventionally implicates" according to his first suggestion, namely, *John was the only person that Mary kissed,* are contradictory. Necessarily if (73) were true, it would be "internally infelicitous." It would be impossible for it to be both true and felicitous.

Halvorsen then suggests that (71c) "conventionally implicates" (71e). He notices, however, that (74) by parity of reasoning ought to "conven-tionally implicate" (75).

(74)   *Was it John and Rick that Mary kissed?*

(75)   *Mary kissed only two persons.*

If so, as he observes, the answer (76) should be infelicitous, as Halvorsen (1978, p. 2) in effect claims earlier in his essay. But it is not. Furthermore (77) should also be infelicitous, but it is not.

(76)   *No, she kissed John, Rick, and Mart.*

(77)   *No, she kissed only John.*

Consistent with his view of the "implicatum" of (74), Halvorsen could have claimed that *no* is a special "contradictory negation" that blocks the "implicature" in the discourse. (For a suggestion of this kind, see Kart-tunen and Peters, 1979; for a rejoinder see Atlas, 1980.) Such an explana-tion is prima facie much less plausible for the evident cancelability of the "implicatum" in the negative sentence (78).

(78)   *It wasn't John that Mary kissed—it was Mart and Rick.*

If *Mary kissed only one person* (or for that matter *Mary kissed at most one person*) were "conventionally implicated" by *It wasn't John that Mary kissed,* Sentence (78) would be anomalous. It is not; the negative sentence does not have these so-called "conventional implicata."

On the basis of his mistaken semantic claims, Halvorsen offers a Mon-taguvian formalization of clefts. He adapts Thomason (1976) and Kart-

tunen and Peters (1979) to this end. The meaning of an expression is given
by a three-tuple consisting of a representation of its contribution to truth
conditions (extension expression), a representation of its "conventional
implicata" (implicature expression), and an expression that allows the
grammar to plug, filter, or flush the implicata of the parts to yield the implicata of the whole expression (heritage expression). A formalization of
It is John that Mary kisses would be approximately as in (79)

(79)   a. *It is John that Mary kisses.*
       b. Extension expression
          $Kiss^e(m,j)$
       c. Existential "implicatum"
          $(\exists x)Kiss^e(m,x)$
       d. Exhaustiveness "implicatum"
          $(\exists x)(\forall y)(Kiss^e(m,y) \rightarrow x = y)$

and a formalization of *It isn't John that Mary kisses* would be approximately as in (80).

(80)   a. *It isn't John that Mary kisses.*
       b. Extension expression
          $\neg Kiss^e(m,j)$
       c. Existential "implicature"
          $(\exists x)Kiss^e(m,x)$
       d. Exhaustiveness "implicature"
          $(\exists x)(\forall y)(Kiss^e(m,y) \rightarrow x = y)$

The "implicature" expressions in (c) and (d) constitute two of the conjuncts in the implicature expression for the sentence. From various passages in Halvorsen (1978, pp. 54, 79), it is clear that he takes the formulae
in (d) to say that there is one and only one person that Mary kisses. The
EXHAUSTIVENESS "implicatum" is described as a UNIQUENESS implicatum. A problem in the formalization is that (d) merely says that some x is
such that all non-xs are not kissed by Mary. Queries about the range of 'x'
aside, this exhaustiveness condition does not entail that there is one and
only one individual that Mary kisses. In general, $(\exists x)(\forall y)(A(y) \rightarrow y = x)$
$\not\models E!\iota x A(x)$. Halvorsen's formula is instead a boundedness implicatum
that says that there is AT MOST one individual kissed by Mary. The existential and the boundedness "implicata" taken together are equivalent to
the uniqueness "implicatum."

  This small distinction matters. If the focus constituent gives rise to a
uniqueness "implicatum," as Halvorsen apparently believes but incorrectly formulates, the existential "implicatum" of the presupposition constituent is redundant. The latter would be entailed by the former. On the

other hand, if the focus constituent gives rise to a boundedness "implicatum," the existential "implicatum" is not redundant. The two views make different predictions about the data.

On the first view, Halvorsen's intended view, (81) is predicted to be infelicitous. It is compatible with the second view that the discourse be felicitous, which in fact it is.

(81)   a. McX: *Was it Mart and Rick that Mary kissed?*
         McY: *She kissed only John.*
       b. *It wasn't Mart and Rick that Mary kissed—she kissed only John.*

Similarly, on Halvorsen's view, (82) is predicted to be infelicitous. It might be compatible with the second view that (82) be felicitous, which in fact it is.

(82)   a. McX: *Was it John that Mary kissed?*
         McY: *She didn't kiss anybody.*
       b. *It wasn't John that Mary kissed—she didn't kiss anybody.*

If felicitousness is to be possible on the second view, we cannot conjoin the boundedness and existential "implicata," which together would entail the uniqueness condition *Mary kissed (exactly) one person*. The "implicata" would themselves have to be preferentially ordered by the syntactic form of the sentence. The "implicatum" of the (main clause) focus constituent is preferred to the "implicatum" of the (subordinate clause) presupposition constituent. Thus on the second view *Mary kissed at most one individual* is ranked above *Mary kissed someone*. The response *Mary didn't kiss anybody* is logically compatible with the preferred "implicatum," and so the discourse is felicitous, even though the response is incompatible with the less preferred "implicatum."

Analogous connections between entailments and surface syntax were discussed by Chomsky (1972) and have been exploited by Wilson and Sperber (1979). Neither "implicatum" is what Wilson and Sperber call a GRAMMATICALLY SPECIFIED ENTAILMENT OF THE SENTENCE (GSE). The sentence "directly entails" (Wilson and Sperber, 1979, p. 313) the GSE *It was someone that Mary kissed*, which is the FIRST BACKGROUND ENTAILMENT (Wilson and Sperber, 1979, p. 314) because it arises by existential closure of the open sentence *It was x that Mary kissed*, where a variable has been substituted for the focus constituent of the sentence. On Halvorsen's view this BACKGROUND is logically equivalent to his "implicatum" *Mary kissed someone*. Halvorsen's uniqueness "implicatum" *Mary kissed (exactly) one person* is not identical to any GSE, nor is the boundedness condition *Mary kissed at most one person* identical to any

GSE. GSEs must be linked to surface structure by substitution of existentially quantified variables for syntactic constituents. And, of the sentences that Halvorsen takes as equivalent to his "implicata," namely, *It was someone that Mary kissed* and *It was (exactly) one person that Mary kissed,* only the former is a GSE. On his view the latter is not an entailment of *It was John that Mary kissed.*

Nonetheless the uniqueness condition does entail the background. This would place it on par with what Wilson and Sperber (1979, p. 315) call THE FOREGROUND. Their foreground consists only of the GSEs that entail the background of a sentence. As the uniqueness condition is not a GSE, it cannot be in their foreground. Propositions in the foreground are given a pragmatic interpretation by Wilson and Sperber. If *A* and *B* are in the foreground and $A \models B$, *A* is "more relevant" than *B* to "the point" of the utterance, to that content the sentence contains over and above its background. The background and its entailments are presuppositional in their behavior. According to Wilson and Sperber (1979, pp. 317–319) they are preserved under denial or questioning. Incompatibility between the presumptions of a context and the background propositions of an assertion leads to its infelicity. A proposition that entails the background, that is entailed by the sentence uttered, and that is not a GSE of the sentence uttered may be part of "the point" of an utterance, but "there is no LINGUISTIC indication that [it] should be . . . (Wilson and Sperber, 1979, pp. 318–319)." Such a proposition, on Wilson and Sperber's view, need exhibit no presuppositional behavior; it can be questioned and denied without infelicity.

According to Halvorsen the uniqueness condition is a "conventional implicatum" (presupposition). As it is "conventional," it depends on the meanings of the words and the syntax of the sentence giving rise to it. If it were, contrary to Halvorsen's view, an entailment of the sentence, it would be a proposition of the sort characterized in the previous paragraph. It would be entailed by the sentence uttered; it would entail the background; it would not be a GSE of the sentence uttered. Since it is a "conventional implicatum" for Halvorsen, it must exhibit presuppositional behavior. According to Wilson and Sperber, on the other hand, it can exhibit assertoric, nonpresuppositional behavior. It can be denied or questioned without making the original utterance infelicitous. On Halvorsen's view, if it is denied, the original sentence cannot be felicitously asserted.

Shall we resolve this contradiction by simply saying that in fact the uniqueness condition is NOT an entailment? Suppose it were a conventional implicatum (in Grice's original sense). It would be part of the "meaning" of the utterance. One could quite plausibly argue that Wilson and Sperber's conclusion could be expanded to include conventional implicata (in Grice's sense) that have the properties required by their argument. Then their theory would more adequately describe the behavior of the sentence. On the other hand, suppose it were a presupposition—"conventional implicatum" (in Halvorsen's sense). It is not part of Wilson and Sperber's background propositions. Their theory of linguistically ordered entailments, which has as its aim a semantically based explanation of presuppositional behavior, would manifestly fail to explain a crucial case of presupposition. Halvorsen's theory would more adequately describe the behavior of the sentence. The status of the uniqueness condition is therefore a crucial test of rival theories.

For the sake of argument we suggested earlier that it might prove useful in explaining the felicitousness of (81) and (82) to split the uniqueness condition into its component parts. We hypothesized an effect of superficial syntactic form: the preferential ranking of the (main clause) uniqueness implication above the (subordinate clause) existential implication of *It was John that Mary kissed*. Further, we hypothesized that it was the relative strength of the preferred uniqueness condition with respect to the existential condition (i.e., of the boundedness condition *Mary kissed at most one person*) that was essential in determining the felicitousness of (81) and (82). But consider the following:

(83)   a. McX: *Was it John that Mary kissed?*
              McY: *She kissed Mart and Rick.*
      b. *It wasn't John that Mary kissed—she kissed*
         Mart and Rick.

These examples are felicitous, which suggests that *It wasn't John that Mary kissed* has no boundedness presupposition *Mary kissed at most one person*. Halvorsen (1978, p. 16) considers examples like (83) but fails to draw the obvious conclusion. The conclusion he does draw is that *Was it John and Rick that Mary kissed?* has a "conventional exhaustiveness implicatum" *Mary kissed n persons* for NO PARTICULAR VALUE of *n* (*n* is an integer such that $1 \leq n$)! The charitable interpretation of this remark is that the sentence's "conventional exhaustiveness implicatum" is *Mary kissed some number of persons*. But that, of course, is just to say *Mary kissed a person/people*. And that is to reject the idea that there is an exhaustiveness/uniqueness condition at all, for the condition has now become just the existential condition *Mary kissed someone*. In conclusion, THERE IS NO UNIQUENESS PRESUPPOSITION FOR CLEFTS. Instead, the affirmative sentence *It was John that Mary kissed*, but not the preferred (choice negation) understanding of the negative sentence *It wasn't John that Mary kissed*, entails *Mary kissed (exactly) one person*.[5]

7. THE OPPOSING DESCRIPTIONS OF CLEFTS

Halvorsen's (1978) account makes the following claims:

1. *It was John that Mary kissed*
   a. Expresses the same proposition as (is logically equivalent to) *Mary kissed John*
   b. "Conventionally implicates" (presupposes) *Mary kissed someone*
   c. "Conventionally implicates" (presupposes) *Mary kissed (exactly) one person*
   d. Entails *Mary kissed someone*.
2. *It wasn't John that Mary kissed*
   a. Expresses the same proposition as (is logically equivalent to) *Mary didn't kiss John*
   b. "Conventionally implicates" (presupposes) *Mary kissed someone*
   c. "Conventionally implicates" (presupposes) *Mary kissed (exactly) one person*.
3. *It was John that Mary didn't kiss*
   a. Expresses the same proposition as (is logically equivalent to) *Mary didn't kiss John*
   b. "Conventionally implicates" (presupposes) *There is someone Mary didn't kiss*

---

[5] Wilson and Sperber account for the behavior of the uniqueness sentence better than Halvorsen. But negative sentences present a difficulty for their theory. The sentences (a) and (b) have the presupposition (c), but the first background entailment of (b) is (d), which entails (e).

(a)   *It was John that Mary kissed.*
(b)   *It wasn't John that Mary kissed.*
(c)   *Mary kissed someone.*
(d)   *There is someone such that it wasn't he that Mary kissed.*
(e)   *There is someone that Mary didn't kiss.*

The background (d) is not the presupposition (c). It is an explicit claim of the theory that background is preserved under denial or questioning (Wilson and Sperber, 1979, p. 317) and that background acts as a presupposition (Wilson and Sperber, 1979, p. 321). It would seem a little difficult to defend this claim in light of examples like this one.

    c. "Conventionally implicates" (presupposes) *There is (exactly) one person Mary didn't kiss*

    d. Entails *There is someone Mary didn't kiss.*

4. *It wasn't John that Mary didn't kiss*

    a. Expresses the same proposition as (is logically equivalent to) *Mary kissed John*

    b. "Conventionally implicates" (presupposes) *There is someone Mary didn't kiss*

    c. "Conventionally implicates" (presupposes) *There is (exactly) one person Mary didn't kiss.*

We propose that in fact a theory of clefts must account for the following observations:

I. *It was John that Mary kissed*

    a. Entails *Mary kissed John;* the latter does not entail the former

    b. Entails *Mary kissed someone*

    c. Entails but does not "presuppose" *Mary kissed (exactly) one person.*

II. *It wasn't John that Mary kissed*

    a. Entails *Mary didn't kiss John;* the latter does not entail the former

    b. "Presupposes" or its use implicates *Mary kissed someone*

    c. Does not "presuppose" *Mary kissed (exactly) one person.*

III. *It was John that Mary didn't kiss*

    a. Entails *Mary didn't kiss John;* the latter does not entail the former

    b. Entails *There is someone Mary didn't kiss*

    c. Entails but does not "presuppose" *There is (exactly) one person Mary didn't kiss.*

IV. *It wasn't John that Mary didn't kiss*

    a. Entails *Mary kissed John;* the latter does not entail the former

    b. "Presupposes" or its use implicates *There is someone Mary didn't kiss*

    c. Does not "presuppose" *There is (exactly) one person Mary didn't kiss.*

A Radical Pragmatics theory must account for both the semantics (the entailments) and the pragmatics (the "presuppositions" or implicata) of sentences in a coherent way. Before we can proceed with our study of clefts, we must reconsider a Standard Version of Radical Pragmatics.

8. NEGATION AND IMPLICATURE:
A PROBLEM FOR THE STANDARD
VERSION OF RADICAL PRAGMATICS

A Standard Version of Radical Pragmatics holds that the meaning of natural language negation is unambiguously that of an exclusion/wide-scope/sentential/external negation and that the usually preferred interpretation as a choice/narrow-scope/predicate/internal negation is pragmatically induced. This view has assumed that the internal negation interpretation could be explained by a straightforward account on Gricean lines. The argument involved has been assumed to be an application of Grice's first maxim of Quantity ("Make your contribution as informative as is required for the current purposes of the exchange") that would induce a more informative interpretation of "what is said." For example, there seems to be a natural parallel between saying (84) and communicating the more informative proposition (85) and saying (86) and communicating the more informative (87).

(84)   *John has three children.*

(85)   *John has three children and no more than three children.*

(86)   *The king of France is not bald.*

(87)   *There is a king of France and he is nonbald.*

The inference whereby (84) is used to communicate (85) by GENERALIZED CONVERSATIONAL IMPLICATURE has been much discussed (Horn, 1972; Gazdar, 1976, 1977, 1979). The parallel suggested that a similar account might be given for the negative sentences. However, closer inspection indicates that the parallelism between the implicatures induced by scalar items and those induced by negation is illusory. The apparent parallelism exists merely because the conjunction of any implicatum, however arrived at, with the logical consequences of "what is said" will typically be more informative than those consequences alone.[6]

In the case of scalar categories, we may construct an ordering of items that meets at least this condition: For an appropriately defined class of sentences, any sentence containing the ith term of the ordering will entail a sentence like the original except for "containing" the $i + 1$st term of the

---

[6] We assume that "what is implicated" is not a logical consequence of "what is said." Here informativeness is narrowly understood so as to satisfy the condition that if p is more informative than q, q does not entail p, and p is neither logically true nor logically false. See Atlas (1975a, 1975b), Harnish (1976, p. 362, n. 46), O'Hair (1969), Quine and Ullian (1978, p. 68), Smokler (1966).

ordering at one occurrence of the *i*th term in the original sentence. Such an ordering we will call a HORN SCALE. (We ignore several complexities; see Gazdar, 1979, pp. 55–58.) For example, consider the Horn scales in (88).

(88)   a.   (. . . , *n, n* − 1, . . . , *four, three, two, one*)
       b.   (*necessarily, possibly*)
       c.   (*all, most, many, some, few*)
       d.   (*know, believe*)
       e.   (*must, should, may*)
       f.   (*and, or*)

Sentences employing scalar words have generalized conversational implicatures of these sorts:

1. If a speaker asserts a sentence containing a later, "weaker" term in the scale, for example, A(*three*), A(*possibly*), A(*some*), he implicates the falsity of the "stronger" scalar variants, for example, the falsity of A(*four*), of A(*necessarily*), and of A(*all*).
2. If a speaker asserts the negation of a sentence containing an earlier, "stronger" term in the scale, for example, *not*-A(*four*), *not*-A(*necessarily*), *not*-A(*all*), he implicates a "weaker" variant, for example, A(*three*), A(*possibly*), A(*some*).

The explanation of the first sort of scalar implicature involves Grice's first maxim of Quantity and the maxims of Quality. If a speaker is in a position to assert that John has five children, he should not say that John has three children; if he does assert the latter, he may be taken to be in no position to assert a stronger statement, for example, *John has five children,* and, in conformity with a consequence of the maxim of Quality— namely, "Do not say what you do not know"—be taken not to know whether John has five children. Thus from the fact that the speaker has NOT asserted the stronger variant it will be inferred that he does not know whether the stronger variant is true. Gazdar (1979) argues that in the case of Horn scales, it will be inferred that the speaker knows that the stronger variant is false.

If a similar explanation were to be give for ordinary negation, we should posit a logical scale (89) where internal

(89) $(\sim\!A, \neg A)$

negation $\sim\!A$ precedes external negation $\neg A$. Then there should be two scalar implicatures: (*a*) if a speaker asserts an external negation, he implicates the falsity of the internal negation; (*b*) if a speaker asserts the negation of an internal negation, he implicates the external negation. Thus it is predicted that the external negation understanding of (86) will pragmatically imply (90) and (91).

(86)   *The king of France is not bald.*

(90)   *The speaker does not know that there is a king of France and that he is non-bald.*

(91)   *The speaker knows that it is not the case that there is a king of France and that he is non-bald.*

Of course, what should be pragmatically implied is (92).

(92)   *The speaker knows that there is a king of France and that he is non-bald.*

One response to the conflict between the pragmatic implications would be to abandon the Gricean claim that the literal meaning of negation in English is that of external negation. A recent account of negation introduces an updated version of the traditional scope distinction and identifies ordinary negation with internal negation (Karttunen and Peters, 1979), but it has been argued that this suggestion has serious defects (Atlas, 1980). An alternative account argues that the literal meaning of natural language negation is neither an internal negation nor an external negation (Atlas, 1975a, 1975b, 1977, 1978, 1979). But no matter whether classical or nonclassical semantics is preferable, it will still be necessary to find a pragmatic principle, different from the one involved in scalar implicatures, that will offer an account of the inference from (86) to (87). An obvious problem to be solved is the conflict between such inferences and the typical Gricean arguments involving the maxim of Quantity, that is, the conflict between the inferences from (86) to (91) and from (86) to (92). The difference between the scalar expressions and ordinary negation that we have described is a general difference between kinds of pragmatic inference for two classes of expressions. The Gricean Inference from Quantity accounts for one class but not for the other.

We are concerned with the pragmatic principles that could be used to explain how and why what is conveyed or communicated by an utterance is more definite or more precise than the literal/conventional meaning of the sentence uttered. For convenience in exposition, we will follow Grice (1961, 1967, 1975, 1978) in identifying "what is said" with the sense of THE SENTENCE, that is, with a logical form or other semantic representation. Where we intend to refer to those inferences falling under maxims of conversation we shall speak of CONVERSATIONAL IMPLICATURES.[7] The

---

[7] Grice uses "conversational implicature" in the narrow sense for inferences from floutings of the maxims.

conjunction of "what is said" with "what is implicated" will be "what is communicated," the meaning a speaker conveys. We are interested in data in which "what is said" is augmented by generalized implicatures so that "what is communicated" is standardly more informative than "what is said." Here are familiar examples in which the (b) sentences are implicata of saying the (a) sentences (Gazdar, 1979, Chapter 3; Horn, 1972, 1973; Grice, 1961, 1967, 1975).

(93) a. *Some of the boys are at the party.*
      b_1. *Not all of the boys are at the party.*

(94) a. *Paul may be in his office.*
      b_1. *Paul may not be in his office.*

(95) a. *Morton has three children.*
      b_1. *Morton has no more than three children.*

(96) a. *Not all of the boys are at the party.*
      b_1. *Some of the boys are at the party.*

(97) a. *Rick is a philosopher or a poet.*
      b_1. *Rick is not both a philosopher and a poet.*
      b_2. $\begin{cases} \textit{Rick may be a philosopher.} \\ \textit{Rick may not be a philosopher.} \\ \textit{Rick may be a poet.} \\ \textit{Rich may not be a poet.} \end{cases}$

(98) a. *If John is at home, the phonograph will be on.*
      b_1. $\begin{cases} \textit{John may be at home.} \\ \textit{John may not be at home.} \\ \textit{The phonograph may be on.} \\ \textit{The phonograph may not be on.} \end{cases}$

(99) a. *It's not the case that Rick is both a philosopher and a poet.*
      b_1. *Rick is either a philosopher or a poet.*

(100) a. *Marjorie believes that Babette is a Phi Beta Kappa.*
      b_1. *Marjorie does not know that Babette is a Phi Beta Kappa.*
      b_2. $\begin{cases} \textit{Babette may be a Phi Beta Kappa.} \\ \textit{Babette may not be a Phi Beta Kappa.} \end{cases}$

These implicata limit "what is said" by shrinking the range of possible states of affairs associated with "what is said" to a smaller range of those states of affairs associated with "what is communicated." "What is communicated" is MORE DEFINITE than "what is said." We shall argue that these more definite propositions are derivable by the Gricean Inference from Quantity.

Other implicata enrich "what is said" by reshaping the range of the possible states of affairs associated with "what is said" to a narrower range of possible states of affairs associated with "what is communicated." "What is communicated" is MORE PRECISE than "what is said." Some examples follow.

(101)   a. *If you mow the lawn, I'll give you five dollars.*
        b₁. *If you don't mow the lawn, I won't give you five dollars.*

(102)   a. *Mart turned the switch and the motor started.*
        b₁. *First Mart turned the switch and then the motor started.*
        b₂. *Mart's turning the switch indirectly caused the motor's starting.*
        b₃. *Mart's turning the switch directly caused the motor's starting.*

(103)   a. *Kurt went to the store and bought some wine.*
        b₁. *Kurt went to the store in order to buy some wine.*

(104)   a. *Mart and David moved the cabinet.*
        b₁. *Mart and David moved the cabinet together.*

(105)   a. *Mikael ate the cake.*
        b₁. *Mikael ate the whole cake.*

(106)   a. *Eve ate the apples.*
        b₁. *Eve ate all the apples.*

(107)   a. *The baby cried and the mother picked it up.*
        b₁. *The baby cried and the mother of the baby picked it up.*

(108)   a. *It was a vase made of bronze and on the base of the vessel was the maker's mark.*
        b₁. *It was a vase made of bronze and on the base of the vase was the maker's mark.*

(109)   a. *Mikael said "Hello" to the secretary and then he smiled.*
        b₁. *Mikael said "Hello" to the (female) secretary and then he (Mikael) smiled.*

(110)   a. *Do you know the time?*
        b₁. *If you know the time, please tell me what it is.*

(111)   a. *The president of Princeton does not have a Ph.D. in rolfing.*
        b₁. *There is a president of Princeton.*

(112)   a. *Pythagoras did not regret that he never tasted soybeans.*
        b_1. *Pythagoras never tasted soybeans.*

(113)   a. *It's not HP sauce that Grice adores.*
        b_1. *Grice adores something.*

(114)   a. *Maybe it's HP sauce that Grice adores.*
        b_1. *Grice adores something.*

(115)   a. *Peter says that it is HP sauce that Grice adores.*
        b_1. *Grice adores something.*

(116)   a. *If the president of Princeton has a Ph.D. in rolfing, at least he'll know how to pummel the faculty.*
        b_1. *There is a president of Princeton.*

Clearly this is a heterogeneous class of examples. They have been discussed under many distinct rubrics, for example, (101) under CONDITIONAL PERFECTION (Geis and Zwicky, 1971), (103) under CONJUNCTION REDUCTION (Schmerling, 1975), (107) under MEMBERSHIP CATEGORIZATION DEVICES (Sacks, 1972), (108) under DEFINITE REFERENCE (Hawkins, 1975, 1978) and BRIDGING INFERENCES (Clark and Haviland 1977), (110) under INDIRECT SPEECH ACTS (Heringer 1976; Searle 1975), and (111)–(116) under PRESUPPOSITION. We shall argue that there is a general principle that licenses an inference from "what is said" to the MORE PRECISE content of "what is communicated" even though the particular ways in which the more precise proposition is selected may differ from case to case. We are interested in understanding the character of this Inference from Informativeness. But first we shall discuss the Gricean Inference from Quantity.

9. THE INFERENCE FROM QUANTITY AND ITS LIMITATIONS

The implicata in (93)–(100) are derivable essentially by appeal to Grice's first maxim of Quantity, namely, "Make your contribution as informative as is required for the current purposes of the exchange." A prototypical Gricean argument for this class of implicatures goes as follows (Grice, 1975):

(117)   a. The speaker S has said p.
        b. There is a proposition q, related to p by virtue of entailing p and/or by being more informative than p, which it would be de-

sirable to convey in view of the current purposes of the exchange. (Here there is reference to the maxim of Relation "Be relevant.")

  c. Proposition q can be expressed as briefly as p, so S did not say p rather than q simply in order to be brief, that is, to conform to a maxim of Manner.
  d. So S must intend the hearer to infer *not-q* or at least *It's not the case that S knows that q,* for if S knew that q, he would have infringed the first maxim of Quantity by uttering p.
  e. Therefore, saying p implicates *not-q* or at least *It's not the case that S knows that q.*

Various versions of this argument have been rehearsed by Gazdar (1979), Harnish (1976), and Horn (1972). Schema (117) will suffice to represent these various arguments. For purposes of our discussion, the salient feature of such an argument is its derivation of implicata from what is NOT said. Given that there is available an expression of roughly equal length that is logically stronger and/or more informative, the failure to employ the stronger expression conveys that the speaker is not in a position to employ it. The inference will always result in a delimitation of what has been said, in a MORE DEFINITE proposition being conveyed.

The argument relies crucially on the existence of equally brief expressions that can be ordered in a Horn scale of relative informativeness. When the items in the scale are elements in a semantic field, and where alternatives are psychologically salient, then the stronger inference to *The speaker knows that the more informative alternatives do not obtain* is licensed. These are the well-known scalar implicatures illustrated in (93b$_1$), (94b$_1$), (97b$_1$), (100b$_1$) and formalized by Gazdar (1979, pp. 58–59) relying partly on the work of Horn (1972).[8]

In other cases the assertion of p will implicate that the speaker is not in a position to assert a stronger, more informative statement q. Instead of an inference from p to S *knows that not-q* as in the scalar cases, there is an inference from p to S *does not know that q* and so to *It's compatible with what S knows that q* and to *It's compatible with what S knows that not-q.*

[8] It seems to have been assumed in the literature that only Horn scales give rise to these strong implicatures. Other types of cases exhibit the same behavior. The implicatum of *Jane's skirt is blue* (Harnish, 1976) is not *The speaker doesn't know whether the skirt is any other color* but rather *The speaker knows that the skirt is not any other color.* Similarly to say *Jones is a doctor* is to imply *The speaker knows that Jones is not (e.g.) an architect* rather than *The speaker does not know whether Jones is an architect.* It may be sufficient that a set of lexical items be "about" the same domain and provide presumptively exclusive alternatives of equal saliency in order for the stronger implicata to obtain.

Some of these cases have been formalized by Gazdar (1979, p. 59) as CLAUSAL IMPLICATURES. These will arise when a compound sentence p has a constituent sentence q such that p entails neither q nor *not-q* and, on Gazdar's theory, presupposes neither as well. As there is usually a similar assertion that would entail q, or its negation, the speaker is presumed not to know whether q is true or whether q is false. This theory accounts for $(97b_2)$, $(98b_1)$, and $(100b_2)$.[9]

The implicata of (101)–(116) are not derivable by the Inference from Quantity. Indeed, the Inference from Quantity yields results inconsistent with the data of (101)–(116). For example, saying (101a) intuitively implicates $(101b_1)$ and thus communicates the conjunction of (101a) and $(101b_1)$, given in (101c).

(101) a. *I'll give you five dollars if you mow the lawn.*
   b_1. *If you don't mow the lawn, I won't give you five dollars.*
   c. *I'll give you five dollars if, and only if, you mow the lawn.*

But by the first maxim of Quantity, the speaker should have said the stronger sentence (101c). As the speaker has not said (101c), the hearer must be intended to infer its denial. Therefore, according to the Inference from Quantity, (101a) implicates either its own falsehood or the falsehood of its intuitive implicatum $(101b_1)$. Saying (101a) cannot implicate $(101b_1)$ through an Inference from Quantity, but there is an implicature nonetheless.[10] We must explain the data by appeal to another form of argument, one that yields interpretations that supplement "what is said" by positing that "what is meant" is a stronger proposition compatible both with presumptions in the context and with "what is said."

---

[9] The data of (96) and (99) seem to require a more elaborate theory (q.v. Horn, 1972). It is tempting to suggest that *not all* derives from an underlying *some are not* and *none* derives from an underlying *all are not*. Then by the usual scalar implicature, saying *not all* (i.e., *some are not*) implicates *not all are not* (i.e., *not none*), which is equivalent to *some*. Thus the pragmatic quantity scale, ordering "deeper" or otherwise "designated" readings, motivates a particular hypothesis about syntactic/semantic representations. We shall not discuss this hypothesis here. A more "surfacey" alternative would be the positing of scales of items: *(impossible, improbable/unlikely, . . .), (none/no, . . . ,not all, . . .)*.

[10] Sentence $(101b_1)$ is only an implicatum; not all conditionals convey a biconditional, indicating the defeasibility of the inference. Compare

(a)   *I have a key in my pocket if the door is locked.*
(b)   *I have a key in my pocket if, and only if, the door is locked.*

Sentence (b) is not implicated by saying (a) because (b) is incompatible with noncontroversial background presumptions and so is blocked, a mechanism formalized in Gazdar 1979.

10. THE INFERENCE FROM INFORMATIVENESS

It seems that at least three notions may enter into intuitive judgments that A is more informative than B: (a) the set of logical consequences of B is contained in the set of logical consequences of A; (b) the set of sentences incompatible with B (its potential falsifiers) is contained in the set of sentences incompatible with A; (c) what B is "about" is contained in (is a part of) what A is "about." These notions are semantical; they do not reflect the relativity of the informational content of an utterance to the context in which it is uttered. Yet it is also a basic intuition that the information an utterance gives an addressee depends in part on what he already knows, believes, presumes, or takes for granted, in short, on what is normally left unsaid.

We believe that there will prove to be some explanatory value in a theory embodying in some form the following propositions:

Maxims of Relativity
1. Do not say what you believe to be highly noncontroversial, that is, to be entailed by the presumptions of the common ground.
2. Take what you hear to be lowly noncontroversial, that is, consistent with the presumptions of the common ground.

Conventions of Noncontroversiality (among which are)
1. **Convention of Intension (Common Knowledge):** The obtaining of stereotypical relations among individuals is noncontroversial.
2. **Convention of Extension (Exportation):**
   If A is "about" t, then
   a. If $\ulcorner t \urcorner$ is a singular term, $\ulcorner \exists x(x = t) \urcorner$ is noncontroversial[11]
   b. If $\ulcorner t \urcorner$ denotes a set, $\ulcorner \exists x(x \in t) \urcorner$ is noncontroversial
   c. If $\ulcorner t \urcorner$ denotes a state of affairs or a proposition, $\ulcorner t$ is actual$\urcorner$ and $\ulcorner t$ is true$\urcorner$ are noncontroversial.

Principle of Informativeness
Suppose a speaker S addresses a sentence A to a hearer H in a context K. If H has n COMPETING interpretations $A^{u_1}, A^{u_2}, \ldots, A^{u_n}$ of A in

---

[11] Gazdar (1977) dismisses a similar idea. He writes, "Naturally one can add to Grice's maxims, perhaps along the lines of: Assume referents exist unless you know they don't, but then one can always invent no less unreasonable sounding conversational maxims to deal with any example at all [p. 127]." The resemblance between our suggestion and Gazdar's straw man is only superficial. We do not conceive the Convention of Extension as a "maxim" of conversation at all. It is part of a theory of background presumption, of noncontroversiality. Its role is emphatically not that of a conversational maxim. Its acceptability will rest upon its value within such a theory of background presumption and upon its contribution to our theory as a whole.

the context K with information contents $INF(A^{u_1})$, $INF(A^{u_2})$, . . . , $INF(A^{u_n})$, and G_A is the set of propositions that are noncontroversial in K, then the "best" interpretation A^{u*} of A for H is the most informative proposition among the competing interpretations that is consistent with the common ground.[12]

Let A^{u*} be A^{u_j} for the least j, $1 \le j \le n$, such that $INF(A^{u_j} + G_A) = \max INF(A^{u_i} + G_A)$, $1 \le i \le n$.[13]

The sentence A will tend to convey the pragmatic content $PRON(A)$ to the hearer H: $PRON(A) = INF(A^{u*} + G_{A^{u*}})$ where $G_{A^{u*}}$ is the set of propositions that are noncontroversial in the context and that are "about" what A^{u*} is "about."[14]

If a predicate Q is semantically nonspecific with respect to predicates P_i, $1 \le i \le n$, but for some j, $1 \le j \le n$, P_j is stereotypical of Qs, then in saying $\ulcorner Qt \urcorner$ a speaker will convey $\ulcorner P_j t \urcorner$ in accordance with the second maxim of Relativity and the Convention of Intension. This is illustrated by Sentences (109a) and (118a)–(120a), which communicate (109b$_1$) and (118b)–(120b), generalized implicata that are more informative than "what is said."

(118) a. *The secretary smiled.*
      b. *The female secretary smiled.*

(119) a. *John had a drink.*
      b. *John had an alcoholic drink.*

(120) a. *John was reading a book.*
      b. *John was reading a non-dictionary.*

The standard application of Grice's first maxim of Quantity does not ex-

---

[12] The notion of "competing interpretations" is left as a primitive notion in this formulation of our theory. It is a complex function of the literal meaning of the sentence uttered, stress, tone, *etc*. The context will enter to fix reference, *etc.*

[13] Two explications of the qualitive concept of a statement's informational content have long been familiar to philosophers; they were proposed by Sir Karl Popper (1959), by Rudolf Carnap (1942), Carnap and Bar-Hillel (1952), John Kemeny (1953), and by Carl Hempel (1960). The first explication identifies the informational content of a statement with the set of its logical consequences, that is, $IN(A) = \{B : A \models B\}$. The second identifies the content with the set of possible falsifiers of the statement, descriptions of possible states of affairs incompatible with it, i.e. $CON(A) = \{B : B \models \neg A\}$. The two views are subsumed under one notion of "semantic content" in Carnap and Bar-Hillel (1953–1954) and a quantitative concept introduced. A Popperian notion related to the falsification content is that which a statement is "about". The Carnapian definition given by Smokler (1966) restricts $\models$ somewhat (see Smokler, 1966, pp. 207, 210).

[14] We shall say more about *about*.

plain the data. On Grice's view a speaker should tailor the form of his utterances to what he thinks his hearer's needs or interests in the conversation might be. If a specification would enable the hearer to satisfy his needs or interests, there is a presumption that the speaker should issue such a specification in his utterance. If the speaker fails to be specific, it is assumed that he cannot be (Grice, 1975, p. 57). Thus it would be predicted that in saying (109a) or (118a)–(120a) a speaker would not implicate that the secretary was female, that the drink was alcoholic, that the book was not a dictionary.

Temporal, causal, and teleological relations between events are stereotypical in our "common sense" conceptual scheme. Thus (102)–(103) also fall under the maxim of Relativity and the Convention of Intension. The (a) sentences of (102)–(103) may be understood in several different ways. In any particular context of utterance, the chosen understanding results from an INFERENCE TO THE BEST INTERPRETATION, the understanding that best "fits" both the shared background presumptions in the context and the communicative intentions attributable to the speaker in light of "what he has said." We have formulated this notion of best interpretation in our Principle of Informativeness.

The Conventions of Noncontroversiality and the Principle of Informativeness also explain the presuppositional sentences (111a)–(116a). If (111a) is "about" the president of Princeton; (112a) is "about" Pythagoras's never tasting soybeans; (113a)–(115a) are "about" what Grice adores; (116a) is "about" the president of Princeton, then in accordance with the Convention of Extension, $(111b_1)$–$(116b_1)$ are noncontroversial. By the Principle of Informativeness, $(111b_1)$–$(116b_1)$ are in turn part of what (111a)–(116a) convey in the pragmatic content PRON for each sentence. These implicata are the traditional presuppositions, including the presupposition of the cleft (113a).

The semantic aspects of the intuitive notion of "aboutness" that we are employing have been in part explicated in Putnam (1958). Generalizing from a suggestion of Popper (1959) we shall say that if a statement A is "about" the set $\mathcal{A}$ and a statement B is "about" the set $\mathcal{B}$, A is more informative than B if $\mathcal{B}$ is properly contained in $\mathcal{A}$ (Popper, 1959, p. 122). For example *All birds have wings* and *All crows have wings* are "about" birds and crows, respectively, but not "about" winged creatures, and the first statement is more informative than the second. On Putnam's explication of "aboutness," A is "about" $\mathcal{S}$ if and only if B is "about" $\mathcal{S}$ provided that A and B are logically equivalent. *All birds have wings* and *All crows have wings* are also "about" the nonwinged, as they are equivalent to *All nonwinged things are nonbirds* and *All nonwinged things are noncrows*. Thus the sentences may be taken to be "about" the set-theoretic union of birds and the non-winged and "about" the set-theoretic union of crows and the nonwinged respectively. Because the former set properly contains the latter, by Popper's criterion *All birds have wings* is the more informative.

It is a feature of Putnam's account that a sentence and its negation are "about" the same thing and that $\ulcorner Fa \urcorner$ is "about" $\{a\}$. A further feature of "aboutness" worthy of mention is its intentionality. This is indicated by the nonreferential occurrence of $\ulcorner t \urcorner$ in $\ulcorner A$ is "about" $t \urcorner$. The sentence *All winged horses are unridable* is "about" winged horses; *All golden mountains are unclimbable* is "about" golden mountains. As sets these are identical, being the null set $\emptyset$. But *All winged horses are unridable* is not "about" golden mountains, nor is *All golden mountains are unclimbable* "about" winged horses. The inference from $\ulcorner A$ is "about" $t \urcorner$ to $\ulcorner \exists x(A$ is "about" $x) \urcorner$ is an instance of an inference dubbed EXPORTATION by W. V. O. Quine (1956). Quine, in a happy choice of terminology, called his inference IMPLICATIVE, and so do we. However logically dubious our inference is, it is dubious in precisely the way exportation is dubious. Quine's classic example of exportation is that inference from *Ralph believes that Ortcutt is a spy* to *Ralph believes z (z is a spy) of Ortcutt*, from which it follows $(\exists x)$ *(Ralph believes z (z is a spy) of x)*. Our need for $\ulcorner \exists x(A$ is "about" $x) \urcorner$ is as pressing as the need Quine recognizes for relational statements of belief. By the Convention of Extension, the exported existential proposition is a matter of presumption in the context of utterance. The proposition does not need to be true; it merely needs to be taken for granted by the parties to the discourse. It is their propositional attitudes that affect how utterances in the context will be understood.

11. THE APPARENT CLASH BETWEEN GRICEAN MAXIMS AND OUR PRINCIPLE OF INFORMATIVENESS: ITS RESOLUTION

We have sketched how our maxims of Relativity, the Conventions of Noncontroversiality, and our Principle of Informativeness explain the data of (102), (103), (109), (111)–(120) that Gricean Inferences from Quantity will not explain. The Quantity implicata are inconsistent with the Informativeness implicata. Yet both forms of inference are needed for explanation of all the data. We must ask why speakers do not intuit contradictions when the Inferences from Quantity and from Informativeness produce propositions inconsistent with each other.

We have already discussed scalar implicatures. It was observed that internal and external negation might be considered a Horn scale ($\sim A$, $\neg A$).

By the Inference from Quantity, asserting $\neg$**A** implicates *not* $\sim$**A** in the same way that asserting $\ulcorner \exists x A(x) \urcorner$ implicates $\ulcorner not \; \forall x A(x) \urcorner$. This is an incorrect account of negation. Typically asserting $\neg$**A** implicates $\sim$**A**, which is the result of an Inference to the Best Interpretation of what the speaker said (by our Principle of Informativeness).

Again, the biconditional and conditional seem to form a Horn scale $(A \leftrightarrow B, A \rightarrow B)$. By the Inference from Quantity asserting $A \rightarrow B$ implicates *not* $(A \leftrightarrow B)$. But this is incorrect. Typically asserting $A \rightarrow B$ implicates $A \leftrightarrow B$.

Sentences like (102a) suggest a possible scale (*A because B, A and then B, A and B*). The Inference from Quantity yields that the assertion *A and B* implicates *not* (*A and then B*) and *not* (*A because B*). Again this is incorrect. If *A and B* is asserted in a context, it will be understood as the strongest proposition in the scale in light of the common ground, the apparent intentions of the speaker, and the literal meaning of the sentence uttered.

We wish to resolve these apparent clashes between the Gricean Inference from Quantity and our Inference from Informativeness. Our strategy is to argue that these cases are not scales properly so-called. If they are not, then there are no scalar implicatures of the sort just described, and so no clash between Informativeness and Quantity. Only Informativeness actually applies to these cases. In fact, there are natural and independently motivated restrictions to put on Horn scales. First, to constitute a genuine scale for the production of scalar implicatures, each item must be lexicalized to the same degree. Second, to constitute a genuine scale, each item in a position on the scale entails those in positions to its right, and all the items are "about" the same thing (Gazdar, 1979, pp. 57–58; 1977, pp. 72, 181). The first restriction will eliminate the Quantity implicatures incompatible with "negation strengthening" and with "conditional perfection." There is no scale $(\sim A, \neg A)$ because there is no free morpheme in English that standardly means the internal negation. There is no argument of the form "Since the speaker did not say *The king of France is nonbald,* he cannot mean it. And so he knows that it is false." Similarly, because there is no unitary lexeme in English like *if* that standardly means the same as *if and only if* (*iff* does not count), there is no Horn scale $(A \leftrightarrow B, A \rightarrow B)$. The second restriction will eliminate the Quantity implicatures incompatible with "conjunction buttressing." There is no Horn scale (*A because B, A and then B, A and B*), as *because* and *and then* introduce relations other than the kind the Horn scale is "about," the paradigm of which is logical conjunction.

Of course there are further cases of apparent clash between Quantity and Informativeness. Saying *not* (*A and B*) seems to implicate *A or B*. Thus, saying *It's not the case that Rick is both a philosopher and a poet* seems to implicate *Rick is either a philosopher or a poet.* The principle involved is the implication of the weakest item on the Horn scale by the denial of a strong one. The scale is (*and, or*). On the other hand, saying *It's not the case that Kurt went to the store and bought some wine* (colloquially, *Kurt didn't go to the store and buy some wine*) does not implicate *Kurt went to the store or he bought some wine.* The Inference from Informativeness results in "conjunction buttressing." *A and B* is informatively understood as *A in order to B.* The two actions described separately in *A* and in *B* are teleologically related as means to end. The sentence indicates one action under a complex description. The implicature from the saying of *not (A and B)* to *A or B* that implicates the possibility of independent alternatives cannot coherently arise. Indeed, saying *Kurt didn't go to the store and buy some wine* implicates *Kurt neither went to the store nor bought some wine.* So, for some *A, B,* saying *not (A and B)* implicates *not-A and not-B.*

However, for Gazdar (1979, p. 59) *not (A and B)* potentially clausal implicates, by appeal to Quantity, *It's possible for all the speaker knows that A* and *It's possible for all the speaker knows that B.* If the Inference from Informativeness yields *The speaker knows that not-A* and *The speaker knows that not-B* in cases like the one in question, Informativeness is inconsistent with Gazdar's rule.

A simplified version of that rule is phrased informally by Gazdar (1979, p. 60) as follows: *X* potentially clausal implicates that for all the speaker knows *Y,* and, for all the speaker knows, *not Y,* if and only if *Y* is a part of *X* but neither *Y* nor its negation is entailed by *X.* In our example *X = not (A and B)* and *Y = A,* where in the stereotypical course of things *A* is necessary for *B. A* is a part of *not (A and B),* and neither *A* nor its negation is entailed by *not (A and B).* Thus *not (A and B)* potentially clausal implicates *It's possible for all the speaker knows that A.* Apart from *Y* (or *not Y*) being entailed by (or being presupposed by) *X,* Gazdar's rule takes no semantic relations into account; in particular, no consideration is given to semantic relations between PARTS of *X.* But that relation is crucial to this example.

The same issues arise for potential scalar quantity implicatures. Saying *A or B* implicates *not (A and B).* But if one says *Socrates is mortal or everyone is mortal,* which is equivalent to *Socrates is mortal,* does one thereby implicate *not (Socrates is mortal and everyone is mortal),* which is equivalent to *not (everyone is mortal)*? The contexts in which one could appropriately employ *Socrates is mortal or everyone is mortal* may be a little odd; it is not as if it were a premise for an argument that continues *Socrates isn't mortal; therefore, everyone is mortal.* No such argument could possibly be sound, though it certainly has a valid form. The fact remains that, whatever ah appropriate context might be, use of a disjunctive sentence equivalent to *Socrates is mortal* is predicted to implicate a sentence equivalent to *Someone is not mortal* in the same way that use of *A or B* is predicted to implicate *but not both*. If it is not obviously false, it also is not obviously true that there is this implicature. We take it that it is an open question whether Gazdar's rules are adequate as they stand. Properly reformulated in light of the semantic relations between *A* and *B*, Gazdar's rules for the sentence *not (A and B)* may not yield scalar or clausal implicata that would contradict the implicata derived by the Principle of Informativeness. So it is an open question whether there is an irresolvable conflict between Quantity and Informativeness.

As our third class of examples in which Quantity and Informativeness apparently conflict, we discuss cases examined by Harnish (1976). When a speaker asserts (121) he implicates (122), and when a speaker asserts (123) he implicates (124).

(121)   *Russell wrote "Principia Mathematica".*

(122)   *Only Russell wrote "Principia Mathematica".*

(123)   *Russell and Whitehead wrote "Principia Mathematica".*

(124)   *Russell and Whitehead jointly wrote "Principia Mathematica".*

By Quantity we may infer that as the speaker of (121) failed to be specific where it would be informative and generally useful to be so, the speaker was in no position to asert (122). Yet this conclusion conflicts with a stereotypical relationship between books and authors, the NORM of "one author per book" (cf. Harnish's example *Leibniz and Newton invented the calculus*). Given that it is held, for example by Gazdar, that possible implicata inconsistent with background presumptions are defeated, it is plausible to analyze the defeat of the Quantity implicatum as one of this kind. However, incorrect Inferences from Quantity will not always be neutralized through the fortuitous intervention of contextual assumptions —the very ones that are employed in our Principle of Informativeness. Perhaps we will finally find a real clash between Gricean maxims and our Informativeness.

For example, there is a strong intuition that (125b), (126b), and (127b) are the preferred interpretations of (125a), (126a), and (127a).

(125)   a. *Mart and David moved the cabinet.*
         b. *They moved it together.*

(126)   a. *Mart and David bought a piano.*
         b. *They bought it together.*

(127)   a. *Mart and David went to San Francisco.*
         b. *They went together.*

Harnish (1976, p. 328 ff.) argues, correctly we believe, that the (a) sentences are not ambiguous between ''independent'' and ''cooperative'' understandings. The preferred interpretation is implicated. Harnish (1976, p. 358 ff.) points out that it is not at all clear that the maxim of Quantity can explain this implicatum. (He does not explicitly say what the Quantity implicatum would be. The hearer might argue that the speaker is in no position to make a relevant ''cooperative'' claim, as he did not say *Mart and David bought a piano together.* Thus the hearer would infer the ''independent'' understanding of the sentence. However, he could also argue that because the speaker did not say *Mart and David bought pianos separately,* the speaker was in no position to make that claim. So the hearer understands him to mean the ''cooperative'' understanding of the sentence. The Quantity implicatum is not well defined.) But Harnish proposes a Gricean submaxim of Manner, namely, in so far as possible, if objects $a, b, c, \ldots F$ together, put their names together when reporting this F-ing. This maxim is intended as one instance of a more general Grice-type maxim: Make your sayings mirror the world (Harnish, 1976, p. 359).

But such Gricean maxims and submaxims of Manner will not account for all the data. For example, the preferred interpretation of (128a) (e.g., in reply to *Who took a shower?* or in reply to *What did Mart and David do?*) is (128b) rather than (128c).

(128)   a. *Mart and David took a shower.*
         b. *Mart and David took showers separately.*
         c. *Mart and David took a shower together.*

In this example the ''independent'' interpretation is the preferred one. Sentence (128a) conveys (128b), and given our social norms, (128b) is predicted by the second maxim of Relativity, the Conventions of Noncontroversiality, and the Principle of Informativeness. The Inference to the Best Interpretation of the utterance (128a) yields the ''independent'' understanding (128b). Because the Quantity implicata for (125)–(128) are not well defined, there is no clash between Quantity and Informativeness. And Manner is simply not a general explanation. We shall now sketch an account of the implicata of (125)–(127).

The literal meaning of the sentence (126a) *Mart and David bought a piano* leaves it open whether there was one piano-buying or two. The usual implicature restricts the understanding to one. If the sentence is indeed a reduced form of *Mart bought a piano and David bought a piano,* the literal meaning, under the assumption that this reduction preserves meaning, is predictable. The conjunction also leaves it open whether one or two pianos were bought. The same observation holds for *Mart bought a piano and so did David*, which requires identity of sense of the deleted constituent. Atlas (1977, pp. 329–330) argued that it would follow from the last sentence that David did what Mart did. The sentence requires sameness of action, but that does not determine whether one or two piano-buyings are involved unless the relevant criteria of identity of actions have been fixed. Given the meaning of the sentence, at least it is clear that the criteria cannot require that the action-token (as contrasted with action-type) be the same for David as for Mart. Thus the piano need not be one and the same.

The "independent" implicatum entails that the action-tokens are different. Normally this would mean that more than one piano were involved, but it is imaginable that in a short period of time Mart could buy and then sell a piano, which David then bought, perhaps from Mart himself. It would not be semantically unacceptable, and though unusual because incomplete it certainly would not be false, to describe that situation—one piano, two buyings—by (129a). We should represent such a situation, following Davidson (1967), by (129b). The normal case would be (129c).

(129)   a. *Mart and David bought a piano.*
      b. $\exists x \exists e \exists e'(Piano(x)\ \&\ Buy(m,x,e)\ \&\ Buy(d,x,e')\ \&\ e \neq e')$
      c. $\exists x \exists y \exists e \exists e'(Piano(x)\ \&\ Piano(y)\ \&\ x \neq y\ \&$
        $Buy(m,x,e)\ \&\ Buy(d,y,e')\ \&\ e \neq e')$
      d. $\exists x \exists e(Piano(x)\ \&\ Buy(m,x,e)\ \&\ Buy(d,x,e))$

By contrast the "cooperative" implicatum entails that the action-token (including the piano) is the same for David as for Mart. *Mart and David bought a piano* would then convey (129d). These implicata are not directly comparable—neither (129c) nor (129d) entails the other. Nonetheless we intuitively feel that the "cooperative" implicatum (129d) is more specific or precise, perhaps because it is in Popper's sense a "riskier" proposition, more easily refuted. The fewer existential quantifiers there are in an affirmative sentence the more highly valued the sentence is. This is a case in which the relevant notion of information is that determined by the class of possible falsifiers of a proposition. Such a proposition is preferred as an interpretation by our Principle of Informativeness unless it contradicts our background Conventions of Noncontroversiality, as described in our Principle.

As examples of our fourth class of cases in which the Principle of Informativeness may clash with the maxim of Quantity, we consider sentences discussed by Grice (1975, p. 56).

(130) a. *John is meeting a woman this evening.*
   b. *The person to be met is someone other than John's wife, mother, sister, or perhaps even a close platonic friend.*

(131) a. *I broke a finger yesterday.*
   b. *The finger is mine.*

Grice argues plausibly that an Inference from Quantity will yield (130b) from (130a). The failure to use a more informative expression than the indefinite description *a woman* suggests that the speaker is in no position to provide a more specific description of the kind normally relevant. The reverse implicatum in (131), which Grice mentions in passing, presents an explanatory difficulty for the Inference from Quantity. According to Quantity if the speaker meant his own finger, he should have said so. Because he did not, he is assumed not to be in the position to make that claim, that is, the finger was not his. But the negation of this proposition is actually implicated. Once again the explanation of the inference lies in what speakers take as stereotypical or conventional behavior. The use of the indefinite description *a finger* leaves it open whose finger was broken, but the speaker's breaking someone else's finger would be regrettable if unintentional and contrary to our social norms if intentional. As noted in the second maxim of Relativity, we are loathe to interpret the utterance so as to impute an abnormal or unnatural act unless there are specific indications to that effect. A similar explanation accounts for the implicatum in (132).

(132) a. *I lost a book yesterday.*
   b. *The book is mine.*

On the other hand Quantity implicatures seem in force in the following cases (133)–(135).[15]

(133) a. *I slept on a boat last night.*
   b. *The boat is not mine.*

(134) a. *I slept in a car last night.*
   b. *The car is not mine.*

(135) a. *I found a ring yesterday.*
   b. *The ring is not mine.*

[15] Data in (132)–(135) are from Grice (1975, p. 56) and Harnish (1976, p. 350). Our intuitions differ from Harnish's on (133); he does not believe saying (133a) implicates (133b). Harnish provides no explanation of his data. We shall provide a partial explanation in what follows.

Quantity is part of an account of cooperative communicative behavior. Informativeness is part of an account of efficient communicative behavior. If one can communicate some specified proposition p by asserting a less specified proposition q, then in general it will be more efficient to assert q and let the hearer make his INFERENCE TO THE BEST INTERPRETATION (Atlas, 1975b). In light of the distinct roles of Grice's maxims and of the Principle of Informativeness, it is no surprise that conflict might be possible. For the class of indefinite descriptions just discussed, the upshot seems to be that where there is an implicature at all (not all indefinite descriptions yield them) Quantity takes precedence over Informativeness unless the result contradicts our background Conventions of Noncontroversiality. If that occurs, the Informativeness implicatum is adopted. This is the first genuine case of clash between Quantity and Informativeness that we have discussed. It is resolved by a general preference for the Quantity implicatum. After all, where the Quantity implicature may be employed appropriately, it is reasonable to do so on the grounds that speakers are being cooperative. In particular, it is reasonable to assume that they are being relevant, perspicuous, and thus informative in what they say. Speakers must share responsibility for successful uptake with their hearers.

12. THE LOGICAL FORM OF CLEFTS AND ITS EXPLANATORY VALUE

One attraction of Grice's views has always been its semantical conservatism. The Fregean notion that "sense" is truth conditions, the identification of a set of English expressions, which are frustratingly resistant to systematization, with the logical constants, which are our paradigm of semantic systematization, and the scrupulous adherence to a policy of austerity in positing senses have contributed to theoretical simplicity in our theory of language. Simplicity is indeed a virtue of theories; simple-mindedness is not. There has been a regrettable temptation to adopt a logical primitivism when theorizing about implicature. The canonical languages of our logical theories are constructed to achieve pellucidity, but a certain measure of complexity is compatible with, indeed on our view required by, a satisfactory use of truth-conditional semantics within a pragmatic theory.

Logical primitivism would take the familiar claim that (136) and (137) have the same truth conditions to imply (fallaciously) that (136) and (137) have the same logical form (138). A less primitive suggestion would give (136) the logical form (139).

(136)   *It was John that Mary kissed.*

(137)   *Mary kissed John.*

(138)   *Kiss(Mary, John)*

(139)   λx(Kiss(Mary, x))(John)

In adopting a logical form we are locating the sentence in a network of
entailment relations that is described by the particular logical theory we
are employing. But we are also interested in hypothesizing logical forms
that are EXPLANATORY, that account for entailment relations by exhibiting
semantically significant structure in the sentence. Such an account will
begin to explain how the relations between the parts of the sentence contribute to the meaning of the whole. It will illuminate the similarities and
differences between related sentences. It will (on the standard view) provide the extensional sentence ''meaning'' upon which inferential mechanisms must operate to yield the understanding of an utterance. The assignment of logical form to a sentence is not only relative to the logical
theory employed, it is relative to the comprehensive theory in which logical forms have an explanatory place. Indeed, even the pragmatic features
of the sentence, its use in the language, can in principle bear on the assignment of logical form, especially if the resulting form increases the overall
coherence and explanatory power of the theory.[16]

The logical forms in (138) and (139) are logically equivalent, but they
are distinct: Whereas (138) has a primitive two-place predicate-symbol
true of Mary and John, (139) has a complex one-place predicate-symbol
true of John. Whereas (138) expresses a relation between Mary and John
—it is ''about'' the pair (Mary, John)—(139) expresses a property of
John; it is ''about'' him. And it is precisely here that the flaws of (139)
become obvious.

If one recalls the semantical similarities between clefts and pseudo-
clefts, the pseudo-cleft (140) will highlight the properties of (136).

(140)   *What Mary kissed was John.*

This sentence is ''about'' what/whom Mary kissed, which is specified or
identified as John. Likewise (136) is actually ''about'' whom Mary kissed,
which is then specified or identified as John.

We expand our description of the behavior of clefts as follows (cf. Section 7):

---

[16] Our indebtedness to the writing and teaching of Donald Davidson shows itself here, as
does our divergence from his views (cf. Davidson 1967, 1970).

I. *It was John that Mary kissed*
   a. Entails *Mary kissed John;* the latter does not entail the former
   b. Entails *Mary kissed someone*
   c. Entails but does not "presuppose" *Mary kissed (exactly) one person*
   d. Is "about" what/whom Mary kissed.

II. *It wasn't John that Mary kissed*
   a. Entails *Mary didn't kiss John;* the latter does not entail the former
   b. "Presupposes" or its use implicates *Mary kissed someone*
   c. Does not "presuppose" *Mary kissed (exactly) one person*
   d. Is "about" what/whom Mary kissed.

The logical forms (138) and (139), and their negations, obviously cannot satisfy these conditions. Is there any logical form that will meet ALL these conditions and in the process yield the correct pragmatic inferences in the Revised Standard Version? The answer, of course, is *yes*. It is just a more complex logical form than is typically suggested.

The correct logical form for (141a) *It was John that Mary kissed* involves λ-abstraction (Carnap, 1958, pp. 129–131) to formulate a complex one-place predicate-symbol and our COLLECTION OPERATOR γ to formulate a singular term.[17] The logical form (141b) of (141a) has precisely the properties described in (I). It may be paraphrased in English by (141c).

---

[17] If $\hat{x}A(x) = \{a\}$, that is, the extension of $\ulcorner A(x) \urcorner$ is just one object a, Hilbert's (1927) term $\ulcorner \epsilon x A(x) \urcorner$ designates the descriptum of $\ulcorner \iota x A(x) \urcorner$. If the extension of $\ulcorner A(x) \urcorner$ is larger, ϵ is a choice function; $\ulcorner \epsilon x A(x) \urcorner$ designates SOME ONE of the individuals in the extension (but we do not know which). The expression $\ulcorner \epsilon x A(x) \urcorner$ may be paraphrased by *an x such that if anything has A, x has A*. The basic axioms governing the use of the term are $\vdash \exists x A(x) \leftrightarrow A(\epsilon x A(x))$ and $\vdash \forall x A(x) \leftrightarrow A(\epsilon x \neg A(x))$. Thus the selection operator allows one to make a statement the force of which is PURELY existential while employing a designating singular term.

Paul Ziff, Jaakko Hintikka, and independently Jay Atlas have remarked on the need for ϵ-terms in giving the logical forms for sentences of a natural language. Ziff and Hintikka noted it for coreference phenomena, as in *John wants to catch **a fish** and eat **it** for supper* (Hintikka, 1973). Atlas (1972) makes the first systematic use of the ϵ-term within Donald Davidson's program of giving a theory of truth for English; the problem was to characterize the circumstances in which *I met the man who wrote "Lolita"; therefore, the man I met wrote "Lolita"* would be an acceptable inference. Once again, the heart of the matter is coreference—the coreference of event–terms.

The indeterminateness of Hilbert's ϵ-term makes it attractive to some, e.g., R. M. Martin (1979:214), as a paraphrase of indefinite plural noun phrases. Though we are in agreement with Martin's suggestions in some respects, his claim that Hilbert's ϵ-term, that is, the selection description, correctly formalizes indefinite plural noun phrases seems to us mistaken. It also seems incorrect to define contextually the ϵ-term as Martin (1958, p. 55; 1979, p. 214) does. Attributing the definition to Frederic B. Fitch, Martin (1958) contextually defines the ϵ-term by: $\ulcorner B(\epsilon x A(x)) \urcorner$ is defined as $\ulcorner \exists x A(x) \& \forall x(A(x) \rightarrow B(x)) \urcorner$. The second conjunct of the

(141) a. *It was John that Mary kissed.*
      b. $\lambda x(x = John)(\gamma x Kiss(Mary,x))$
      c. *A group of individuals kissed by Mary is identical to John.*

The advantages of this semantic representation are manifold. First, it explains the data in (I). It is easy to see that the entailment relation is as claimed in (Ia), as $\lambda x(x = John)(\gamma x A(x)) \models A(John)$, but $A(John) \not\models \lambda x(x = John)(\gamma x A(x))$. Condition (Ib) then follows immediately from (Ia). It is easy to prove that $\lambda x(x = John)(\gamma x A(x)) \models E! \iota x A(x)$, so part of (Ic) is explained. It may be worth remarking on the reasons for this entailment.

The formula $\ulcorner \lambda x(x = John)(\gamma x A(x)) \urcorner$ is definitionally equivalent to $\ulcorner \exists x A(x) \ \& \ \forall y(A(y) \rightarrow y = John) \urcorner$, from which $\ulcorner \exists x A(x) \ \& \ \exists x \forall y(A y) \rightarrow$

---

definiens seems too inclusive to be an accurate analysis of the definiendum. (For discussion of the ϵ-term, see Leisenring (1969).) But the condition in the definiens does capture an important concept in mathematics and in linguistics of which we can make use in the analysis of collective terms and so of clefts. Just as the ι-operator attaches to a formula A to produce an individual term $\ulcorner \iota x A(x) \urcorner$, so our γ-operator attaches to a formula A to produce a collective term $\ulcorner \gamma x A(x) \urcorner$. By a collective term we mean one that denotes a group. For example, the plural noun phrase *the boys* may be used as a collective term in *The boys* (collectively, that is, a group of boys) *are at the party;* the sentence is true if and only if there are boys and every boy (in the group) is at the party. We contextually define $\ulcorner B(\gamma x A(x)) \urcorner$ as $\ulcorner \exists x A(x) \ \& \ \forall x(A(x) \rightarrow B(x)) \urcorner$.

The γ-operator is indifferent to the distinction between singular and plural; $\ulcorner \gamma x A(x) \urcorner$ is consistent with both singular $\ulcorner$the A$\urcorner$ and plural $\ulcorner$the As$\urcorner$ and so captures a linguistic feature of collective nouns. Collective nouns in English are sometimes grammatically plural, for example, *cattle, clergy,* sometimes grammatically singular, for example, *furniture,* and sometimes either, for example, *family.*

A collective noun can designate a group collectively, and so behave as a denoting term, or designate a group distributively, for example, (in the U.S.) *The Administration, who have . . . , are . . . ;* (in the U.K.) *The Government, who have . . . , are . . . ;* plural count nouns, like *The boys* in our example above, which can mimic the behavior of collective nouns. Martin's definiens, which we accept as roughly correct for $\ulcorner \gamma x A(x) \urcorner$, though not for $\ulcorner \epsilon x A(x) \urcorner$, captures the distributive use of the collective term in the truth-conditions for sentences containing it.

It is also linguistically possible for a collective noun, and so even for plural count nouns, to designate a group of one as well as a more normal group of more than one. It is a virtue of our γ-operator that it allows this possibility. The cleft sentence *It was John that Mary kissed* is "about" the collectivity, not excluding a group of one, that Mary kissed. It can easily be demonstrated that the logical form for clefts that employs our γ-operator explains precisely those characteristics of clefts that we have argued are properly attributable to them.

There is one final observation supporting formalization of collectivity by our γ-operator. Collective nouns like *flock, herd, library, forest,* and *group* can act as "sortal classifiers" when attached to count nouns, for example, *flock of sheep.* And it has been claimed that "sortal classifiers" have properties in common with determiners (Lyons 1977, p. 464). If so, there is a suggestive analogy between a determiner like *the* and a "sortal classifier" like *group.* Likewise, there is an analogy between the ι-operator and our γ-operator, which we have exploited.

$y = x)^1$ follows immediately—that is, *Mary kissed (exactly) one person.*
The sentence *Mary kissed someone* follows from the contribution of *that
Mary kissed* to *It was John that Mary kissed.* But the proposition *Mary
kissed (exactly) one person* follows because of the CONTINGENT fact that
the specification in the (surface) main-clause focus constituent of *It was
John that Mary kissed* lists but one item, namely, John. That "asserted"
fact adds *Mary kissed (at most) one person* to the "presupposed" *Mary
kissed someone* to give *Mary kissed (exactly) one person.*

The felicitousness of the discourse (142)

(142)   McX: *Was it Mart and Rick that Mary kissed?*
        McY: *She kissed only John.*

which was inexplicable to Halvorsen, is explained without the machinery
of "ordered implications" (cf. Wilson and Sperber, 1979) that we
sketched in Section 6. What is being contradicted is not a "presupposition" but an assertion, and there is no problem of felicitousness.

Furthermore, the fact that lists can be of any finite length receives a
natural accomodation. Lists are sequences (or vectors), and can be the
values of individual variables. The expression *kiss* can be treated as a
"multigrade" predicate **Kiss,** so a sequence of any length (including infinite length) can be one of its arguments. The sentence schema *It was N_1,
N_2, . . . N_{i-1}, and N_i that Mary kissed* specifies a sequence $[s_a]_{a=1}^i$ of i
terms where $s_a = N_a$. The logical form is $\lambda \mathbf{x}(\mathbf{x} = [s_a]_{a=1}^i)(\gamma \mathbf{xKiss}(m,\mathbf{x})$ with
$\mathbf{x}$ ranging over i-term sequences of individuals. If we wish to accomodate
ANY number of terms, we may let sequences be infinite and identify the
subsequence $[s_a]_{a=1}^i$, $s_a = N_a$, with the sequence $[t_a]_{a=1}^\infty$ such that $t_a = s_a$,
$a = 1,2, . . . ,i$ and $t_a = \mathcal{D}, i + 1 \leq a$, where $\mathcal{D}$ is the domain of individuals.

The logical form preserves the intuition that the cleft is a property
rather than relation statement. In so doing it shows that it is "about" its
logical subject, removing the incoherence between the semantics and
pragmatics noted in Section 5; thus it explains datum (Id). It is "about"
what/whom Mary kissed, that is, "about" $\gamma xKiss(Mary,x)$.[18]

---

[18] If the reader still believes in a uniqueness implicature, so that he believes that (Ic)
should read '"presupposes" *Mary kissed (exactly) one person*' he can be satisfied by the
logical form $\ulcorner \lambda x(x = John)(\iota xKiss(Mary,x))\urcorner$. The logically equivalent form $\ulcorner \iota x$-
$Kiss(Mary,x) = John\urcorner$ resembles an underlying syntactic structure adopted for clefts by
Harries-Delisle (Contrastive emphasis and cleft sentences. In J. H. Greenberg *et al.* (Eds.)
Universals of Human Language, Volume 4: Syntax, Stanford: Stanford University Press,
1978, pp. 419–486). Harries-Delisle produces syntactical arguments to show that the underlying structure of the "equational sentence" *The one whom Mary kissed is John* also under-
lies *It was John that Mary kissed,* where *the one* is a neutral head noun marked for person
(third) and in English at least for number and for humanness. Logically the sentence is rec-

Radical Pragmatics posits the external negation (143b) for the negative sentence (143a). The Revised Standard Version of Radical Pragmatics, by the Principle of Informativeness, yields as a generalized conversational implicatum of (143a) the internal negation (143c).

(143) a. **It wasn't John that Mary kissed.**
       b. $\neg\lambda x(x = John)(\gamma xKiss(Mary,x))$
       c. $\lambda x(x \neq John)(\gamma xKiss(Mary,x))$

On either understanding of (143a), (IId) is explained. Condition (IIc) is explained as the implicatum (143c) does not entail *Mary kissed (exactly) one person.* This completes the explanation of (Ic). The implicatum (143c) entails, so (143a) implicates, *Mary kissed someone.* Thus (IIb) is explained. And finally, the implicatum (143c) entails *Mary didn't kiss John,* but the converse is not the case. So (IIa) is explained.

In Section 6 we discussed the peculiarity of Halvorsen's and Sadock's analysis of *Mary kissed no one and it wasn't John that Mary kissed,* a sentence that was allegedly true but "internally" infelicitous (self-contradictory). Radical Pragmatics predicts that on the literal understanding of (143a) it is true and, because the implicatum is canceled, felicitous, even if redundant. On the conveyed understanding (143a) is false and "odd" because straightforwardly contradictory. (These truth-values are determined by the assumption in the case that *Mary kissed no one* is true.) These theoretical descriptions of the behavior of *Mary kissed no one and it wasn't John that Mary kissed* seem empirically adequate and pleasantly nonparadoxical.

In general, with the qualifications that Jay Atlas has consistently made about the Radical Pragmatics treatment of negation, which strikes him as another instance of logical primitivism, the Radical Pragmatics view is a coherent and empirically adequate account of the entailment and "presuppositional" behavior of cleft sentences.[19]

---

ognized to involve identity, but grammatically the underlying structure is subject/predicate, and there are various complications about the occurrence of the copula in the underlying structure. Our work begins from roughly the same semantic intuitions, but refines and supports a logical analysis by semantic and pragmatic rather than syntactic data. It is now reassuring to discover syntactical arguments in support of an underlying structure whose basic features at least approximate those of the logical form that we have posited. Critical assessment of Harries-Delisle's arguments we must leave to syntacticians.

[19] Atlas (1975a, 1975b, 1977) argued that negation was univocal; that it was general/nonspecific rather than ambiguous. He also suggested how a Radical Pragmatics theory could accept an identification of negation in English with the external negation in ordinary logic, namely, by giving up the identification of external negation with the "literal meaning" of a sentence. Instead the theory would rest content with describing the understandings of utterances, and for the sake of theoretical simplicity make the external negation the "unmarked" case (see Atlas, 1979).

13. THE INTERACTION OF SEMANTICS AND PRAGMATICS

Within the philosophy of language and linguistic theory over the last decade, there have been attempts to investigate the relationship between semantics and pragmatics, to map a boundary between the two domains, and to understand the mechanics of their interaction. The aim of this chapter has been to exemplify one approach through which our understanding might be improved and to make evident the explanatory power of such an approach. A benefit for linguistics is the retrieval of the hope, now largely and prematurely abandoned, that the phenomena known as "presupposition" can be reduced to matters of entailment on the one hand and nonconventional conversational inferences on the other. The ingredients making this hope viable are (*a*) a refinement of the role of logical form and (*b*) the formulation of general principles of conversational inference.

The original intuition that we have tried to explicate is that there is significant semantic structure, explicable by logical form, over and beyond truth conditions. This structure meshes closely with pragmatic principles to produce informative, defeasible implicata. There were two problems. First, we needed to find some independent condition on logical forms that express the same truth conditions. This condition would distinguish a semantic representation of an English sentence from another logically equivalent to it. Second, we needed to make explicit that in fact there are two crosscutting pragmatic principles governing informativeness, not simply a hodgepodge of conflicting inferences. No doubt our formulations can and will be improved. Our aim here has been to show that, contrary to most expectation, progress can be made towards a coherent, explanatory theory.

The successful development of our approach would have several benefits. The one that we have focused on here is the reduction of some well-known presuppositional phenomena to matters of semantic structure interacting intimately with pragmatic principles of the sort used for a serious philosophical purpose by H. Paul Grice. Alternative theories treat presupposition as irreducible, a special species of conventional, non-truth-conditional inference that requires specific lexical items and syntactic structures to be associated with the inferences. This is accomplished not by rule but item by item (Gazdar, 1979; Karttunen and Peters, 1979). On our theory a few general principles will explain a wide range of data. Apart from the strength and simplicity of theory thereby achieved, our account attempts to answer to the intuition that presuppositions arise in part because of the semantic structure of the sentences yielding them, but it avoids the incoherencies of accounts of "semantic presupposition" (Atlas, 1975a, 1975b; Boer and Lycan, 1976; Gazdar, 1976, 1977, 1979; Karttunen, 1973; Kempson, 1975; Wilson, 1975; Atlas, 1977).

One example of a simplification attributable to a more delicate use of logical form is the unification of the presuppositional behavior of clefts, factives, and definite descriptions, as illustrated in (144).

(144) a. *It was John that Mary kissed.*
       b. $\lambda x(Gx)(\gamma xFx)$
       c. *Mikael knows that California is exciting.*
       d. $K(m, \iota P(P = {}^\wedge A \ \& \ Tr(P))$
       e. *The prince of Wales is clever.*
       f. $G(\iota xFx)$

But whatever the success of this semantic and pragmatic reduction, the issues raised here bear on how the relation between semantics and pragmatics should be construed: what the relationship between truth conditions, implicata, and logical forms is; what conditions of adequacy (e.g., predicting "aboutness" and reading off implicata) semantic representations should satisfy. These problems are central to a theory of meaning, especially since sole reliance upon a theory of truth and logical form manifestly fails, as has been argued by Atlas (1978, 1979). Classical semantics is inadequately explanatory, in either its extensional or intensional varieties.

ACKNOWLEDGEMENTS

The collaboration on which this chapter is based was made possible by funds provided to Stephen Levinson by the Small Grants Research Fund in the Humanities of the British Academy. Both authors would like to express their gratitude to the Academy. Jay Atlas would like to acknowledge his indebtedness to the Department of Philosophy, Princeton University for a Visiting Fellowship in 1979, to the President and Fellows of Wolfson College, Oxford, to Paul Benacerraf, Michael Dummett, S. Feferman, Paul Grice, Dan Isaacson, Mart Pearson, Dana Scott, and Frederick Tibbetts. The authors would also like to thank Kent Bach, Gerald Gazdar, Larry Horn, Lauri Karttunen, Stan Peters, Ellen Prince, Andy Rogers, Jerry Sadock, and Deirdre Wilson. Jay Atlas is also grateful to Hugh Collins, Mark Shepherd, and Charlie Tomson for their assistance.

REFERENCES

Allwood, J. (1972). Negation and the strength of presupposition. *Logical Grammar Reports No. 2*. Department of Linguistics, University of Göteborg, Sweden.

58   Jay David Atlas and Stephen C. Levinson

Akmajian, A. (1970). On deriving cleft sentences from pseudo-cleft sentences. *Linguistic Inquiry*, **1**, 149–168.

Atlas, J. D. (1972). *A Davidsonian approach to demonstrative inference*. Paper presented to the Rutgers University Colloquium on Logic and Language, April 1972.

Atlas, J. D. (1975a). Frege's polymorphous concept of presupposition and its role in a theory of meaning. *Semantikos*, **1**, 29–44.

Atlas, J. D. (1975b). Presupposition: A semantico-pragmatic account. *Pragmatics Microfiche*, **1.4**, D13–G9.

Atlas, J. D. (1977). Negation, ambiguity, and presupposition. *Linguistics and Philosophy*, **1**, 321–336.

Atlas, J. D. (1978). On presupposing. *Mind*, **87**, 396–411.

Atlas, J. D. (1979). How linguistics matters to philosophy: Presupposition, truth, and meaning. In C-K Oh and D. Dinneen (Eds.), *Syntax and Semantics 11: Presupposition*. New York: Academic Press. Pp. 265–281.

Atlas, J. D. (1980). A note on a confusion of pragmatic and semantic aspects of negation. *Linguistics and Philosophy*, **3**, 411–414.

Boer, S. A., and Lycan, W. G. (1976). The myth of semantic presupposition, *Ohio State Working Papers in Linguistics, No. 21*. Department of Linguistics, Ohio State University. Pp. 1–90.

Brown, P., and Levinson, S. C. Universals in language usage: Politeness phenomena. In E. Goody (Ed.), *Questions and Politeness: Strategies in Social Interaction*. Cambridge: Cambridge University Press. Pp. 56–310.

Carnap, R. (1942). *Introduction to Semantics*. Cambridge, Mass.: Harvard University Press.

Carnap, R., and Bar-Hillel, Y. (1952). *An Outline of a Theory of Semantic Information* (Technical Report No. 247). Cambridge, Mass.: Research Laboratory of Electronics, MIT.

Carnap, R., and Bar-Hillel, Y. (1953–1954). Semantic information. *The British Journal for the Philosophy of Science*, **4**, 147–157.

Chomsky, N. (1972). Deep structure, surface structure, and semantic interpretation. In N. Chomsky, *Studies on Semantics in Generative Grammar*. The Hague: Mouton. Pp. 62–119.

Clark, H., and Haviland, S. E. (1977). Comprehension and the given–new contrast. In R. Freedle (Ed.), *Discourse Production and Comprehension*. Hillside, N.J.: Erlbaum. Pp. 1–40.

Cresswell, M. (1978). Semantic competence. In F. Guenthner and M. Guenthner-Reutter (Eds.), *Meaning and Translation: Philosophical and Linguistic Approaches*. London: Duckworth. Pp. 9–28.

Davidson, D. (1967). The logical form of action sentences. In N. Rescher (Ed.), *The Logic of Decision and Action*. Pittsburgh: University of Pittsburgh Press. Pp. 81–95.

Davidson, D. (1970). Action and reaction. *Inquiry*, **13**, 140–148.

Fogelin, R. (1967). *Evidence and Meaning*. New York: Humanities Press.

Gazdar, G. (1976). *Formal Pragmatics for Natural Language Implicature, Presupposition, and Logical Form*. Doctoral dissertation, University of Reading, U.K.

Gazdar, G. (1977). *Implicature, Presupposition, and Logical Form*. Bloomington: Indiana University Linguistics Club.

Gazdar, G. (1979). *Pragmatics: Implicature, Presupposition, and Logical Form*. New York: Academic Press.

Geis, M. L., and Zwicky, A. M. (1971). On invited inferences. *Linguistic Inquiry*, **2**, 561–565.

Grice, H. P. (1961). The causal theory of perception. *Proceedings of the Aristotelian Society*, Supplementary Volume 25, 121–152.

Grice, H. P. (1965). The causal theory of perception. In R. J. Schwartz (Ed.), *Perceiving, Sensing, and Knowing*. New York: Doubleday. Pp. 438–472.

Grice, H. P. (1971). Utterer's meaning, sentence-meaning, and word-meaning. In J. Searle (Ed.), *The Philosophy of Language*. Oxford: Oxford University Press. Pp. 54–70. (Reprinted from *Foundations of Language*, 1968, **4**.)

Grice, H. P. (1975). Logic and conversation. In P. Cole and J. L. Morgan (Eds.), *Syntax and Semantics 3: Speech Acts*. New York: Academic Press. Pp. 41–58. (From H. Paul Grice's Williams James Lectures, Harvard University, 1967.)

Grice, H. P. (1978). Further Notes on Logic and Conversation. In P. Cole (Ed.), *Syntax and Semantics 9: Pragmatics*. New York: Academic Press. Pp. 113–127.

Halliday, M. A. K. (1967). Notes on transitivity and theme in English, Part 2. *Journal of Linguistics*, **3**, 199–244.

Halvorsen, Per-Kristian. (1978). The syntax and semantics of cleft constructions. *Texas Linguistic Forum*, **11**, Department of Linguistics, University of Texas, Austin.

Harman, G. H. (1965). The Inference to the Best Explanation. *Philosophical Review*, **74**, 88–95.

Harman, G. H. (1968a). Enumerative induction as Inference to the Best Explanation. *Journal of Philosophy*, **65**, 529–533.

Harman, G. H. (1968b). Knowledge, inference, and explanation. *American Philosophical Quarterly*, **5**, 164–173.

Harnish, R. M. (1972). *Studies in Logic and Language*. Unpublished doctoral dissertation, MIT, Cambridge, Mass.

Harnish, R. M. (1976). Logical form and implicature. In T. G. Bever, J. J. Katz, and D. T. Langendoen (Eds.), *An Integrated Theory of Linguistic Ability*. New York: Crowell. Pp. 313–391.

Hawkins, J. A. (1975). The pragmatics of definiteness. *Pragmatics Microfiche, 1.3*, C2–G10.

Hawkins, J. A. (1978). *Definiteness and Indefiniteness*. London: Croom Helm

Hempel, C. G. (1960). Inductive inconsistencies. *Synthese*, **11**, 439–469.

Heringer, J. (1976). *Some Grammatical Correlates of Felicity Conditions and Presuppositions*. Bloomington: Indiana University Linguistics Club.

Hilbert, D. (1927/1967). The foundations of mathematics. In Jean van Heijenoort (Ed.), *From Frege to Gödel: A Sourcebook in Mathematical Logic, 1879–1931*. Cambridge, Mass.: Harvard University Press. Pp. 464–479.

Hintikka, K. J. J. (1973). Grammar and logic: Some borderline problems. In K. J. J. Hintikka *et al.* (Eds.), *Approaches to Natural Language: Proceedings of the 1970 Stanford Workshop on Grammar and Semantics*. Dordrecht: Reidel. Pp. 197–214.

Horn, L. (1972). *On the Semantic Properties of Logical Operators in English*. Bloomington: Indiana University Linguistics Club.

Horn, L. (1973). Greek Grice: A brief survey of proto-conversational rules in the history of logic. In *Papers from the Ninth Regional Meeting of the Chicago Linguistic Society*. Department of Linguistics, University of Chicago. Pp. 205–214.

Horn, L. (1978a). Remarks on Neg-Raising. In P. Cole (Ed.), *Syntax and Semantics 9: Pragmatics*. New York: Academic Press. Pp. 129–220.

Horn, L. (1978b). Some aspects of negation. In J. H. Greenberg *et al.* (Eds.), *Universals of Human Language Volume 4: Syntax*. Stanford: Stanford University Press. Pp. 127–210.

Karttunen, L. (1973). Presuppositions of Compound Sentences. *Linguistic Inquiry*, **4**, 169–193.

Karttunen, L. and S. Peters. (1977). Requiem for presupposition. *Proceedings of the Third Annual Meeting of the Berkeley Linguistics Society.* Department of Linguistics, University of California, Berkeley. Pp. 360–371.

Karttunen, L. and S. Peters. (1979). Conventional implicature. In C-K Oh and D. Dinneen (Eds.), *Syntax and Semantics 11: Presupposition.* New York: Academic Press. Pp. 1–56.

Kemeny, J. (1953). A logical measure function. *Journal of Symbolic Logic*, **18**, 289–308.

Kempson, R. (1975). *Presupposition and the Delimitation of Semantics.* Cambridge: Cambridge University Press.

Kempson, R. (1977). *Semantic Theory.* Cambridge: Cambridge University Press.

Leisenring, A. C. (1969). *Mathematical Logic and Hilbert's ∊-symbol.* London: Macdonald.

Levinson, S. C. (1978). *Pragmatics and Social Deixis.* Manuscript, Department of Linguistics, University of Cambridge.

Lewis, D. K. (1969). *Convention.* Cambridge, Mass.: Harvard University Press.

Lyons, J. (1977). *Semantics.* Cambridge: Cambridge University Press.

Martin, R. M. (1958). *Truth and Denotation.* Chicago: Chicago University Press.

Martin, R. M. (1979). *Pragmatics, Truth, and Language.* Dordrecht: Reidel.

O'Hair, S. G. (1969). Implication and meaning. *Theoria.* **35**, 38–54.

Popper, K. (1959). *The Logic of Scientific Discovery.* New York: Basic Books.

Popper, K. (1963). *Conjectures and Refutations.* New York: Basic Books.

Prince, E. (1978). A comparison of WH-clefts and *it*-clefts in discourse. *Language*, **54**, 893–906.

Putnam, H. (1958). Formalization of the concept "About". *Philosophy of Science*, **25**, 125–130.

Quine, W. V. O. (1956). Quantifiers and propositional attitudes. *Journal of Philosophy*, **53**, 177–187.

Quine, W. V. O. (1977). Review of *Truth and Meaning*, G. Evans and J. McDowell (Eds.). *Journal of Philosophy*, **74**, 225–241.

Quine, W. V. O., and Ullian, J. (1978). *Web of Belief.* New York: Random House.

Rogers, A. (1978). On generalized conversational implicature and preparatory conditions. In S. F. Schmerling and C. S. Smith (Eds.), *Texas Linguistic Forum 10.* Department of Linguistics, University of Texas, Austin. Pp. 72–75.

Rogers, A., and Gazdar, G. (1978). *Conventional implicature: A critical problem.* Manuscript, Department of Linguistics, University of Texas, Austin.

Rozeboom, W. W. (1964). Discussion: of selection operators and semanticists. *Philosophy of Science*, **31**, 282–285.

Sacks, Harvey. (1972). On the analyzability of stories by children. In J. Gumperz and D. Hymes (Eds.), *Directions in Sociolinguistics: the Ethnography of Communication.* New York: Holt, Rinehart and Winston.

Sadock, J. M. (1975). Larry scores a point. *Pragmatics Microfiche, 1.4*, G10–G13.

Sadock, J. M. (1978). On testing for conversational implicature. In P. Cole (Ed.) *Syntax and Semantics 9: Pragmatics.* New York: Academic Press. Pp. 281–297.

Schmerling, S. F. (1975). Asymmetric conjunction and rules of conversation. In P. Cole and J. L. Morgan (Eds.), *Syntax and Semantics 3: Speech Acts.* New York: Academic Press. Pp. 211–232.

Scott, D. S. (1970a). Advice on modal logic. In K. Lambert (Ed.), *Philosophical Problems in Logic: Recent Developments.* Dordrecht: Reidel. Pp. 143–173.

Scott, D. S. (1970b). Semantical archaeology: A parable. *Synthese*, **11**, 150–158.

Searle, J. (1975). Indirect speech acts. In P. Cole and J. L. Morgan (Eds.), *Syntax and Semantics 3: Speech Acts*. New York: Academic Press. Pp. 59–82.

Smokler, H. (1966). Informational content: A problem of definition. *Journal of Philosophy*, **63**, 201–211.

Stoppard, T. (1972). *Jumpers*. New York: Grove.

Strawson, P. F. (1974). On understanding the structure of one's language. In P. F. Strawson, *Freedom and Resentment and other Essays*. London: Methuen. Pp. 198–207. (Also published in G. Evans and J. McDowell (Eds.), *Truth and Meaning: Essays in Semantics*. Oxford: Clarendon. Pp. 189–198.)

Thomason, R. H. (1973). *Semantics, pragmatics, conversation, and presupposition*. Manuscript, Department of Philosophy, University of Pittsburgh.

Thomason, R. H. (1976). Some extensions of Montague grammar. In B. Partee (Ed.), *Montague Grammar*. New York: Academic Press. Pp. 77–119.

Thomason, R. H. (1977). Where pragmatics fits in. In A. Rogers *et al.* (Eds.), *Proceedings of the Texas Conference on Performatives, Presuppositions, and Implicatures*. Arlington, Va.: Center for Applied Linguistics. Pp. 161–166.

Wilson, D. (1975). *Presuppositions and Non-truth-Conditional Semantics*. New York: Academic Press.

Wilson, D. and D. Sperber. (1979). Ordered entailments: An alternative to presuppositional theories. In C-K Oh and D. Dinneen (Eds.), *Syntax and Semantics 11: Presupposition*. New York: Academic Press. Pp. 299–323.

Zwicky, A., and Sadock, J. M. (1975). Ambiguity tests and how to fail them. In J. P. Kimball (Ed.), *Syntax and Semantics 4*. New York: Academic Press. Pp. 1–36.

On Time, Tense, and Aspect:
An Essay in English Metaphysics

Emmon Bach

1. THE PROBLEM

In 1936, Benjamin Lee Whorf wrote a justly famous paper entitled "An American Indian Model of the Universe" (Carroll, 1956). In that paper, Whorf criticized the easy assumption that people in different cultures, speaking radically different languages, share common presuppositions about what the world is like. He contrasted the Hopi view of space and time with what he called elsewhere the Standard Average European view. For the Hopi, space and time are inherently relativistic; for the speaker of Western European languages, like English, the universe is basically Newtonian, time and space are absolute, "containers" of things and events.

It is not my purpose here to discuss Whorf's assessment of Hopi metaphysics. Rather I would like to consider a little more carefully than Whorf did the other side of the comparison. This essay may be thought of as an exercise in "ethnometaphysics," an attempt to dig out the hidden assumptions made by speakers of English about the way the world is. My topic will be Time.

What methods can we use in such an enterprise? One approach would

63

be to ask the native speakers what they think about various questions. Is time dense, discrete, or continuous? Is there a single time line into the future or do we have to allow for branching futures, reflecting different ways we might choose or expect the world to be tomorrow? Can events recur in all their particularity? Many philosophers, members of "Standard Average European" cultures, have sought answers to such questions, and their answers have been far from uniform. So it seems we must take a different and more difficult approach.

The tack that I will take is this: We attempt to find out about the hidden structures of meanings in a language and culture by constructing formal theories about the syntax, semantics, and pragmatics of the language. We seek indirect evidence for our hypotheses by trying to give the most accurate and general explanations for various facets of linguistic knowledge. In carrying out this task we find that we can account for a number of seemingly disparate facts—intuitions about sentences, their well-formedness, interrelations, truth conditions—by separating out certain assumptions that seem to be metaphysical in character, rather than semantic or syntactic. Thus, the validity of our conclusions rests ultimately on the coherence and explanatory value of our entire picture.

In the context of such an inquiry I would like to consider a number of puzzles about the English tense–aspect system and its interaction with temporal expressions. I will try to show how a number of these puzzles can be solved by positing certain metaphysical assumptions made by speakers of the language. I believe that my conclusions have a wider application than just English and hope that I will be able to show that the facts we uncover about English point toward a more basic human matrix of assumptions about the world, that the Hopi and English world views are not at bottom incompatible, but rather are different orchestrations of material that is part of our common human heritage.

The framework within which I work draws on two main sources, the work in generative grammar initiated by Chomsky and the philosophical and logical methods first applied fruitfully to the study of natural languages by Richard Montague. Even though the paper is presented in an informal way, it is to be judged ultimately on the extent to which I am able to translate it into a precise account of English syntax, semantics, and pragmatics. To the extent that my account is successful I think that it supports the view that the bewilderingly complex facts of natural languages are best understood as resulting from the interplay of a number of relatively simple and autonomous subsystems. In particular, it will support the view that it is a good move to think of semantics itself as a relatively narrow and simple system.

2. ENGLISH TENSE LOGIC

There is by now a vast literature on tense logic. Philosophers and logicians have studied the properties of a wide variety of different systems. Montague's treatment of some English tenses, set forth primarily in his paper "The proper treatment of quantification in ordinary English" (Paper 8 in Montague 1974, henceforth PTQ) falls within this tradition. Montague's semantics is model-theoretic and intensional. Truth is defined relative to a possible world and a time. We might begin by outlining the system of PTQ.

The interpretation of English given in PTQ assumes among other things two sets, I and J, the set of possible worlds and the set of times, respectively. There is a simple ordering relation, $\leq$, with J as its field and J is understood to be the set of moments of time. To illustrate the method, *John has loved Mary* is taken to denote the Truth at a world i and time j just in case there is a time j', strictly earlier than j, such that *John loves Mary* is true at i, j'. If we unpack the terse definitions and terminology of PTQ that relate to time we can restate what I have just said as follows:

1. Time is absolute across possible worlds. It is always possible to relate temporally things that happen in different possible worlds. From this it follows also that things that happen in THIS world can always be temporally related in a unique way.
2. The relation $\leq$ is transitive, reflexive, and antisymmetric (cf. Montague, 1974, p. 106, fn. 6). (A relation R is antisymmetric iff $x\,R\,Y$ and $y\,R\,x$ always entail $x = y$.)

No other assumptions are made, but this much already commits us to certain conclusions:[1]

(i)   Newtonian physics is correct; Einsteinian physics is wrong. This follows because by (1) it is always possible to establish an ordering between two events, independent of observer.
(ii) Time travel is logically impossible.
(iii) Sentences about time relations in different possible courses-of-events (worlds) always have a definite truth value, example:

---

[1] Strictly speaking, this is not quite right. In any model it will be the case that two events are temporally related in a unique way. It is unclear whether Montague intends his interpretation of English to be making any claims about the real world. One could also interpret his semantics for English as saying that Einsteinian physics is inexpressible in (ordinary) English.

(1)   *If Mary had left on the space probe yesterday she would now be eating breakfast.*

   (iv) The fundamental units of the time series are moments, not intervals (taking "moments" to mean "instants," cf. Paper 5 in Montague 1974).

Certain other questions are left open:

   (v) Is the set of times infinite or finite?
   (vi) Is there a first (last) moment of time?
   (vii) Is time discrete, dense, continuous?

Again, answers to each of these questions imply certain conclusions about our judgments about English sentences. For example, suppose the set of times is finite. Then, certain sentences will be logically false, and their negations logically true. Let N be the cardinality of the finite set J. Then any sentence of the form "ϕ_1 and then ϕ_2 . . . and then ϕ_{N+1}" will be true at no possible world and its negation true at all possible worlds. If the answers to (vi) are yes, then at the last (first) moment of time any future (past) sentence will be false at all worlds and hence any implication with it as antecedent will be logically true. And so on.

   Considerations such as these lead me to the view that our specifications of THE tense logic of English, if there is such a thing, should be cast in a very liberal way.

3. PRAGMATICS

   More particularly, my framework is this: English is a pragmatic language, by which I mean that it contains expressions like *I, now, here* and tenses, that must receive a value from a context before the expressions in which they stand can be evaluated. *I am here now* spoken by me at 8:03, May 10, 1979, in such and such a room in such and such a place must be turned into a proposition by filling in all the values for the indexical expressions. Thus, I adopt the view of Stalnaker (1972) and others according to which the interpretation of expressions of a language like English is accomplished in two stages. In particular, declarative sentences receive sentence meanings which are functions from contexts to propositions, the latter in turn are functions from worlds (or histories as I prefer to call them) to truth values.

   It is usual to say that among the elements of the context is a time of utterance. This is not quite accurate, as there may not be an actual utterance (think of a street sign). So I will speak instead of a context of evaluation, thought of as a kind of performance. As we are interested here in time and tense, I will confine attention to this element or index: the time of the evaluation. So declarative sentences will be thought of in the first place as functions from times to propositions (see Kratzer, 1977; von Stechow, 1977, on the problems of a theory of contexts).

4. EVENTS, STATES, PROCESSES

There is a well-known typology that has its roots in Aristotle but has been brought into linguistic and philosophical thinking in recent times mainly by Anthony Kenny (1963) and Zeno Vendler (1957). It has to do with different kinds of sentences (or verb phrases) and the kinds of states-of-affairs that they describe. According to this view we need to contrast STATES, PROCESSES, and two kinds of EVENTS: PROTRACTED and INSTANTANEOUS (the latter correspond to Vendler's ACCOMPLISHMENTS and ACHIEVEMENTS, respectively). Some sentences illustrating the four types are these:

(2)   *Mary is in New York.*   (STATE)

(3)   *John ran (for an hour).*   (PROCESS)

(4)   *Mary built a cabin.*   (PROTRACTED EVENT)

(5)   *Mary found a unicorn.*   (INSTANTANEOUS EVENT)

(You should note that these terms are not uniformly used in the literature.) There is another dimension which crosscuts these distinctions, in English at least, having to do with the notions of agentivity, volition, and the like. The necessity for taking the distinctions into account for the semantics of English has become most evident in a series of papers by various philosophers and linguists who have dealt with the English progressive and similar constructions in other languages.[2] Let us note some contrasts in the acceptability and interpretation of sentences in the progressive. A state sentence cannot occur in the progressive:

(6)   **Mary is being in New York.*

(I will discuss apparent exceptions to this in what follows.) The other three types can:

---

[2] Dowty (1972, 1977), Vlach (forthcoming) are two examples.

(7)   *John was running.*

(8)   *Mary was building a cabin.*

(9)   *Mary was finding a unicorn.*

If we follow Vlach (forthcoming), who has given to my mind the best account of the English progressive, in the idea that the progressive construction itself is stative, then it follows that there can be no progressives of progressives:[3]

(10)   **John was being running.*

Further, if the English perfect forms state expressions, it also follows that we will not have progressives of perfects:

(11)   **John is always having been hurt.*

The necessity to keep processes apart from events can be seen, among other things, in the semantics of the progressive. It is necessary to give different truth conditions for sentences involving progressives of processes and events (cf. Vlach, forthcoming). Various writers (e.g., Dowty, 1977) have tried to give an account of the semantics of the progressive as a uniform function of the semantics of corresponding simple sentences. This works only for processes. For example, we can say that on one understanding, a sentence like *John was running for an hour* is true just in case the sentence *John runs* is true at sufficiently many subintervals (or moments) of some hour. This is clearly wrong for sentences like *Mary was building a cabin for three years* or *Mary was finding a unicorn yesterday*.

The hardest distinction to understand, so far, is that between processes and states. That there must be such a distinction is clear from the interpretations we must give to simple present sentences:

(12)   *Mary loves John.*

(13)   *Mary runs.*

The latter but not the former has two understandings: On the one hand it can be telling us something about Mary's habits or dispositions (call this the gnomic sense); on the other hand it can be used as a vivid description of an entire event (so-called ''reportive'') or as a historical present: ''Last night I go downtown. I see Mary. She runs.'' (It is possible that these last

---

[3] This idea was also put forward by various linguists. I have been unable to find a reference, but I recall discussion of this point in the late sixties among especially generative semanticists.

two understandings should be assimilated.) I say "understandings," rather than "meanings" or "readings," as I do not want to prejudge the question whether such sentences are genuinely ambiguous. (Of course, we can give nonce nonstative meanings to stative verbs like *love;* these come out when the verbs are in the progressive: *Mary is loving John,* I'll return to these in what follows.)

There have been a number of attempts to explicate these notions on the basis of time structures. For example, Montague (1974, Paper 5) proposed that generic instantaneous events be analyzed as properties of moments of time. I prefer to go in the other direction and analyze our notions of time on the basis of the typology given earlier, taking it as primitive. One reason for this is of purely autobiographical interest. I find it much easier to understand these notions than various abstract properties of time. But there are more interesting reasons for taking this approach, which will emerge in what follows.[4]

For my semantics, I take as basic the notion of a POSSIBLE HISTORY. This is in a sense nothing but a possible world, but I use the word history to stress the fact that the temporal relations that will come out of the analysis are world-imminent, not as in PTQ independent of worlds. Along with a collection of possible individuals (in the ordinary sense) I will assume as given a set of EVENTUALITIES, this being the generic term for the things we have just been considering: states, processes, and events (of two kinds).

Following mainly Whitehead (1920, but cf. Note 4), I will assume that there are two primitive relations that can hold between eventualities; one is a relation of strict precedence ($<$) for which I will write BEFORE, the other is a notion of covering (Whitehead's notion of "extending over"), for which I will use the term WHILE. (These words are chosen advisedly, but should be considered technical terms that will not be used quite in the way the English words that they resemble are used.) About these relations I will assume the following:

  (i) *Before* is transitive, asymmetric, and hence irreflexive.
  (ii) *While* is transitive, asymmetric, and hence irreflexive.
  (iii) *Before* and *While* are mutually exclusive.

(Thus *While* is to be interpreted as "properly covering": In time talk, the duration of the second eventuality is a nontangential proper part of that of

---

[4] The idea of constructing "time" on the basis of primitive relations among events may be found in Russell 1929 and Whitehead 1920. More recently, it has been taken up by Kamp (1980) and Van Benthem (1980). Kamp shows the usefulness or necessity of this approach for two applications: a theory of discourse and a treatment of temporal relations for the interpretation of sentences involving vague predicates.

the first.) A HISTORY is now taken to be a set of eventualities and relations among them. Please take note that it is explicitly not assumed that every pair of eventualities in a history is related by *Before* or *While*. A maximal set of eventualities that ARE so related I will call a LOCAL HISTORY. (Thus, if the actual history of the universe is a local history, then it is a Newtonian history.) We can define SIMULTANEITY as another relation between eventualities as follows:

(iv) $Sim(e,e') =_{df}$ for all eventualities e'', $(While(e'',e)$ iff $While(e'',e'))$
      and $(While(e,e'')$ iff $While(e',e''))$

Now, although I cannot say exactly what the various kinds of eventualities are, we can say something about some of their properties (the following owes a great deal to unpublished work and lectures by Lauri Carlson, cf. also Mourelatos, 1978). First of all, there is a natural affinity between the kinds of things that we are thinking about and theories of MEREOLOGY, that is the logic of part–whole relations. Such a theory takes as its basis a single binary relation, that of being a part, and a single operation, that of forming a new individual out of several individuals. Using these ideas it is possible to state intuitively reasonable characteristics of the various kinds of eventualities. Consider first two typical events: a finding of a unicorn and a building of a cabin. Whatever else is true of such events, no proper part of one can be an event of the same kind. Call this property ANTISUB-DIVISIBILITY. This property is clearly not shared by processes. Note that it is not correct to say that a process can always be subdivided into parts that are also processes of the same kind. The point is that sometimes processes can be so subdivided but events never can. Further, if you have two distinct events of the same kind, their sum is never an event of the same kind; but if you sum two or more processes of the same kind you will or may have a process of the same kind: call the latter ADDITIVITY. Thus we can say that events are antisubdivisible and nonadditive; processes lack these properties (Note: Again it is not the case that processes are necessarily subdivisible and additive). We are reminded of the similar distinctions having to do with the nominal system of English and the difference between bare plurals (*dogs*) and mass terms (*gold*) on the one hand and count nouns (*dog*) on the other.

   The foregoing considerations provide a strong argument against all attempts to reconstruct events and the like on the basis of times. For example, if an event is a property of a certain kind of interval, we simply can not say that no proper part of the interval is also an event of the same kind. Further, certain entailments that have been noted in the literature can be captured in a very direct way. Consider, for example, the "entailment" (cf. Kenny, 1963):

(14)   *If Mary is finding a unicorn, Mary has not found a unicorn.*

Although this entailment is clearly false, there is a valid intuition behind it. The intuition is something like this: If Mary is finding a unicorn, then THAT finding of a unicorn by Mary is not over. This statement uses the notion of an individuated event directly. Another sort of "entailment" has to do with processes:

(15)   *If John is running, then John has run.*

Although again I do not think that this is literally a semantically valid entailment (consider the very beginning of John's running), what I have said about subdivisibility makes it a natural kind of pragmatic "entailment."

Within the preceding framework of contrasts, what can we say about states? The ontological status of states is considerably more obscure than that of events and processes. Moreover, the relation between states and temporal notions often seems mysterious. In the case of events and processes we were led naturally to think about their temporal parts. Events may have beginnings and ends and possibly "middles." We think easily about a process going on for a time and think about smaller chunks of the same process. States have an atemporal and abstract quality. Think about the questions: Where did a certain event take place? Where is a certain process going on? Now think about the questions: Where is the state of John's being in New York located? Where does Mary know algebra? It is hard to make sense of these last sentences. The atemporality of states (at least some states) can be brought out in the following Gedankenexperiment: Imagine a possible history (world) with only one time (which in a sense amounts to having no time); it is possible to think of various states that might obtain in such a world, but impossible to imagine events and processes that occur or go on in such a world.

Bennett and Partee (1978) have suggested using (among others) the "subinterval" property to distinguish event predicates from states and processes. If a sentence has a subinterval verb phrase as its main predicate and is true at some interval I, then it will be "true at every subinterval including every moment of time in I." This is an important idea (and clearly related to the notion of antisubdivisibility). However, taken literally it is applicable only to states, not processes. If we take a process verb like *run* and consider an instant included in some interval of running, then the plain predicate *run* will NOT hold for the argument. But a stative predicate, including in particular the progressive predicate *be running* (Vlach, forthcoming), does have this property.

Rather tentatively, we can sum up these differences as follows. We will require that if *e* is an event, then there must be at least one other event connected to *e* by the relation *Before,* and if *e* is a process then there must be at least two events overlapped by *e* that stand in the *Before* relation. States will have no such requirement. Thus possible histories that contain events or processes are guaranteed to have a certain temporal "thickness." Our world does have such thickness, hence the abstract character of states.

In any case, there are certain facts about states that should be explained in any adequate theory. Here are some:

(i) The naturalness of simple present tense sentences We have already noted this, and its concomitant: the oddity or downright anomalousness of progressives for states.

(ii) The semantics of *when*-clauses Vlach (forthcoming) notes that for a sentence combining a *when*-clause rooted in a state sentence with an event sentence to be true the time of the event has to be in the interval defined by the state:

(16)   *When John was in New York, Mary left.*

In time talk, there must be at least an instant of John's being in New York coincident with Mary's leaving. We can sharpen this intuition by a sentence like (17):

(17)   *?When I was in bed, I got up.*

The question mark serves to indicate that on the ordinary understanding of getting up (i.e., getting out of bed) this sentence is anomalous.

5. TIME ADVERBIALS

The distinctions just reviewed play a role in the interpretation of time adverbials and combinations of tense and aspect. I will first consider adverbials, restricting the discussion in this section to sentences in the simple past tense.

Following Bennett and Partee (1978), we can distinguish three main classes of adverbials:

1. FRAME ADVERBIALS:
        Point: *at 3 o'clock*
        Interval: *on the 23rd of June, today*
2. DURATION: *(for) three hours, all day*
3. FREQUENCY: *twice, frequently*

Frame adverbials occur only with event or state descriptions, thus forcing an event or state interpretation when combined with a process phrase.

(18)   *Mary found a unicorn at dawn.*

(19)   *Last year Bill built a cabin.*

(20)   *In 1943, Sam was in New York.*

(21)   *John ran yesterday.*

(22)   *John ran last year.*

Sentence (21) requires us to think of a particular event of which running is a part, say, running for a specific length of time, starting to run, or the like. Sentence (22) also has available a stative, generic reading.

   Some peculiarities arise when we make various specific choices.

(23)   *At 4 o'clock, Bill built a cabin.*

(24)   *At 3 o'clock, Mary knew physics.*

Sentence (23) is peculiar only because we know that building a cabin, in the real world, is a protracted event. If Bill were a magician, then it would be perfectly acceptable. Sentence (24) is, I think, an unlikely but not anomalous sentence. For many states, it is odd to pin them to particular times and we tend to reinterpret the stative predicates as event predicates (come to know). On that understanding (24) would be unlikely, again for real world reasons (compare *At 3 o'clock Mary knew the answer*).

   Point-time adverbials name events: in conventional time schemes, periodic events like dawn, the summer solstice, positions of hands on a clock, vibrations of the cesium atom. Sentences involving them are true just in case an event described in the sentence is simultaneous with the named event or a state described holds "at" the event in question. What happens when we have a process predicate like *run* is that the truth conditions force us to take a "piece" of running which is simultaneous to some named event or we take the process in a generic sense. We can offer the same explanation for interval adverbials if we provide for them a semantics that incorporates the idea of a reference event ("time") within the named interval.

   We find just the opposite pattern for events and processes in much discussed examples involving durational expressions (not necessarily time expressions):

(25)   *John ran for an hour.*

(26)   *?For 3 hours, Mary found a unicorn.*

(27)   *?John built a cabin for 3 days.*

(28)   *For 3 days, John was in New York.*

(29)   *?For 3 years, Mary knew physics.*

State descriptions occur with durationals (with the same proviso, it is odd to think about—not just say something about—someone knowing something for a definite period of time). Event descriptions with durationals are anomalous, not just odd, process descriptions are fine. How are we to account for this difference?

The combination of a specific durational adverbial with a process predicate (or sentence) acts in every way like an event predicate (or sentence):

(30)   *It took John an hour to run for an hour (naturally).*

(31)   *?John ran for an hour for an hour.*

Once again the analogy with the count–mass distinction comes to mind. Durational expressions stand to verbal expressions as amount expressions stand to nominal expressions. Just as we do not use expressions like *3 pounds of* with singular count nouns like *a horse,* we do not use the expressions that chunk up our experience with (singular) expressions that provide that experience already chunked up. Another way to see the same thing is this: Suppose durationals have something like the following truth condition: for I, p (p a sentence, I an interval) is true just in case p is true at all (or sufficiently many scattered) subintervals of I. Then (26) (cf. Vlach, ms.) would be literally true if Mary finds a unicorn sufficiently often over the 3 hours in question. But as speakers of English we know that the right way to say THAT is *Mary found unicorns for 3 hours.*

Finally, frequency adverbials like *often* co-occur with all sorts of descriptions but again with a difference.

(32)   *Mary often found a unicorn.*

(33)   *People frequently went to the country.*

(34)   *Sometimes Bill ran.*

(35)   *John was in New York twice.*

In event sentences like (32) and (33) the adverbials are acting like direct quantifiers over events. With processes and states we have to say a little more. For (34) to be true it must have been true on several occasions that Bill started to run, ran, and stopped. Similarly for (35). Thus by their nature frequency adverbials like these require that the processes or states involved constitute parts of events.

Sentences like (33) are particularly interesting for my basic thesis that time is a derivative notion. Sentence (33) does not mean that there were frequent "times" at which someone went to the country. Similarly, *John was hit twice* requires that there be two hittings but they may have occurred at the very same instant (gratia Terry Parsons). What is needed is some notion like "occasion" or "case" (Lewis, 1975). Such examples provide direct evidence against any theory that combines PTQ's treatment of time and Montague's analysis of events as properties of moments of time (1974, Paper 5).

The possibilities for combining various sorts of time adverbials in a single sentence are literally endless, and I cannot begin to do justice to the topic in this chapter. But it is worth looking at a few examples to show how metaphysical assumptions can be used to explain certain judgments. Consider this sentence:

(36)   *?At 3 o'clock, John left at 4 o'clock.*

Such examples are sometimes taken as showing that the grammar of English should contain a restriction (syntactic or semantic) that limits the number of point time adverbials in a simple sentence to one. But this is unnecessary. It follows from the stipulation that *Before* is irreflexive and the semantics of the particular time expressions that (36) could be true in no possible "standard" history. Similar considerations apply to mismatches between temporal expressions and tenses:

(37)   *John will leave yesterday.*

(38)   *Mary left tomorrow.*

6. TENSE AND ASPECT

In this section I wish to take up several problems in the interpretation of the English tense–aspect system. Once again, I can only skim the surface and give a few examples that show the interaction of the typology of eventualities with this system.

The first set of puzzles has to do with the interpretation of the simple present tense. Indeed, it was in part the behavior of simple present tense sentences and contrasts between simple present and progressive that led Vendler and others to set up the typology we have been examining. If *be* + progressive is itself a state-describing expression (Vlach, forthcoming), then we can say that most "ordinary" present tense sentences are state descriptions:

(39)   *Mary loves John.*

(40)   *Three plus two equals five.*

(41)   *John is in New York.*

(42)   *John is building a cabin.*

(43)   *Mary is running.*

These are to be contrasted with simple present tense sentences involving single events and processes:

(44)   *Mary finds a unicorn.*

(45)   *Harry builds a cabin.*

(46)   *Sam runs.*

These sentences require "special" interpretations: a so-called reportive reading; a futurate present (*The Mets play at 3*); or in the case of (46) a generic or gnomic reading (itself stative). And we find that a process verb like *run*, interpreted in the reportive way, requires us to think of some singular event involving running.

This configuration of facts reminds us of what we have seen about past-tense sentences with frame adverbials. This is not surprising. I have suggested that such sentences can be true in just two circumstances: an event described is simultaneous with the reference event (time) explicitly or implicitly present in the frame adverbial or a state described covers the reference event. Following our earlier discussion we can take present tense sentences to be functions from an event ("time") of evaluation (from context) to propositions. Thus the truth conditions are to be considered "at now." Moreover, if we assume that the event of evaluation (a performance) is thought of as instantaneous we can provide an explanation for a number of facts.

Consider first the problem of the reportive interpretation. I suggest a basically Gricean explanation. Suppose we take the account that was given literally: The event described must be simultaneous with the performance event. There are two circumstances when we can really be sure of this. One of these is when such sentences are used to PERFORM events, as with verbs like *christen, promise, pronounce.* Such verbs are used in the simple present with first person subjects in performative sentences. As we might expect, with other subjects they act like any other kind of event sentences: (*He christens the child*). The second is when we are, so to speak, creating a fictional history or recreating actual history. Here, by fiat, the events described are thought of as simultaneous with the evaluation; hence the use of such sentences in poetry, narrative, historical present, and so on. The reportive use falls into the same slot.

Support for the idea that the time of evaluation is thought of as an instant comes from the consideration of sentences like these:

(47)   *I utter a sentence.*

(48)   *I tell the truth.*

If the performance of a sentence were identified with an utterance (something that happens in the physical world and takes time) then the temporal condition for such sentences would always be satisfied, and they should be perfectly ordinary. In fact, they have the same range of interpretations as any other event sentences. I believe the key to understanding such facts and others that have received attention in the literature (the habits of verbs like *recognize*) lies in the assumption that it is above all, or exclusively, mental acts that are felt to be truly instantaneous.

The second puzzle I would like to consider is illustrated in sentences like these:

(49)   *?I am knowing the answer.*

(50)   *?John is believing that the earth is flat.*

Every English grammar tells us that such sentences are peculiar if not ungrammatical or "unsemantic." But in every list of such "stative" verbs I have ever seen I have been able to find natural examples of progressives with stative verbs (with the sole exception of *be* when it combines with a prepositional phrase or nominal):

(51)   *I'm really loving the play.*

(52)   *I'm understanding you but I'm not believing you.*

We have already considered one class of such examples, where a normally stative verb is given a nonce meaning of a nonstative sort (*Mary is loving John*). But examples like (51) and (52) do not seem to fall into this usage.

I mentioned earlier the idea that the progressive is simply not defined for states (this is Vlach's position, forthcoming). If we accept this idea then we are forced to conclude that examples like (51) and (52) involve different predicates from the simple counterparts, that is, we would have to assume different lexical items: $love_1$, $love_2$, *etc.* But I believe the phenomenon is more systematic that that. To focus our ideas, let us consider a more perspicuous example:

(53)   *I live in Massachusetts.*

(54)   *I am living in California.*

The conditions under which I would use these two sentences are fairly
clear. Sentence (54) suggests or means that I am living in California tem-
porarily. Sentence (53) has no such implications. For (54), there is the
feeling that we are thinking of some bounded interval (this year, these
days). The same obtains for progressives of gnomic sentences:

(55)   *John drives a truck.*

(56)   *John is driving a truck (these days).*

If we take these facts seriously we will have to abandon the idea that the
progressive is not defined for states and add yet another case to the statement of the truth conditions for the progressive.

Let us call the kind of state described by a progressive of a stative verb
TEMPORARY and the kind of state described by simple statives—including
in particular the gnomic situation as in (55)—NONTEMPORARY. This distinction can also be seen in adjectives: on the one hand *tall, intelligent,
sane;* on the other *drunk, present, sick.* Greg Carlson (1977) has explicated this difference as follows. Suppose we distinguish two kinds of entities in our universe: ordinary individuals and their temporally limited
manifestations (or "realizations"). Then we can say that adjectives are
divided into those that denote properties of individuals and those that denote properties of their manifestations over some limited length of time.
This distinction can be used to account for the kind of difference seen in
the examples just given. For Carlson, a progressive verb phrase denotes
the property of being an individual such that there is a manifestation (or
realization) of that individual of which the basic predicate holds. In
mereological terms we can identify the manifestation of an individual with
some temporally limited proper part of the individual. Thus, the
progressive of a stative verb like *love* (e.g., (51)) has to do with a temporary state more or less directly connected with the meaning of the more
basic nonprogressive predicate.

A consequence of the decision to let the progressive operator or construction occur with statives is that we must seek some new explanation
for the lack of a progressive of a perfect or progressive:

(57)   *?John is always having been hurt.*

(58)   *?Mary is being running in the park.*

For the first case, the explanation is straightforward. Suppose *John has
been hurt* is true in a history. Then forever after in that history it will be
true. Hence, there is no temporary state corresponding to the stative

predicate *have been hurt*. More generally, "eternal" sentences (*Two plus two equals four*) do not have progressive forms. There is also a straight-forward explanation for (58) on Carlson's account of the progressive (or any parallel explanation using a distinction between individuals and their manifestations). The semantics assigns to Sentence (58) the following interpretation: Sentence (58) is true just in case (at history *h* at the contextually determined time of evaluation) Mary has the property of being an individual such that there is a Mary-manifestation that has the property of being an individual such that some manifestation of that individual runs. But (in Carlson's terms) this meaning is sortally incongruous: Manifestations cannot stand in the realization relation to manifestations.

7. CONCLUSIONS

I hope to have shown how certain metaphysical assumptions are essential to an understanding of English tenses and aspects. These assumptions have to do with the way reality—or our experience of it—is structured. I believe that our more sophisticated and abstract ideas about time have their roots in the fundamental types of eventualities and their relationships (as perceived by us). Whatever truth there may be in Whorf's account of Hopi metaphysics, I believe that he was simply wrong about the "Standard Average European" metaphysical assumptions about time. The minimal assumptions we must make about temporal relations in order to explain our intuitions about sentences lend themselves just as well to the construction of an Einsteinian as a Newtonian world view. Moreover, I believe that the notions we have been examining are universal: I have yet to encounter a language in which there is no reflection of the contrasts between states, events, and processes. This is not to say that the use they are put to or the reflexes that we find are identical across languages.

Certain aspects of human experience are common to all people. It is this matrix of common experience that is the stuff of which grammars are made: causation, human responsibility and intentionality, temporal and spatial relations, important classifications of the things in the world (animateness, sex), number, social hierarchy, family relations. Such notions probably enter in one way or another into every human language either as covert or overt categories (to use Whorf's terms). I believe that many universal aspects of language will be understood in the end as resulting from an interaction between the innate language-creating gift of the human animal and this common matrix.

I have said very little about the technical problems of incorporating such metaphysical distinctions into a linguistic description. I do not intend to address such questions here. But I think we can draw one conclusion (and I believe I am in agreement with Chomsky here, though probably not on the question of what to do about it): A formal semantics for a natural language, if it is to be truth-conditional, cannot ignore metaphysical questions. If it is correct that the truth conditions related to tense, aspect, and temporal adverbials must make reference to the event structures we have posited, and if these distinctions are basically metaphysical, this conclusion is inescapable. Moreover, since what is required to work this out is reference to particular words, we cannot draw a sharp line between truth-conditional "structural" semantics and "lexical" semantics (to borrow Partee's terminology). To do justice to such aspects of language in an explicit theory is a challenging task. But even partial solutions cannot fail to tell us something important about language, people, and their place in the world.

ACKNOWLEDGEMENTS

The research reported on here was initially undertaken at the Center for Advanced Studies in the Behavioral Sciences, Stanford, under support from the Center and the National Endowment for the Humanities. I wish to express gratitude for this support and for the help of the Center staff, particularly Mary Tye. For criticism and discussion I would like to thank the following friends and colleagues (none of whom, of course, should be held responsible for my mistakes or misunderstandings): Greg Carlson, Lauri Carlson, David Dowty, Terry Parsons, Mark Stein, and especially Barbara H. Partee. I am also indebted to the late Michael Bennett for many good discussions.

REFERENCES

Bennett, M., and Partee, B. H. (1978). *Toward the Logic of Tense and Aspect in English*. Bloomington: Indiana University Linguistics Club.

Carlson, G. N. (1977). A unified analysis of the English bare plural. *Linguistics and Philosophy*, **1**, 413–458.

Carroll, J. B. (1956). *Language, Thought, and Reality: Selected Writings of Benjamin Lee Whorf*. Cambridge, Mass.: MIT Press.

Dowty, D. R. (1972). *Studies in the Logic of Verb Aspect and Time Reference in English*. Unpublished doctoral dissertation, University of Texas, Austin.

Dowty, D. R. (1977). Toward a semantic analysis of verb aspect and the English 'Imperfective' progressive. *Linguistics and Philosophy*, **1**, 45–79.

Kamp, H. (1980). Some remarks on the logic of change, Part I. In C. Rohrer (Ed.), *Time, Tense, and Quantifiers*. Tuebingen: Niemeyer. Pp. 135–179.

Kenny, A. (1963). *Action, Emotion, and Will*. New York: Humanities.

Kratzer, A. (1977). Kontexttheorie. Universität Konstanz: Sonderforschungsbereich 99 Linguistik 18.

Lewis, D. (1975). Adverbs of quantification. In E. L. Keenan (Ed.), *Formal Semantics of Natural Language*. Cambridge: University Press.

Montague, R. (1974). *Formal Philosophy,* edited by Richmond Thomason. New Haven: Yale University Press.

Mourelatos, Alexander P. D. 1978. Events, processes, and states. *Linguistics and Philosophy,* **2**, 415–434.

Russell, B. (1929). *Our Knowledge of the External World.* Chicago and London: Norton.

Stalnaker, Robert. 1972. Pragmatics. In D. Davidson and G. Harman (Eds.), *Semantics of Natural Language.* Dordrecht: Reidel. Pp. 380–397.

Stechow, A. von (1977). Occurrence-interpretation and Context-theory. Universität Konstanz: Sonderforschungsbereich 99 Linguistik 14.

van Benthem, Johan. (1980). Points and periods. In Christian Rohrer (Ed.), *Time, Tense, and Quantifiers.* Tuebingen: Niemeyer. Pp. 39–57.

Vendler, Z. (1957). Verbs and times. *Philosophical Review,* **56**, 143–60.

Vlach, F. (Forthcoming). *The semantics of the progressive.* (Paper presented at Brown University conference on tense and aspect, to appear in the proceedings.)

Vlach, F. Manuscript. *The semantics of tense and aspect.* Manuscript.

Whitehead, A. N. (1920). *Concept of Nature.* Cambridge: University Press.

Stalnaker on Pragmatic Presupposition

Charles E. Caton

1. INTRODUCTION

In this chapter I try to improve upon Stalnaker's account of what pragmatic presupposition is.[1] A concept of this sort is sufficiently widely used
in recent philosophy and linguistics and other fields that I will not attempt
to motivate the pursuit of this subject further here. Stalnaker's account
needs improvement in two ways that I will primarily focus on: first, a relatively minor one, a certain indefiniteness as to the relation between what
is pragmatically presupposed and what is uttered in an utterance, and,
second, a major one, the problem he explicitly leaves unsolved as to what
the propositional attitude is in which a speaker stands to a proposition he
pragmatically presupposes. In the course of my discussion, improving the
former will be seen to involve illocutionary acts; and the solution of the
latter will be seen to involve the phenomenon I have elsewhere called

[1] I will deal primarily with Stalnaker's "Pragmatic Presupposition", which appears in
Munitz and Unger (1974) and in Rogers, Wall, and Murphy (1977). Page references to these
will be given in the form m/n, m being the former printing and n the latter. There are also the
earlier "Pragmatics" (1972, Section III "Presuppositions"), "Presuppositions" (1973), and
the later "Assertion" (1978).

RADICAL PRAGMATICS

epistemic qualification.[2] Various other related matters require discussion, including mutual knowledge,[3] semantic presupposition (as distinct from but related to pragmatic presupposition), certain principles of what may be termed discourse grammar, and certain uses of *if* and *would*.

2. STALNAKER'S "FIRST APPROXIMATION" AND ITS ADDENDUM

Early on in "Pragmatic Presupposition", Stalnaker gives what he regards as only a "first approximation" to a definition of what it is to pragmatically presuppose something:

> A proposition *P* is a pragmatic presupposition of a speaker in a given context just in case the speaker assumes or believes that *P*, assumes or believes that his audience assumes or believes that *P*, and assumes or believes that his audience recognizes that he is making these assumptions, or has these beliefs. [p. 200/p. 137].

After some discussion of cases in which a speaker pretends that these conditions are satisfied, knowing they are not, Stalnaker adds:

> Where a conversation involved this kind of pretense, the speaker's presuppositions, in the sense of the term I shall use, will not fit the definition sketched above [given in the preceding quote]. That is why the definition is only an approximation. I shall say that one actually does make the presuppositions that one seems to make even when one is only pretending to have the beliefs that one normally has when one makes presuppositions [p. 202/p. 138].

A speaker and his audience (or, really, an addressee) being involved, Stalnaker's definition–sketch then might appear to be this:

(1)   A speaker pragmatically presupposes that *p* by uttering an expression *e* in a certain context just in case
        (i) the speaker assumes or believes that *p*,
        (ii) the speaker assumes or believes that his addressee assumes or believes that *p*, and
        (iii) the speaker assumes or believes that in the context his addressee will recognize that the speaker is making these assumptions or has these beliefs [= the ones in (i) and (ii)]
        —or else (i.e., rather than all three of these being true)
        (iv) the speaker acts as if or pretends that (i)–(iii) are true.

---

[2] See Caton 1966.
[3] In the sense of Schiffer 1972.

However, this definition–sketch would be insufficiently explicit about the relation between the speaker's uttering what he does and his pragmatically presupposing what he does when he issues that utterance. For what a speaker will be understood to be presupposing will not, in general, depend just on what expression it is that he utters in a context; it will also depend on what speech act he is understood to be performing thereby. I am inclined to think and will here assume that what is in question is, in Austin's terms,[4] the illocutionary act performed, not just the locutionary act but also not the full perlocutionary act (if any) that the speaker may be attempting.[5] I have no argument to present that the latter is not involved, except that it does not seem to be in the examples of pragmatic presupposition that are typically alleged. However, an argument that it is the illocutionary and not just the locutionary act that is in question is that the same statement may, for example, be made either in asserting something or in denying its opposite and yet the speaker will be understood in the latter, but not (necessarily) in the former, case to be presupposing that the suggestion or statement has been made that the thing he is denying is true. So a reference to the illocutionary act is necessary in characterizing the desired concept of pragmatic presupposition. Such a reference will also conveniently fix that part of the speaker-meaning necessary to settle what the propositional content of his utterance is; it is necessary to do this because of the referential and possibly lexical ambiguity of the expression uttered taken by itself. That is, what a speaker is presupposing depends, in general, on how ambiguities in the expression uttered are resolved.

Furthermore, not only is the propositional content[6] of the illocutionary act relevant to what the speaker is presupposing, but it or it together with the utterance used to make it are what CONVEY the presupposition. That is, it is BY performing that illocutionary act BY uttering that expression in that context that the speaker indicates that he is presupposing a certain thing. The "recognizing" that Stalnaker refers to [cf. clause (iii) of (1)] is the addressee's seeing what the speaker is presupposing from WHAT the speaker has illocuted and from HOW he has illocuted it.[7]

---

[4] Austin (1962).

[5] By the illocutionary act here I mean the specific illocutionary act, so not the locutionary or generic illocutionary act. Some doubt the concept of the locutionary act, for example, Searle (1968); but this question does not, I think, affect this chapter.

[6] In the sense of Searle (1969, p. 30).

[7] That Stalnaker intends this is clear from his discussion of examples. He seems, though, a bit uncertain of the point. But obviously there is a useful concept of pragmatic presupposition to be distinguished from (though it is related to) mutual knowledge in Schiffer's sense. I know you know $2 + 2 = 4$, you know I do, *etc.*, but this does not mean we are constantly or even ever presupposing it when we converse (cf. also Stalnaker 1973, pp. 456–457, fn. 5).

For these reasons, a better statement of Stalnaker's definition–sketch is this:

(2)   A speaker pragmatically presupposes that p by illocuting that q by uttering e in a certain context just in case
   (i) the speaker assumes or believes that p,
   (ii) the speaker assumes or believes that his addressee assumes or believes that p, and
   (iii) the speaker assumes or believes that his addressee will recognize, from his illocuting that q by uttering e in the context, that the speaker is making these assumptions or has these beliefs [= the ones in (i) and (ii)]
  —or else
   (iv) the speaker acts as if or pretends that (i)–(iii) are true.

This version, in clause (iii), makes the required connection between the speaker's utterance and his presupposing that p.

3. PROPOSITIONAL ATTITUDES, EPISTEMIC QUALIFICATION, AND PRAGMATIC PRINCIPLES GOVERNING DISCOURSE

3.1. The Propositional Attitude[8] ("Assumes or Believes") in the Definition

One reason Stalnaker offered his account only as a "sketch" of a definition of pragmatic presupposition was that it involved the unanalyzed notion he expresses in the definition as the speaker's "assuming or believing" that the proposition presupposed is so [I have retained this feature in (2)]. It is plain that Stalnaker thinks that the propositional attitude relating to the speaker in clauses (i)–(iii) is the same in all three and is also the same as that relating to the addressee in clause (ii). I think he probably also thinks that the "recognizing" in clause (iii) is simply COMING TO assume or believe the proposition there in question as a result of hearing the utterance. But I will urge that this appearance of uniformity in the propositional attitudes involved is ONLY an appearance, one resulting from fail-

---

[8] This term is used in the sense familiar in the philosophical literature. I am not sure how to define it, but it is not necessary to do so for the discussion here. The various things here so called are stock examples. It suffices to know that a person and a proposition are always involved. [I believe it is correct to call pragmatic presupposition itself a propositional attitude, as Stalnaker does in his 1973 paper, even with clause (ii).]

ing to consider the phenomenon I call "epistemic qualification", which is involved throughout and which when considered aright leads to an account that is more general and more nearly adequate. Also, the reason for the appearance of uniformity can, in these terms, be seen to result from one particularly important special case of the more general account. It will be seen that the speaker's propositional attitude referred to in (ii) and (iii) and the addressee's in (iii) are fixed at a certain (strong) level of epistemic qualification, whereas the speaker's in (i) and the hearer's in (ii) vary (together) in different cases. [This is apart from clause (iv), which depends entirely on (i)–(iii) in these respects.]

3.2. Epistemic Qualification Briefly Expounded

By the EPISTEMIC QUALIFICATION (EQn) of a proposition, I mean the modification of it in such a way as (perhaps among other things) to involve the speaker's state of knowledge with respect to the proposition, that is, whether he knows or is certain that it is true, just believes or thinks that it is true, or thinks that it is probable, very probable, quite possible, *etc.*, or none of these but just thinks it possible. The linguistic devices employed to convey this nearly ubiquitous sort of modification vary from special lexical items and constructions (like those just used) to tenuous conversational implicatures.[9] Variations in strength are exhibited in EQn and three broad types of strength of epistemic qualifiers (EQs) may be distinguished: (*a*) strong, like those expressed by the EQ expressions *I know, I'm certain, It's certain, undoubtedly, etc.* as well as by "flat statement" (including the case of no EQ expression); (*b*) moderate, like those expressed by *I believe, I think, It's likely, It's probable, The chances are, It's very possible;* and (*c*) weak, like those expressed by *It's possible* (POSSIBLE), *It may be, perhaps.* Epistemic qualification is not just a main clause or even just an asserted clause phenomenon, but seems to be involved in the lexicon (because, e.g., of the EQn involved in factive expressions and individual words such as *fear,* and *hope*), in subordinate clauses [e.g., the use of declarative *if*-clauses seems to regularly imply that the speaker thinks the proposition they express to be possibly true and *or*-disjunctions that the speaker does not know the disjuncts to be true (or false)[10]], felicity conditions for illocutionary acts (e.g., for a promise to be appropriate the speaker must think he knows that the promised act will benefit the addressee[11]), Gricean conversational maxims (notably the submaxims of

[9] In the sense of Grice 1975.
[10] This is discussed by Grice and others.
[11] See Searle, 1969, p. 58.

Quality, "Do not say what you believe to be false" and "Do not say that for which you lack adequate evidence"[12]), *etc*. A particularly important case of EQn is that involved in presupposition, semantic and pragmatic, discussed in what follows.

Some technical terms will be useful. I will say that a proposition OCCURS IN a discourse if it figures in it in any way whatever, for example, through being ILLOCUTED (i.e., being the propositional content of an illocutionary act that is performed in the discourse), presupposed, conventionally or conversationally implicated,[13] or even an obvious logical consequence of something illocuted or otherwise occurring. To occur in this sense in a discourse a proposition need not be asserted or even tentatively claimed to be true; it might occur, for example, through being denied or questioned or just referred to. It is useful to have a term for the occurrence of a proposition in a discourse when it IS being said to be so or to be thought to be so or being presupposed or obviously entailed by something asserted or suggested, *etc.;* I will call this the proposition being PROPOUNDED. I will use the notation "*f(p)*" to refer to the epistemically qualified (EQed) proposition *p*, with *f* variable over EQs. In conjunction with this notation, I will speak of what a speaker "would say" (e.g., that he would say that is probable that *p*), on the strength of the fact that this is one way we ordinarily use this phrase.[14]

In terms of EQn, a generalization useful in the later discussion is possible of Schiffer's notion of "mutual knowledge" of a proposition *p*, namely, the notion of the mutual ACCEPTANCE of a QUALIFIED proposition *f(p)*. I will say that two people *x* and *y* MUTUALLY ACCEPT THAT *f(p)* in case *x* would say that *f(p)*, *y* would say that *f(p)*,[15] *x* knows (or is certain, *etc.*) *y* would say that *f(p)*, *y* knows (*etc.*) *x* would say that *f(p)*, *y* knows *x* knows *y* would say that *f(p)*, *etc.*, in the fashion of Schiffer.[16]

---

[12] Grice, 1975, p. 46.

[13] In the sense of Grice 1975.

[14] Compare saying what something is or is like by saying what one *would call* it or how one *would describe* it. (I suppose the *would* here means "would if asked" and the question one would be asked in the case of *f(p)* would presumably be the question whether *p*.)

[15] In the case of personal EQ expressions (like *I think*, as distinct from the impersonal *probably*), a problem may be felt here that does not attend impersonal ones, namely, how is *f(p)* to be expressed if it is to be shared by *x* and *y*? I mean to count two people as both such that they would say that *f(p)* where they would both (candidly) say "*f(p)*," for example, would both say *I think that p*.

[16] Schiffer (1972, p. 30ff.). Mutual knowledge is then just the special case of mutual acceptance where *f(p)* = *I know that p /It is certain that p*, etc.

3.3 Propositional Attitudes Reconsidered in the Light of EQn.

Given the variations in strength of the several EQs, the various ways in which EQn is expressed linguistically, and the large variety of propositional attitudes there are, the question arises how these articulate. The name of a propositional attitude may lexically MEAN a certain state of knowledge (like *know* or *think*), it may semantically[17] presuppose one (like *discover* in any person or tense or *fear* in the first person present), or, in the right context, its use may conversationally implicate one (as in *No one seems to know, but Jones thinks that . . .*). It seems plain that, in connection with linguistic questions involving propositional attitudes, we should always ask how the propositions that are involved relate to the structure of EQn. In particular, we should ask whether the propositions involved must be EQed or not in order to figure the way they do in whatever is under consideration.

Applying this advice to the version given in (2) of Stalnaker's definition –sketch of pragmatic presupposition, consideration of examples seems to show that the propositional attitude of the speaker referred to in clauses (ii) and (iii) and the one of the hearer called ''recognizing'' in clause (iii) should be regarded as fixed at the strong level of EQn, whereas the speaker's attitude in (i) and the hearer's in (ii) vary and vary together in different cases. To begin with, it is clear that ordinary semantic presuppositions of illocutions are EQed, as Moorean paradoxes[18] can be generated using the presupposed propositions as well the proposition itself, as in

(3)   *I think I've been to Grantchester, but I haven't.*[19]

in which the strong EQ of flat statement in the second conjunct is ruled out by one having just advanced the opposite proposition with moderate EQn in the first conjunct: This paradox has to do with logical relations of the propounded proposition itself. But similar paradoxes are generable off presuppositions of the other part, as in

(4)   *I think I've been to Grantchester, but there isn't any such place.*

which again would involve strong EQn of the second conjunct, here the

---

[17] I argue in what follows for the existence of semantic presuppositions. I think my discussion would not be seriously affected if there were not any.

[18] Often so called in the philosophical literature because of their having been first discussed by G. E. Moore (1912, pp. 125–126). See also Moore (1951, pp. 203–205). These are also called or are a subclass of the examples called ''pragmatic paradoxes.''

[19] Due to A. M. MacIver (1937–1938), who credits F. P. Ramsey.

denial of the presupposed proposition. But moderate strength will do, as in

(5)   *I think I've been to Grantchester, but I don't think there is any such place.*

in which the moderate strength EQ of *I think* in the second conjunct is ruled out by one's having in the first conjunct just advanced with moderate EQn a proposition presupposing (or illocuting which presupposes) the opposite proposition.[20] All of these examples apparently involve the presupposition occurring with strong EQn implicit on it.

But a proposition may be presupposed by an illocution without being qualified with strong strength. Such a proposition can be qualified with moderate strength and this in either of the two ways a presupposition can be made, either being mutually accepted and tacit in the discourse or having been prepared for by being explicitly propounded earlier. Each of two parties to a conversation may know that the other thinks (but does not know) that there is a king of Siam; that is, it can be that they mutually accept that they think that there is a king of Siam. And they can then refer to him as such and in the usual related ways (*he, who, etc.*)—Refer to whom?—To the king of Siam they think there is. That is, the referential presupposition is here occurring with only moderate EQn. The case is the same if one of the parties has, earlier in the conversation, explicitly said something to the effect that he (or they) thinks (but does not know) that there is a king of Siam and this has, perhaps tacitly, been accepted in the conversation. For example, it might go:

(6)   (a) *I **think** there's a king of Siam. . . .* (b) *He lives in Paris.*

If the speaker who had said that (a) were asked who he meant/was referring to (by *he*) in (b) he would or anyhow could candidly and accurately say that he was referring to the king of Siam that he thinks there is (or that he thinks there is a king of Siam and he was referring to him). (It would not be accurate to answer: *To the king of Siam,* as this answer would presuppose that there was one and imply that the speaker knew or was certain there was, unless the speaker meant this answer in the former way.)

However, there appears to be a constraint on such handling of presuppositions that has to do with the strength of the EQn with which they are propounded in the discourse. Namely, it appears that what has just been said about moderate-strength EQn of presuppositions is not true of weak-

---

[20] On the other hand, *I think I've been to Grantchester, but there may not be such a place* is possible, at least with *think* stressed. That this is possible appears to require the presupposition to be construable as only moderately EQed in the first conjunct. This is further discussed in what follows.

strength EQn of presuppositions. The difference here might be missed because of the fact that it could be that it was mutually accepted or earlier propounded in a discourse that, for example,

(7)   *It's **possible** that there is a king of Siam.*

and that later the referring expression *the king of Siam* was used to refer to him—that is, to the king of Siam that (the speaker thinks) it is possible there is. But the case is different from that where the proposition is mutually accepted with, or has been propounded with, moderate strength. The difference is revealed by the discourse ungrammaticality of the analogue of (6):

(8)   (a) *It's **possible** that there is a king of Siam. . . .* (b) *He lives in Paris.*

in which, assuming no change of mind or retraction or modification on the part of the speaker of his earlier remark (a), the speaker can no longer correctly say (just[21]) (b). In the present case, a certain type of *if*-clause tends to occur or main verbs will acquire the auxiliary *would* or, though the expressions used are the same as in the moderate-strength case, they are understood differently, that is, as though *if*s and *would*s were present. For example, a discourse of this sort might occur:

(9)   (a) *It's possible that there is a king of Siam. But,* (b) *if so, he must live in exile,* (c) *probably in Paris.*

This contains the sort of *if*-clause that I have in mind; it is what may be termed a PRESUPPOSITION-DISCLAIMING (P.-D.) IF-CLAUSE, that is, one that expresses the proposition that is semantically presupposed by (the proposition expressed by) the following *then*-clause. Note here that the proposition in question is apparently unqualified in the p.-d. *if*-clause; in any case, what is disclaimed is that the proposition presupposed is KNOWN or CERTAIN or so, rather than that proposition more weakly qualified or the bare proposition.

This use of *would* in English is similar to that of the p.-d. *if*-clause as far as the effect on presupposition is concerned. Thus instead of (9), there could occur:

(10)   (a) *It's possible that there is a king of Siam. But* (b) *he surely would live in exile,* (c) *probably in Paris.*

---

[21] I mean in the ordinary way, analogous to (b) in (6). I would here (by "just" or "modification") mean to accommodate the fact that the conversation might, for example, go: *A: It's **possible** that there is a king of Siam. B: Well, let's talk as though there definitely is. Where does he live? A: He lives in Paris.*

In (10), the referent of *he* would be explained in the same way as in (9). No one would understand statement (b) in (12) or (13) to presuppose or entail that there really WAS a king of Siam, that is, that it was KNOWN or CERTAIN that there was or that it could be taken as being so. That is, no one would who remembered (the unmodified and unretracted) remark (a). Also, the EQ expressions *surely* in (b) and *probably* in (c) would be understood as applying to a propositional content the presuppositions of which had been affected in that same way by the presence of *would*. [The same is true with *if* in (9).] And, of course, a p.-d. *if*-clause can be combined with a *would* auxiliary on the main verb of the following *then*-clause, with the same effect on presuppositions.[22]

It thus appears that there is a principle of what may be termed DIS-COURSE GRAMMAR to the effect that

(11)   **Pragmatic Principle I:** If a proposition is pragmatically presup-posed in a discourse, whether tacitly through mutual acceptance or through earlier propounding, it must be EQed with either strong or moderate strength.

Thus four sorts of cases of pragmatic presupposition in connection with an EQed proposition *p* apparently can occur: where it is tacit in the discourse and mutually accepted (*a*) at strong strength or (*b*) at moderate strength; or where it is in some way propounded earlier in the discourse, it being there qualified (*c*) with strong strength or (*d*) with moderate strength. Where *p* is mutually accepted or earlier propounded with WEAK strength, illocutions will, in English, be conditionalized with p.-d. *if*-clauses or with *would* auxiliaries or both or will be understood as though they were.

3.4. An Argument for Semantic Presupposition

It seems to me that the fact that a proposition can be taken for granted in a discourse without being explicitly propounded or even having oc-curred in it tends to argue for the existence of SEMANTIC presuppositions, that is, ones that can be stated as two-termed relations between a presup-

---

[22] The hypothesis crosses one's mind that sentences whose main verb has the auxiliary *would* and that do not have p.-d. *if*-clauses but that are understood as though they did are elliptical for ones that do, the missing clauses being recoverable from a knowledge of what the presuppositions of the (nonconditional) statement would be without the *would*. For example, *He would go to Podunk* might be understood the way it is (in a conversation about some person's plans) with respect to presuppositions, because it was elliptical for *He would go to Podunk, if he went to college*, the *if*-clause in the latter disclaiming the presupposition that he will go to college.

posing illocution and the presupposed proposition.[23] I will pause here to give an argument that uses the fact just mentioned, together with the familiar fact that a speaker S may convey to an addressee A that p by illocuting something that involves taking it for granted that p rather than saying that p. In a conversation between S and A, it can occur that p is not mutually known to S and A, though it is known to S. In some such cases, at least, there will be illocutions q such that S can illocute q and thereby (among other things) convey to A that p. (For example, S says to A that S's sister lives in Michigan, when it had never occurred to A to wonder whether S had a sister.) HOW can he? Ex hypothesi, p is not mutually known and in fact is not, before the utterance, known to A at all. Further, it need not be that S ASSUMES that A knows or believes that p; S may know he does not and be deliberately using his utterance to convey this information to A. Further still, S need not be assuming that A is aware of certain features of the context of utterance which, together with the fact that S illocutes q, would enable A to see or infer that p; there need not be any. No, it must, it seems, be that there is some relation between p and q as such (a two-termed relation) that enables S to convey that p to A in this way. Furthermore, all this can occur when, not only does illocuting that q behave this way, but illocuting not-q (i.e., the "inner negation" of q) does so too (e.g., saying that his sister does not live in Michigan).—But this relation between p and q would be readily explainable given what semantic presupposition was explained as being and therefore argues for its existence.

3.5. Rationale of Pragmatic Principle I

Like Grice, Stalnaker recommends trying to understand pragmatic phenomena in terms of what rational cooperative behavior would urge. I do not know whether the present phenomena can be explained in that fashion. But if the force of the EQs of the different strengths is kept in mind, there is an obvious reason why a language might have its pragmatic principles, its rules of discourse grammar, arranged in the present way. It is that propositions that are strongly or moderately EQed EXCLUDE other propositions in a way that weakly EQed ones do not: If propositions p and q are logically incompatible (in a narrow, possible-truth-conditions sense), then propounding one of them with one of the stronger forces commits one to not propounding the other with either of the strong forces but with at most weak force and, if with strong force, then to not propounding the other at

---

[23] As in Strawson 1952 and of course numerous other places.

all.[24] But this does not hold for weakly EQed propositions: One CAN pro-
pound both of two incompatible propositions weakly EQed. That is, to
say that it may be that p does not exclude saying at the same time and
without retracting anything or announcing a change of mind that it may
(also) be that q, where p and q are logically incompatible.[25] (This is not, of
course, to say that it may be that BOTH p and q are true.) Thus if weakly
EQed propositions could be presupposed as a result of mutual acceptance
or earlier propounding in a discourse, as moderately and strongly EQed
ones can, then incompatible propositions could be presupposed, producing an incoherent communication situation.

Principle I has to do with the propositional attitude (there expressed by
"assumes or believes") that is referred to in clause (i) of definition (2) as
the speaker's and in clause (ii) as the addressee's, not the speaker's attitude in (ii) and (iii), that is, not the "assumption or belief" the speaker
makes about the addressee and not the addressee's "recognizing" in (iii).
We must deal now with the latter and, as might be expected, it will turn
out that the variation involved in the earlier case does not attach to this
latter one. I say this might be expected, because the intuitive idea of pragmatic presupposition involves that of something one indicates by one's
utterance that one assumes. Because (as Stalnaker's sketch goes) a
speaker can, through clause (iv), pragmatically presuppose a proposition
without actually having the propositional attitude toward it that he purports to have, the question here is what propositional attitude the speaker
PURPORTS to have in clause (ii) toward the proposition that his addressee
assumes or believes that p and in clause (iii) toward the proposition that
his addressee will recognize from what he says that he, the speaker, is
making the previous assumptions or has the previous beliefs.

My hypothesis is that the speaker's propositional attitude in clauses (ii)
and (iii) must be of such a sort as to entail strong EQn of the propositions
toward which the speaker is said to have the attitude and that cases of
pragmatic presupposition where this is not so are best regarded as falling
under clause (iv), according to which the speaker acts as if or pretends
that (i)–(iii) are satisfied. For consider what is the most likely other possibility, namely, that the speaker's propositional attitude in (ii) and (iii)
should be such as to involve only moderate, not strong, strength of EQn
on the propositions about the addressee. Here the EQn fitting the speaker

---

[24] This principle also belongs to discourse grammar, but does not relate as narrowly to
pragmatic presupposition as those singled out as such in the text.

[25] In fact, in a sense, whenever one says merely that something may be so there is *always*
another incompatible proposition that one is also propounding as possibly so, namely, the
denial of the first. To say something may be so is also to say (i.e., really, to say what implies)
that it may not be so.

in (i) and the addressee in (ii) might be of any strength, but the speaker does not know (*etc.*) that the latter obtain, but rather only THINKS they do. For example, it might be that (i') the speaker thinks that there is a king of Siam, but that (ii') the speaker only THINKS[26] that the addressee also only thinks that there is, and (iii') that the speaker only thinks that the addressee will recognize, from what he illocutes by uttering a certain expression *e* that the speaker ''is making these assumptions or has these beliefs'', here that the speaker only thinks that there is a king of Siam and that the speaker only thinks that he, the addressee, only thinks that there is.

Can this sort of case occur in pragmatic presupposition? I do not think so and the reason that I do not is the difficulty of seeing what the expression *e* might be that the speaker is supposed to have uttered. Note that it is not just a question of whether (ii) holds, that is, of whether the speaker might only think the addressee only thought that *p* (this would often hold), but of whether (ii) holds along with (iii). Now either the same surface expression *e* could also be used in the case where the presupposed proposition was strongly EQed or it could not. But I cannot imagine what sort of expression it could be that would be able to express the present sort of pragmatic presupposition but not the sort in which the EQn in (ii) and (iii) is strong rather than moderate. And if it could also be used in the other case, then clearly some sort of information about the context of utterance would have to be assumed on the part of the addressee; and it would have to be information such that, knowing it, the addressee would know that the speaker's using *e* in that context meant (if he was speaking candidly), not that (ii) and (iii) were true in such a form that the speaker would say he was certain, but rather that (ii) and (iii) were true where the speaker would say he only THOUGHT that the addressee thought that *p* and that he would recognize, from his uttering *e*, that he (the speaker) only thought that *p* and only thought that he (the addressee) thought that *p*. It seems plain that this sort of conversational context would be quite rare at best. I cannot show any incoherence in it, but my suspicion is that it does not occur.

There is a similar problem for the supposed case where moderate EQn is involved in (ii) and (iii) about the satisfaction of the pretence clause (iv). If the speaker's propositional attitude in (ii) and (iii) is capable of different EQ strengths, then it would, in accordance with (iv), have to follow that the speaker could pretend to have different propositional attitudes, as per (ii) and (iii). Again, I do not see what difference in the expression *e* chosen to be uttered could be relied on to effect this difference in presupposition

---

[26] To avoid repetition, let me use ''only thinks'' as short for ''only thinks (but doesn't know).''

without the special background knowledge. The point about this knowledge being of a rather special sort is simply that it cannot then be plausibly supposed to be very often involved in the mundane, ubiquitous phenomenon of pragmatic presupposition.

For these reasons, I conclude that, although the propositional attitudes related to the speaker in (i) of the definition–sketch (2) and to the hearer in (ii) can vary across the board with respect to the strength of EQn in question, nevertheless the propositional attitude related to the speaker in (ii) and (iii)—and by reference in (iv)—must be of STRONG strength. That is, in order (candidly) to illocute something that pragmatically presupposes that $f(p)$, a speaker must EITHER actually be certain [cf. (ii)] that his addressee would say that $f(p)$ and [cf. (iii)] that his addressee will recognize, from his illocution, that the speaker would say that $f(p)$ and is certain that his addressee also would, OR [cf. (iv)] the speaker must act as if or pretend that this is the case.[27]

It thus appears that there is another principle of discourse grammar, to the effect that

(12)   **Pragmatic Principle II:** If an EQed proposition $f(p)$ is pragmatically presupposed in a discourse, then it must be the case that the speaker is certain[28] that the addressee would say that $f(p)$ and that the speaker is certain that the addressee will recognize, from what he illocutes, that the speaker would say that $f(p)$ and that the speaker is certain that he (the addressee) would say that $f(p)$.

Principles I and II relate to clauses (i)–(iii) of the definition (2) of pragmatic presupposition, but not to the pretense clause (iv), because the latter is parasitic upon the former; the principles of discourse grammar, like those of any grammar, must define what is correct in the way of linguistic behavior and thus what it is that one pretends to do in linguistic pretense. As far as I can see the preceding discussion need not assume any particular view of what the nature of discourse grammar is, beyond the fact that it contains or somehow yields pragmatic principles conformity to which partly defines what it is to speak correctly in a discourse.[29] The principles, together, would define (at least in the sense of constrain-

---

[27] Stalnaker's (1973) discussion of *as if* and *pretense* is interesting, suggesting the phenomenon is both common and rational.

[28] I use "is certain" to avoid the factivity of "knows," since the speaker may be pretending or may be mistaken as to $f(p)$. And a speaker is not regarded as speaking incorrectly just because he thought he knew something he did not in fact know and spoke accordingly.

[29] A recent philosophical dispute seems to be centered further back, so to speak; there seems to be general agreement that there are conventions of a pragmatic sort, the question being how they might have arisen as principles of rational cooperative behavior.

ing) what it is for a conversation to be discourse-grammatically correct, no doubt as any (serious) interchange of remarks that does not violate any of the principles. The definition of pragmatic presupposition is not a principle of discourse (or any other) grammar, but of course it relates importantly to it and its constraints on conversational correctness in that (*a*) some principles of discourse grammar are (or can be) formulated employing the notion of pragmatic presupposition (which fact confirms the utility of the notion in pragmatics), and in that (*b*), as mentioned earlier, some principles of discourse grammar restrict what can (discourse-grammatically) be pragmatically presupposed.

3.6. The Rationale of Principle II

It would be appropriate here to insert an account of the rationality of Principle II, that is, of its being a principle of discourse grammar that a speaker should KNOW or BE CERTAIN that his addressee would say that $f(p)$ and will recognize from his illocuting that he would too, rather than that he should only THINK that these things were so, when he wanted (candidly) to make a certain presupposition in a conversation. However, I do not have one on a par with the one given earlier for Principle I, concerning the strength that can be involved in pragmatic presupposition. But it should at least be noted that there is an obvious efficiency, convenience, and economy in having a phenomenon like pragmatic (and semantic) presupposition in a language and that these would be impaired if there were any ambiguity about what the speaker wishes to imply concerning this background acceptance, that is, about in what WAY it was accepted or taken for granted, regardless of what specifically it is that is being so accepted. With, but not without, the present principle, one would seem to have the best of both worlds, as far as efficient communication is concerned in this respect, in that WHAT is being taken for granted to be known, only thought, or thought possible, *etc.* can vary indefinitely as to its EQn, while the WAY it is being taken for granted (assumed, "believed," *etc.*) is definite and fixed, the same in every context.

3.7. Stalnaker's Definition–Sketch Revised

We have now determined what the propositional attitudes are that are involved in the first three clauses of Stalnaker's definition–sketch. Using the "would say that $f(p)$" device introduced on p. 88, a revised version of his sketch can be stated as follows:

(13)   A speaker PRAGMATICALLY PRESUPPOSES that $f(p)$ by illocuting that q by uttering e in a context c just in case either

(i)   the speaker would say that $f(p)$,
(ii)   the speaker is certain[30] that his addressee would say that $f(p)$, and
(iii)   the speaker is certain that his addressee will recognize, from his illocuting that q by uttering e in c, that (i) and (ii) are true, or else
(iv)   the speaker acts as if or pretends that (i)–(iii) are true.

As above, here p ranges over unEQed propositions and f is any EQ or at least fixes the strength of the EQn of p. Also, the "recognizing" in clause (iii) is to be understood as coming to be certain, that is, the addressee's coming to be certain that the speaker would say that $f(p)$ and is certain that he would.

4. CONCLUSION

4.1. Summary of the Main Contentions Leading to the Revised Definition

The extension of the notion of pragmatic presupposition is, in actual normal conversation or discourse, strongly constrained by the pragmatic principles of discourse grammar discussed earlier, no doubt among others.[31] The phenomenon of EQn is involved in the principles mentioned and in the revised definition; in particular, the fact that EQs vary in strength is involved.[32] Especially noteworthy was the fact that pragmatic presupposition is of *EQed* propositions, not unqualified ones, between which latter logical relations in the familiar senses definable in terms of possible-truth-conditions hold.[33] In connection with the statement and discussion of this definition and these principles, a generalization of Schiffer's concept of mutual knowledge has been useful, that is, what I termed "mutual acceptance" of a qualified proposition $f(p)$, where both parties would say that $f(p)$ and each know they would, *etc*.

[30] I again use "is certain" as the strong EQ expression here to avoid the factivity of "knows".

[31] See also Note 24 and Note 34.

[32] If one is inclined to doubt the reality of the phenomenon of EQn itself, one can view the explanations that appeal to it makes possible as evidence of its reality.

[33] The strict analogue for pragmatic presupposition of the question once debated in the philosophical literature concerning semantic presupposition over whether presupposition entails entailment is thus seen not to exist. Perhaps the nearest analogue would be the question whether if p is pragmatically presupposed by illocuting q it follows logically that q entails p. This of course is not so, because pragmatic presuppositions often have to do with contextual factors extraneous to the propositional content illocuted.

4.2. Some Unsolved Problems

One major question left by the preceding discussion is that concerning the relation between EQn and semantic presupposition. An argument was presented for assuming that the latter exists (contrary to what seems to be the prevailing opinion in the linguistic and philosophical literature). Some of the things that had been classed as semantic presuppositions seem to involve unqualified propositions as what was presupposed, whereas others do not; I do not know of a principled way to separate the two classes.[34] For example, in referential semantic presupposition, it seems to be the unqualified proposition that is presupposed, whereas, for example, in the case of the verb *fear* (as in *He is, I fear, in some sort of trouble*) the item is apparently lexically associated with moderate strength EQn. It seems clear that there cannot be a simple rule that will predict the EQn involved in pragmatic presupposition simply from the information as to what is semantically presupposed. To treat semantically presupposed propositions uniformly as being EQed perhaps does some violence to the term "semantic," as EQn is inherently pragmatic in nature; but then the term was not a good one to begin with—"logical" (which is sometimes used) would have been better for a two-termed relation between propositions.[35]

The problem about semantic presupposition, however, seems to me to be not whether there is some such thing, but rather what its nature and range are. Perhaps it is some special case of the concept with which this chapter has dealt and a clear account of which is in any case desirable, that is, of pragmatic presupposition in the sort of sense Stalnaker attempted to characterize.

REFERENCES

Austin, J. L. (1962). *How to Do Things with Words* (J. O. Urmson, Ed.). Oxford: Oxford University Press.

Caton, C. E. (1966). On the general structure of the epistemic qualification of things said in English. *Foundations of Language*, 2, 37–66.

Grice, H. P. (1975). Logic and conversation. In P. Cole and J. L. Morgan (Eds.), *Syntax and Semantics 3: Speech Acts*. New York: Academic Press. Pp. 41–58.

MacIver, A. M. (1937–1938). Some questions about 'know' and 'think'. *Analysis*, 5, 43–50.

[34] Complicating the question is the fact that a speaker ordinarily pragmatically presupposes anything his illocution semantically presupposes (another principle of discourse grammar).

[35] As it originally was in Strawson 1952. But both earlier (Strawson, 1950) and later (Strawson, 1964, but already implicit in Strawson, 1954), he used a concept (called "implying" in 1950) that involved a pragmatic factor, the speaker in 1950 and the topic of conversation in 1964.

Moore, G. E. (1912). *Ethics,* London: Williams & Norgate.

Moore, G. E. (1951). Russell's 'Theory of Descriptions'. In P. A. Schilpp (Ed.), *The Philosophy of Bertrand Russell (3rd ed.).* New York: Tudor. Pp. 177–225.

Munitz, M. K., and Unger, P. K. (Eds.). (1974). *Semantics and Philosophy,* New York: N.Y.U. Press.

Rogers, A., Wall, R., and Murphy, J. P. (Eds.). (1977). *Proceedings of the Texas Conference on Performatives, Presuppositions, and Implicatures.* Arlington, Va.: Center for Applied Linguistics.

Schiffer, S. R. (1972). *Meaning,* Oxford: Oxford University Press.

Searle, J. R. (1969). *Speech Acts.* London: Cambridge University Press.

Searle, J. R. (1968). Austin on locutionary and illocutionary acts. *The Philosophical Review,* **77**, 405–424.

Stalnaker, R. C. (1972). Pragmatics. In D. Davidson and G. Harman (Eds.), *Semantics of Natural Language.* Dordrecht: Reidel.

Stalnaker, R. C. (1973). Presuppositions. *Journal of Philosophical Logic,* **2**, 447–457.

Stalnaker, R. C. (1974/1977). Pragmatic Presupposition. In M. K. Munitz and P. K. Unger (1974) and in A. Rogers, R. Wall, and J. P. Murphy (1977).

Stalnaker, R. C. (1978). Assertion. In P. Cole (Ed.), *Syntax and Semantics 9: Pragmatics.* New York: Academic Press. Pp. 315–332.

Strawson, P. F. (1950). On referring. *Mind,* n.s., **59**, 320–344.

Strawson, P. F. (1952). *Introduction to Logical Theory.* London: Methuen.

Strawson, P. F. (1954). A reply to Mr. Sellars, *The Philosophical Review,* **63**, 216–231.

Strawson, P. F. (1964). Identifying reference and truth-values. *Theoria,* **30**, 96–118.

Syntactic and Semantic Indeterminacy Resolved: A Mostly Pragmatic Analysis for the Hindi Conjunctive Participle

Alice Davison

1. INTRODUCTION

It is not always immediately clear what kinds of syntactic and semantic relations, observed through speakers' intuitions, are direct and relevant evidence for the syntactic and semantic structures incorporated into linguistic description. As Morgan (1978) points out, semantic relations are not directly observable, as they are accessible only through speakers' intuitions about particular sentences in particular uses. In Schmerling 1978, sentences from English are considered about which speakers have intuitions which, if taken as syntactic evidence, lead to two distinct syntactic accounts of what would otherwise be considered the same construction. Schmerling demonstrates that the perceived differences are really due to real-world knowledge which is independent of a particular syntactic structure. In similar cases, where speakers' intuitions give conflicting indications of structure, a significant gain in generality and elegance of description can be made by taking this approach. It involves disregarding as linguistic evidence those features of a sentence that are the effects of con-

RADICAL PRAGMATICS

textual factors. These include real-world knowledge about the referents of lexical items in the structure, conversational inferences from context and propositional contents, as well as from other properties of the linguistic structures in question.

In this chapter, I want to demonstrate the value of this approach in accounting for the varied, variable, and conflicting properties of a specific construction, the CONJUNCTIVE PARTICIPLE -*kar* in Hindi, which has the approximate meaning 'having V-ed'. The analysis I want to propose illustrates how certain apparently syntactic or semantic relations alternatively might be accounted for outside the syntax and semantic structure of the language. To do otherwise would not necessarily exceed the capacity of linguistic theory, but it would lead to a complex and uninteresting, unrevealing account of the relations expressed by -*kar*. This construction has analogues in many other languages, including related languages of northern India (cf. Dwarikesh, 1971 for a study of dialects of Hindi), and unrelated languages. The analogous participial construction in Tamil has been discussed in a detailed and insightful way in Lindholm 1975. One of the curious features of the perfective adverbial constructions is that they appear to be syntactically a subordinating construction, but also have a number of features in common with coordinate structures. Conjunctions in Japanese, some similar to -*kar* in Hindi, also exhibit indeterminacy between subordination and coordination with respect to the possible scope of negation, question, and modals (Kuno, 1973, pp. 180–210). Thus the problems of description invoked by Hindi -*kar* have a somewhat more general import, and the solution offered in this case will have general application to the analysis of similar constructions.

In the following sections, I will first illustrate the different readings and equivalent paraphrases of -*kar* sentences, then give syntactic evidence for its being a subordinate construction. Following that, two sections will illustrate the variable properties of -*kar,* scope relations with question and negation, and the lexical meaning of the affix. Arguments will be given for a single, very general meaning. In the last section, I will describe the inferences necessary to derive the range of readings that occur.

2. COORDINATION VERSUS SUBORDINATION

The conjunctive participle construction in Hindi links clauses syntactically, as in (1) and (2):

(1)   *Poorbandar-see   pita   -jii   [raajasthaanii koorT-kee*
        -from father-hon. Rajasthani   court -of

*sadasy **ban**   -kar] raajkooT gayee.*
member become-CP   go-perf.-mpl.
'My father, having become a member of the Rajasthani court,
went from Poorbandar to Raajkoot.'   (M. Gandhi, 1957, p. 3.)

The verb of the internal clause marked in brackets is a tenseless verb stem
combined with *-kar*. The subject of the clause is identical with the subject
of the higher clause.

Example (2) illustrates the contrast between coordinate conjunction of
finite clauses, and the conjunctive participle construction:

(2)   *Kumaar-nee ghaRii-mēē vaqt deekhaa   aur [[saamnee*
                   -erg. watch -on   time look at-perf. and   in front
        *kee kaagazōō- kaa pulandaa **uThaa -kar**] Tree mēē*
        of   papers-obl. of   bundle   raise -CP tray -in
        Daal   diyaa.]
        throw give-perf.
        'Kumar looked at the time on his watch and, having picked up the
        bundle of papers in front of him, he tossed them into the
        tray.'   (Raakesh, 1972, p. 1.)

I mention this difference of surface syntax because one of the features of
the construction that I want to discuss and find an explanation for is the
fact that it is very close in meaning and discourse function to coordinate
constructions.

For example, if the subjects of the two clauses are not alike, it is necessary to use a coordinate structure, as in (3). Except for the difference of
subject, (3a) is not distinguishable in meaning from (3b):

(3) a. *Baniee   -kee beeTee -nee [ciTThii **likh-kar**] Daak   -mēē*
        shopkeeper-of   son-obl.-erg. [letter(f) write-CP] postoffice -in
        Daalii
        throw-perf. -f.
        'The shopkeeper's son wrote a letter and mailed it at the postof-
        fice.''   (Bailey, 1956, p. 146.)

     b. *[baniee   -nee ciTThii   **likh lii**]   aur phir [beeTee*
        [shopkeeper-erg. letter   write-take.perf]. and then [son
        -nee Daak   -mēē Daalii.]
        -erg. postoffice-in   throw-perf.]
        'The shopkeeper wrote a letter and his son mailed it at the postof-
        fice.'

Each clause in the coordinate structure (3b) has a finite verb. Differences
between the coordinate structure in (3b) and the subordinate structure in
(3a) will be discussed in later sections of the chapter.

But it is not the case that the conjunctive participle construction always has the syntactic form of a subordinate structure and the other properties, semantic and pragmatic, of coordinate constructions. It is possible to paraphrase some *-kar* sentences with other subordinate constructions which take nonfinite verbs:

(4) a. [*Wahãã jaa -kar*] *mujhee pataa*   *calaa*   *ki . . .*
          [there go -C.P.] me-Dat. information proceed-perf. that
          'When I went there, I found out that . . . .'

      b. [*Wahãã calaanee*   *-par*] *mujhee pataa*
          [there proceed-inf.obl.-on] me-Dat. information
          calaa   *ki . .*
          proceed-perf that
          'When I got there, I found out that . . . .'

The constituent marked with *-kar* may be perceived as though it were not a full subordinate clause, but rather a manner adverbial:

(5) a. [[*dauR-kee*] *jaaoo*]   *varnaa* [*naraaz hũũgaa*]
          [[run -CP go-imp.-fam.] or (else) [annoyed be-fut. lps. masc.]
          'Go quickly or I will be annoyed.'

      b. *Jaldii -see* *calee*   *jaaoogee too mujhee acchaa nahii*
          hurry-with go along-perf. got-fut. then me-too good   not
          lageegaa.
          will strike
          'If you leave in a hurry, I won't be pleased.'

---

[1] A SYNTACTIC DERIVATION analysis would postulate three underlying structures: Structures (a)–(c) would undergo various possible, but not generally motivated, movement rules and lexical substitutions so as to become the surface structure (d):

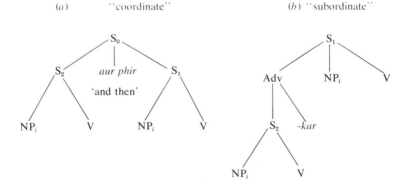

The conjunctive participle in (5a) corresponds to an adverbial formed by the combination of a nominal *jaldii* 'haste' and in the instrumental postposition.

Thus *-kar* constructions have something in common with coordinate structures, other subordinate constructions, and with nonclausal adverbials. Some *-kar* sentences can be paraphrased with only one other kind of structure, whereas others have multiple interpretations. For instance, (6a) has two equally plausible interpretations paraphrasable by the English glosses (6b) and (6c):[1]

(6) a. *Us   -nee [sooc -kar] kaam kiyaa.*
        3rd p.-obl.-erg [think-CP] work do-perf.
     b. 'Having thought, he/she did the work; He/she did the work after thinking.'
     c. 'He/she did the work carefully.'

Some of the problems of the analysis of *-kar* are to specify the association between sentences with *-kar* and the interpretations they may have and to define what distinguishes subordinate from coordinate constructions.

3. SYNTACTIC ARGUMENTS FOR *-KAR* CONSTRUCTIONS AS SUBORDINATE

Before describing the semantic and other properties of *-kar*, I want to establish at the beginning that all the syntactic evidence points to *-kar* constructions being subordinate and not coordinate constructions. First,

---

Footnote 1 continued:
Only structure (*b*) is well motivated. Conversely, a SEMANTIC INTERPRETATION analysis could derive from (*d*) various readings (*a*)–(*c*), which would be relevant for determining scope relations with respect to question and nagation.

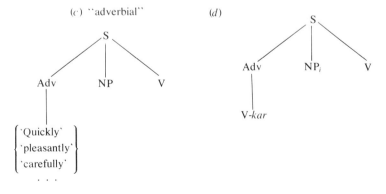

the verb is nonfinite. Although not all subordinate constructions in Hindi have nonfinite verbs, there are no nonfinite verbs in main or coordinate clauses. Although verb stems may be combined, as later examples will show, there is always one verb that bears tense–aspect information in a finite clause.

Second, the use of -kar requires that the subject of the nonfinite clause be identical to the subject of the higher clause, with a small class of permitted exceptions. The following sentences are all ungrammatical because this condition has not been met:

(7)   *Baniyaa   [ciTThii **likh -kar**] beeTee -nee Daak   -mẽẽ
      shopkeeper [letter   write-CP] son-obl.-erg. postoffice-in
      Daalii.
      throw-perf.
      'The shopkeeper having written a letter, his son mailed it at the post-office.'

(8)   *Mãĩ [un   -ciizõõ   -koo **deekh-kar**] mãã   -koo gussaa
      I   [those-obl.-things-obl.-dat. see   -CP] mother-dat. anger
      aayaa.
      come-perf.
      'I having seen those things, mother got very angry.'

(9)   *Raam [**dauR-kar**,] tum   jaaoo . . .
      Ram [run   -CP] you-fam. go-imp.-fam. . . .
      'Ram having run, you go. . .'

(10) *Raam [**sooc -kar**] laRkii-nee kaam kiyaa.
      Ram [think-CP] girl   -erg. work do-perf.
      'Ram having thought, the girl did the work.'

In sentences such as (1)–(6), the like-subject condition must be met, and, as Kachru (1978) has shown, one of the NPs must be deleted. Pronominalization is not possible. Although one NP may be deleted in a coordinate construction, by identity with another coreferential NP in another clause, such deletion is usually not obligatory. Subordinate constructions do undergo obligatory deletion, as in cases of Equi-NP deletion where the antecedent precedes and commands the coreferent.

Some evidence that the NP associated with the verb marked with -kar is deleted comes from the case marking of the surviving NP subject. Verbs in Hindi govern different case marking on their subjects; some require zero or nominative marking, others the dative–accusative marker -koo. Some verbs with nondative subjects require ergative marking with -nee in the perfective. Where the -kar verb requires -nee marking and the finite verb does not, or vice versa, the requirements of the finite verb win out. We can assume that its subject is not deleted, and instead the subject of the subordinate clause disappears. For instance, *aa* 'come' requires a nominative subject, and *banaa* 'cause to be made' requires *-nee* in the perfective:

(11)   *Mistrii -nee [kal   **aa**   -kar] sanduuq banaayaa.*
        carpenter-erg. [yesterday come -CP] box   make-perf.
        'The carpenter came yesterday and made the box.'

Finally, coordinate and subordinate constructions have different alternative word orders. Constituents may be moved to the left or right for stylistic emphasis. In (12a), the direct object of the main clause verb, *caay* 'tea', may be moved to the left of the *-kar* clause, as in (12b).

(12)   a. *[∅[Akeelee   **baiTh-kar**] caay pii   thii.]*
          [alone-obl. sit -CP] tea   drink-perf. (f.) be-past (f.)
          'He used to sit alone and drink tea.'   (Raakeesh, 1972, p. 1.)

     b. *∅[Caay [akeelee   **baiTh-kar**] pii‍ₗ   thii.]*
         tea   alone-obl. sit   -CP drink-perf. be-past)(f.)

Example (13a) is a coordinate sentence equivalent to (12a), just as (3b) is equivalent to (3a). But movement of *caay* in (13b) produces an ungrammatical sentence.

(13)   a. *[∅   akeelee   baiThaa] aur[∅ caay pii   thii.]*
               alone-obl. sit-perf. and   tea drink-perf. be-past (f.)
         'He sat alone and drank tea.'

     b. **[ₗcaay akeelee   baiThaa] aur[ⱼpii   thii.]*
         [tea   alone-obl. sit-perf.] and drink-perf. be-past (f.)

Similarly, movement of a NP to the right past the verb is possible in a coordinate structure, but not in a *-kar* construction, if movement is to preserve meaning.

(14)   a. *Us   -nee [apnee   doost-kee baaree   -mēē **sooc -kar**]*
          3rd p.-obl.-erg. [own-obl. friend-of about-obl.-in   think-CP]
         patra likhaa.
         letter write-perf.
         'He/she, having thought about his/her friend, wrote a letter.'

     b. **Us   -nee [ₗ**sooc -kar**] apnee   doost -keeₗ*
         3rd p.-obl.-erg. [think-CP] own-obl. friend -of
         baaree   -mēē patra likhaa.
         about-obl.-in   letter write-perf.

(This sentence is well-formed if the meaning is 'letter about his/her friend'.) The coordinate version of this sentence does allow the object of *sooc* 'think' to be permuted to the right of the verb:

(15) a. *Us   -nee apnee   doost-kee baaree   -mēē soocaaa*
        3rd p.-obl.-erg. own-obl. friend-of about-obl.-in   think-perf.
        aur patra likhaa.
        and letter write-perf.
        'He/she thought about his/her friend and wrote a letter.'

      b. *Us   -nee soocaa   apnee doost-kee baaree-mēē aur*
        3rd p.-obl.-erg. think-perf. own   friend-of about in   and
        patra likhaa.
        letter wrote

Sentences (12)–(15) show clear syntactic differences, illustrating the differences between a coordinate construction and the subordinate -*kar* construction. The differences noted here follow from a general restriction on permuting constituents outside of clause boundaries (cf. Ross, 1967). No special conditions are needed to account for the data if -*kar* is analyzed as a subordinating conjunction. But, having emphasized the syntactically subordinate properties of -*kar,* in the next sections I will describe other properties of -*kar* which appear to be at variance with the syntactic structure of -*kar* clauses for which I have just given arguments.

4. SCOPE OF NEGATION AND QUESTION

Clauses containing -*kar* differ from both subordinate and coordinate clauses in that in certain cases the scope of question or negation over -*kar* is obligatory or else blocked entirely. There do not seem to be any clear syntactic or semantic principles governing such cases. For example, yes/no questions usually include both clauses of a coordinate structure, while subordinate clauses usually have two interpretations, one in which the question has scope over the whole structure, including the subordinate clause, and one in which the question has scope over the subordinate clause alone. In the case of -*kar* clauses, the first kind of interpretation is ruled out in some cases, where only the subordinate clause is in the scope of the question. It is as though the higher clause were 'transparent', or pragmatically subordinate to the clause contained within it syntactically. For example:

(16) *Woo   [bartan saaf **kar** -kee hii] gaii   thii   na?*
      3rd ps. [pots   clean make-CP only] go-perf. f. be-past neg

`   She cleaned the pots before she left, didn't she?'   (Bailey
       1956; p. 145.)

(Lit. 'She left having cleaned the pots, didn't she?')
Sentence (16) is not understood as a question about whether she left, but
about whether she cleaned the pots. The import of (17), as reported in the
context in which it was uttered, was to ask if the addressee was going to
make a certain telephone call, not if she was coming or not.

(17)   *tum*   [*Teelifoon* **kar** **-kee**] *aaoogii?*
        you. fam. [telephone make-CP] come-fut.-2nd psg.fam.f.
        'Are you going to make the telephone call?'   (R. Moag, per-
        sonal communication)
        (Lit. 'Are you coming having made the telephone call?')

Contrast these cases with sentence (18), where the higher clause is in the
scope of the question:

(18)   [*Woo*   *šaraab* **pii**   **-kar**] *kyaa*   *gaaRii calaayeegaa?*
        [3rd ps wine   drink-CP] question car   go-caus.-fut. 3ps.
        'Can he drive when he is drunk?' (Lit. 'When he is drunk, will he
        drive?')   (Dwarikesh, 1971, p. 123.)

The position of the question particle *kyaa* may indicate that the higher
clause is its scope; normally the particle is sentence initial.
    The scope of negation is also variable. If the positive sentence (19) a. is
negated, it no longer has sequential interpretation of -*kar*. Instead the -*kar*
clause itself is negated, as in (19) b.

(19) a. *Woo*   [*doostōō*   *-see* **mil** **-kar**] *aa*   *gayaa*
         3rd ps. [friends.obl.-with meet-CP] come go-perf.
             'He met his friends and came.'

      b. [*Woo*   [*doostōō*   *-see* **mil** **-kar**] *nahīī* *aayaa*
         3rd ps. [friends.obl.-with meet-CP] not   come-perf.
             'He didn't meet his friends; he came without having met his
             friends.'

The causal interpretation of (19b), is not possible, namely that he did not
come on account of meeting his friends. The causal interpretation is not
possible in a similar sentence which is a question, though the causal adverb -*kee kaaraN* may express the meaning which might be expected for
(19b) and (20a), but which is not possible:

(20) a. ??*Kyaa*   *woo*   [*doostōō-see* **mil** **-kar**] *deer* *-see*
         question 3rd ps. [friends -with meet-CP] delay-with

aayaa?
come-perf.
'Did he come late having met his friends; did he come late because of meeting his friends?'

b.   *Kyaa*   [*woo*   *doostōō*   *-see*   **milnee**   **-kee**   **kaaraN**]
     question [3rd ps. friends.obl.-with meet-inf. obl.-of cause]
     deer-see aayaa?
     delay-with come

     'Did he come late on account of meeting his friends?'

Similarly, the causal adverb *kee kaaraN* may be either in or outside the
scope of negation, while *-kar* in (21b) *is not* in the scope of negation.

(21) a. *Woo* [*doostōō*   *-see*   **milnee**   **-kee kaaraN**] *nahīi aayaa*
          3ps. [friends.obl.-with meet-inf.-of cause]   not   come-perf.
          (i)   'He didn't come, because of meeting friends'.
          (ii) 'He came, not because of meeting friends'.

      b. [*Yah baat*   **sooc -kar**] *woo*   *ghar*   *nahīi aayaa*
          [this matter think-CP] 3rd ps house not   come-perf.
          'Having thought of this matter, he did not come to the house',
          'He did not come to the house because of thinking of this
          (other/unpleasant) matter'.

In these sentences, the higher, main clause is negated (21b), or negatable
(21a), and the causal relationship between the two clauses is conveyed.

Though not the sole determining factor, the 'transparency' of the higher
clause noted in connection with questions in examples (16) and (17) may
be responsible for the lower *-kar* clause having prominence over the
higher clause. Compare the positive and negative sentences in (22), which
both contain higher clauses which would be clearly redundant when spoken by someone who was in fact present in the situation:

(22) a. *Mãī* [*abhii*   **khaa-kar**] *aayaa*   *hũū*
         I   [now-emph. eat -CP] come-perf. am
         'I had a meal just before I came.' (Lit. 'I have come having eaten
         just now'.   (Bailey, 1956, p. 145.)

      b. *Mãī* [*yah sooc   -kar*] *yahãā nahīi aayaa*
         I   [this matter-CP] here   not   come-perf.
         'I didn't come here to fight with you; I came not thinking of this
         matter.' (Lit. 'I did not come here having thought of this mat-
         ter.')

Discourse prominence is given to the subordinate clause in (22a), which
clearly contains more information than the higher clause. If the same is

the case in (22b), the negation will be taken with the subordinate clause rather than the redundantly true higher clause.

In summary, scope relations between -*kar* and question, negation and even assertion are not what would be expected if -*kar* had the properties for which evidence has just been given. This evidence, in (12)–(15), has pointed strongly towards -*kar* being a subordinating conjunction with temporal or causal meaning. Where a causal interpretation is possible, it ought to have the same properties as -*kee kaaraN* 'on account of, because of', in particular two possible scope interpretations, as in (21a). We have seen in (16)–(22) that one or other interpretation is ruled out entirely. In cases like (16)–(18), (19b) and (22), the interpretation is ruled out which puts the higher clause in the scope of question, negation or assertion. The subordinate -*kar* clause is therefore in the scope of these operators, but it generally has no causal interpretation; compare (19a,b), with temporal meaning, to the similar but causally interpreted sentence (21b), where negation goes with the verb of the higher clause.

Nothing in the syntactic structure or lexical items of these sentences seems to predict which readings will be possible. The possible interpretations depend rather on the overall content of the sentence, the speaker's knowledge of what is being talked about, discourse context or subjective factors such as whether the higher clause is perceived as redundant or uninformative. It appears to be generally true that if the lower clause is in the scope of a higher operator, it does not have the causal interpretation. The question of the variability of the causal interpretation will be taken up in more detail in the next subsection, in the discussion of -*kar* clauses and the emphatic particles *hii* 'only', and *bhii* 'also'.

The emphatic particles tend to be associated with particular readings of -*kar,* according to Dwarikesh (1971, p. 141–43). *Hii* 'only' emphasizes the temporal relation between the clauses:

(23)   [*is   -baat -kaa sooc* **-kar hii**]   *us   -nee*
        [this.obl.-matter-of   think-CP only] 3rd ps.obl. -erg.
        jawaab diyaa
        answer give-perf.
        'He gave an answer only after thinking the matter over.'

The particle bhii 'also' emphasizes a causal, or rather adversitive, relationship between the clauses, especially when the higher clause is negative:

(24)   *tum   [ustaad **hoo-kar bhii**] yah nahũ jaantee?*
        you.fam. [teacher be -CP also] this not   know.imperf.pl.
        'You don't know this even though you are a teacher?' (Bailey, 1956, p. 146.)

The conjunction -kar has a causal interpretation in (24) in that the addressee would be expected to know something *because of* being a teacher. The same is true in (25), where it is implied that hearing a certain matter would provoke the referent into answering:

(25)   [yah baat **sun -kar bhii**] us   -nee jawaab
        [this matter hear-CP also] 3rd ps.-erg. answer
        nahīī diyaa
        not   give-perf.
        'He didn't answer even after hearing this matter.'

Note that the particles have the effect of blocking the scope of negation in these sentences, though *bhii* often marks constitutents which are in the scope of negation (Bhatia, 1977, Davison, 1978). Again, one possible reading for causal or temporal adverbials in subordinate structures is ruled out.

In sentences having negation and perfective aspect, the use of -*kar* with this adversitive causal reading is possible only with *bhii*:

(26) a.   [Yah baat **sun -kar bhii**] usee   kroodh
            [this matter hear-CP also]3rd ps.-dat. anger
            nahīī aayaa
            not   come.perf.
            'Even though he heard this matter, he didn't get angry.'

      b. ??[Yah baat **sun -kar hii**] usee   kroodh
            [this matter hear-CP   ] 3rd ps.dat. anger   not   come-perf.
            nahīī aayaa
            not   come.perf.
            'He did not get angry only after having heard this matter.'

      c. ??[Yah baat **sun -kar** ∅] usee   kroodh nahīī aayaa
            [this   matter hear-CP   ] 3rd ps.dat. anger   not   come-perf.
            'Having heard this matter, he did not get angry.'

(26b) and (26c) are not possible, unless, in the case of (26c), the sentence is said in contrast to some previous assertion. Thus, in some neutral discourse context, *bhii* is required with -*kar* when negation is in a higher clause where it must not have the -*kar* clause in its scope, and the adversitive causal reading is intended. The same is true in negative future sentences like (27) where there is both temporal and causal order.

(27) a   Woo [caay **pii -kar bhii**] nahīī jaaeegaa
           3rd p. [tea   drink-CP also] not   go-fut.3rd p.masc.
           'He won't go even after drinking tea.'

b. ??*Woo*   [*caay **pii**   -**kar*** ∅] *nahīī jaaeegaa*
   3rd p. [tea   drink-CP   ] not   go.fut.3rd p.masc.
   'He won't go having drunk tea.'

In questions about temporal sequence alone, however, -*kar* itself may be questioned:

(28)   [*caay **pii**   -**kar***] *jaaoogee?*
       [tea   drink-CP] go.fut.2nd p.sg.fam.
       'Will you have tea before you go; will you go having drunk tea?'

Here the higher clause is, again, pragmatically less prominent than the -*kar* clause, which is in the scope of the question, and lacks a protecting particle.

While speakers disagree about particular cases, the Hindi speakers I have consulted find something less acceptable about cases of -*kar* alone in sentences on the general order of (26) and (27), compared with -*kar* followed by *bhii*. Though not all -*kar* sentences have this property, it is sufficient for my argument to point out that -*kar* sentences are not predictable as to scope of negation, by comparison with lexical conjunctions of time and causality.[2]

The adverbial reading of -*kar* does allow scope of negation over -*kar*:

(29)   a. *Woo*   [***dauR-kar***] *aayaa*
          3rd p.dir. [run   -CP] come-perf.
          'He/she came quickly.'

---

[2] For example the following sentences illustrate the occurrence of embedded causal and temporal clauses within the scope of question and negation:

(i)   *Kyaa   woo   zyaadaa kaam **karnee**   -see   biimaar hoo   gayaa.*
       question 3rd p. much   work do-inf.-obl. -from ill   become-perf.
       'Did he become ill from too much work?'

(ii)   *Woo   khaanaa **khaanee**   -kee-baad nahīī sooyaa.*
       3rd p. food   eat.-inf.-obl.-of -after not   sleep-perf.
       (a) 'After eating, he did not sleep.'
       (b) 'He did not sleep after eating (but after some other event).'

Nonclausal adverbials may also be in the scope of question or negation if they occur in pre-verbal, focus position:

(iii) a. *Kyaa   laRkii **bazaar-see**   tarkaarii laayii?*
          question girl   bazar -from vegetable bring-perf.
          'The girl brought the vegetables from the bazar?'   (Steffensen, 1971)

       b. *Kyaa   laRkii tarkaarii **bazaar-see**   laayii?*
          question girl   vegetable bazar -from bring-perf.
          'Was it from the bazar that the girl brought the vegetables?'

    b. *Woo*   [***dauR-kar***] *nahīi aayaa*
    3rd p.dir. [run -CP] not   come-perf.
    'He/she didn't come quickly.'

    c. *Woo*   ***jaldii -see*** *nahīi/* ***dhiiree*** *aayaa*
    3rd p.dir. haste-with not   slowly come-perf.
    'He/she didn't come quickly/ came slowly.'

(30) a. *Us*   *-nee* [***sooc -kar***] *kaam kiyaa*
    3rd p.obl.-erg. [think-CP] work do-perf.
    'He/she did the work carefully.'

    b. *Us*   *-nee* [***sooc -kar***] *kaam nahīi kiyaa.*
    3rd p.obl.-erg. [think-CP] work not do-perf.
    'He/she didn't do the work carefully; he/she did the work without thinking.'

    c. *Us*   *-nee* [***binaa***   ***soocee***   ] *kaam kiyaa.*
    3rd p.obl.-erg. [without think-perf.] work do-perf.
    'He/she did the work without thinking.'

Sentences (28b)–(30b) also have negative counterparts with adverbs in the scope of negation, (28c)–(30c).

Note that the *-kar* clauses that come closest to ordinary adverbials with respect to negative scope are the *-kar* clauses that have adverbial meaning. Words like *hās-kar* and *dauR-kar*, 'having smiled' and 'having run' respectively, modify verbs of speaking and verbs of motion as though they were simple adverbials like *khušii-see* 'pleasantly' and *jaldii-see* 'with haste', and have this preferred interpretation (Y. Kachru, personal communication). The literal meaning of *hās-naa* 'to smile' cannot be expressed with *-kar;* instead a finite verb must be used, as in (31):

(31)   *Woo* ***hāsaa***   *leekin kuch*   *nahīi* ***kahaa***.
    3rd p. smile-perf. but   something not   speak-perf.
    'He smiled but didn't say anything.'

Sentences (28)–(29) and (31) might suggest that the "adverbial" reading of *-kar* constituents is derived from a underlying syntactic structure different from that other *-kar* clauses. Adverbial *-kar* in this hypothetical analysis would bear a different relation to negation than nonadverbial *-kar*, if only syntactic and semantic explanations are available. But this hypothetical analysis offer no general explanation for the fact that (30a) has both the adverbial reading, which is given as the gloss for it, and (6c), and also a sequential reading, shown in (6b). The negative version (30b) has a reading somewhat different from the preceding sentences. The agent is described as having done the work 'not having thought', but here this does not suggest 'carelessly', whereas (29b) and (29c), suggest negative adverbs 'unpleasantly', 'slowly'.

So if underlying syntactic relations are the only means of indicating semantic differences of negative scope, there would have to be separate underlying structures for adverbial and sequential readings. In such an analysis it would be an accident that main verbs of the classes of verbs of motion and verbs of speaking allowed only the adverbial reading for -*kar,* whereas verbs of other classes occurred as the main verb with both readings. Sentences such as (30a) would be ambiguous, derived from two separate underlying structures. It will be argued that the two readings are actually not distinct in meaning and thus not derived from distinct underlying forms. Further, if the relation between V-*kar* and negation is different in the sequential reading, (26) and (27), versus the adverbial reading, (28)–(30), then (30b) would be predicted to be ambiguous, as *sooc-naa* 'to think' allows both the adverbial and the sequential reading. But (30b) is not ambiguous and has only the reading in which V-*kar* is negated, though not in exactly the same way as in other negative sentences with the adverbial reading. Thus a purely syntactic representation of differences is complex and does not explain the relation between form and meaning in a satisfying way.

Negation inside -*kar* clauses is ill-formed except under certain pragmatically defined circumstances. Negation, in the form *na,* may occur in other subordinate constructions:

(32)   [*Icchaa na* **hoonee**   -*par bhii*] *gaanee   lagaa.*
        [desire   not be-inf.-obl.-on even] sing-inf. strike-perf.
'He began to sing although he didn't want to.'   (Porizka, 1963, p. 343)

But, in sentences like (33)–(35), negated subordinate clauses are not possible:

(33)   a.   *Woo*   [*dauR-kar*] *aayaa.*
             3rd p. [run   -CP] come-perf.
             'He came running.'   (Bhatia, 1977, p. 157.)

        b.   **Woo*   [*na   dauR-kar*] *aayaa.*
             3rd p. [not run   -CP] come-perf.
             'He didn't come running.'

(34)   a.   *Raajaa* [*aa   -kar*] *kitaab paRhnee   lagaa.*
             king   [come-CP] book   read-inf.-obl. strike-perf.
             'The king having come began to read the book.'   (Bhatia, 1977, p. 142.)

        b.   **Raajaa* [*na aa   -kar*] *kitaab paRhnee   lagaa.*
             king   [not come-CP] book   read-inf.-obl. strike-perf.
             'The king not having come began to read the book.'

(35) a. *Woo   patra [**paRh-kar**] boolaa.*
          3rd p. letter [read -CP] speak-perf.
          'He spoke after reading the letter.'   (Bhatia, 1977, p. 142.)

      b. **Woo   patra [**na   paRh-kar**] boolaa.*
          3rd p. letter [not   read-CP] speak-perf.
          'He spoke after not reading the letter.'

But it is not possible to prohibit *na* entirely in *-kar* clauses, as (36a) demonstrates. According to Bhatia (1977), (36a) is synonymous with (36b).

(36) a. *Woo   [ghaas **na   khaa-kar**] pattee khaa rahaa hai.*
          3rd p. [grass not eat -CP] leaves eat   prog. is
          'Instead of eating grass, he is eating leaves.'   (Bhatia, 1977,
          p. 159.)

      b. *Woo   [ghaas **khaanee   kii jagah**] pattee khaa rahaa hai.*
          3rd p. [grass eat-inf.-obl. of place] leaves eat   prog. is
          'He is eating leaves instead of/in place of eating grass.'

What makes (36) a different from (33b)–135b) seems to be world knowledge rather than grammatical principles. In the acceptable case (36a) (and others cited in Bhatia, 1977), the two clauses linked by *-kar* express some combination of incompatible but mutually relevant circumstances. In the unacceptable cases, it is hard to imagine how the events expressed COULD be incompatible, although I imagine that the unacceptable cases could become more acceptable, given the right context of background knowledge.

5. THE MEANING OF *-KAR*

In the preceding sentences which contain *-kar,* various synonyms in Hindi and glosses in English have been given as the meaning of *-kar* in a particular case. There has been considerable variation among the sentences; *-kar* has been described as equivalent to:

(37) a. *aur phir* 'and (then)'
      b. V-inf.-*par* 'on V-ing'
      c. Adv, N-*see* 'Adj-ly'
      d. V-inf.-obl.-conj. *bhii* 'even though, although'
      e. V-inf.-obl. *kii jagah* 'in place of, instead of'

To this list we might add the overt expressions of time and causality that are implied by *-kar;* V-inf. *kee baad* 'after' and V-inf. *kee kaaraN* 'because of', and the conditional.

Note that use of *-kar* in sentences that refer to future or nonpast events conveys no special supposition of truth of the event referred to:

(38)   [*Aisee*   **kar-kee**] *tum*   *kuursii tooR dēēgee.*
         [that way do -CP] you-fam. chair   break give-fut.-you-fam.
         'If you do that you'll break the chair.'

Other sentences discussed earlier do convey this supposition, by virtue of the perfective aspect of the main verb, as in sentences (1) and (2), or the presence of *bhii* 'also' following *-kar*. The conjunction *-kar* does not by itself presuppose the truth of its complement even in sentences where the truth of the complement is supposed or suggested.

On the basis of the facts summarized in the preceding paragraphs it looks as though we could not propose a single meaning for *-kar* in all its uses. We would be forced to a fragmentary and complex semantic analysis which has the same defects as the syntactic analysis which required a separate underlying structure for each possible scope relation of *-kar* and question or negation. Even if such analysis were not considered complex and lacking in generality, it would still provide no overall explanation for why a particular combination of main clause and subordinate clause would be related by a given sense of *-kar,* or why some combinations of clauses, in sentences like (34) and (35), could not be related by *-kar*. What determines the particular interpretation that *-kar* has in a particular instance is a combination of other features of the sentence, constituents like emphatic *bhii,* the presence of negation, the verb of the main clause, the semantic contents of the two clauses, and the speaker's knowledge of the world and context of utterance.

Thus a more satisfactory analysis of the meaning of *-kar* would be to assign a very general meaning to *-kar,* such as 'perfective aspect', and to allow the other constituents of the sentence and contextual information to determine clause relations more fully. Contextual information determines the exact interpretation directly, instead of being specified as part of a complex list of semantic environments for the lexical insertion of *-kar₁*, *-kar₂, etc.*

The single meaning 'perfective' includes both the temporal sequential reading and the causal relation, which also involves temporal sequence. The only reading that does not derive from this meaning in any obvious way is the adverbial reading, which I will discuss shortly as part of a general discussion of how conversational inference operates on sequences of syntactically linked clauses. First, I want to provide some justification for assigning *-kar* the meaning 'perfective'.

The argument that *-kar* means 'perfective' has two parts. First, I will call attention to the fact that V-*kar* V-tense combinations are nearly identical in meaning to V V-tense combinations, or compound verbs, as noted by Bahl (1964) and Hook (1974). Hook (1974, 1980) argues that compound verb combinations (which are distinct from single main verbs) are found in association with perfective aspect relative to some other proposition. Second, I will note that compound verbs do not occur in -*kar* clauses, although they do not occur in other kinds of subordinate clauses. These facts taken together argue that -*kar* marks one clause as perfective relative to the other, main clause.

In sentences like (39) and (40), the (a) version with -*kar* is nearly synonymous to the (b) version without -*kar;* the difference will be discussed more fully in a later section.

(39) a. *Pulis -nee* [*coorŏŏ   -koo **aa**   **-kar**] **pakaR liyaa.***
          police -erg. [thieves-obl. -dat. come -CP] seize   take-perf.
          'The police nabbed the crooks.'   (Hook, 1974, p. 52.)

      b. *Pulis -nee coorŏŏ   -koo **aa**   **pakRaa.***
          police-erg. thieves-obl.-dat. come seize-perf.
          'The police nabbed the crooks.'   (Hook, 1974, p. 52.)

      c. *Pulis -nee **aa**   **-kar** coorŏŏ/   -koo₊pakaR*
          police-erg. come-CP thieves-obl./-dat. seize
          liyaa/pakRaa.
          take-perf./seize-perf.
          'The police came and seized the crooks.'

Sentence (39c) has constituents in the same order as sentences previously discussed in this chapter, with the main clause subject and the conjunctive participle adjacent. The order in (39a) is the result of a scrambling rule which may move the -*kar* clause to the right in the main clause.

(40) a. *Us   -nee* [*apnee   pati   -koo šaraabii **banaa -kar***]
          3rd p.-obl.-erg. [own-obl. husband-dat. drunkard make -CP]
          chooR   diyaa   thaa.
          abandon give-perf. was
          'She made her husband into a drunkard and then left him.'
          (Hook, 1974, p. 106.)

      b. *Us   -nee apnee pati   -koo šaraabii **banaa chooRaa***
          3rd p.-erg. own   husband-dat. drunkard make abandon-perf.
          thaa.
          was
          'She irresponsibly/recklessly turned her husband into a drunkard.'   (Hook, 1974, p. 106.)

Bahl (1964) observes that the equivalence between V_1-*kar* V_2 and the conjunct verb sequence V_1 V_2 holds in the cases where the second verb is in the perfective aspect. He proposes a rule of -*kar* deletion to explain the presence in second position of V_1 V_2 sequences of verbs that normally do not occur in this way (V_2 is usually one of a fairly small set of verbs that occur as explicators of the main verb, V_1). The combinations *pakaR liyaa* in (39a) and *chooR diyaa* in (40a) are more normal exemplars of the construction. The combination of *aa pakRaa* in (39b) and *banaa chooRaa* in (40b) are anomalous as conjunct verbs but make far more sense if regarded as V_1-*kar* V_2 expressions of sequential events. The deletion of -*kar* can thus be regarded as a case of deletion of redundant material, if -*kar* expresses perfective aspect and the main verb *pakaR* has perfective aspect also.

Hook (1974, p. 103) notes a number of parallels between the syntactic behavior of conjunct verb combinations and -*kar* constructions. In a more recent paper (Hook, 1980), he notes that conjunct verb sequences are used in preference to a single perfective verb in clauses that express events completed or perfective relative to another event.

(41) a. [*Jab -tak   us   -nee mujhee paisee diyee*]   [*tab -tak*
        when-up to 3rd p.-erg. me-dat. money give-perf.] [then -to
        *tum   yahãã **pahūc gaee**   thee.*]
        you-fam. there   arrive go-perf. was]
        'You **had arrived** there by the time he gave me the money.'

      b. *Jab -tak tum yahãã pahūcee   tab -tak us   -nee mujhee*
        when-to you there   arrive-perf. then-to 3rd p.-erg. me-dat.
        *paisee **dee diyee**   thee.*
        money give give-perf. was.
        'He **had given me** the money by the time you arrived there.'

The pluperfect aspect of the first clause relative to the second is expressed by the use of a compound verb, *pahūc gaee* in (41a) and *dee diyee* in (41b), versus a single verb inflected for tense, *diyee* and *pahūcee*.

The argument is an indirect one; Hook (1974, 1980) notes an association between compound verbs and perfective aspect. Bahl (1964) and Hook (1974) note an association between -*kar* and compound verbs, dependent on perfective aspect. If these facts are related, then it is plausible to assumed that -*kar* is associated nonaccidentally with perfective aspect. Assuming that it MEANS perfective aspect allows us to postulate a general meaning for -*kar* and to explain some of its properties, such as the resemblance to conjunct verbs. Failing to make such an assumption forces us to postulate a number of unrelated meanings for -*kar* and to express facts about the behavior of -*kar* as though they were unrelated.

A further fact that would go unexplained is the nonoccurrence of compound verbs in -*kar* clauses, although subordinate clauses allow compound verbs to occur.

(42) a. [[*KhiRkii-kee baahar sããjh* **utar** **aanee** **-par**]
         [window -of   outside evening descend come-inf. -on]
         jhõõpRii-mẽẽ raat **ghir** **aatii** **hai.**]
         hut   -in   night encircle come-imperf. be pres.]
         'When evening descends outside the window, night rushes into
         the hut.'   (Hook, 1974, p. 37.)

      b. [*Kabhii* *kabhii* *woo* *bhaay-see* **kããp** **uThtii**]
         [sometime sometime 3rd p. fear -from tremble rise-impf.]
         aur [*pachtaatii.*]
         and [regret-imperf.]
         'From time to time she would start trembling with fear and she
         regretted everything.'   (Hook, 1974, p. 22.)

Compound verbs occur in *-par* subordinate constructions, and in the first
clause of a coordinate construction, as in (42a) and (42b). Compound
verbs inside *-kar* clauses do not occur, unless the verb sequence has become a fixed or idiomatic expression:[3]

(43)   *Raat [khiRkii -kee baahar **utar** **aa** **-kar**] jhõõpRii -mẽẽ*
       night [window -of   outside descend come-CP] hut   -in
       ghir *aatii* *hai.*
       encircle come-imperf. be.pres.
       'Night having descended outside the window, comes rushing
       into the hut.'

This restriction makes *-kar* clauses unlike EITHER subordinate or coordinate clauses, both of which allow compound verbs. But it would follow
from the semantics of *-kar* in particular, if *-kar* means perfective and compound verbs also express perfectiveness. Compound verbs in a *-kar*
clause would be radundant, unless the V - V combination had fixed or
conventional meaning. This in itself is not enough to make V - V *-kar* combinations ungrammatical, though it would be sufficient to ensure that they
do not normally appear in discourse.
    There is another factor related to discourse that sheds some light on the
meaning of *-kar*. I have proposed that *-kar* means 'perfective aspect', but
there is also an inflected affix which means 'perfective aspect', and occurs
in finite, main verbs. Staneslow (1980) notes that the perfective aspect
affix is used in the verbal element of sentences that indicate transitions
from one episode to another, in narrative. When the perfective aspect is
demanded by the meaning of the proposition, but the sentence is not intended by the writer to indicate a transition in the narrative, the perfective
meaning is expressed by *-kar*.

---

[3] For example, the V - V combination *hoo jaa-naa* 'be-go' contrasts in meaning, 'become'
with *hoo-naa* alone, 'be'.

(44) a. [*Mantrii -nee vinay -see sir **jhukaayaa***]   *aur*
         [minister-erg. humility-with head incline-perf.] and
         [*dhiiree-see   jawaab diyaa.*]
         [slowly -rather answer give-perf.]
         'The minister inclined his head modestly and slowly gave his an-
         swer.'   (Staneslow, 1980.)

      b. *Mantrii -nee*[*vinay- see sir **jhukaa-kar***]
         minister-erg. [humility -with head incline-CP]
         dhiiree-see   jawaab diyaa.
         slowly -rather answer give-perf.
         'The minister inclining his head modestly slowly gave his an-
         swer.'

Sentence (44a) occurs in paragraph initial position in the passage cited by
Staneslow, whereas (44b) would be its counterpart when the writer did
not wish to focus the first clause.[4] If this is generally the case, we have
both some evidence for the meaning of *-kar,* and an explanation for why a
coordinate structure like (44a) and a subordinate structure like (44b) are
fully equivalent in some ways—semantically—but not identical syntactically.

6. CONVERSATIONAL INFERENCES FROM
-KAR CLAUSES

The structure that I want to propose as the syntactic and semantic representation underlying *-kar* constructions of all types is the following:

(45)

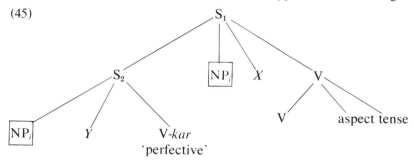

---

[4] A similar phenomenon was noticed independently by Paul Hopper and Wallace Reid for
French narrative prose. The imperfect and passé simple forms of the verb have some aspectual meaning, imperfect versus perfective. Certain verbs may have meaning more compatible with one than the other. Yet, as Hopper and Reid have noted, the imperfect is consistently used for background propositions, whereas the passé simple, like the perfective in
Hindi, is used to focus on the events described in the sentence. Examples are given in Reid
and Gildin (1979).

Coreferential NP deletion applies to the NP subject in the -*kar* clause, provided that it is identical in reference to the higher NP subject (with a restricted class of permitted exceptions).[5] A scrambling rule, probably motivated by considerations of emphasis and focus, allows the -*kar* clause to be permuted to the right of the higher clause subject and other constituents as well [cf. (39) and (40)]. The structure in (45) would be subject to general restrictions on movement rules which do not allow elements to be dislocated outside of clause boundaries [cf. (12)–(15)].

In this analysis, the syntactic features of -*kar* clauses are no different from those of other subordinate constructions in Hindi, and the derivation of the surface forms from the underlying structure (45) is uncomplicated. If, on the contrary, three separate underlying structures were postulated (see Note 1) for the coordinate, subordinate, and adverbial readings of the construction, the derivations would be much more complicated, and less well motivated by general patterns of the language.

The simple subordinate structure (45) leaves unexplained many of the features of -*kar* just outlined in preceding sections. These include (*a*) the variety of lexical paraphrases of -*kar*, given in (37); (*b*) the differences between the coordinate, subordinate, and adverbial interpretations of the same surface configuration; and (*c*) the variable scope relations between -*kar* and question and negation. I propose to account for all of these properties of -*kar* by pragmatically motivated means, that is, conversational inference from various syntactic and semantic properties of the sentence as a whole and from contextual factors.

6.1. Meaning Variation

In the preceding section I argued that there is a close connection, though not absolute identity, between -*kar* and the finite, inflected perfective aspect marker that occurs in main clauses. If -*kar* has the aspectual meaning 'perfective', then it would be normal for the hearer to infer a

---

[5] The permitted exceptions are very similar to those allowed in Tamil (Lindholm, 1975), though in both languages it is hard to see exactly what factors must be present for the like subject condition to not be met. The subjects of the two clauses may be different:

(i)   *Diwaar **gir -kar** patthar gir gaee.*
       wall   fall-CP stones   fall go-perf.-pl.
       'The wall having fallen, stones fell.'

The deleted NP in the lower clause may be a nonsubject:

(ii)   *BaaN (hiraN-koo)   **lag -kar** hiraN mar gayaa.*
       arrow deer -dat./acc. strike-CP deer   die go-perf.
       'The arrow having struck (the deer) the deer died.'

I am grateful to Rajeshwari Pandharipande for having pointed out this example to me.

temporal and sometimes also a causal connection between the first non-finite -*kar* clause and the following main clause. As the conditional reading of (38) shows, -*kar* does not in itself establish past time reference relative to the speech event. Rather it conveys perfective aspect relative to the time reference of the main clause. But the initial position of the -*kar* clause and its perfective aspect conveys temporal priority by Grice's maxims of Relevance and Manner (Grice, 1975). Causal priority, which is a stronger inferred relation, is a further inference from temporal order. The case of *and* in English, about which similar inferences are made, is discussed by Schmerling (1975), who points out that the exact relationship between clauses conjoined by, *and* is often indeterminate and context dependent, so that if one were to propose a fully specified lexical connective in underlying structure, it is not clear in every case what it would be.[6]

The main difference between *and* and -*kar* is that *and* conjoins finite clauses which may have independent temporal reference indicated by tense affixes and adverbs,[7] whereas -*kar* only suggests temporal reference by means of perfective aspect. Both *and* and -*kar* are in a sense "unmarked" conjunctions, in that their semantic content is minimal compared to other conjunctions like *because, so, although,* and *but,* and their Hindi counterparts. Neither *and* nor -*kar* stipulates that one of the conjoined clauses is presupposed to be true. Hence it is not surprising that the semantic content of the clauses, the connective itself, and position of the clauses in discourse serve as the basis for inferences which more fully specify the relation between the conjoined clauses.

Note that the presence of negation in the main clause and the emphatic particle *bhii* 'even, also' following -*kar* reverses the causal relation, as in (21)–(27). If *bhii* parallels *even* in English, for which Horn (1969) proposes a presuppositional meaning, then *bhii* cancels the causal relationship by presupposing the existence of some other proposition. This other proposition, rather than the -*kar* clause, is presumably what counts as the

---

[6] Very similar points were made about the Tamil adverbial participle by Lindholm (1975), although he did not make use of conversational inference per se as an explanation.

[7] If -*kar* does not have independent time reference except by inference, this feature may explain why at least one speaker (R.P.) finds that (i) and (ii) differ in acceptability:

(i) ??*Mistrii   aaj   sanduuq banaa-kar kal   laaeegaa.*
     carpenter today box   make -CP tomorrow bring-fut.
     'The carpenter, having made the box today, will bring (it) tomorrow.'

(ii) *Ham sTaaks aaj   khariid-kar doo saal -kee-baad beec dēēgee.*
      we   stocks today buy   -CP two years-of -after sell give-fut.
      'We have bought stocks today and will sell them in two years.'

Pragmatically, the gap in time in (ii) is somehow more plausible or permissible than the gap in time in (i).

temporal and causal antecedent of the main clause proposition. As the main clause is negated, one is less likely in any case to infer a cause, as the clause expresses a negative state rather than a positive event.

The inferred, or inferrable, causal and temporal relations are also canceled in cases like (33)–(36), where negation occurs in the subordinate clause, and emphatic particles are not a factor. According to Bhatia (1977) sentences with -*kar* attached to negative clauses are possible only if the two conjoined clauses are—or can be conceived of as—contrastive. In the cases where contrast is possible, the temporal or causal relation is not inferred, partly because of the negation in the first clause, and partly because of the close similarity of the clauses. It is at least POSSIBLE to imagine a negative antecedent cause, but it is hard to do so if the supposed effect is a very similar clause [cf. (36a)]. Thus the only inferrable relationship seems to be 'instead of'. Perfective aspect predicated of a negative event is hard to interpret in any meaningful way.

Independent temporal reference to a separate event is another inference associated with -*kar,* derivable from its perfective aspect meaning and the maxim of Relevance. The cancellation of this inference is what characterizes the adverbial reading as distinct from the coordinate and subordinate readings, each of which suggests reference to a sequence of two independent events. The semantic class of the main verb determines whether the adverbial interpretation is preferred. The presence of a verb of motion or of speaking cancels the inference of independent time reference, making the adverbial reading the only one possible. Other main verbs either require or allow the inference of independent time reference to be made, depending on whether or not it is possible to imagine that the first clause specifies a manner of action that is relevant to the main clause. The examples that I have found of the adverbial reading, such as (5a) and (6), do not suggest that there is any real semantic difference from other uses of -*kar,* nor that sentences like (6) are truly ambiguous in that one interpretation would be true under some conditions in which the other would be false. The -*kar* clause describes circumstances that enable the act or event described in the second clause to occur, and thus the effect of the first event persists in or overlaps with the second. If one runs, one is able to come quickly; if one smiles, one is able to speak pleasantly; if one thinks, one is able to work carefully.

6.2. Variability of Scope Relations

In this section, I want to explain the relationship between -*kar* and question and negation, in terms of the analysis I have proposed for -*kar* and the temporal–causal inferences that can be made from it. The general approach will be to say that all the scope relations that would be possible for subordinate constructions are possible in principle for -*kar*, but if they are not, then the failure is the result of other, independently occurring factors.

Cases of "pragmatic reversal" of syntactic dominance relations, like (22) and (23), can be assimilated to the case of question having scope over the whole structure, including the subordinate clause. The content of the higher clause is redundant, and thus contributes little or no information pragmatically. The lower clause appears more prominent in a discourse context, though there is no real reason to suppose that the underlying structure is any different from other cases of -*kar*.

The failure of -*kar* itself to be in the scope of question, illustrated in (20a), is relative to the counterparts of these sentences, like (20b), which have the clause connection indicated by a fully specified lexical item, like *kee baad* 'after', -*tee hii* 'immediately upon', and -*kee kaaraN* 'because of'. The -*kar* counterparts as statements would allow these clause relations to be inferred. But if the inferences themselves are not able to be questioned, which we would expect them not to be if they are not part of lexical content nor of presuppositions, then the questions would be questioning, in one reading, the perfective aspect of a verb. They would not be ungrammatical, but would be pragmatically odd, unless the context strongly suggested causal priority, *etc*. Where causal relations are not at issue, the perfective aspect can be questioned.

Negation should be able to have -*kar* clauses in its scope. This seems to be generally the case with the adverbial or nonindependent temporal cases, that is, the cases in which no temporal inference is made, and presumably no causal inference either, as the manner event does not directly cause the event described in the main clause. The adverbial reading is thus the case where no inferences are made, and the scope of negation is normal [(29)–(30)]. The presence of *bhii* in (26) and (27) blocks the scope of the negation from including -*kar*. As we have seen, *bhii* causes the usual inferences to be canceled and also (following Horn, 1969) allows the constituent it is associated with to be asserted. Thus the reading in which the -*kar* is both asserted and in the scope of negation and denied would be contradictory.

The versions of (26) and (27) without *bhii* are ill-formed, whether one takes the negation as negation on the higher verb or on the lower subordinate clause. One would assume that the usual temporal and causal inferences hold, as they are not canceled by *bhii* or the higher main verb. In that case, one would have either a cause with a negative effect, or a negative cause, a negative state without independent time reference, causing an actual event. Neither of these readings is very informative, though presumably the same contents would be expressible with other constructions, for example connectives that stipulated as true a negative proposition. The third possible reading is one in which the negation negates -*kar*. But this reading would also be uninformative, because all that could be negated would be "perfective." The temporal and causal meanings, being only inferences, cannot be the sole meaning components which are negated.

7. CONCLUSION

In this chapter I have described an array of syntactic and semantic relations that one would want to describe as part of the grammar of Hindi in a reasonably general way. Yet all of the facts, taken together, do not directly point to any such general analysis. In fact, attempting to describe all of the facts in terms of differences of underlying form, exception features and conditions on lexical insertion, or rules of interpretation, constitutes a sort of reductio ad absurdum, even though all the formal devices needed are available in principle. On the contrary, even though such a complex and unrevealing description is available, I think it is imperative to look for a more parsimonious description if one is possible. In the one that I have proposed here very little is assumed to be part of the syntax or semantics of Hindi, just a single syntactic form underlying all occurrences of -*kar* and a single lexical meaning. From this combination of subordinate structure and perfective aspect the other properties of -*kar* constructions can be derived if one assumes that not all "meaning" perceived by speakers of the language is relevant to meaning in a strict truth conditionally defined sense. Much of the variability in interpretation and well-formedness is attributed to nongrammatical factors, to real-world knowledge and pragmatic purposes, such as being informative or obeying Grice's maxims of Cooperative Conversation. Although such an analysis has the defect that it is hard to distinguish genuine counterexamples from cases where the context explains some relation, or where the message fails to be well-formed, I think that I have shown that the inferences I have proposed do conform to the properties of conversational inferences in general, in being cancelable, and therefore being absent when -*kar* is in the scope of negation or other predicates that cancel the temporal or causal inference. But the features of the analysis I propose are self consistent, whereas alternative approaches offer no overall generalizations.

ACKNOWLEDGEMENTS

I would like to acknowledge here a long-standing debt to Jim Lindholm's work on the Tamil adverbial participle, which has been of very great help to me in defining the problem of subordination in general and the Hindi conjunctive participle in particular. Rajeshwari Pandharipande has been very generous with her time in suggesting and judging example sentences, as have Tej Bhatia and Beena Gokhale. I am particularly grateful for insights and helpful criticism to Y. Kachru. Many thanks to Rodney Moag for encouragement and useful information. An earlier version of this chapter was presented at the Second International Conference on South Asian Languages and Linguistics, Osmania University Hyderabad, which I attended with support from the American Institute of Indian Studies.

REFERENCES

Bahl, K. C. (1964). *A Study in the Transformational Analysis of the Hindi Verb*. Chicago: University of Chicago South Asian Language and Area Center.

Bailey, T. G. (1963). *Urdu*. London: English Universities Press.

Bhatia, T. K. (1977). *A Syntactic and Semantic Description of Negation in South Asian Languages*. Unpublished doctoral dissertation, University of Illinois.

Davison, A. (1979). Some mysteries of subordination. *Studies in the Linguistic Sciences*, **9**,1 105–128.

Dwarikesh, P. P. S. (1971). *The Historical Syntax of the Conjunctive Participial Phrase in the New Indo-Aryan Dialects of the Madhyadesa ("Midland") of Northern India*. Unpublished doctoral dissertation, University of Chicago.

Grice, H. P. (1975). Logic and conversation. In P. Cole and J. Morgan (Eds.), *Syntax and Semantics 3: Speech Acts*. New York: Academic Press, Pp. 41–58.

Hook, P. (1974). *The Compound Verb in Hindi* (Michigan Series in South and Southeast Asian Languages and Linguistics, No. 1). Ann Arbor, Michigan.

Hook, P. (1980). *The distribution of the functions of the compound verb in New Indo-Aryan*. Paper presented at the Second International Conference on South Asian Languages and Linguistics, Osmania University, Hyderabad.

Horn, L. R. (1969). A presuppositional analysis of *only* and *even*. In Binnick, R. *et al.* (Eds.), *Papers from the Fifth Regional Meeting of the Chicago Linguistic Society*. Department of Linguistics, University of Chicago. Pp. 98–107.

Kachru, Y. (1978). On relative clause formation in Hindi-Urdu. *Linguistics*, **207**, 5–26.

Kuno, S. (1973). *The Structure of the Japanese Language*. Cambridge, Mass.: MIT Press.

Lindholm, J. (1975). *The Conceptual Basis of the Tamil Adverbial Participle*. Unpublished doctoral dissertation, University of Chicago.

Morgan, J. L. (1978). Two types of convention in indirect speech acts. In P. Cole, (Ed.), *Syntax and Semantics 9: Pragmatics*. New York: Academic Press. Pp. 261–280.

Porizka, V. (1963). *Hindstina, Hindi Language Course*. Prague: Statni pedagogicke nakladatelstvi.

Reid, W., and Gildin, B. (1979). Semantic analysis without the sentence. In P. Clyne, W. F. Hanks, and C. L. Hofbauer (Ed.), *The elements: A Parasession on Linguistic Units and Levels*. Chicago Linguistics Society Department of Linguistics, University of Chicago. Pp. 163–174.

Ross, J. R. (1967). *Constraints on Variables in Syntax*. M.I.T. doctoral dissertation.

Schmerling, S. (1975). Asymmetric conjunction and rules of conversation. In P. Cole and J. Morgan (Eds.), *Syntax and Semantics 3: Speech Acts*. New York: Academic Press. Pp. 211–231.

Schmerling, S. (1978). Synonymy judgements as syntactic evidence. In P. Cole (Ed.), *Syntax and Semantics 9: Pragmatics*. New York: Academic Press. Pp. 299–313.

Staneslow, P. (1980). *Discourse structure in a Hindi short story*. Paper presented at the South Asian Languages Roundtable, University of Illinois.

Steffensen, M. (1971). A deverbal analysis of adverbials in Hindi. *Studies in the Linguistic Sciences*, **1**, 136–179.

Intuitions and Presuppositions

Keith S. Donnellan

Although much of the space in this chapter is devoted to the notion of linguistic presuppositions, as developed by Frege and Strawson, my target may be said to be "intuitions"—the term favored by many analytic philosophers and some linguists for what we would say about certain hypothetical situations—the notion of presuppositions being a sustained example. Even though the topic of linguistic presuppositions is one philosophers, I fear, are somewhat weary of (from my knowledge of the literature, this seems not to be the case among linguists) I will on the way have some things to say about the notion, although it will not be my main concern. My remarks about presuppositions and about intuitions will, I believe, have relevance to the linguists' interests, but there is the possibility that one could argue, for example, that the intuitions linguists rely on are different in nature from those philosophers use. Still, on this particular issue it is difficult to see how that could be the case. What I think needs looking at, in the end, is the source of these intuitions.

1. HISTORICAL BACKGROUND

In the philosophical literature the notion of linguistic presuppositions has been discussed mainly in connection with what we may call "singular referring expressions," in particular, singular definite descriptions and

RADICAL PRAGMATICS

proper names. Failure of reference and what to do about it in the face of certain theoretical considerations about how singular referring expressions work has been the dominant motivation. In contrast, linguists have used the notion for a much larger range of cases, singular referring expressions and the problems of reference failure being only one among many examples of the same phenomenon. (This is not to say that linguists in general have accepted the notion—there has been opposition in that field just as there has been in philosophy.)[1] This difference is not, I believe, an instance of two disciplines developing along independent, but fortuitously somewhat similar, lines with different aims in mind. Most linguists who employ the notion, I think, would acknowledge a debt to the philosophical literature, especially to definitions of "presupposition" introduced by Strawson.

Some fifty odd years before Strawson brought the notion of presuppositions back to philosophers' attention, Frege had used it to handle what he took to be a somewhat regrettable fact about natural languages, that they allow for the possibility that singular referring expressions fail to refer. Frege's brief introduction of linguistic presuppositions was clearly a consequence of his views about referring expressions. So far as I know there was no idea that it might be extended to other cases.

Strawson's philosophical motivation, given that his target was Russell on definite descriptions, was obviously the same—what happens when there is failure of reference? Strawson's definition of "presupposition," however, is unlike Frege's in an important respect and allows an extension far beyond problems about reference failure. Strawson also did something else that one does not find in Frege; he appealed to intuitions. And, as I have said, it is the danger of doing this that ultimately I want to ask about.

How, for both Frege and Strawson, did a theory about presuppositions arise from thoughts about reference? As is well known Frege (1892/1952) used the term "name" (the English translation, of course) to cover both proper names and definite descriptions. Frege scholars may dispute this, but for the purposes of this chapter I will assume that proper names have a sense, on Frege's view, which can be specified by some set of definite descriptions—so, for example, "Aristotle" might have as its sense 'the author of the Metaphysics, the teacher of Alexander the Great, ...'. Definite descriptions wear their sense on their sleeves. In any event every Fregean name, as I will call this combined group of expressions, has a sense and the sense determines the referent of the name, if it has one. In using a Fregean name one refers to whatever its sense determines. In this

---

[1] See, for example, Wilson (1975).

simplified account we can think of the referent as being whatever has the properties specified by the definite description which either explicitly or implicitly gives the sense of the name.

For simplicity, let us restrict ourselves to ASSERTIONS involving Fregean names (we could construct a view for other speech acts, questions, commands, etc.) Although there is a complex mechanism involved, I believe that Frege (unlike Russell) and Strawson also might be fairly characterized as holding that Fregean names function simply to refer to some person, thing, place or whatever. The point can be put by giving the following directions for deciding whether an assertion[2] containing Fregean names is true or false:

1. Divide the assertion into the Fregean names it contains, the remainder to be called the "predicate."
2. Determine what the Fregean names refer to.
3. If there is only one Fregean name, determine whether the predicate correctly applies to its referent; if there is more than one Fregean name, determine whether the relation specified by the predicate holds among the referents of the names.

In the simplest sort of example, say, the assertion "The author of "On Denoting" was a pacifist," we first find the referent of "the author of "On Denoting""—Bertrand Russell—and ascertain whether or not he satisfies the predicate, whether or not he was a pacifist. If so, we pronounce "true," if not "false." Of course this oversimplifies. In particular, one might know that a certain predicate (e.g., "is identical with itself") applies to everything or applies to nothing and so one might skip, in practice, the step of determining what the Fregean name applies to. But, on the view I am attributing to Frege and Strawson, one would still assume that the more direct method would, in theory, work out.

On what, for the moment, I will call the Frege–Strawson view, the apparent need for presuppositions comes in when we consider an assertion together with its denial. In each case we segregate out the Fregean names and determine whether the property ascribed or the relation posited holds. What happens when a Fregean name has no referent? What happens when, to use the previous example, there is no author of "On Denoting" (the reader can make up circumstances in which this would be true)? We cannot, it seems, carry out the instructions that were outlined. The

---

[2] I use the term "assertion" where others might prefer "statement", "proposition", or "sentence". I also use quotation marks without great regard for niceties. I do so partly because I begin with a discussion of Frege, some quoted passages from whom use "assert" and "assertion" followed by material in quotation marks, partly for simplicity and with the justification that I do not think it makes much difference to the points I want to make.

instructions require that we determine the referent of the Fregean names first and then determine whether the property or relations hold. Using the simple example of "the author of 'On Denoting,'" we cannot proceed because, as Frege says, "Whoever does not admit the name has a reference can neither apply nor withhold the predicate [p. 62]." It seems to follow from this that when a Fregean name in an assertion fails to refer nothing true nor false can have been asserted.

Frege introduces the notion of presupposition in this way: "If anything is asserted there is always the obvious presupposition that the simple or compound names have reference. If one therefore asserts 'Kepler died in misery', there is a presupposition that the name 'Kepler' designates something . . . [p. 69]." And the same presupposition exists for the negative assertion, "Kepler did not die in misery."

Notice that Frege's formulation is metalinguistic: The presupposition of the example is not the proposition that Kepler existed; it is rather a proposition about the name "Kepler," that it has a reference. If we extend this treatment to definite descriptions—as Frege meant us to—it represents an interesting difference from Strawson's treatment in which the presuppositions are propositions which have the form "the ϕ exists." There is at least no simple and obvious way to extend Frege's formulation so that it applies to features of language other than Fregean names. For example, if one is inclined to say that the pair of assertions, "John has stopped smoking" and "John has not stopped smoking" share, aside from any connected with the name "John," a presupposition, the obvious suggestion (and one people have made) is that both presuppose that John has been smoking. But that is not a metalinguistic proposition and it is difficult to see how to generate from what Frege says about presuppositions behind Fregean names a general formula which will apply to such a case. This provides another reason for thinking that for Frege, at least, the notion of a presupposition was thought of as supplying a solution to a special problem presented by referring expressions—Fregean names.

2. RUSSELL'S TREATMENT

By the time of Strawson's early writings on the subject, there had been for some decades a rival analysis of how Fregean names, as I shall continue to call them, function and that, of course, was Russell's famous theory of definite descriptions.[3] Ignoring Russell's "names in the strict logical sense," this was a theory about Fregean names because Russell held

---

[3] First put forward by Russell in his 1905 paper, "On Denoting."

that ordinary proper names are really concealed definite descriptions and so fall under his theory. To use our previous example Russell would have analyzed "The author of 'On Denoting' was a pacifist" as asserting that (*a*) there was an author of "On Denoting" and (*b*) there was at most one author of "On Denoting" and (*c*) if anyone was an author of "On Denoting" he was a pacifist. With suitable changes "Kepler died in misery" would get a similar analysis, for the name "Kepler," on Russell's account, is a concealed definite description—perhaps "the discoverer of the elliptic shape of the planetary orbits."

There are two main ways in which Russell's treatment of Fregean names differs from Frege's. First, on Russell's view Fregean names do not function simply to refer—in fact, Russell might be seen as holding that they do not refer at all. In any event they perform a much more complicated job on Russell's account; they introduce quantifiers and (in the straightforward cases we are looking at) the assertions in which they occur are in reality completely general. Second, the true negation of a statement of the form "*N* is ϕ," where "*N*" is a Fregean name, is a disjunction. So the true negation of "The author of 'On Denoting' was a pacifist" is "Either there was no author of 'On Denoting' or there was more than one author of 'On Denoting' or it is not the case that if anyone was the author of 'On Denoting' he was a pacifist."

What this means is that if Russell is correct then Frege's "obvious presupposition that the simple and compound names have a reference" does not exist. For if, as Frege would put it, in our examples "The author of 'On Denoting' " or "Kepler" lacked a reference, the result on Russell's theory would simply be that the corresponding assertions using the Fregean names are false. Neither lacks a truth-value.

3. STRAWSON'S VIEW AND INTUITIONS

I am sure that almost no one will find what I have said so far news; I have rehearsed some well-known facts to emphasize that the notion of presuppositions entered the philosophical literature as a result of certain theoretical considerations about what I have called Fregean names. At the time Strawson was writing on the issue there seemed to be two contenders for the correct analysis of Fregean names (today things are a bit more complicated, but I will not go into that here): Russell's analysis and Frege's. Frege's view seems to lead to the necessity for some notion of presupposition to account for failure of reference; Russell's completely excludes the notion. How is one to decide which is correct, assuming that they are the only possibilities? Neither, of course, can be faulted on strictly formal grounds. Neither leads to inconsistency or paradox. On Frege's view we shall, it seems, have to drop the requirement that every assertion be true or false, but many-valued logics come to the rescue there. Both theories about Fregean names are embedded by Russell and Frege in more general theories of language. We might then think of assessing the more general theories on whatever criteria such theories are judged by. But it seems unlikely that this will provide an answer because, among other things, it is not clear that either general theory necessitates the particular treatment given to Fregean names. Perhaps more ingenuity would suggest some other way of settling this dispute, but there is available the well-trod road of appealing to "intuitions"—to what we would say if. . . . And this, I believe, is where Strawson rested his case. A bit of evidence for this is the following passage from Strawson's early and well-known essay, "On Referring":

> Now suppose someone were in fact to say to you with a perfectly serious air: 'The King of France is wise'. Would you say, 'That's untrue'? I think it quite certain that you would not. But suppose he went to *ask* you whether you thought that what he had just said was true, or was false; whether you agreed or disagreed with what he had just said. I think you would be inclined, with some hesitation, to say that you did not do either; that the question of whether his statement was true or false simply *did not arise*, because there was no such person as the king of France. You might . . . say something like: 'I'm afraid you must be under a misapprehension. France is not a monarchy. There is no king of France." . . . when . . . we say (as we should) 'There is no king of France', we should certainly *not* say we were *contradicting* the statement that the king of France is wise. We are certainly not saying that it is false. We are, rather, giving a reason for saying that the question of whether it is true or false simply does not arise [1950/1971, p. 12].

Given the rather bare scene setting Strawson gives us here, I think we have to agree that our initial intuitions lie on his side. But later even Strawson admits that with this very example, "The king of France is wise," filling in the picture in a certain way is likely to change our minds. In any event, it becomes evident that our intuitions do not go across the board in favor of the uncompromising view. It seems obvious that we will all suppose that a serious assertion that the king of France exists or that the king of France does not exist will have a truth-value despite the presence of a definite description with no denotation. But then perhaps ascriptions of existence and nonexistence are well-known troublemakers and perhaps some exception can be made for them without abandoning the general principle. There are, however, any number of other cases where a minimal scene setting will produce intuitions contrary to the uncompromising view: I ask you, for example, what you would say were someone seriously to assert that among the readers of this paper will be the king of

France and then want to know whether you think his assertion true or false. I believe that your raw, uninstructed (or uncorrupted by theory) answer would be that you would say that it was false. And so too with the lunatic's assertion that he is the king of the French.

4. STRAWSON'S LATER VIEW

Faced with such conflicting intuitions Strawson attempted in "Identifying Reference and Truth-Values," published in 1964, to hold on to at least his attack against Russell and to account for the conflict. Russell, of course, also gave us an uncompromising view about definite descriptions and ordinary proper names. If there were a clear range of cases in which one were forced into adopting Strawson's presupposition—truth-value gap—account, that would do at least great damage to the Russellian view. As Strawson puts it in that paper:

> One who accepts the Theory of Descriptions [Russell's] as a correct analysis is bound to accept the falsity theory for certain cases and reject the truth-value gap theory. One who accepts the truth-value gap theory is bound to reject the Theory of Descriptions as a *generally* correct analysis [1964/1971, p. 86].

In Strawson's early writings on this subject and in this paper up to now very little scene setting is done. We are asked, in effect, to consult our intuitions about particular assertions, where the definite description, for example, has no denotation, in isolation from the conversational circumstances in which the assertion is made. When asked to do this about various assertions our intuitions seem to vary capriciously. We might try to systemitize the data by attempting to find some rule about kinds of assertions. This is not what Strawson attempted in his 1964 paper—and I believe he was probably correct. Instead he suggested a very ingenious theory which uses as its central idea the conversational circumstances, in particular, what he calls the "topic of conversation."

Although he does not, I believe, emphasize this, I think he would have agreed that presented with various assertions involved in this dispute, more or less in isolation, we are inclined to think of them as used in their most natural conversational circumstances. That is to say, even though we have not been given any substantial conversational surroundings, we are naturally inclined to supply some because particular sentences are most naturally or usually used in certain kinds of circumstances. If conversational circumstances make the difference in our intuitions, this would account for differing intuitions about assertions given to us in isolation. Another consequence would be that with the very same assertion our intuitions might differ if we were to be given somewhat unusual conversational circumstances in which is it embedded—and Strawson argues that is so even with the standard example, "The king of France is wise."

If I am correct, then, Strawson, in this later paper finds his earlier uncompromising view wrong because our intuitions do not always go along with him. He then gives us a theory that brings in the conversational circumstances, a theory that I think I can show will not work. My main point, however, is that Strawson relies on our intuitions; if they do not fit this theory then we will just have to get a new theory.

Strawson's theory in this later paper, as I understand it, is this: Although the notions of subject and predicate (I only deal here with assertions) may not be part of the common person's intellectual equipment, the common person nevertheless does divide assertions up that way. It is well known that formal logic recognizes no such distinction. "John loves Mary" and "Mary is loved by John" would be translated the same way into the symbolism of logic.

Strawson's suggestion is that in the context of actual use there will be a TOPIC of conversation. (It seems to me to be in the spirit of Strawson's view that there may be more than one topic of conversation, but to keep things simple I will follow him in assuming that there is only one.) Even though other things, people, places, *etc.* may get mentioned in a particular conversation they may not be the topic of the conversation. Support for this would seem to come from the fact that asked what the participants in some conversation are talking about, we are unlikely to reel off everything mentioned in its course, but rather settle on one or a few. (We would, however, have to deal with the fact that we might answer by giving something to which no overt reference has been made at all, e.g., a conversation could be about the energy crisis without the phrase "the energy crisis" nor any other way of referring to it being an overt part.)

Strawson's suggestion is that, depending on the topic of conversation, the very same sentence may be carved up into subject and predicate in different ways in different contexts:

> In the case of a statement containing more than one, say two, referring expressions, it is open to us to cast one of these for role of subject expression, while the other is regarded as absorbed into the predicate term which is attached to the subject-term to yield the statement as a whole [1964/1971, p. 88].

As an example, consider "Among the readers of this paper will be the king of France." If this is asserted in the midst of a conversation whose topic is the readers of this paper, for example, someone has just asked whether there will be anyone of interest reading this paper, we would naturally take the subject of the assertion (or "statement," as Strawson puts it) to be "the readers of this paper" and the definite description "the king of France" would be treated as absorbed into the predicate.

As opposed to what I have called the uncompromising view of Strawson's early discussions, our intuition about the example is that given that there is no king of France what is asserted is simply false. Strawson's explanation for this depends on the fact that we are viewing the offending definite description as being absorbed into the predicate. The source of our intuition is the thought that, to paraphrase Strawson, whoever will be among the readers of this paper, among them will NOT be the king of France, since there is no such person.

It is, however, possible to imagine a conversation in which the assertion (or statement) in question is used where the topic is not the readers of this paper, but the king of France. Perhaps one party to a conversation in which the participants are all under the mistaken impression that France is a monarchy asks, "Do you suppose the King of France ever reads philosophical papers?" and receives that as an answer. In such a case, Strawson believes our intuition will be that the answer has no truth-value and this because "the King of France" is now to be regarded as the subject and, since there is no king of France, nothing can be truly or falsely predicated of him. About Russell's well-known example Strawson says,

> We feel very squeamish indeed about 'the king of France is bald' presented abruptly, out of context, just because we don't naturally think of the context in which interest is centered, say, on the question, 'What bald notables are there?' rather than on the question 'What is the king of France like?' or 'Is the king of France bald?'. Of course, to either of *these* two questions the statement would not be just an incorrect answer. These questions have no correct answer and hence, in a sense, no incorrect answer either [1964/1971, p. 91].

5. TROUBLES WITH STRAWSON'S LATER VIEW

Strawson's later view as outlined in the last section is both ingenious and plausible. But does it capture and correctly delimit our intuitions? It seems to do so for the sort of examples he uses. It also seems to give some rational foundation for those intuitions. Unfortunately it will not work for other examples.

Before turning to those let me mention schematically and as an aside a matter of logic with which Strawson's new account would have to deal. In his earlier work Strawson, as against Russell, maintained that assertions (statements) of the following two forms are, when they have a truth-value, true contradictories:

1. The ϕ is ψ

2. The ϕ is not ψ

Russell would have said about (2) that it is either ambiguous or not really the negation of (1). A main contention of Strawson's earlier work was that this is not so. There is, so far as I can see, nothing in the 1964 paper to show that he has abandoned that position. (If he has, much of the argument with Russell evaporates.) That position, however, cannot be maintained on the newer view. We have to read (1) and (2), on the new view, not in the usual way, but rather as schemata which show that in a certain context "The ϕ" is the subject and "ψ" is the predicate. But "ψ", the predicate, might contain a definite description which has been "absorbed" into it and which also lacks a denotation. This should make both (1) and (2) false, which, of course, is not possible for true contradictories.

Putting aside this *ex consessus* difficulty, there is at least one class of cases for which Strawson's attempt to account for our intuitions simply will not work. The cases I have in mind are what I will call "comparisons of the existent with the nonexistent." In discussing these cases I will appeal to my intuitions and the readers'. Where, following Strawson, the topic of conversation is "the readers of this paper," it seemed that we should say that the assertion, "Among the readers of this paper will be the king of France," given that there is no king of France, should be pronounced false. But now contrast this, the topic of conversation being the same, with the assertion, "The readers of this paper will know more about presuppositions than does the king of France" (said in all seriousness, of course). Insofar as I find myself agreeing with Strawson about truth-value gaps, when I consult my intuitions, my intuition is just as strong here that there is no truth-value as it is about any of the more familiar cases.

Am I a better volleyball player than the king of France? Suppose that I am the topic of conversation and that I am being compared with various people—if I claim that I am better than, among others, the king of France, have I said something true or false? It does not seem a question of what the topic of conversation is; if we have intuitions that some assertions have no truth-value, this is, contrary to Strawson's later view, surely an example.

With a couple of easily characterized exceptions I believe comparisons of the existent with the nonexistent in general will, contrary to Strawson's later view, yield the same result: It does not matter what one chooses to call the "topic of conversation," our intuitions will tend toward "no truth-value."

The exceptions will not help Strawson's case, but they may be worth mentioning. We can truly or falsely compare an existent thing with something in fiction, legend, etc. or something that has been thought to exist and around which there has been some accumulation of beliefs. In both cases, however, the clear intuition that what is asserted has truth-value seems only to be there when characteristics involved in the comparison derive from the characteristics ascribed or believed to be true about the fictional or nonexistent thing. So, I guess, even Mohammed Ali has never been as strong as Paul Bunyon, but my intuitions tell me that I cannot decide the truth-value of the assertion that Mohammed Ali is a better poet than Paul Bunyon. If Homer did not in fact exist, I still might be able, with truth or falsity, to compare, say, Auden to Homer in regard to poetic ability; but comparing them in regard to strength would give rise to the same intuition: no truth-value. In giving these exceptions, it seems clear to me that the topic of conversation would make no difference.

6. INTUITIONS

If Strawson's attempt at explaining our seemingly capricious intuitions about truth-value in cases of denotation failure does not work, what is the explanation? It cannot be simply that whenever a denoting expression fails to have a denotation we refuse to assign a truth-value to an assertion using it—it was just because our intuitions do not go in that direction in a variety of cases that Strawson offered the new explanation. And, as we have now seen, his notion of the "topic of conversation" founders on the class of cases I have called "comparisons of the existent with the nonexistent."

There is a third explanation that we need to look at briefly. This is one that, I believe, entered the literature first in an article by Wilfred Sellars (1954) defending Russell's theory of definite descriptions against Strawson's original challenge. In effect what it says is that our intuition in certain cases involving a nondenoting definite description that nothing true or false has been asserted is not really what it seems to be. Rather, what we are hesitant about is that the simple verdict "false" would have, in Paul Grice's terminology, a conversational implicature which we do not want to let stand. On Russell's view if someone asserts that the king of France is bald and there is no king of France what he has asserted is false. But an assertion of the form "The ϕ is ψ" can turn out false for anyone of three reasons: (a) there is nothing which is ϕ; (b) there is more than one thing which is ϕ; or (c) there is one and only one ϕ but that thing does not have the property of being ψ. Faced with an assertion of this form in isolation and asked to pronounce on truth-value when we know that there is no ϕ, we hesitate, according to this view, not because we take the assertion to have no truth-value, but because the simple answer "false" does not distinguish among the three reasons we might have for so pronouncing. And it may be that in giving the simple verdict there is a presumption that we are doing so on the basis of the third kind of reason, that we are generally presumed to be asserting a contrary, not the contradictory. Why there should be such a presumption might stem from conversational rules of practice in line with those Grice has suggested. This defense of Russell can be extended to other cases where truth-value gaps have been invoked and presuppositions given as the explanation, for example, the well-known question, "Have you stopped beating your wife?"

Plausible as this explanation of our intuitions is—and it is an explanation, not a defense, if we represent our intuitions in various cases as involving lack of truth-value—it also founders on the very sorts of examples Strawson's later view tried to explain. Given that there is no king of France, we should have the same hesitation, if Russell's analysis is correctly the source, about "Among the readers of this paper will be the king of France," but we do not—even though on Russell's view what would be said could be three-ways false.

Returning to comparisons of the existent with the nonexistent, none of the explanations so far explored tell us what to do about all cases and thus not about this case. The explanation that perhaps first comes to mind is that when one compares one thing to another there is a noncomparative property of each thing in virtue of which the assertion is true or false. So, if A is larger than B is true, this is because A has a certain size and B has a certain size and the first size is greater than the second. But if one of the terms in the assertion of comparison does not denote anything, then there will not be, unless there is some fictional or other kind of accretion of properties, its noncomparative property to determine the truth-value of the comparison. So, because there is no king of France, there is no way of determining his skill at volleyball, for example. And thus whatever level of skill I possess there is not in this instance the necessary ingredient for determining the truth-value of the assertion that I am a better volleyball player than the king of France.

Let us suppose that this is the background for our intuitions in the case of comparisons of the existent with the nonexistent. We still do not have a systematic explanation of our intuitions.

The difficulty is that this is the same sort of explanation of our intuitions that can be given for the sort of examples Strawson, rightly in my opinion, tried to account for. Because there is no king of France, the king of France cannot be found among the readers of this paper. But with Strawson's sort of example we are, at least I am, inclined to give different verdicts depending on the conversational circumstances. Even though the most plausible explanations of the source of our intuitions seem on a par with each other in the two cases, comparisons with the nonexistent do not seem to depend on circumstances in the way Strawson's examples do. How do we explain that difference?

Whatever the explanation in the end, and this chapter does not provide one, if we want to depend on intuitions, matters are clearly more complicated than one might initially suppose. If there is a principle behind our intuitions it cannot be the simple one that referential terms with no reference result in a truth-value gap when they are used. No other easy principle comes to mind.

One possibility, of course, is that our intuitions are ill-founded. This would be a Humean sort of conclusion, which I do not feel prepared to endorse, but suppose as an end to this exercise we try it out for a moment.

Suppose that our hesitation about giving truth-value to comparisons between the existent and nonexistent (where the exceptions I have mentioned do not have application) stems from the thought that if A does not exist there can be no property of being ϕier or not ϕier than A. So, given that the king of France does not exist, there just is no property of being a better volleyball player than him and none of being worse. So, I cannot have or fail to have either property and so it cannot be true or false that I have or lack either property. This SOUNDS very close to the "plausible" explanation of our intuitions I gave earlier. But it will not do. There is the property of being a better volleyball player than the king of France and also the property of being worse. If, to take an analogous case, the color red were to be wiped off the face of the universe, nothing would have the property of being redder than anything else, but it would not destroy the property. The only result would be that nothing has it. So too, without a present king of France around, I do not have the property of being a better volleyball player than he nor worse nor an equal. But that does not mean that there are no such properties. In possible worlds talk, there are possible worlds in which my spikes and bump-shots blow the king of France off the court and others in which I have to admit that the monarch of France is better than I am.

Suppose we try adding into this supposed source of our intuition that the properties we think not to exist are the properties of being better than, worse than or equal to the ACTUAL king of France. There being no king of France, I think there are, indeed, no such properties. So, I agree that I cannot have any nor lack any. The difficulty here is that the same move

could be made about the sorts of examples Strawson tried to explain. If
this is the source of our intuition, then why do we not have the same intuition about the assertion that among the readers of this paper will be the
king of France (with, if you will, "the readers of this paper" as subject)?
There is equally no property of having the ACTUAL king of France among
the readers of a paper.

I find no easy way to organize the explanation for our intuitions about
the sorts of examples philosophers have been primarily concerned with—
reference failure. And I have not tried to deal with the much broader application of the notion of presuppositions that linguists have made.
Nothing I have said supports or denies that assertions have presuppositions or that, about the sorts of examples philosophers have been interested in, Russell was or was not correct as against Strawson. I do suggest that intuitions are not simple things to account for.

REFERENCES

Frege, G. (1892/1952). On sense and reference. In P. Geach and M. Black (Eds.), *Transla-
tions from the Philosophical Writings of Gottlob Frege*. Oxford: Blackwell. Pp. 56–78.
Russell, B. (1905). On denoting. *Mind*, **14**, 479–493. [Reprinted in R. C. Marsh (Ed.), *Logic
and Knowledge*, London: Allen and Unwin, 1956.]
Sellars, W. (1954). Presupposing. *The Philosophical Review*, **63**, 197–215.
Strawson, P. F. (1950/1971). On referring. *Mind*, **59**, 320–344. [Reprinted in P. G. Strawson,
Logico-Linguistic Papers. London: Methuen.]
Strawson, P. F. (1964/1971). Identifying reference and truth-values. *Theoria*, **30**, 96–118.
[Reprinted in P. G. Strawson, *Logico-Linguistic Papers*. London: Methuen.]
Wilson, D. (1975). *Presuppositions and Non-Truth-Conditional Semantics*. New York: Aca-
demic Press.

Pragmatics and the Description of Discourse[1]

Charles J. Fillmore

In this chapter I will state for linguistics an interpretation of the terms SYNTAX, SEMANTICS, and PRAGMATICS; I will suggest an approach to the analysis of discourse that I favor—an approach that consists in describing the pragmatic conditions of different types of discourse and in identifying the lexico-grammatical concomitants of these conditions; and I will demonstrate this approach by identifying a number of properties of a particular type of fictional narrative.

1. SYNTAX, SEMANTICS AND PRAGMATICS

I use the terms SYNTAX, SEMANTICS, and PRAGMATICS in ways that Charles Morris did not have in mind when he first set up this famous three-way distinction (Morris, 1938). I assume three ways of looking at linguistic facts, the three viewable as independent from each other or not, depending on whether we are thinking of classes of facts or explanations. In the broadest sense, I believe that syntactic, semantic and pragmatic

---

[1] This chapter originally appeared in Schmidt, Siegfried (Ed.), *Pragmatik II*, Munich, Wilhelm Fink Verlag, 1976. Reprinted by permission.

RADICAL PRAGMATICS   ISBN 0-12-179660-4

FACTS can be distinguished from each other, but I also believe that some syntactic facts require semantic and pragmatic explanations and that some semantic facts require pragmatic explanations. Put differently, interpreters sometimes use semantic and pragmatic information in making judgments about the syntactic structure of a sentence, and they sometimes use pragmatic facts in making semantic judgments.

Observations that belong to syntax more or less without question are observations about the structural organization of sentences and observations about the distributional possibilities of lexical items within lexically and grammatically defined contexts. Semantics, by contrast, is concerned with the relation between linguistic forms and what the users of the language can DO with those forms, both in terms of the propositional content they can be used to give expression to, and the illocutionary acts they can be used to perform.

Syntax, in short, characterizes the grammatical forms that occur in a language, whereas semantics pairs these forms with their potential communicative functions. Pragmatics is concerned with the three-termed relation that unites (*a*) linguistic form and (*b*) the communicative functions that these forms are capable of serving, with (*c*) the contexts or settings in which those linguistic forms can have those communicative functions. Diagrammatically,

Syntax	[form]
Semantics	[form, function]
Pragmatics	[form, function, setting]

To the extent to which the types of observations one is dealing with are distinct, one can regard these three fields as more or less autonomous; but to the extent to which observations in one of these areas yield to explanations drawing on another, they are interdependent.

2. PRAGMATICS IN PARTICULAR

Among the products of an adequate account of the semantics of a language is the establishment of explanations for significance, ambiguity, contradiction, *etc*. Although it seems clear that judgments of ambiguity fall within semantics, it is not always clear when one is dealing with ambiguity rather than with something else. I believe that the English sentence

(1)   *Can you come to my party next Friday night?*

can be said to be ambiguous in a way in which the sentence

(2)   *Can you come to my party next Monday night?*

is not. The fact is that when spoken early in the calendar week, the phrase *next Friday* can designate either the Friday of the current week or the Friday of the succeeding week, as many speakers of English know who have had the experience of showing up one week too early or one week too late for a cocktail party. The phrase *next Monday,* on the other hand, is not ambiguous in the same way. The expressions can only designate the Monday of the week following the calendar week in which the sentence containing it is pronounced.

Those of us who were brought up on the semantic theory of Katz and Fodor have been taught to believe that semantic facts should be explained by a semantic theory, and that a semantic theory must be independent of a theory of beliefs, usage, or settings. The explanation in the case of our examples would accordingly have to take the form of our recognizing in the lexical description of the word *next* and the words *Friday* and *Monday* those semantic features and combinatorial properties that together would account for the phenomena just observed. Either that, or the phenomena would have to be ruled out of semantics—what I have described as an ambiguity would have to be described as something else.

Whatever the phenomenon is, its explanation requires an understanding of the pragmatics of several types of expressions. First, although there are alternative conventions for determining the beginning of the calendar week cycle, to be sure, all speakers of English agree (I think) that it begins on either Sunday or Monday. Second, one does not use a day-indicating expression of the "next *X*-day" form for indicating a day which is either one day or two days in the future, because for such purposes the expressions *tomorrow* and *day after tomorrow* are pre-emptive. These pragmatic realities, together with the fact that *next* in a calendric expression can either designate the (future) nearest unit or the unit of the (future) nearest cycle, guarantee that *next Monday* can designate only the Monday of the succeeding week. That is, there is simply no time when it is appropriate to say *next Monday* without in fact being in the calendar week which precedes the designated Monday.

An account of the ambiguity of one expression and the nonambiguity of a related expression has required, in short, an appeal to knowledge of how the institution of calendar-keeping in our culture works, how the days of the week are organized, when the week cycle begins, and how the choice of a day-of-the-week expression is constrained by the speaker's knowledge of the time of the speech act. I assume that these are pragmatic, and not purely semantic, facts, and I assume furthermore that there is no a priori notion of ambiguity according to which the different possibilities of interpretation for our two sentences could have been described as not being within the scope of semantics proper.

Consider now another example—this time the fact that the sentence

(3)   *We'll go there right away.*

is ambiguous between the inclusive and the exclusive interpretation of the pronoun (i.e., *we* can be either "you and I" or "somebody other than you or I"), while the sentence

(4)   *We'll come there right away.*

can only be given the interpretation by which the *we* is taken as exclusive of the addressee. The explanation has to do, of course, with the difference between *come* and *go,* but not in ways that can be directly explained from the semantic analysis of those two verbs.

The conditions for the most straightforward use of *come* are, briefly, that when I am talking to you, I can use the word *come* to speak of the movement of something toward my location or toward your location. In *We'll come there right away* I cannot be speaking of movement toward my location, since I am one of the travelers; hence the movement must be movement toward your location. If, for the use of *come* to be appropriate, you must be located at the destination of the movement, you cannot be among the travelers; and thus *we* must designate somebody else and me, not you and me. Since the verb *go* is not constrained in the same way, both possibilities for *we* are available in the *go* sentence.

The analysis is inescapably tied up with knowledge of the conditions limiting the use of the verb *come,* assumptions about how the personnel in a conversation can be distributed in space with respect to each other, etc., and this is information that can surely be thought of as pragmatic (see Fillmore, 1972). In other words, it is by means of establishing the pragmatic conditions for the sentence that we can discover its interpretation possibilities.

3. METHODS OF DISCOURSE DESCRIPTION

There are in linguistics many approaches to the description of discourse, these being united solely by the shared conviction that it is wrong for linguistic theory to limit its scope to the properties of individual sentences. The different approaches I am thinking of include the study of the proper sequencing of sentences in texts; the study of the architectonic or constituent structure organization of texts and their parts; the study of discourse as an entity which develops in time; the study of the statistical properties of various types of texts; the pragmatic or sociolinguistic analysis of the real or potential occasions-of-use of texts; and the study of the ways in which the grammatical, organizational and rhetorical choices made by the creators of texts have determined their rhetorical or esthetic effect.

Scholars emphasizing the proper sequencing of sentences try to establish the characteristics of coherent, as opposed to incoherent, sentence sequences. Where the sentence grammarian separates the well-formed from the ill-formed to match intuitive judgments he refers to as GRAMMATICALITY and NONGRAMMATICALITY, the discourse grammarian relies on judgments we can refer to as SEQUITURITY and NONSEQUITURITY. Some of the scholars of sequiturity emphasize the use of sentence connectives, others the maintenance of pronominal reference, others the maintenance of such semantic categories as topic, setting, or the identity of the experiencing psyche.[1] Scholars who seek to describe the architectonic structure of texts provide a kind of outline or table of contents for the texts analyzed and then classify texts according to characteristic features of such outlines (see, e.g. Longacre, 1968). Efforts to discover statistical regularities in texts of various kinds range from observations of mean sentence length and type–token ratios for lexical items, through frequency counts of words taken from particular registers or vocabulary fields, to studies of characteristic uses of transformations, characteristic types of surface structural organizations of sentences, or characteristic ways of distributing background and foreground information in a sentence.[2]

With the pragmatic approach, an analysis is carried out in sociolinguistic terms in which the identity, location, and relative social statuses of the participants in the communication act are taken into account, together with a description of the social or institutional occasion within which the discourse was observed or within which it could be produced. Of particular interest, of course, is the correlation of these items with formal linguistic phenomena.[3] An extension of the pragmatic approach is what might be called the dynamic or developmental approach, the analysis of a text which emphasizes its development in time. Here discourse is seen not as a purely architectonically structured entity, and certainly not as merely a set of messages whose semantic organization can be captured through an amalgamation of the semantic content of the total set of its constituent sentences, but rather as something which is experienced in time, both on the part of the creator(s) of the text and on the part of its interpreters. Analysis of literary texts must be able to take the time-development into account, in order to make intelligible such interpreter experiences as ex-

[1] For useful surveys of such approaches, see van Dijk (1972), Chapters 1–3; Grimes (1972), Chapter 2; and Stratton (1971), Chapter 1.

[2] For a study near the more sophisticated end of this continuum, see Smith 1971.

[3] See Grimes, 1972, especially Chapter 5, ''The speaker and hearer in discourse.''

pectation, suspense, surprise, etc.; and workers in conversation analysis cannot avoid this aspect of discourse, if only to be able to distinguish between discourse that is preplanned and discourse that is produced in response to ongoing events.

The text line that goes from the beginning to the end of a text defines a precedence relation, an earlier–later scale, both from the point of view of the creator of text and from the point of view of the hearer or reader. Because of this fact, each point in the text line can be seen as a present moment, with what appears earlier and later in the text seen, with respect to that point, as past and future respectively. In the analysis of an ongoing conversation, of course, this point is trivial, but it is important to realize that even in written texts, the tenses of a sentence are typically "centered" on the point in the textual time line where the sentence occurs. (It is a rare thing, though it is certainly possible, for a writer to regard his entire production as something completed in the past, and for him to write in, say, Chapter Two, something like "I have discussed this phenomenon in greater detail in Chapter Eight.") Knowledge of the development of a discourse in time figures importantly in stating the principles for regulating a conversation, in the treatment of anaphora, ellipsis, topic-maintenance, and in the analysis of jokes.

An aspect of the time development of a text that is particularly important for spoken language is the way in which the text develops in response to ongoing events, internal or external. There are many features distinguishing discourse which is being composed "on the run" from discourse for which there has been a certain amount of preplanning. There are grammatical differences between the two types, exemplified most easily with the difference between planned coordination ("Who was at the party?"— "Jimmy, Mabel, Clara, and George.") and unplanned coordination ("Who was at the party?"—"Jimmy, and Mabel, and Clara, and George"). There are also differences in coherence standards between preplanned texts and texts that are produced partly in response to on-going events. There is no oddness to sudden shifts of topic if these can be understood as ongoing experiences on the part of the speaker. ("Yes, I've enjoyed living in California a great deal. My, this soup is magnificent! And in fact I can't imagine ever wanting to live anywhere else. Oh my God, what's happening? The whole house is moving!")

Lastly, then, it is possible to examine a piece of discourse as a work of art. For this the analyst seeks to discover, appreciate, and evaluate the devices which the author made use of, consciously or unconsciously, in achieving the results he was after. In this area, for example, we can compare the "story" with the "plot," that is, the chronology of events that the author has in mind can be compared with the sequence in which and the extent to which the details of this history are revealed to the reader. Another much-discussed area is that of "point of view," the particular perspective or orientation assumed in a fictional work. Here the analyst is concerned with such matters as the identity and role of the narrator, the perceptual or psychological vantage point from which the reader is invited to experience the narrative, the confidences which the narrator has with the reader, the degrees of objectivity or omniscience that the narrator assumes, and so on.

4. CONTEXTUALIZATION

The approach to discourse that I favor is the pragmatic, emphasizing deixis and dynamic development. It seems to me that the discourse grammarian's most important task is that of characterizing, on the basis of the linguistic material contained in the discourse under examination, the set of worlds in which the discourse could play a role, together with the set of possible worlds compatible with the message content of the discourse.

There is, thus, both an external and an internal aspect to this process, the difference depending on whether we are determining the nature of the worlds in which the discourse could serve as part of a communication event, or on whether we are determining the possible properties of the world depicted or implied by the text. I am interested, in other words, in how formal properties of texts can be related both to what the participants (the producers and interpreters of the texts) are doing and what they are mentally experiencing.

I will refer to the analytic process of determining the character of such "world sets" as CONTEXTUALIZATION. In EXTERNAL CONTEXTUALIZATION our concern is with the worlds in which the text can appropriately be used; with INTERNAL CONTEXTUALIZATION our concern is with the worlds in the imagination of the creator and interpreters of the text.

The following sentence can serve to exemplify the external contextualization process:

(5)   *Do you like this one better than this one?*

If we are to imagine a situation in which this sentence has been used appropriately, we must assume that the speaker was able to index two things for the addressee, one at a time, and that he indexed one of the two things at the time he pronounced the first token of *this one,* the other at the time he pronounced the second token of the phrase. Although other contextualization possibilities exist, the most easily imagined context for the sentence is one in which the two participants are in visual contact with each other, the indexing being done by appropriate acts of presenting or gesturing.

For an example of what I mean by internal contextualization, consider now a sentence like

(6)   *She never* **had** *enjoyed listening to her husband lecture, and this time was no exception.*

On hearing or reading this sentence, a sensitive interpreter of English finds himself imagining a woman experiencing discomfort during a lecture by her husband, and he furthermore experiences the text as something which more or less represents her feelings at that time. These impressions are created by a number of properties of the sentence, including the particular tenses it contains, the expressive relative position of *never* and *had,* the emphatic stress on *had,* and the use of the phrase *this time.* The sentence in question has, of course, an external contextualization as well. We would expect to find it in a narrative, rather than in an ordinary conversation; and we would expect either that it is preceded in the same text by a passage in which *she* and *her husband* had been previously identified and in which the time referred to by the simple past tense had been set up, or that the absence of such a preceding context was to be taken as a deliberate aspect of the narrative, it being presented in a particular mode (we can call it, after Cohn, 1966, narrated monologue), the episode beginning *in media res.*

The analyst of discourse needs to become clear about how it is that interpreters of texts can know such things. I will have some suggestions about that later on, but there are still, unfortunately, a few additional preliminary issues to get out of the way first.

5. POSITIONS ON THE PROPER DESCRIPTION OF DISCOURSE

There are certain positions on the study of discourse that I would like to associate myself with; and, even though these may not be particularly novel or controversial, I feel that it may be wise to make them explicit anyway.

The first of these has to do with the question of whether there is a clear boundary between sentence grammar and text grammar, that is, whether there is an essential difference between the sorts of things one can say about sentences and the sorts of things one can say about discourses. I am inclined to think that judgments of grammaticality and judgments of sequitury are intuitively different sorts of things, but I cannot believe that this difference imposes a boundary between different kinds of linguistic units. In particular, sequiturity judgments, judgments about the coherence of sequences of clauses, are just as important for determining the fittingness of clauses within sentences as they are for determining the fittingness of sentences within texts; and grammatical rules involving pronominalization, deletion, stress assignment, *etc.,* operate in accordance with essentially the same principles within texts as within sentences.

A second position that I would like to take has to do with the interpretation of a contextualization description. The concern is neither with prediction nor with prescription, but rather with norms of interpretation. Discourse grammarians are responsible, not for making probabilistic statements about what people will actually say in given situations, nor for giving advice on what people should say, but rather for characterizing the competence reliable interpreters of a language possess which enables them to judge the appropriateness of given utterances in given contexts.

This last point can be easily misunderstood, so let me give an example of what I have in mind, together with an example of one way in which the point can be misunderstood. At the 1972 Georgetown University Roundtable meeting, I gave an invented discourse that I said would be particularly difficult to contextualize (Fillmore, 1973). The discourse was this:

(7)   *Hello. This is Chuck Fillmore. Could you send over a box about yea big?*

The challenge to contextualization comes from the following collection of facts: The *Hello* indicates that it is the beginning of a conversation, and that it is a conversation that begins, in fact, with the establishment of contact between the speaker and the addressee. From that it is likely that the next sentence, *This is Chuck Fillmore,* is used in self-identification rather than being something said while introducing a friend or pointing to a photograph. That being so, it further becomes necessary to believe that the conversation is taking place over a telephone, since the "This is X" locution as a means of self-identification is not used in face-to-face conversation nor in letter-writing. And this whole accumulation of facts renders the last sentence difficult to accept, since the expression *yea big* is used (in American English) only when the speaker is presenting some dimensional estimate by means of a manual gesture. But, of course, if the conversation is being conducted over the telephone we assume that the participants are not in visual contact.

The conflict, then, is that one part of the discourse requires that the communication not be face-to-face, another requires that the speaker be presenting something to the addressee's view. It is our knowledge of the separate pragmatic conditions of several separate linguistic properties of the discourse which helps a speaker of English to sense that it is a bizarre piece of discourse, and it is also that knowledge which would make it possible for a particularly inventive speaker to imagine a situation—such as one involving communication by videophone—in which the sentence would indeed be appropriate. My purpose was to show that speakers possess this kind of knowledge, and that it is knowledge about the contextualization of individual linguistic usages.

A friend heard this demonstration of mine, and has referred to it here and there as an example of the dangers of introspectionism in linguistics. This friend once lost a pet dog and put a notice about it in the newspapers. Somebody who thought that he might have found the dog telephoned my friend and said, "Mr. Labov, I think I have your dog." When asked to describe the dog, the caller said, "Well, he's about so big." That conversation was taken by my friend as evidence that the claim I had made about *yea big*—a claim achieved by introspection about an invented piece of conversation—was simply wrong. My answer to this objection must be that the nature of a contextualization description must be properly understood: I would suggest, too, that the reported actual telephone conversation is an example of failed communication, and that this failure can be accounted for by pointing out that a gestural deictic form was used under conditions when the addressee was not able to witness any accompanying gesture.

A third position on discourse grammar that I would like to maintain is that the language of face-to-face conversation is the basic and primary use of language, all others being best described in terms of their manner of deviation from that base. I assume that this position is neither particularly controversial nor in need of explanation.

6. TEXT TYPOLOGY

I believe, then, that it is useful to classify texts according to the general pragmatic conditions of their production, paying special attention to the use in the texts of linguistic material that has pragmatic import. It will be found that pragmatically different sorts of texts have interestingly different grammatical properties.

One of the criteria for classifying texts along these lines has to do with whether the text is MONOLOGIC, constructed on the model of me-talking-to-myself, or DIALOGIC, constructed on the model of me-talking-to-you, or IMPERSONAL. I assume that monologic texts can be explained as a subtype of dialogic texts, the differences being accounted for by showing that in monologic discourse the addressee and the speaker are the same person.

In dialogic texts one finds both first person and second person references, and one finds such second person appeals as commands, questions, apologies, *etc.* An example of dialogic discourse is

(8)   *Could you move over a bit, please?*

In monologic texts one finds instances of expressive speech and first person references, but usually no second person references. A potential example of monologic discourse is

(9)   *Oh no, a cop!*

In impersonal texts there is no first-person mention of the creator of the text and no second-person mention of the addressee of the text. An example of an impersonal piece of discourse is

(10)   *Printed in Great Britain by Richard Clay Ltd.*

A second major set of criteria by which texts can be pragmatically distinguished from each other has to do with the relationship between the occasion of production and the occasion of interpretation of the text. In FACE-TO-FACE CONVERSATION between people who can hear each other and see each other, it is typical that the situation in which the participants find themselves provides an enormous background of shared information, especially as this situation includes the postures and movements of the participants themselves. Discourse produced under these conditions can contain material of the kind that must be accompanied by gestures and presentations. This basic type of discourse can be compared with a TELEPHONE CONVERSATION in which speech of the kind that must be accompanied by gestures is automatically ruled out. And these can be compared further with dialogic discourse in which the time of production and the time of the interpretation are distinct, as with most instances of WRITTEN COMMUNICATION. That these latter two are derivative of the face-to-face conversational norm is suggested by the fact that, in cases where the sender of a message might be unskilled in maintaining an awareness of the addressee's interpreting task, the telephoner might use forms that normally require the addressee to see what he is doing, or the writer of a message might use time-indicating expressions whose correct interpretation require the addressee to know when the message was encoded. People with this particular problem have been known to leave notes on their office doors that read, ''I'll be back in an hour.''

It is possible to become aware of the effects that different pragmatic conditions have on semantic interpretation by taking sample sentences and seeing whether they can be contextualized in ways that differ according to the basic kinds of pragmatic variables mentioned in the preceding paragraphs. One example that illustrates this is a note that I found on a colleague's office door—let us call the colleague Y. M.—that read: "I may be in room 2114." It is difficult to imagine this sentence used in face-to-face conversation. The note that I observed was intended as an example of dialogic communication using writing in which the addressee is someone who is looking for Y. M., the time at which Y. M. "may be in room 2114" is not the time at which the message was written but that time at which the message was expected to be interpreted, and the uncertainty associated with the word *may* is due to the uncertainty of knowing when somebody might read the note. A totally different possibility for this message has it as an instance of monologic speech: Somebody was drugged and taken off, unconscious, to some room; he later woke and, noticing some familiar objects around him, concluded that he might be in room 2114; he wrote the message down on a piece of paper as a kind of diary-keeping act; somebody found that piece of paper and taped it to Y. M.'s office door. The present-tense uncertainty of the *may* is compatible with the contextualization of this sentence as an example of monologic speech.

7. FEATURES OF EMBEDDED DISCOURSE

Situations that make clear certain kinds of differences between internal and external contextualization are discourses that contain reports of the actions, speech, thoughts, and inner experiences of persons other than those involved in the ongoing communication act, or of participants in the communication act at times other than that of the communication act. There are different ways of exhibiting speech and thought in discourse, and the contextualizing processes work differently for each of these.

There are three different ways of presenting speech or thought in discourse, and these can be called QUOTING, REPORTING, and REPRESENTING. There are also many mixtures of these, but they can be ignored for now.

Examples of quoted, reported, and represented thought are (a), (b), and (c) respectively:

(11) a. *"What to do now?" she thought.*
      b. *She wondered what she should do.*
      c. *What on earth should she do now?*

Examples of quoted, reported, and represented dialogue are Sentences (12), (13), and (14), respectively.

(12) a. *"Can I try it again?" he asked his mother.*
      b. *"No," she answered, "you certainly cannot."*

(13)   *He asked his mother if he could try it again, but she answered that he couldn't.*

(14)   a. *Could he please try it again, he asked his mother.*
         b. *No indeed he could not, she replied.*

There are many systematic ways in which these three methods of exhibiting discourse within discourse differs from each other.

In quoting, one is generally taken as presenting the reported speaker's exact words, or at least an utterance that could be attributed to the subject of the associated verb of saying or thinking. (The difficulties that require some sort of qualification can be seen in sentences like *"I haven't had dinner yet," he seemed to be saying/he said in Chinese.*) In represented speech it is nearly possible to represent his exact words; but in reported speech it is not.

In reported speech and in represented speech, the tenses of the original utterance are sometimes backshifted and sometimes not. When backshifting takes place, an original present becomes past, an original past or present perfect becomes pluperfect.

Within a clause of reported speech, indexical and referencing expressions are transparent, that is, they are selected from the point of view of the reporting speech act, nor the reported speech act. Thus, if I say to you:

(15)   *She thinks that that idiot is a genius.*

I am identifying somebody as an idiot and I am telling you that she regards him as a genius. Although in the surface sentence the noun phrase *that idiot* is commanded by *thinks*, the description can be mine, not hers. Or in a sentence like

(16)   *She told him that she wanted me to be here today*

the words *she, me, here,* and *today* are chosen from the point of view of the speaker of the larger sentence, and not that of the speaker of the reported utterance.

In reported speech, then, we sometimes find in a single clause some material that is relevant for internal contextualization and some that is relevant for external contextualization.

Reported discourse differs from the others in lacking the means for exhibiting certain kinds of utterances. ASSERTIONS are possible, as in

(17)   *He told her that he was ready.*

QUESTIONS are possible, as in

(18)   *He asked her if she was ready.*

and COMMANDS are possible, as in

(19)   *He told her to get ready.*

But exclamations, curses, blessings, *etc.*, are not possible, unless they are cast in the form of one or another of these basic sentence types.

In reported speech, linguistic forms that figure in external contextualization are generally taken from the reporter's point of view rather than that of the original speaker. Thus, to give another example, in

(20)   *He said he'd be here by now.*

the forms *he, would, here,* and *by now* are my words, not his. But there is at least one word for which this generalization does not hold, and that is *come.* In a sentence like

(21)   *He asked her to come to his party.*

the word *come* can be understood as the word HE would have used, not necessarily the word I would use if this were not an instance of reported speech. To show that this is so, we can juxtapose to this last sentence one in which the choice of *come* or *go* must be made from the point of view of the speaker of the outer sentence.

(22)   *He asked her to come to his party. She said that she would, but in the end she decided not to go (*come).*

Backshifting phenomena ("sequence of tenses") appear in reported speech if the relevance of the situation described in the reported clause to the situation of the reporting sentence is not being suggested. If I say something like

(23)   *He said that he was ready.*

I am merely reporting what somebody said; but, by contrast, if I say

(24)   *He said that he's ready.*

it has to be the case that the information contained in the reported clause is also relevant to the external contextualization of the sentence.

This relevance to the external situation of the context of a reported clause with unshifted tenses bears on the observations earlier made about *come.* In a sentence like

(25)   *They told him that she was coming to the party.*

the choice of the word *come* can be relevant to either internal or external contextualization. In a sentence without backshifting however, for example

(26)   *They told him that she's coming to the party.*

the choice of *come* is relevant only to the EXTERNAL contextualization of the sentence. That is, either you or I must be at the party either at the time the sentence is spoken or at the time of her expected arrival.

In represented speech, contextualizing words figure almost exclusively in internal contextualization. The exceptions are pronouns and tenses, these being chosen in the same way as in reported speech. That is, the person whose speech or thought is being represented is always presented in the third person, and his thoughts and utterances are generally converted to the appropriate backshifted tense. Here is an example:

(27)   *He had done it like this before, and he was going to do it again, she just knew it. But why with her?*

8. REMARKS ON A SELECTED TEXT TYPE

I have now presented, I believe, all of the concepts I will need for characterizing a particular type of discourse, a narrative type that is perhaps closest to that labeled by Norman Friedman as the selective omniscience type (Booth, 1965). Its matrix is that of impersonal language use, which means, then, that no representation is made of the author and no reference or appeal is made to the addressee, the reader. By virtue of its impersonal matrix, it is possible for phenomena that reflect a single individual's "point of view" to be associated with a character in the narrative; and, in general, a narrative of the type I have in mind can be segmented into parts such that some of these—the descriptive parts—present what the central character is doing or observing, others—the inner experience parts—present what the central character is thinking and feeling. These latter sections are presented in what I have been calling, after Jespersen (1924), "represented speech," and what others have called "narrated monologue," "erlebte Rede," "style indirect libre," and "semi-indirect discourse." I will take examples of this narrative type from the much-analyzed short story of James Joyce, "Eveline," and from a story by John Updike called "Solitaire."

There is in narrative of this type one character through whose psyche the events of the narrative are presented. The experiences in the story are his. The actions in the story are actions that he witnesses or engages in. Flashbacks are interpreted as his reminiscences. And, with the exception of tenses and pronouns, deictic and expressive elements in the text are to be contextualized from the point of view of this character at the point in the time line of the narrative at which the contextualizing form is found.

In "Eveline," following some reminiscences on Eveline's part about her past life, we read

(28)   "That was a long time ago; she and her brothers and sisters were all grown up; her mother was dead. Tizzie Dunn was dead, too, and the Waters had gone back to England. Everything changes. Now she was going to go away like the others, to leave her home."

Notice that in this passage the word *ago* is presented from the point of view of the time of her experiencing these reminiscences, not the time of Joyce's writing the story or the reader's reading it; and the same is true of the word *now* in the last sentence.

In conversational language, by contrast, there is a difference between *ago* and *earlier*. The one is used in phrases identifying some time point at a measured distance anterior to the time of speaking, the other taking as its reference point some time identified in the text. For conversational language there is a co-occurrence restriction against the combination of *ago* and the pluperfect tense, since the function of the pluperfect is to relate some time point or time period to some given past time reference point. Thus, of the sentences in (29), (29c) cannot be contextualized within normal conversational language:

(29)   a. *He lived there many years ago.*
        b. *He had lived there many years earlier.*
        c. *He had lived there many years ago.*

In the type of third-person narrative that I have been discussing, there is no such restriction, since the pluperfect could result from the backshifting appropriate to represented speech and the word *ago* could be chosen from the central character's point of view at the particular point in the narrative where this "memory" is introduced.

In the "Eveline" passage quoted above, the tense is in the simple past, except for the single sentence "Everything changes," which is in the present. Even though the general form of such narratives is impersonal, the use of the present tense here is in fact relevant to external contextualization; the thesis that "Everything changes" is taken to be true, not only of Eveline's beliefs at the time, but also of the world of the narrator and reader of the story. This will generally be true of generic or timeless statements in past tense narratives of this type.

Within the impersonal matrix, the represented speech is on the monologic model. This is known from the use of personal names in a context that fails to identify the people being named. Personal names, personal pronouns, and definite noun phrases in general, are only used in dialogic speech if the speaker has reason to believe that the addressee can interpret the identifying expression without any further information. Since the reader of the story has not been told who Tizzie Dunn was, or who the Waters were, this sample of discourse has to be understood as representing somebody talking to herself.

There are many other examples, too, in "Eveline," of references to things that Eveline knows about but the reader does not. One such example is

(30)   "She knew it was that that had given her the palpitations."

Nowhere in the story is the reader told anything about "the palpitations." But that fact supports the interpretation that the passage represents Eveline's thoughts; and it is only natural that she feels no need to explain these things to us!

The nondialogic nature of the narrative matrix accounts for the absence of certain lexical and grammatical features in this narrative style. For example, there is no way, while being faithful to this style, for the author to communicate to the reader things which the central character does not himself know. Thus, for example, we cannot expect to find in such a story a sentence like

(31)   *Unknown to our hero, two of his political enemies were hiding behind the drapes.*

For the same reasons, we cannot expect to find, except in the portions that represent the central character's thoughts, evaluations of actions or epistemic qualifications. Thus, sentences like

(32)   *This was probably the last time she would see him.*

(33)   *He had acted unwisely.*

have to be thought of as representing the central character's thoughts.

The opening paragraph of "Eveline," a descriptive portion of the story, is this:

(34)   "She sat at the window watching the evening invade the avenue. Her head was leaned against the window curtains and in her nostrils was the odour of dusty cretonne. She was tired."

It would have an absolutely jarring effect on the reader, I believe, if the last line of the paragraph were to read

(35)   *She was probably tired.*

With the word *probably* in there, either the story would be interpreted as being presented in something other than the narrated monologue style—in which case the reader would wonder why he had not been told from the start who "she" was—or the story would be taken as presenting somebody else's point of view, somebody who was observing Eveline at the beginning of the story—in which case the reader would soon find it puzzling that this observer knows so much about Eveline's inner psychological life.

Later on in the story Eveline looks around the room,

(36)   "wondering where on earth all the dust came from. Perhaps she would never see again those familiar objects from which she had never dreamed of being divided."

The expressive language of "where on earth" supports the view that we are here witnessing Eveline's own thoughts, and here, because of that, the word *perhaps* is not out of place. It is Eveline's *perhaps,* not the storyteller's.

There is more to say about what one might not find in narratives that take some character's point of view. Lexical items like *perhaps* or *unwise* have exclusively epistemic or judgmental meanings; but there are words which seem to have two functions, one as bearers of some descriptive notions, the other something epistemic or evaluative—one part relevant for internal contextualization, the other for external contextualization. One such word is the verb *misunderstand.* If I tell you that Smith misunderstood Jones, I am telling you that Smith had some opinion of Jones, and I am simultaneously telling you that Smith's opinion of Jones was mistaken. It would follow, then, that while a verb like *misunderstand* would be quite appropriate in the thought-representing part of the narrative type I am trying to characterize, it cannot appropriately occur in the descriptive portions. If you find a sentence like

(37)   *She read his note, but she misunderstood his intentions.*

you can be fairly sure that you are not reading a narrative of this type. On the other hand, should you find a sentence like

(38)   *She had read his note, but she had misunderstood his intentions.*

you may well be reading the thought-representing part of such a narrative.

Verbs designating psychological states or events can sometimes occur without any reference to the experiencing subject of these states of events. Where the experiencer is not mentioned in the actual surface sentence, it is generally understood, in conversational language, as being the SPEAKER of the sentence if the sentence is an assertion, or the ADDRESSEE if the sentence is a question. Thus, if I say

(39)   a. *She seemed angry.*
       b. *It was interesting.*
       c. *It tasted good.*

I am speaking about my own impressions; and if I say

(40)   a. *Did she seem angry?*
       b. *Was it interesting?*
       c. *Did it taste good?*

I am asking you about yours. On the other hand it is possible, of course, to mention the experiencer explicitly, as in

(41)   *She seemed to Harry to be angry.*

Now it happens that in narrative of the type that takes some central character's point of view, these same psychological verbs and adjectives can be used without any specification of the experiencer of the event or impression, but in every case the experiencer is taken as being the central character.

Consider a sentence like this one:

(42)   *He looked into her eyes. She seemed angry.*

There are two possible contextualizations of this passage. Either it is an example of dialogic language, and the speaker/witness is telling us his impressions, or it is a sample from the narrated monologue style and it is "his" impression that "she" is angry.

The first sentence in this sequence has him looking into her eyes, which allows us to believe that each is perceiving the other. That being so, it would also be possible to have, for the second sentence, *He seemed angry.* Thus:

(43)   *He looked into her eyes. He seemed angry.*

This passage, too, has two possible interpretations, including one in which both sentences are presented to us from "her" point of view. Further evidence for the correctness of this interpretation is related to the fact that a "point-of-view" narrative style can only represent one person's psyche at a time. Hence a sequence like the following one has to be interpreted as occurring in a sample of dialogic speech; it has to be taken as the speaker informing the addressee that he perceived both persons as angry:

(44)   *He looked into her eyes. He seemed angry, and so did she.*

I indicated earlier that instances of definite reference in narrated monologue passages are "definite" from the character's point of view and need
not meet the conditions for definite reference that characterize dialogic
speech. People and things known to the central character are represented
with pronouns, definite noun phrases, or personal names, whether the
reader has been told about them or not. This being so, the presence in this
type of narrative of an INDEFINITE noun phrase can have its own special
effect.

The first sentence in John Updike's "Solitaire" is this:

(45)   "The children were asleep and his wife had gone out to a meet-
        ing; she was like his father in caring about the community."

This, let me repeat, is the first sentence in the story. We are not told who
"he" is. "The children" are mentioned, but we have not been prepared to
know who they are. The sentence is in the simple past tense, though there
is no preceding context to identify the time being focused on. We assume
therefore, right away, that the passage represents somebody's inner experiences, in his own terms. In that case, quite properly, everything that he
knows about can be represented with definite descriptions, and the simple
past tense can be used to indicate the time during which he is having the
thoughts we are learning about, the pluperfect for indicating the time of
his memories.

We can assume, then, that if the central character knew what meeting
his wife had gone out to, the sentence would contain one more definite
article, and we would be reading that his wife had "gone to THE meeting."
By thus surprising the reader in that expectation, the author immediately
succeeds in giving the reader the impression that the wife's community
activities are not an important part of this man's life, and that he and his
wife do not communicate much about them. This impression is supported
by the rest of the story.

The tense in this kind of narrative is typically the simple past and is understood as that of the time of the central character's actions or impressions. Whereas in dialogic speech the use of the simple past requires the
establishment of some sort of reference time (*this morning, last year,
when the cat died, and then, etc.*), such indications are not necessary in
point-of-view narratives, because here the tenses are to be interpreted as
back-shifted versions of the tenses in some underlying monologue.

Sometimes, however, the past tense is used in a narrated monologue
under the usual conditions (as in first example from "Eveline"). A time
that is anterior to that of the narrative time-line can be specified, and the

events associated with that time can be expressed in the simple past, not necessarily the pluperfect. The pluperfect can be used to introduce a "flashback," but once the new time period has been introduced, the episodes of that anterior period can be represented in the simple past. Then, by using the pluperfect again, together with some time deictic word like *now* or *today*, the author can reorient the reader back to the main time line of the narrative.

In "Solitaire" the main events of the narrative are presented in the simple past, as expected. The central character then recalls some events in his childhood, these being introduced with a pluperfect form. Then there follows a series of memories about that period, all expressed in the simple past. And then, with the help of the word *now* the reader is brought back to the focal time with a paragraph that begins

(46)   "Now he realized that his mother had been disturbed in those days."

Some sequiturity judgments in a narrative depend on the understanding that the event or situations presented in successive sentences represent successive perceptions in the mind of the central character. Since the events are presented from the point of view of a unique observer, the description portion mentions events, not according to the order in which they occur, but in the order in which the observer might have observed them. There is thus nothing odd about a sentence like:

(47)   *The light went on. She was standing by the door.*

if it is a narrative. The sequence is taken as indicating the order of somebody's observations.

By virtue of this latter fact, it is sometimes the case that certain understandings about the position or "angle of vision" of the observer are revealed, not by specific semantic properties of individual sentences, but by virtue of the contextualization possibilities for the implied sequence of observations. Interesting possibilities exist in cases where both contextualizable words and observation-sequence requirements combine to give the intended interpretation.

Hemingway's story "The Killers," to use another much-discussed work, is not written in the narrated monologue style, but it is written from the point of view of a single observer. The first sentence of the story provides a good example of how inferences about the observation point can be drawn from a sentence quite independently of what would ordinarily be considered part of the meaning of the sentence.

The sentence is this:

(48)   ''The door of Henry's lunchroom opened and two men came in.''

Now one way to think about contextualizing for point of view is to imagine how one could most faithfully film the episode, seeking from the text information as to how the scene should be set up, how many actors will be needed, what they should be doing, where the camera should be located, and so on.

In the case of the Hemingway passage, it is clear that the camera should be inside the lunchroom, because of the use of the verb *come*. The scene, then, would have two men, they would open the door, and they would then enter the lunchroom; and the camera would be on the inside the whole time.

Suppose we try to separate out the role of the verb *come* in this contextualization process, and replace it with the verb *go*:

(49)   *The door of Henry's lunchroom opened and two men went in.*

Because of the verb *go* in this version of the sentence, it is clear that the camera must this time be outside the lunchroom, not inside. But that is not the only change we must make. With the observer on the outside, we must now imagine how it is that an observer on the outside would first notice the door open and then notice the two men went in. This time it is more natural to believe that somebody on the inside opened the door, not one of the two men. From the fact that it is ''two men'' rather than ''the two men'' we must imagine either a scene where there are more than two men outside the lunchroom at the beginning, with just two of the assembled men entering after the door opens, or a scene (possibly a close-up of the door) in which the men are not in view at the beginning but come into view after the door opens.

Suppose now that we construct a sentence which more or less gives the outside view of the first version. Such a sentence might be:

(50)   *Two men approached Henry's lunchroom, opened the door, and*
          went in.

This time the scene can be enacted in the same way as for the sentence Hemingway originally wrote, except that the camera has to be outside. But now, just for fun, let us see what would happen if we modified that sentence by replacing its *go* by *come:*

(51)   *Two men approached Henry's lunchroom, opened the door, and*
          came in.

This time, because of *came* we have to put the camera on the inside, but we must also make it possible for the events to be observed in the order in which they are mentioned; and for that it would be most natural to provide the lunchroom with a window or a glass door. The acceptability of the sentence as "sequituritous" requires, in other words, a context in which, from the vantage point required by the lexical material in the sentence, the events could be observed in the order determined by the clauses which describe them.

9. CONCLUDING REMARKS

I have been proposing, in a somewhat rambling way, that samples of discourse that differ in significant pragmatic ways will be structured according to different sets of syntactic and semantic principles, these in turn largely explainable by an appeal to the pragmatic conditions. One of these types of discourse is the one in which the creator of the discourse is telling a story, in which no linguistic forms are chosen by which the author establishes or recognizes contact with the reader, and in which the story is presented from the point of view of some character in the story, as that character's actions, observations, and thoughts. I have tried to suggest that such texts are governed by special privileges and special constraints, and that these concern the use of pronouns, personal names, definite noun phrases, tenses, deictic words, sequencing rules, and the use of epistemic, evaluative, and psychological-experience lexical items.

I would argue that the most straightforward principles of pragmatics or contextualization are to be found in the nature of conversational language, the language of people who are looking at each other or who are otherwise sharing some current experience and in which the hearer processes instantaneously what the speaker says. I believe that once the syntax, semantics, and pragmatics of these basic types of discourse have been mastered, other types of discourse can be usefully described in terms of their deviation from such a base. Heuristically, I believe that many facts about the nature of the basic pragmatic conditions can be discovered by examining deviating types of discourse and paying close attention to those of their properties that stand out. The study of literary conventions can thus lead to greater understanding of the basic workings of language.

ACKNOWLEDGEMENTS

I have profited in the preparation of this chapter from conversations with Shige-Yuki Kuroda and Julian Boyd. Julian Boyd first drew my attention to the force of the passage from "The Killers."

REFERENCES

Booth, W. (1965). *The Rhetoric of Fiction*. Chicago: University of Chicago Press.
Cohn, D. (1966). Narrated monologue. *Comparative Literature, 2*, 97–112.
Fillmore, C. J. (1972). How to know whether you're coming or going. In K. Hyldgaard-Jensen (Ed.), *Linguistik 1971*. Frankfurt: Athenäum. Pp. 369–379.
Fillmore, C. J. (1973). A grammarian looks to socio-linguistics. *Georgetown University Monographs on Languages and Linguistics Number 25*. Pp. 273–287.
Grimes, J. E. (1972). *The Thread of Discourse*. Ithaca: Cornell University Press.
Jesperson, J. O. (1924). *The Philosophy of Grammar*. (Reprinted by the Norton Library, 1965.)
Longacre, R. E. (1968). *Discourse, Paragraph and Sentence Structure in Selected Philippine Languages*. Summer Institute of Linguistics.
Morris, C. W. (1938). Foundations of the theory of signs. *International Encyclopedia of Unified Science*, Vol. 1, No. 2. Chicago: University of Chicago Press.
Smith, C. S. (1971). Sentences in discourse: An analysis of a discourse by Bertrand Russell. *Journal of Linguistics, 7*, 213–236.
Stratton, C. R. (1971). *Linguistics, Rhetoric, and Discourse Structure*. Unpublished doctoral dissertation, University of Wisconsin.
van Dijk, T. A. (1972). *Some Aspects of Text Grammars*. The Hague: Mouton.

Pragmatics, Grammar, and Discourse

Georgia M. Green and Jerry L. Morgan

1. THE QUESTIONS

This chapter is a programmatic discussion of some questions of discourse pragmatics. In this first section we outline what seem to us the basic questions for such a theory. In the second section we discuss a few previous attempts at answers to these questions, and in the third we propose a more promising alternative. In the fourth we discuss some implications. Our main point is that most of the work of accounting for discourse comprehension is to be done not by a linguistic theory of discourse, but by a general theory of common-sense inference, plus certain kinds of language-related knowledge distinct from linguistic competence as presently conceived. The thrust of our program is not to replace the standard view of linguistic competence, nor to subsume it under some more general set of abilities; rather, it is to suggest that the role of linguistic competence in discourse comprehension is smaller than one might suppose.

The first problem is to make clear what the goals of a theory of discourse are—what is the theory to account for? We take it to be obvious that the goal is to provide at least a partial account of the human ability to construct and understand connected discourse of various kinds, both oral

167

ISBN 0-12-179660-4

and written. We shall lump all this together under the term "text," leaving open the question whether different types of texts require radically different treatments.

Given this vaguely stated goal, of providing at least a partial account of the ability to construct and understand texts, we see certain parallels with Chomsky's position on linguistic theory. In particular, we assume that the business of an adequate theory is to provide an account of the mental reality underlying observable behavior, rather than the direct prediction of behavior, on two counts: First, various factors involving memory and other matters undoubtedly intervene as "errors" to make the relation between competence and behavior indirect. Second, we reject as a requirement that the theory predict text production, in the sense of predicting who will produce what texts under what circumstances, since conscious choice is involved in such production; and, even setting aside matters of free will and conscious choice, the number of variables involved is obviously so immense, and their interaction so complex (cf. Green, to appear), as to make such prediction out of the question.

Our goal, then, is to work toward a theory of interpretation, partially on the grounds that how one understands a text is not a matter of conscious choice; though one can certainly decide to APPEAR to understand in a certain way, the interpretation process is clearly not under conscious control.[1] Thus we aim at a theory of interpretive competence, not of production, though it should be obvious that production will be heavily influenced by the speaker/writer's assessment of how an utterance is likely to be interpreted by a real or hypothetical audience.

What, then, is "interpretation"? We mean by this term the process of arriving at an "understanding" of a text. Unfortunately, it is beyond our competence to say more about the nature of "understanding" than is intuitively implied by the colloquial sense of the word, but we can try to point out some of the things involved.

The basic idea is this: that it makes a certain amount of sense to speak of the "meaning" (in some loose sense of this very vague word) of an entire text. To somehow reconstruct or recover this meaning from the text is to arrive at an understanding. But both these terms—MEANING and UNDERSTANDING—are susceptible of several interpretations. To narrow things down, we shall have to discuss some of the things one might have in mind in speaking of the meaning of a text. (In this section we beg the indulgence of semantically sophisticated readers.)

For illustration's sake, we will examine a single sentence; but at least

---

[1] Apparent counterexamples will, we think, turn out to be cases of consciously choosing among multiple interpretations unconsciously arrived at (e.g., deciding to "put the most charitable interpretation" on a passage) or similar kinds of meta-assessments.

some of the separate senses of "meaning" we discuss can be extended to longer passages.

An example like (1) might be said to have a number of different kinds of meaning.

(1)   *He is allergic to chocolate.*

The most obvious kind of meaning we might attribute to (1) has to do with its PROPOSITIONAL CONTENT—roughly, the conditions under which it is true. It is clearly a requirement for any theory of meaning, whether it is based on "truth conditions" or not, that some direct or indirect account be given of how language users are able to know what the world would be like if a given declarative sentence were true, a given imperative obeyed, and so on. We shall refer to this kind of meaning as "propositional content". It is not clear to us whether the notion "propositional content" can be usefully applied to an entire text, apart from the logical sum of the propositional contents of the constituent sentences.

A second, logically prior kind of meaning one might attribute to (1) is the contribution of the meaning conventions of English to the determination of the propositional content of (1). The propositional content of an utterance is not always identical to the meanings of the parts plus rules of composition. Notice that the conventions of English associated with the words in (1) do not determine a referent for the pronoun *he*; that information must be inferred by the hearer in some way influenced by context. Thus the conventional meanings of the words in (1), taken together with the semantic rules of combination, do not fully determine the propositional content associated with a particular use of (1). Still, it makes sense to say that (1) has "meaning" out of context, in the sense that the conventional meanings of the words, together with the semantic rules of composition, restrict in certain ways the range of possible propositional contents that can be assigned to a particular utterance of (1). There is something about the meaning of *he*, for example, that restricts its possible referents to males, though it does not uniquely determine a referent. We shall refer to this kind of meaning as LINGUISTIC MEANING, as distinct from but contributing to propositional content. In some cases, especially where indexical terms are involved, linguistic meaning underdetermines propositional content; in other cases, propositional content may be entirely determined by linguistic meaning.

So far, then, we have isolated two kinds of things one might want to call "meanings": the propositional content associated with a particular use of a sentence, and "linguistic meaning"—the contribution of the forms themselves (via their associated meaning conventions and rules of composition) to the determination of propositional content.

A third is meaning in the sense of the familiar notion SPEECH ACT—a specification of what act is performed in uttering (1). Linguistic meaning and propositional content play a role here; saying (1) clearly does not count as making the same assertion as saying its negation in the same context. It is not clear to us whether speech act notions can be extended to entire texts, apart from the aggregate of the speech acts associated with its separate sentences; possibly they can.

A fourth thing one might take to be a meaning of (1) is its IMPLICATURES, in the sense of Grice (1975). For example, if we say (1) as a reply to the question

(2)   *May we give your child a piece of this chocolate cake?*

we will likely be understood as having given a negative answer, or at least of having done something whose ultimate effect is the same as if we had given a negative answer, though we think it is obvious that we could not reasonably attribute the negative character directly to either the linguistic meaning or the propositional content of (1). Rather, as in Grice's program, this kind of meaning is derived from inferences about the speaker's intentions in uttering (1) in this context.

A fifth kind of meaning we have seen attributed to sentences and texts is the sort of subtle literary interpretation one finds in the work of literary critics. It is obvious that this kind of meaning attaches to a sentence or text (in part) by virtue of (not instead of!) its meaning in the four other senses we have discussed here. Further, critical analysis can also involve inferences about a text that go far beyond what the author intended; this seems to us an entirely different matter from the interpretive abilities involved in simple comprehension of a text. We therefore will not consider this kind of meaning here. On similar grounds we exclude from consideration other kinds of inferences that can be made that are not (or not clearly) part of the author's intention. For example, if someone says (3) to us,

(3)   *Nobody discussed the difference between meaning and reference before the 1970s.*

we may reasonably infer that the speaker has not read much philosophy. Likewise, if our 3-year-old child says (4) we may conclude that we left the water running in the bathtub, even though we know that the child is unaware of the fact.

(4)   *Water is coming out of the ceiling.*

In cases like these, the inference that we can reasonably make is not part of the meaning of the sentence or utterance, in any sense of the word ''meaning'' that interests us here. Such cases are ''meaning'' in the same sense that falling leaves mean winter is coming (cf. Grice, 1957). We do not mean to downplay the potential importance of inferences BASED on the understanding of a text; a sophisticated reader may be able to put two and two together to derive far more information from a news report than a reporter had in mind in writing it, for example. But we think the simpler, bare-facts understanding of discourse is logically prior to such sophisticated interpretation, and any account of the latter therefore presupposes an account of the former. We have in mind the kind of understanding that allows one to successfully carry out a set of instructions, to know what an object looks like from a clear description of it, to "get the facts" from a newspaper report, and so on. A primary goal of a discourse theory, then, is to provide an account of how these four kinds of meaning—linguistic meaning, propositional content, speech act properties, and intended inferences like indirect speech acts—combine to explain at least part of discourse understanding.

A secondary goal is to treat a couple of subsidiary notions whose importance for discourse has often been pointed out: "coherence" and "text structure." In fact in some approaches to discourse these factors are taken as indications of the need to expand linguistic theory to account for discourse. This position is widespread enough that it is worthwhile to argue against it. (For a fuller discussion see Morgan and Sellner, 1980.)

2. SOME PREVIOUS ATTEMPTS

There are two approaches to discourse theory that seem to us particularly misguided. The first is the search for formal linguistic properties that constitute or contribute to coherence and/or text structure. The second is the attempt to construct "linguistic" theories of discourse—theories whose unified domain extends from morphemes to entire texts, designed to generate not just sentences, but discourses. The first approach is exemplified to some extent in the work of Halliday and Hasan (1976), the second is especially clear in the work of van Dijk (1972, 1977).

It is not entirely surprising that such approaches should be taken, especially by linguists. The study of linguistic form is the linguist's primary pursuit, and it is natural that linguists would look first to formal properties for explanations of language-related phenomena, as Halliday and Hasan seem to do in their study of "cohesion." Furthermore, the observation of parallels between sentence and discoure properties has a certain initial appeal. Preliminary consideration of problems of coherence, and of text structure, easily might lead one to conclude that there are important similarities between these two aspects of discourse analysis and more familiar phenomena of sentence syntax. One might even take the parallelism as an indication that it is the same system at work in both cases. It has become a truism that people have intutions of well-formedness about texts, as well as about sentences. Some linguists have gone so far as to speak of the "ungrammaticality" of texts (e.g., van Dijk, 1972). Nonetheless, we think the parallels are only superficial, and disappear on closer inspection.

Halliday and Hasan (1976) propose the property of cohesion as a partial determinant of "texture": "If a passage of English containing more than one sentence is perceived as a text, there will be certain linguistic features present in that passage which can be identified as contributing to its total unity and giving it texture [p. 2]." By texture they seem to mean what other linguists refer to as "coherence": "The concept of TEXTURE is entirely appropriate to express the property of 'being a text'. A text has texture, and this is what distinguishes it from something that is not a text [p. 2]." At one point, they characterize cohesion as a matter not of form but of interpretation, when they say that cohesion "occurs when the IN-TERPRETATION of some element in the discourse is dependent on that of another [p. 4]." But their characterizations are not consistent. Elsewhere they say cohesion is independent of meaning:

> one can construct passages which seem to hang together in the situational-semantic sense, but fail because they lack cohesion . . . [p. 23].

> Cohesion does not concern what a text means; it concerns how the text is constructed as a semantic edifice [p. 26].

And in other places, it is characterized as a matter of linguistic form, or of relations between forms:

> where there is continuity of subject-matter within a text, as we typically find it, the texture is not necessarily the result of this; [an example text on the history of mathematics] is about mathematics, but cohesion is provided, especially in the last sentence, more by the lexical patterns of *complicated . . . difficult . . . easy* and *greater time . . . long . . . short* than by any linking of specifically mathematical concepts [p. 25].

They appear here to claim that coherence of content is not sufficient to make a text coherent. The additional linguistic property of cohesion must be present. This is a striking claim, important if true. One might assume that coherence is a matter of content, with, of course, consequences in the linguistic form of the text. The choice of form is determined by content; if one wants to talk about apples, one is likely to use the word *apples*. In a discussion of mathematics, words referring to mathematical concepts are likely to occur, as well as pronouns when the referent will be clear from context. But it would be a mistake to take the occurrence of a series of words for mathematical concepts as the SOURCE of coherence. One can easily construct gibberish texts which contain such "lexical patterns." The lexical patterns are a symptom, not a cause, of coherence. Halliday and Hasan's examples are misanalyzed in this way, taking matters of form as cause, rather than symptom, of coherence. And it is clear they intend cohesion as a matter of form in such cases of "lexical cohesion": "It is not by virtue of any referential relation that there is a cohesive force set up between two occurrences of a lexical item; rather, the cohesion exists as a direct relation between the forms themselves . . . [p. 284]." It would be an important discovery if one could show that aspects of linguistic form affected coherence, independently of their meanings. But Halliday and Hasan provide no clear argument for this position; there is no reason to believe that coherence has anything to do with linguistic form per se.

A more radical position is found in the work of van Dijk (1972, 1977), who attempts to lay out a LINGUISTIC theory of discourse, arguing for the replacement of standard kinds of grammatical theory by a theory of "text grammar," which generates texts and assigns them a structural description. Van Dijk has clearly mistaken matters of content coherence for matters of linguistic form. He is quite serious about extending the notion "grammaticality" to texts: "We will require of any adequate grammar to predict which combinations (pairs, triples, . . . , n-tuples) of sentences are grammatical and which are less grammatical or fully ungrammatical . . . [1972, p. 41]." But examination of his examples shows that the notion "grammaticality" is misapplied as a treatment of coherence. For example, of the following "ungrammatical text": "The old woman was buried in her native village. She is dying of pneumonia [p. 82]," he says that it is "ungrammatical to predicate something about an individual of which the [actual] nonexistence has been asserted [1972, p. 83]." But surely this kind of "ungrammaticality" is not in the domain of any reasonable theory of discourse. What is wrong with the "text" above is that it reports events that AS EVENTS are very bizarre. Indeed the text could be just a true report of strange goings-on. The fact that they are strange is a matter of our beliefs about the world, not of textual coherence. By van Dijk's approach, any coherent accurate report of bizarre occurrences would count as ungrammatical. The proper business of a discourse theory is not to say what events are strange, but (among other things) to say why a given text is or is not successful as a report of a given chain of events.

In his second (1977) book, van Dijk seems to have abandoned the notion of text grammaticality, but he continues to speak of the "acceptability" of texts as something to be accounted for by discourse theory, repeating the error of his first book. For example, he speaks of the acceptability of (5a) as a continuation of (5b).

(5) a. (. . .) she drank her inkwell (. . .)   [p. 99]
(5) b. Clare Russell came into the *Clarion* office on the following morn-
        ing, feeling tired and depressed. She went straight to her room,
        took off her hat, touched her face with a powder puff and sat down
        at her desk.
           Her mail was spread out neatly, her blotter was snowy and her
        inkwell was filled. But she didn't feel like work (. . .)   [p.
        98].

But in a situation like this wherein Clare Russell DID in fact drink her inkwell, we would be faced with a curious consequence: a true state of affairs
which it was impossible to report in an acceptable text. Surely such a theory is to be rejected out of hand.

As an account of text structure (and simultaneously, as a kind of semantic representation of the text), van Dijk offers the notion "macro-
structure." Insofar as any sense can be made of them, macro-structures
appear to be hierarchically structured layers of progressively less specific
abstracts of the subparts of the text. But van Dijk offers no formally or
informally developed system for assigning structures to texts. Moreover,
in spite of his claim that "text grammar is the only adequate framework
for the description of sentence structure [1972, p. v]" he does not provide
any analyses of sentential syntactic properties. Clearly macro-structures
have no resemblance to the kind of structures necessary for describing the
syntactic structures of sentences. Consequently, van Dijk's work is not to
be taken seriously as a demonstration of any nontrivial similarity between
text structure and sentence structure.

It seems to us that the only approach to discourse problems like comprehension, coherence, and text structure, is one that is based on a simple
but pervasive human ability: the ability to interpret the actions of other
people by forming complex hypotheses about goals, plans, and intentions
that underlie acts. One might plausibly claim that this kind of interpretation is the most pervasive mental activity of human beings. It seems to us
that most of the problems discourse theories might address are really to
be accounted for in such terms, rather than by specifically linguistic
mechanisms. Comprehension obviously depends heavily on this interpretive ability. We suggest that coherence and text structure are to be explained in these terms as well.

Consider the problem of coherence. We can exclude from consideration those texts that are perfectly comprehensible but "incoherent" because they describe bizarre happenings, since their supposed "incoher-

ence," we have argued, is not something to be accounted for in a theory of discourse. That leaves us, then, with a second kind of incoherence: a text that is incomprehensible to some degree, though each of its sentences is perfectly well-formed. We believe the proper treatment of this kind of incoherence is to be found in matters of author's goals, plans, and intentions, and the degree to which it is possible to form consistent hypotheses about them from reading/hearing the text. Similarly with text structure: It is clear, we believe, that the mind imposes structure on a text, but it is a mistake to conclude that this structure is an extension of sentence syntax or anything like it. Insofar as the text is understood, the mind imposes structure on the events or concepts related by the text, just as the mind imposes structure on events directly observed and thoughts directly experienced. This kind of structure is not the business of discourse theory. But there is a structure to the ORGANIZATION of a text, probably (though the facts are not yet clear) hierarchical. It seems to us that this kind of structure is best analyzed as the formation of hypotheses about the author's goal structures—the relation of goal to subgoal, and so on—in constructing the text.

3. MORE PROMISING DIRECTIONS

It seems to us that acts, intentions, and goals are the backbone of a theory of discourse. As Austin (1962) noted, at least five kinds of acts are simultneously involved in uttering a sentence, all of them goal-directed. First there is the phonetic act of producing the articulation of tongue, jaw, diaphragm, larynx, *etc.* that results in connected speech sounds. The presumable goal of this phonetic act is to produce an acoustic object that the addressee will recognize as belonging to a language. Simultaneously, and by means of the phonetic act, the speaker performs the act of producing a concatenated sequence of tokens of forms belonging to a language (Austin's "phatic act"), presumably with the intention that it be recognized as connected discourse intended to convey some attitude. In the service of this goal, the speaker intends these forms to be taken as referring to individuals, actions, events, *etc.* in some real or imaginary world, that is, intends them to be taken as having sense, and referring according to the conventions of the language and culture of a community to which the addressee belongs (Austin's "rhetic act"). Fourth, the speaker intends his actions in producing each sentence of his discourse to be taken as executing an illocutionary act of some sort which will give his utterance of the sentence an illocutionary force. That is, he intends that the addressee will assume that she is intended to take the propositional content of the utterance in particular way (e.g., as a promise, or a prediction, or a question). Finally, from the assumption that speech is a rational act, executed for a purpose, we may infer that the speaker had a reason for making the particular utterance at the time he did to the addressee he chose.

Discourse production is thus the pursuit of goals by performing acts of various sorts. These acts and their goals are hierarchically related; the resulting structure might be called a PLAN. To assign a text structure to a discourse is at least in part to infer such a plan.

In addition to the plan's being complex, its implementation is complex in that, at any given point in the implementation, various subparts of the plan are being carried out simultaneously. The implementation of plans is further complicated by the fact that the process of evaluating choices among possible acts of a given sort may generate new goals (or necessitate changes in the original goal), so the plan may be constantly changing, as well as being implemented simultaneously on several levels. Evidence of making such choices, especially among various possible phatic and rhetic acts, can be seen whenever a speaker hesitates or backtracks to rephrase part of an utterance.

The basic datum of comprehension is not the word or the sentence (or even the paragraph or whole discourse), but the observation that "So-and-so has just said 'Thus-and-such.'" The interpretation of this datum consists in inferring the intentions and goals of the speaker in saying "Thus-and-such," and saying it in exactly the way he said it (Grice 1957, 1975). Relevance and coherence, far from being linguistic properties of texts, are functions of the relation between observed acts on the one hand, and goals, intentions, purposes, and motivations inferred or inferable by the hearer, on the other.

The acts that are relevant to interpretation of intention may include not only speech acts of diverse types—ranging from the phatic act and the classical kinds of illocutionary acts and acts of referring (Searle, 1969), to acts of mentioning, sequencing, intoning, pausing, describing, failing to mention, implicating, *etc.*—but also acts that do not involve speech at all (e.g., gesturing, glancing, staring, winking).

The hearer's task in comprehension is to form a model of the speaker's plan that is consistent with the speaker's acts and the addressee's beliefs about the speaker and the rest of the world. In actual performance, the hearer's hypothesis may change constantly in the course of arriving at an interpretation.

Comprehension of discourse or text thus involves not only knowledge of language, but also knowledge necessary for the use of language. We take the latter category to include at least (*a*) use properties of expressions that cannot be predicted from their literal meanings (cf. Morgan, 1978); (b) knowledge of conversational and literary conventions (e.g., the convention of beginning a narrative in media res, narrator's presence, and author's, narrator's, and characters' points of view); and (c) encyclopedic knowledge about the world, such as knowledge of individuals and kinds, and the consequences of events, and knowledge about human nature and likely motives. In addition, comprehension requires the ability to make inferences from conjunctions of facts of these various types.

Because the link between intentional acts—even speech acts—and their interpretation is so underdetermined by the objective data (that So-and-so has said "Thus-and-such"), and so dependent on the interpreter's beliefs about the actor's goals and motives, it should not surprise us that it is a tenuous one, and that there will be many a slip twixt cup and lip.

It is for this reason that we have chosen to say that a hearer INTERPRETS an utterance or discourse or text, rather than "understands" it. To attempt to describe the means by which a hearer "understood" an utterance might imply a view of discourse in which communication is the simple encoding and decoding of "thoughts" or "meanings" in linguistic packages: A speaker packs thought into words or larger expressions and sends them to be unpacked, unchanged, by the addressee, who then "has" them. This view of discourse and communication has been criticized as not only romantic and simplistic, but pernicious, and we find the arguments (Reddy, 1979) convincing that, speaking metaphorically, what is sent in communication is closer to something on the order of a near-cryptic blueprint for the creation of a model of something inalienably possessed by the speaker, and which the hearer must use all of the linguisitic, real-world, and cultural knowledge at her disposal to interpret.

4. SOME IMPLICATIONS

The view of discourse that we have sketched has a number of implications regarding the nature of the competence required to interpret discourse. For one thing, it implies that it is not a monolithic competence with a single hierarchical organization. Rather, a variety of kinds of knowledge and abilities interact to enable discourse production and interpretation. This should hardly be a surprising conclusion. It amounts to claiming that the whole mind is deployed in producing and understanding discourse. It runs counter to common sense, we think, to claim that such mental activities are the product of "strictly linguistic" processing mechanisms.

It is not our intention to provide a MODEL of communication, or even of speech production or comprehension, but only to indicate some of the relationships among the things that such models will have to include.

In addition to the sine qua non of knowledge of language, language users must employ their knowledge of conventions about the use of the language and about communication, their general powers of observation, memory and imagination, and a number of different kinds of knowledge of the world.

By KNOWLEDGE OF LANGUAGE we mean just the kind of knowledge that could distinguish speakers of English from speakers of Tagalog or Aleut, by virtue of their being speakers of that language (excluding, therefore, differences that arise due to their being members of the culture of that language community). Knowledge of language is roughly the same thing as GRAMMAR in the traditional sense (phonology, morphology, and syntax), plus a compositional semantics of some kind. Universal properties of grammar do not enter into such a characterization insofar as they are either (a) innate, and not learned, and thus, not knowledge; or (b) functional, and evolved to meet communicative needs, and hence only fortuitously universal; if societal needs changed somewhere, they might cease to be universal, and come to be potential distinguishing properties.

We use KNOWLEDGE ABOUT LANGUAGE and KNOWLEDGE ABOUT THE USE OF LANGUAGE to refer to principles and societal conventions (Morgan, 1978) for using or exploiting the forms provided by the grammar of the language to achieve goals. This knowlege is separate from knowledge of language per se, and from knowledge about communicating, but all are required equally for using language effectively. Although knowledge about language might have some culture-specific details, for example, what counts as polite, it does not have language-specific details, in the sense of details that would constitute facts about the language (as opposed to facts about the culture of the people who use the language). Mature speakers of a language will vary much more in their pragmatic competence than in their linguistic competence. Some speakers may be brilliant as it, others barely competent. In this respect there is a striking difference between the relative uniformity of linguistic competence and the wide variation in pragmatic competence. And, unlike the case with the acquisition of linguistic competence, which is pretty much complete by age six, acquisition of knowledge about the use of language and about communication may continue well past middle-age.

As an example of knowledge of the use of language, the language user knows what pragmatic conditions are required for the use of particular syntactic constructions. Among the pragmatic conditions we have in mind are ones that relate to assumptions about discourse topic [affecting, e.g.,

Passive, Cleft (Prince, 1978), Inversion (Green, 1980)], to attitudes about consequences to participants [affecting, e.g., Passive (Davison, 1980)], to beliefs about participants and their relationships [affecting, e.g., Passive (Lakoff, 1971), Raising (Postal, 1974), Dative Movement (Green, 1974)], etc.

Naturally, to make use of this knowledge, the language user also requires knowledge of the history of the discourse (e.g., who has been referred to before, what the current topic is), as well as knowledge of the subject of the discourse, of individuals and kinds, of the Cooperative Principle (Grice, 1975), and of the addressee's model of the world, in order to determine whether such pragmatic conditions are met; for example, to determine whether a subject-cleft like *It was John that ran out of the room* will be appropriate.

We can give several examples of what we mean by KNOWLEDGE OF (conventions of) COMMUNICATING. First and foremost, we take this expression to include assumption of what Grice (1975) has called the Cooperative Principle: "Make your conversational contribution such as is required, at the stage at which it occurs, by the accepted purpose . . . of the [enterprise] in which you are engaged [p. 45]" and the corollaries Grice (1975) phrased as maxims (Grice 1975, pp. 45–46):

1. Quantity: make your contribution as informative as is required. Do not make your contribution more informative than is required.
2. Quality: Do not say what you believe to be false. Do not say that for which you lack adequate evidence.
3. Relation: Be relevant.
4. Manner: Avoid obscurity of expression. Avoid ambiguity. Be brief. Be orderly.

This kind of pragmatic competence must also include knowledge of the highly complex strategies for choosing referring expressions, which involve not only principles for the use of the definite as opposed to the indefinite article, and how to exploit probable inferences of presupposition, but also principles for using the same term, in conjunction with the Cooperative Principle, to designate any of a number of entities of quite different kinds according to what Nunberg (1978) calls "referring functions." These functions are principles according to which the phrase *the newspaper,* for example, might be used to refer to a copy of the *San Francisco Chronicle,* an edition of the *San Francisco Chronicle,* the corporation that publishes the *San Francisco Chronicle,* or, especially to be noted, some person who is believed to be mutually believed to have, or have wanted, or have had some previously mentioned newspaper (on any of the interpretations mentioned). Even the referring possibilities of proper names can be extended according to such referring functions; the phrase *the San Francisco Chronicle* could be used in exactly the same ways we have said *the newspaper* can.

The knowledge of one's interlocutor that is required includes not only the same kinds of knowledge that the speaker has about OTHER individuals, such as personal history, attitudes, affiliations, kinship ties, and the like, but also estimates of her knowledge of the world, including what she can observe at the time of the speech act, and her relevant beliefs. It also includes beliefs about her view of her role in the ongoing conversation, her model of the speaker's model of the world, and beliefs about her goals and plans for the ongoing discourse. Finally, it includes beliefs about her reasoning ability—in particular about the likelihood of her having correctly interpreted acts of the speaker earlier in the discourse.

We conclude with an aside on the domain of linguistics. We have made a distinction between knowledge of language—"linguistic competence," more or less—and other kinds of knowledge and abilities (of quite general scope) that we have claimed are involved in discourse interpretation and production, with the suggestion that knowledge of language plays a relatively small (though indispensable) part. In our recent experience, a very frequent question in informal discussions of matters of the second category is, "Is this linguistics?" Most often the question betrays a parochial concern for professional, rather than intellectual, matters. But it might be charitably interpreted as questioning whether linguists can safely IGNORE the "nonlinguistic" part of the picture. We think they cannot. Nature does not provide an a priori classification of language-related phenomena into those that are to be explained by theories of linguistic competence and those to be explained by more general theories. In fact, it has been argued that a given phenomenon can change in time from a matter of pragmatics to a matter of grammar (see Morgan, 1978 for fuller discussion). Then the theoretical linguist, necessarily interested in determining the domain of linguistic competence, must be aware of what other kinds of nonlinguistic explanations might be used to explain apparently linguistic (or unclassifiable) phenomena. The result of an increase in sophistication in such matters should result in a clarification, perhaps even a narrowing, of the domain of theories of linguistic competence. The theoretical linguist can ignore such matters entirely only at the peril of constructing bloated linguistic theories to account for nonlinguistic problems.

REFERENCES

Austin, J. L. (1962). *How to Do Things with Words*. Cambridge, Mass.: Harvard University Press.
Chomsky, N. (1979). *Rules and Representations*. New York: Columbia University Press.

Davison, A. (1980). Peculiar passives. *Language*, **56**, 42–66.

Green, G. M. (1974). *Semantics and Syntactic Regularity*. Bloomington: Indiana University Press.

Green, G. M. (1980). Some wherefores of English inversions. *Language*, **56**, 582–601.

Green, G. M. (To appear). Linguistics and the pragmatics of language use. In R. Buhr, (Ed.), *Neurolinguistics and Cognition*. New York: Academic Press.

Grice, H. P. (1957). Meaning. *Philosophical Review*, **66**, 377–388.

Grice, H. P. (1975). Logic and conversation. In P. Cole and J. Morgan (Eds.), *Syntax and Semantics 3: Speech Acts*. New York: Academic Press. Pp. 41–58.

Halliday, M. A. K., and Hasan, R. (1976). *Cohesion in English*. London: Longman.

Lakoff, R. (1971). Passive resistance. In *Papers from the Sixth Regional Meeting of the Chicago Linguistic Society*. Department of Linguistics, University of Chicago. Pp. 149–162.

Morgan, J. (1978). Two kinds of convention in indirect speech acts. In P. Cole (Ed.), *Syntax and Semantics 9: Pragmatics*. New York: Academic Press. Pp. 261–280.

Morgan, J., and Sellner, M. (1980). Discourse and linguistic theory. In R. C. Spiro *et al.* (Eds.), *Theoretical Issues in the Study of Reading*. Hillsdale, N.J. Lawrence Erlbaum Associates. Pp. 165–200.

Nunberg, G. (1978). *The Pragmatics of Reference*. Unpublished doctoral dissertation, CUNY.

Postal, P. (1974). *On Raising*. Cambridge, Mass: MIT Press.

Prince, E. (1978). A comparison of WH-clefts and it-clefts in discourse. *Language*, **54**, 883–906.

Reddy, M. (1979). The conduit metaphor. In A. Ortony (Ed.), *Metaphor and Thought*. Cambridge University Press. Pp. 284–324.

Searle, J. (1969). *Speech Acts*. Cambridge: Cambridge University Press.

van Dijk, T. (1972). *Some Aspects of Text Grammars*. The Hague: Mouton.

van Dijk, T. (1977). *Text and Context: Explorations in the Semantics and Pragmatics of Discourse*. London: Longman.

Presupposition and Conversational Implicature[1]

Paul Grice

I want in this chapter to consider, from a certain point of view, whether the theory of descriptions could, despite certain familiar objections, be accepted as an account of *the* phrases, and whether the kind of linguistic phenomena that prompted the resort to the theory of presupposition as a special sort of logical relation (with all the ramifications which that idea would involve) could be dealt with in some other way. One might consider three objections which have at one time or another been advanced by this or that philosopher.

The first is the kind of objection that primarily prompted Strawson's (1950) revolt against the theory of descriptions (Russell, 1905), namely, that when one is asked such a question as whether the king of France is, or is not, bald, one does not feel inclined to give an answer; one does not feel very much inclined to say either that it is true that he is bald or that it is false that he is bald, but rather to say things like *The question doesn't arise* or *He neither is nor isn't bald,* etc. There is, indeed, something unnatural

[1] The material of this chapter was originally delivered as a lecture to the University of Illinois at Urbana in 1970; it has since then been somewhat revised and expanded, but not substantially altered. Its appearance here is intended as a tribute to the work, in this and other philosophical domains, of my friend, former pupil and former Oxford colleague and collaborator, Sir Peter Strawson.

RADICAL PRAGMATICS   ISBN 0-12-179660-4

about assigning a truth-value, as far as ordinary discourse is concerned, to statements made by means of sentences containing vacuous descriptions.

The second objection was also made by Strawson, namely, that, if you take an ordinary conversational remark, such as *The table is covered with butter,* it seems a somewhat unacceptable translation to offer in its stead, *There exists one and only one table and anything which is a table is covered with butter.* To make this kind of remark is not to be committed, as seems to be suggested by the Russellian account, to the existence of a unique object corresponding to a phrase, *the so-and-so;* to suggest that one is so committed is quite unjustified.

The third objection (voiced by Searle, among others) is that one gets into trouble with the Russellian theory where one considers moods other than the indicative. To say, for example, *Give these flowers to your wife* does not look as if it translates into something like *Make it the case that there is one and only one person who is married to you, who is female, and who is given these flowers by you.* And, *Was your wife at the party?,* again does not seem as if it would be properly represented by *Was it the case that you have at least one wife and not more than one wife and that no one is both your wife and not at the party?* There does not seem to be the feeling that the person who asks whether your wife was at the party is, among other things, inquiring whether you are nonbigamously married.

I would first start considering whether one could use, to deal with this sort of difficulty, the notion of CONVERSATIONAL IMPLICATURE which I concocted some time ago (Grice, 1975). I will here just give a brief résumé of the main aspects of it. I was concerned with the kind of implication, on the part of a speaker, which appears in such cases as that when somebody asks me where he can get some petrol and I say that there is a garage around the corner; here I might be said to imply, not just that there is a garage around the corner, but that it is open, and that it has stocks of petrol, etc. Or if, in response to a request for a testimonial for somebody who is a candidate for a philosophical job and whom I have taught, I write back and say that his manners are excellent and that his handwriting is extremely legible, I could be said to be implying that he was not all that good at philosophy. I distinguished a number of what I called CONVERSATIONAL MAXIMS which, I suggested, generally applied to the way we talk. They were such things as "Other things being equal, give neither more nor less information than, or at least give as much information as, is required." Another maxim was "Do not say that which you believe to be untrue or that for which you have inadequate evidence." A third was "Be relevant." These maxims are all concerned with the kinds of things that one might say. Besides them there was also a general bunch of items that fell under the heading of MANNER (the manner in which one says things), including the general maxim "Be perspicuous." These were desiderata that normally would be accepted by any rational discourser, though, of course, they could be infringed and violated. But the general assumption would be that they were not, and that, if there was an apparent violation, then there would be cause for looking to see whether the violation was, in fact, only apparent. I suggested that the presence of some conversational implicata arose from cases where there was at least an appearance of violation of one of these maxims. What was implicated by the speaker would be what he might expect the hearer to suppose him to think in order to preserve the idea that the maxims are, after all, not being violated. That is to say, to take the case of the testimonial, the suggestion would be something like that the hearer might be disposed to have a thought that could be expanded in this way: "It is clearly in point for him [the speaker] to tell me a good deal about this candidate's philosophical abilities. [This is required by the maxim of Quantity.] He hasn't done so; on the assumption that he is not violating conversational procedures, he has some reason why he has not. That reason is likely to be that the things he would say would either be untrue or else bad and he doesn't want to say those things. So the explanation then would be that he had a low opinion of the candidate." Thus this information is conveyed indirectly.

I also distinguished, within this general heading, particular conversational implicatures that depended on particular contextual features (the features of the context) and ones that I thought of as relatively general which I called GENERALIZED IMPLICATURES. These are the ones that seem to me to be more controversial and at the same time more valuable for philosophical purposes, because they will be implicatures that would be carried (other things being equal) by any utterance of a certain form, though, as with all conversational implicatures, they are not to be represented as part of the conventional meaning of the words or forms in question. (It is important that what is conversationally implicated is not to be thought of as part of the meaning of the expressions that are used to get over the implication.) And I thought that this notion of a GENERALIZED conversational implicature might be used to deal with a variety of problems, particularly in philosophical logic, but also in other areas. In these cases there seemed to me to be quite good grounds for suspecting that some people have made the mistake of taking as part of the conventional meaning of some form of expression what was really not part of its conventional meaning, but was rather a nonconventional implication which would normally be carried, except in special circumstances, by the use of that form. It is difficult to find noncontroversial cases just because, if this mistake has been committed, it has been committed on such a wide scale. But plausible examples are perhaps not impossible to find. It was suggested by Strawson, in *An Introduction to Logical Theory*, that there is a divergence between the ordinary use or meaning of the word *and* and the conjunction sign of propositional or predicate calculus, because *He took off his trousers and went to bed* does not seem to have the same meaning as *He went to bed and took off his trousers*. The suggestion here is, of course, that, in order properly to represent the ordinary use of the word *and,* one would have to allow a special sense (or subsense) for the word *and* which contained some reference to the idea that what was mentioned before the word *and* was temporally prior to what was mentioned after it, and that, on that supposition, one could deal with this case. I want to suggest, in reply, that it is not necessary, if one operates on some general principle of keeping down, as far as possible, the number of special sense of words that one has to invoke, to give countenance to the alleged divergence of meaning. It is just that there is a general supposition which would be subsidiary to the general maxim of Manner ("Be perspicuous.") that one presents one's material in an orderly manner and, if what one is engaged upon is a narrative (if one is talking about events), then the most orderly manner for a narration of events is an order that corresponds to the order in which they took place. So, the meaning of the expression *He took off his trousers and he got into bed* and the corresponding expression with a logician's constant "&" (i.e., "he took off his trousers & he got into bed") would be exactly the same. And, indeed, if anybody actually used in ordinary speech the "&" as a piece of vocabulary, instead of as a formal device, and used it to connect together sentences of this type, they would collect just the same implicata as the ordinary English sentences have without any extra explanation of the meaning of the word *and.*

I should say that I did suggest, in the paper on implicature, two sorts of tests by which one might hope to identify a conversational implicature. I did not mean to suggest that these tests were final, only that they were useful. One test was the possibility of cancellation; that is to say, could one, without logical absurdity, attach a cancelling clause. For instance, could I say *He took off his trousers and got into bed, but I don't mean to suggest that he did those things in that order*? If that is not a linguistic offense, or does not seem to be, then, so far as it goes, it is an indication that what one has here is a conversational implicature, and that the original suggestion of temporal succession was not part of the conventional meaning of the sentence. The other test was a related sort of test; it consisted in looking for other ways of saying just what was being said by the original thing which would not carry the same implication. And if one found that all the other ways seemed to be infected in just the same way (to carry the same implication) as the original, then that, so far as it went would be a good indication that the implicature did not attach to any par ticular words, but was something to do with conversational rules. But neither of these tests was regarded by me as being final; the final test for the presence of a conversational implicature had to be, as far as I could see, a derivation of it. One has to produce an account of how it could have arisen and why it is there. And I am very much opposed to any kind of sloppy use of this philosophical tool, in which one does not fulfill this condition.

Now, what about *the present king of France*? As far as I could see, in the original version of Strawson's truth-gap theory, he did not recognize any particular asymmetry, as regards the presupposition that there is a king of France, between the two sentences, *The king of France is bald* and *The king of France is not bald;* but it does seem to be plausible to suppose that there is such an asymmetry. I would have thought that the implication that there is a king of France is clearly part of the conventional force of *The king of France is bald;* but that this is not clearly so in the case of *The king of France is not bald.* Let us abbreviate *The king of France is not bald* by $\bar{K}$. An implication that there is a king of France is often carried by saying $\bar{K}$, but it is tempting to suggest that this implication is not, inescapably, part of the conventional force of the utterance of $\bar{K}$, but is rather a matter of conversational implicature. So let us apply the tests of cancellability and detachment.

First, the implication seems to be explicitly cancellable. If I come on a group of people arguing about whether the king of France is bald, it is not linguistically improper for me to say that the king of France is not bald, since there is no king of France. Of course, I do not have to put it that way, but I perfectly well can. Secondly, the implication seems to be contextually cancellable, that is, cancellable by circumstances attending the utterance, $\bar{K}$. If it is a matter of dispute whether the government has a very undercover person who interrogates those whose loyalty is suspect and who, if he existed, could be legitimately referred to as the loyalty examiner; and if, further, I am known to be very skeptical about the existence of such a person, I could perfectly well say to a plainly loyal person, *Well, the loyalty examiner will not be summoning you at any rate*, without, I would think, being taken to imply that such a person exists. Further, if I am well known to disbelieve in the existence of such a person, though others are inclined to believe in him, when I find a man who is apprised of my position, but who is worried in case he is summoned, I could try to reassure him by saying *The loyalty examiner won't summon you, don't worry.* Then it would be clear that I said this because I was sure there is no such person.

Furthermore, the implicature seems to have a very high degree of nondetachability. Many of what seem to be other ways of saying, approximately, what is asserted by $\bar{K}$ also carry the existential implicature, for example, *It isn't the case the king of France is bald*, *It is false that the king of France is bald*, *It is not true that the king of France is bald*. Of course, if the truth-gap theory is wrong, then there will be a way of asserting just what is asserted by $\bar{K}$ that lacks this implicature, namely, a Russellian expansion of it, for example *It is not the case that there is one and only one person who is the king of France. . . .* But all that this breakdown of nondetachability would show would be that the presence of the implicature depends on the manner of the expression, in particular on the presence of the definite description itself. No implicature, however, could be finally established as conversational unless the explanation of its presence has been given and been shown to be of the right kind, as involving conversational maxims in an appropriate way. That is what I shall try to deal with next.

Before we go further, it would be expedient to define the task somewhat more precisely.[2] If we are looking for a possible formal counterpart for such a sentence as *The king of France is bald*, we have two candidates to consider: (a) $(\iota x.Fx)\, Gx$, in which the iota-operator is treated as being syntactically analogous to a QUANTIFIER; and (b) $G\,(\iota x.Fx)$, in which the iota-operator is treated as a device for forming a TERM. If we select (a), then, when we introduce negation, we have two semantically distinguishable ways of doing so; $\sim((\iota x.Fx)\, Gx)$ and $(\iota x.Fx)\sim Gx$. The second will, and the first will not, entail the existence of an x that is uniquely F. But if we select the latter, there is only one place (prefixing) for the introduction of negation; and in consequence $\sim G(\iota x.Fx)$ will be an ambiguous structure [unless we introduce a disambiguating scope convention]; on one reduction to primitive notation the existence of a unique F will be entailed, on the other it will not. (Call these respectively the strong and the weak readings.) Now if there were a clear distinction in sense (in English) between, say, *The king of France is not bald* and *It is not the case that the king of France is bald* (if the former demanded the strong reading and the latter the weak one), then it would be reasonable to correlate *The king of France is bald* with the formal structure that treats the iota-operator like a quantifier. But this does not seem to be the case; I see no such clear semantic distinction. So it seems better to associate *The king of France is bald* with the formal structure that treats the iota-operator as a term-forming device. We are then committed to the structural ambiguity of the sentence *The king of France is not bald*. The proposed task may now be defined as follows: On one reading *The king of France is not bald* entails the existence of a unique king of France, on the other it does not; but in fact, without waiting for disambiguation, people understand an utterance of *The king of France is not bald* as implying (in some fashion) the unique existence of a king of France. This is intelligible if on one reading (the strong one), the unique existence of a king of France is entailed, on the other (the weak one), though not entailed, it is conversationally implicated. What needs to be shown, then, is a route by which the weaker reading could come to implicate what it does not entail.

If one looks for some prima facie plausibility for the idea of regarding the definite description as carrying an implicature of a nonconventional and conversational kind, where is one to find it? Well, one would have to select, first, (and the case would have to be argued for) one or another of the different Russellian expansions as being that for which such an expression as *The king of France is bald* (or *The king of France is not bald*) is to be regarded as a definitional contraction. And I think there will be some case for selecting one particular one, namely, the one that would run *There is at least one king of France, there is not more than one king of France, and nothing which is the king of France is not bald*. It seems to have a particular feature that recommends it and might fit in with some general principle of discourse; namely, there are no conjunctions occurring in it within the scope of quantifiers. That is to say, it sets out separately three distinct clauses, and each one of these can be false while both of the others are true. I think this is perhaps appropriate because it may well have some connection with something that I am going to mention in a moment, namely, that this particular expansion is constructed in a way that makes it particularly suitable for denial on the part of somebody (a hearer) to whom it might be uttered. I would be inclined to suggest that we add to the maxims of Manner which I originally propounded some maxim which would be, as it should be, vague: "Frame whatever you say in the form most suitable for any reply that would be regarded as appropriate"; or, "Facilitate in your form of expression the appropriate reply." It is very clear that one of the appropriate replies to something that you have asserted is the denial of what you say. If your assertions are complex and conjunctive, and you are asserting a number of things at the same time, then it would be natural, on the assumption that any one of them might be challengeable, to set them out separately and so make it easy for anyone who wanted to challenge them to do so. So, let us make the assumption that we accept some such maxim and also agree that denial is a natural and suitable form of response to an assertion. Let us also adopt the following abbreviational scheme: "A" is to represent *There is at least one king of France*, "B" is to represent *There is at most one king of France*, "C" is to represent *whatever is king of France is bald*, "ABC" is to represent the conjunction of A, B, and C, which we are taking as the favored Russellian expansion of "D." which represents *The king of France is bald*.

Now we may hope to reach the conclusion that the production of this abbreviation (D) would violate our newly introduced maxim of Manner unless one could assume that the speaker thought he was within his rights, in that he did not consider that a distinct denial of A or of B would be appropriate (that this was a response not to be looked for, in his view). As a start, given that SOME kind of denial has to be thought of as appropriate, as that is a natural response to any form of assertion, we might claim that one who employs the abbreviated form D ought EITHER to be thinking it likely that, if there is to be a denial, it will be a wholesale denial, OR ELSE, to be thinking that, though the hearer may be going to reject one conjunct, one particular conjunct is, in some way, singled out as the one that is specially likely to be denied. It must, indeed, be the second possibility that is to be seriously considered, as the conjuncts cannot all be denied together consistently. If it is false that there exists at least one king of France, then it is vacuously true that whatever is king of France is bald (that nothing is both king of France and not bald). So that leaves us with the demand to show that, in some way, one particular conjunct is singled out. Now this would be the case if it would be reasonable to suppose that the speaker thinks, and expects his hearer to think, that some subconjunction of A and B and C has what I might call common-ground status, and, therefore, is not something that is likely to be challenged. One way in which this might happen would be if the speaker were to think or assume that it is common knowledge, and that people would regard it as common knowledge, that there is one and only one F. But that would be only one way in which it could arise.

For instance, it is quite natural to say to somebody, when we are discussing some concert, *My aunt's cousin went to that concert*, when one knows perfectly well that the person one is talking to is very likely not even to know that one had an aunt, let alone know that one's aunt had a cousin. So the supposition must be not that it is common knowledge but rather that is is noncontroversial, in the sense that it is something that you would expect the hearer to take from you (if he does not already know). That is to say, I do not expect, when I tell someone that my aunt's cousin went to a concert, to be questioned whether I have an aunt and, if so, whether my aunt has a cousin. This is the sort of thing that I would expect him to take from me, that is, to take my word for. So, we have now got into the position that we might well be in the clear, as far as concerns representing the existential implication as a conversational implicature, if we could show that, in general, there should be a reasonable expectation, other things being equal, that, in the favored Russellian expansion of a definite description, two of the clauses (in fact, the first and the second) would be matters that would have this common ground status, and so not be controversial or likely to be open to challenge. We might, then, assume that, so far, it looks as if the hearer would be justified in concluding that two of the items must be given common ground status, the only question is which two. Now the third clause (C) is general in form. And we can think of a general statement as being either something the establishment of which depends on the complete enumeration of a set of instances, or as something to be an inductive step.

Let us take the first possibility. Let us suppose it is enumeratively based. That is, one is to think of *Nothing that is F is not G* as to be reached by finding the instances of *F* and seeing that none of them fail to be *G*. For it to be possible to establish this enumeratively if the whole sentence (D) is true, it must be the case that there exists just one *F* which is the basis of the enumeration. And so we have, in effect, a conjunctive statement that tells you there are a certain number of cases (just one) that would test a certain generalization, and then gives you the generalization. It would seem to be very peculiar to imagine that anybody could be in the situation in which he was prepared to speak of C, but not as being common ground, because he would have to be put in the position of saying something like, "I can accept that nothing is *F* but not *G*, that 'what is *F* is *G*' is true, and is also to be established by complete enumeration. But what I am uncertain about is whether you are right about whether there are any instances of *F*, or, if so, how many." It is not necessary that it should be IMPOSSIBLE for somebody to be in that position, but that it is certainly not to be expected; and what is to be generally assumed may depend, not on something being universally the case, but merely on its being expectable.

Again, we can take the other possibility. Suppose we take the last clause, C, not as being an enumerative generalization, but as an open one. And there may be some cases in which that is how it is to be thought of. Even so, it is prima facie not to be expected that you would find somebody in the position of being prepared to concede the generalization but being concerned about whether and how often that generalization is instantiated. Again, I am not saying that that is not possible. But that would certainly be not the kind of situation that one would think of as being the natural one; and the implicature depends on what is to be expected, not on what is universally true.

If this line of argument (or something like it) goes through, then we could perhaps explain why it is that somebody who says it is not the CASE that the present king of France is bald (someone who denies what is expressed by D) would also be implicating, though not explicitly stating, that there is a unique king of France. It is as if he is countering a remark which might be made to him, in which the speaker has indicated that he is expecting the challenge, to come, if at all, in a particular direction, namely, to C; and he just says, "No, that is not so." He denies that the present king of France is bald, and so naturally he will be taken to be going along with the expected restriction of comment that is implicitly carried by the presentation of the original statement in the abbreviated form (D), rather than in the full form in which each clause would have been set up for him to object to if he wants to. The position that I am outlining might be presented, in summary fashion, as follows:

A speaker S, who utters D (the affirmative form of a sentence having as subject a definite description) might expect a hearer H to reflect (or intuit) as follows:

"1. (By the conversational "tailoring" principle) S has uttered D rather than its Russellian expansion; so there is one particular Russellian conjunct that S expects me (if I reject anything) to reject, while accepting the other conjuncts.
2. That is, all but a particular one of the Russellian conjuncts are thought of by him as likely to possess common ground status (to be treated as noncontroversial).
3. The first two conjuncts would, in most natural circumstances, be items which anyone would have to know or accept in order to have a good ground for accepting the third.
4. So the first two conjuncts are the ones to which he attributes common-ground status."

A speaker S', who utters D̄ (the negation of D) might expect a hearer H' to reflect (or intuit) as follows:

"1. Speaker S' has uttered the negation of D; so he is speaking as if he were responding negatively to S (above), i.e., to one who utters D.
2. So S' is fulfilling the expectations that S would have had about H, that is, he is accepting the first two conjuncts and rejecting the third."

We may note, before moving on, that for a very large range of cases a different account of the existential implication carried by the negative forms of statements involving descriptions might be available. Consider utterances of such a sentence as *The book on the table is not open*. As there are, obviously, many books on tables in the world, if we are to treat such a sentence as being of the form *The F is not G* and as being, on that account, ripe for Russellian expansion, we might do well to treat it as exemplifying the more specific form *The F' which is φ is not G*, where 'φ' represents an epithet to be identified in a particular context of utterance ('φ' being a sort of quasi-demonstrative). Standardly, to identify the reference of 'φ' for a particular utterance of *The book on the table is [not] open*, a hearer would proceed via the identification of a particular book as being a good CANDIDATE for being the book meant, and would identify the reference of 'φ' by finding in the candidate a feature, for example that of BEING IN THIS ROOM, which could be used to yield a composite epithet ("book on the table in this room"), which would in turn fill the bill of being an epithet which the speaker had in mind as being uniquely satisfied by the book selected as candidate. If the hearer fails to find a suitable reference for 'φ' in relation to the selected candidate, then he would, normally, seek another candidate. So determining the reference of 'φ' would standardly involve determining what feature the speaker might have in mind as being uniquely instantiated by an actual object, and this in turn would standardly involve satisfying oneself that some particular feature actually is uniquely satisfied by a particular actual object (e.g., a particular book). So utterances both of *The book on the table is open* and of *The book on the table is not open* would alike imply (in one way or another) the existence of a particular book on a table.

We might, indeed, if we regard this apparatus as reasonably well set up, try to use it to deal with the difficulty raised in the third main objection mentioned, namely, the difficulty about applying the Russellian expansion to needs other than the indicative. First, I think a distinction is needed. I think that the objection, as I presented it, is put in a bad form. I think it is important to notice a distinction between what I might call CAUSING something to be the case and what I might call INSURING that it is the case. If I tell somebody to cause it to be the case that a particular person has somewhere to live and enough to live on, it looks certainly as if I am thinking that he has to operate in order to promote both clauses; I mean, that he will have to find him somewhere to live and give him enough to live on. And it seems possible that he could hardly claim to have caused him to have somewhere to live and to have enough to live on unless he had done both of these things. But, if I merely tell somebody to insure that the person has somewhere to live and enough to live on, then I think he could also, afterwards, claim that he had insured this, even though, in fact, when he got onto the scene, he found that the man already had somewhere to live and that all he needed was something to live on. All he has to do, so to speak, is to bring the state of affairs up to completion, if that is required. What exactly one is entitled to say if one finds not only that the man has somewhere to live, but also has enough to live on, after one has been told to insure that he has both of these things, perhaps is not quite so clear.

So to the question of the imperatives: part of the paradoxical character of the suggested Russellian account comes from the fact that I began with *Make it the case that,* which suggests that if I were to say, *Give these flowers to your wife,* the expansion of that imperative must begin *Make it the case that . . .* And then, when you put in the full Russellian expansion, it looks as if I am instructing you to make three changes, one corresponding to each clause. But if I put in *Insure that . . . ,* instead, then there would not be this implication. All that would be required is that you should bring the thing to completion, so to speak, insofar as there is a gap. And so it may well turn out, also (indeed, in some cases it turns out as a matter of logical fact or something like it), that you CANNOT do anything about some of the clauses.

You cannot now make it the case that you are now married to one and only one person. Either you are or you are not. That is outside your control; so, in many cases, the only clause left with respect to which you can act is the one covered by *Make it the case that she has the flowers.* But, of course, there will be some cases where this particular provision would not work. If I tell somebody who is not presently married and, as far as I know, has no immediate prospect of getting married, *See that your next wife looks after you properly,* I do not necessarily think that he is going to get married. Nor, I think, am I instructing him to get married. It would be possible, presumably, on a Russellian account, for him to take my instruction as telling him to select a wife, first, and then, second, to make sure that she looks after him properly. So we would need something to insure that it was not taken this way.

At this point, if one supposed that it is being taken as an assumption by me, as common ground between us, as not to be questioned, that he will at some time or other have another wife (and the point is that when the time comes she should look after him properly), then he will not take the imperative force, so to speak, as attaching to the selection of a particular wife. So, if there is a conversational implicatum that he will at some time or other have a wife, then this will be excerpted from the instructions. I am inclined to think that this particular dodge works reasonably well for the range of cases considered; but I am not wholly happy about it, as it stands, because this general phenomenon of presupposition (or cases that look like presupposition) is one that occurs in a large number of places. In recent years, linguists have made it increasingly difficult for philosophers to continue to keep their eyes glued to a handful of stock examples of (alleged) presupposition, such as the king of France's baldness and the inquiry whether you have left off beating your wife.

There is, in fact, an enormous range of cases in which the questions about presuppositions arise, not least in connection with psychological verbs. One can distinguish, perhaps, a number of such cases in connection with psychological verbs. Let us take, first, *think*. If I say that somebody thinks (or believes) that such-and-such, there is no indication that what he thinks or believes is true. Supposing, however, I take the verb *discover*, and I say *Somebody discovered that the roof was leaking*. Here, it is not logically possible to discover that one's roof is leaking unless one's roof is leaking. On the the other hand, I do not think (though, perhaps, this is doubtful) that so-and-so didn't discover *P* also implies that *P* is true. I think I can say that some explorer went off to some place expecting to discover that the natives were very interesting in certain respects, but he did not discover that because they were not. So here we have a case where there is a logical implication on the part of the affirmative, but not on the part of its denial. (That looks like a case of entailment.)

Then there is a third case, which perhaps is exemplified by the word *know*, in which to say that somebody did know that so-and-so was the case and to say that he did not know that so-and-so was the case both imply that it was the case. This is a specimen, I think, of the kind of verb that has been called FACTIVE. There is a distinction between this and a fourth case, because, though both the affirmation and denial of statements about particular people knowing that *P* carries with it a commitment to *P*, you can weaken the verb in such a way that this implication is lost. *He knew that P* and *He didn't know that P* both carry this implication, but *He thought he knew that P* does not. When I say *He thought he knew that P*, I am not committing myself to its being the case that *P*, but there some verbs in which even the weakened forms also seem to carry this implication, particularly, perhaps, a verb like *regret* (i.e., *He thought he regretted his father's death, but it afterwards turned out that he didn't*, as far as it makes sense, would, I think, still imply the committal to his father's death). I am not sure about the last distinction and I think perhaps it does not matter very much. These are cases where there is some kind of a commitment on the part of a normal speaker, by using both the affirmative and the negative forms, to some common element being true; and I do not see that it is going to be particularly easy to represent the implication in the case of *regret* as being one of a conversational kind. It does not look as attractive as the Russellian case. So, I would be interested in having recourse to a conventional device which would be a substitute in standard cases for an original conversational implicature. In my *William James Lectures* I considered a treatment of some ordinary conditionals as material conditionals with certain standard conversational implicata, but I was worried about negating conditionals. It seems to me that I had to depart from the original nonconventionalist treatment by introducing a conventional element, but one that did not introduce any new concepts or anything like that. In its original form it can be given a syntactical account. And so I had the thought of representing *if P, Q* by use of a square bracketing notation. This square bracket can be placed around any expression which, when attached to another sentential form, results in the production of a further sentence. In its original form, the general nature of this device was to take a sequence of elements *ABC* which form a sentence and put square brackets around *B*, yielding *A[B]C*; then this has to be rewritten as *BAC*. The general rule would lay down that, provided *A* is of a certain sort (to be determined), *A[B]C* is to be rewritten as *BAC*; if *A* is not of that sort, or is null, the square brackets are simply emitted in the rewrite.

In application to conditionals, this rule is designed to ensure that *if P, Q* ([P ⊃]Q) is equivalent to $P \supset Q$, while *It is not the case that if P, Q* (~([P ⊃]Q)) is equivalent to $P \supset \sim Q$; the effect would be (I hoped) to provide a representation for ONE reading of the negation of a conditional, while using only the notion of the material conditional together with what is, in fact, merely a scope device, and, thus, syntactical in character.

A revised and somewhat more complicated characterization of the square brackets device may have greater general utility. The revised rules might be roughly as follows:

1. (*a*) If expression *A* is of the denominated type *T*, then *A[B]C* is rewritten as *BABC*.
   (*b*) If expression *A* is not of type *T*, or is null, then *A[B]C* is rewritten as *ABC*.
2. In rewriting, nested brackets are eliminated, seriatim, from exterior to interior.
3. If no connective directly precedes a closing (R.H.) square bracket, "&" is supplied in rewriting, where needed, to preserve syntactical admissibility.
4. Any open (L.H.) parentheses introduced in rewriting are closed terminally.
5. In preposing an expression containing a bound variable, the variable is changed.

Using the revised version, ~([P ⊃]Q) will be rewritten as

$P \supset \sim(P \supset Q)$, which is equivalent to $P \supset \sim Q$ [the rewrite of $\sim([P \supset]Q)$ on the original version]. We could use the revised version to handle the alleged existential presuppositions of *some* and *every*, *every F is G* could be represented as $\sim[(\exists x)\ (Fx \&]\sim Gx)$, with the rewrite $(\exists y)$ $(Fy \& \sim(\exists x)(Fx \& \sim Gx))$. We may also use the revised device in the formal representation of such a factive verb as *regret*.

Accordingly, *x regrets* ϕ (e.g., that Father is ill) is defined as

1. $[x$ knows* ϕ &$]$ x is anti ϕ
   x *knows** ϕ is defined as x *thinks* $[\phi]$
   So, x regrets ϕ emerges as
2. $[x$ thinks $[\phi]$ &$[$ x is anti ϕ
   So, *x does not regret* ϕ would be expressible as

1. $\sim([x$ thinks $[\phi]$ & $]$ x is anti $\phi)$
   Replacing exterior square brackets, we get
2. x thinks $[\phi]$ & $\sim(x$ thinks $[\phi]$ & x is anti $\phi)$
   Replacing remaining square brackets, we get
3. ϕ & x thinks ϕ & ϕ & $\sim(x$ thinks ϕ & x is anti $\phi)$
   Eliminating redundant occurrence of ϕ, we get
4. ϕ & x thinks ϕ & $\sim(x$ thinks ϕ & x is anti $\phi)$
   which is equivalent to
5. ϕ & x thinks ϕ & $\sim(x$ is anti $\phi)$

We may, finally, consider the employment of the square brackets device to handle the possible difficulties for the Russellian account connected with the appearance of definite descriptions in sentences couched in a mood other than the indicative.

1. *Arrest the intruder*
   could be thought of as representable (using "!" as an imperative operator) as
2. ! $([[(\exists_1 x)\ (x$ is an intruder) &$]\ (\forall y)\ (y$ is an intruder $\supset$ you will arrest $y))$
   Provided "!" is treated as belonging to the denominated type T, (2) will be rewritten (on the original version of the square bracket device) as
3(a). $(\exists_1 x)\ (x$ is an intruder) & ! $(\forall y)\ (y$ is an intruder $\supset$ you will arrest $y)$
   and (on the revised version) as
3(b). $(\exists_1 z)\ (z$ is an intruder) & ! $((\exists_1 x)\ (x$ is an intruder & $(\forall y)\ (y$ is an intruder $\supset$ you will arrest $y))$

Since the first clause of 3(b) STATES that there is just one intruder, the imperatival clause cannot be taken as enjoining that the addressee see to it that there be just one intruder.

In conclusion, let me briefly summarize the course of this chapter, primarily in order to distinguish what I have been attempting to do from what I have not. I have endeavoured to outline, without aligning myself with it, an exposition of the thesis that the existential presuppositions seemingly carried by definite descriptions can be represented within a Russellian semantics, with the aid of a standard attachment of conversational implicature; I paid attention both to the possibility that such implicata are cancelable and detachable and also to the availability of more than one method of deriving them from the operation of conversational principles. Promising though such an account may seem, I have suggested that it may run into trouble when it is observed that the range of cases of presupposition extends far beyond the most notorious examples, and that perhaps not the whole of this range would prove amenable to the envisaged mode of treatment. At this point I took up the idea of a minimal strengthening of a Russellian pattern of analysis by the addition of a purely syntactical scope device, which could at the same time be regarded as a conventional regimentation of a particular kind of nonconventional implicature. I have not, in this chapter, given any consideration at all to what might well turn out to be the best treatment of definite descriptions, namely to the idea that they are, in the first instance at least, to be regarded as being, semantically, a special subclass of referential expressions.

REFERENCES

Grice, H. P. (1975). Logic and conversation. In P. Cole and J. L. Morgan, *Syntax and Semantics 3: Speech Acts*. New York: Academic Press. Pp. 107–142.
Russell, B. (1905). On denoting. *Mind* **14,** 479–499.
Strawson, P. F. (1950). On referring. *Mind* **59,** 320–344.

Validating Pragmatic Explanations

Geoffrey Nunberg

1. INTRODUCTION

In his 1978 paper "On Testing for Conversational Implicature", Jerrold Sadock offers a number of observations about methodology in pragmatics that lead him to a bleak conclusion about the state of the art: "There is, then, given the existing methodology, no way of knowing for sure whether an implicature is conversational. . . . To solve the problem of the thorny cases and shore up the foundations of linguistic pragmatics, more powerful tools will have to be developed [p. 296]." I think it is fair to say that Sadock is only expressing a general dissatisfaction here; linguists often complain that pragmatic explanations, on the whole, lack the rigor of explanations in syntax and phonology. What I want to do here is to show that the criticism is inappropriate, that it arises out of a native conception of what a pragmatic explanation should look like, based on the assumption that semantics and syntax ought to have the same methodology. This assumption is practically the last of the dogmas offered by Katz and Fodor 1964 to go unchallenged, and is what leads, for example, to the hope that there should be "tests" for conversational implicature that parallel the "tests" for raising or derived constituent structure. And this

RADICAL PRAGMATICS

is what leads Sadock, I think, to draw the wrong moral from his own observations, as important as they are.

Sadock begins his discussion by assuming that it is the task of natural-language semantics to determine which parts of a particular message are conveyed conventionally, and which nonconventionally. He asks, "How can we make this decision in a reasoned and reasonable way?" Looking at the six characteristics that Grice (1975) assigns to conversational implicatures, he finds three that are "candidates for practical tests." (The others, such as "Conversational implicata are . . . nonconventional," are obviously circular.) They are (not in the order Sadock gives them):

(1) a. Conversational implicata are CANCELABLE.
     b. Conversational implicata are NONDETACHABLE.
     c. Conversational implicata are capable of being "worked out" on
        the basis, *inter alia,* of the Cooperative Principle. That is, they
        are CALCULABLE.

Sadock then argues that none of these three provides us with a satisfactory operational measure for sifting out conversational implicatures. (I will assume here, as I believe Sadock does, that the problem of identifying conversational implicatures is equivalent to the problem of identifying nonconventional uses in general.)

The problem with (1a)—cancelability—Sadock observes, is that is does not distinguish implicatures from cases of fortuitous homonymy. Alongside (2), for example, we can also say (3):

(2)   *John took off his trousers and got into bed, but not in that order.*
(3)   *John dropped a file on my foot, and I don't mean a dossier.*

This is just what we would expect, on reflection; all that "cancelability" means is that whenever an utterance is liable to two interpretations, for whatever reason, a speaker is free to clarify his purpose with an extra clause. So the fact that an inference is cancelable entails nothing with regards to its status as conventional or nonconventional. And we can note as well (though Sadock does not make this point), that as EVERY utterance has potentially more than one interpretation when the context is not adequately specified. It is possible to cancel any conventional meaning, as well as any implicature; the expression *but I don't mean that literally* does very nicely in most cases. So cancelability proves nothing at all.

The test of detachability—substituting synonymous expressions to see if implicatures are preserved—fares even worse. As with cancelability, it does not distinguish conventionally and nonconventionally conveyed inferences, for semantic entailments are of course also preserved when one synonym is substituted for another. Moreover, it presumes that we have an independent means of determining synonymy, which is to say, a way of determining when two expressions carry the same conventional entailments; but the test itself is supposed to tell us which entailments are conventional. (Grice and Sadock point out other shortcomings of the test—for example, it is inapplicable when a maxim of "manner" is violated. There is no need to belabor the point here, however.)

Cancelability and detachability were to have been "tests" in the sense of "diagnostics"—rules of thumb that would enable us to sort out conventional and nonconventional uses of expressions in a ready way. But Sadock's third criterion, calculability, is not really a "test" at all, but a good deal more than that. As Grice presents it—early on, apart from the list of features at the end of the article from which Sadock's other characteristics are drawn—an implicature is calculable if the hearer can work it out on the basis of his knowledge of "the conventional meanings of the words used, together with the identity of any references which may be involved," together with his knowledge of the conversational postulates, "the context linguistic and otherwise," "other items of background knowledge," and the fact that all of this information is part of what can be presupposed by all participants. In short, we say that an implicature is calculable when we can demonstrate that it would be a reasonable inference in the context of utterance. And since we assume that no convention would be necessary to ensure conformity to a practice that makes sense without one—in fact, that such a practice could NOT be conventional, for the situation involved would not satisfy the necessary condition of being a "coordination problem," in the terms of Lewis 1969—then a demonstration that an implicature is "calculable" amounts to a proof that it is not conventional. (Put otherwise, a demonstration of calculability is simply an explanation of a nonconventional use of an expression.) So when Sadock claims that calculability is not a sufficient "test" for conversational implicature, he claims in effect that pragmatic explanation is not always possible, that there are circumstances in which we CAN'T know what the conventions of language are. This is not a "state-of-the-art" problem for Sadock, either: His arguments for the inadequacy of calculablity as a test of implicature have nothing to do with methodological limitations. If Sadock is right, then, the distinction between conventional and nonconventional uses cannot be validated, no matter how many "more powerful tools" are developed.

Now I find myself in a bind here: I think there are good grounds for accepting this last conclusion, but these have little to do with the arguments that Sadock actually offers.[1] So let me assume for purposes of argu-

---

[1] See Nunberg (1979).

ment that Sadock's conclusion—or rather, our interpretation of Sadock's conclusion—is intolerable, and proceed to see where his discussion of calculability goes wrong.

Basically, Sadock suggests that calculability overdetermines the class of implicatures in two ways: It allows us to explain some uses that do not occur, and to explain others that must be conventional. His argument for the first point is familiar: The conversational maxims are necessarily so powerful and vague that they will have to be "strong enough to do certain things they shouldn't." The only example he gives in the service of this point is unfortunately rather complicated and in his terms "improbable," but we could turn the point a bit to apply it to another well-known example that he cites in his discussion of detachability: the observation that '*Can you* . . .' has uses in indirect requests that the apparently synonymous '*Are you able* . . . ' does not; a satisfactory explanation of the use of the first would also explain the use of the second to the same purpose. (This particular example is also unhappy: *Can* in its "root" sense may not be exactly synonymous with *be able*—I think not—and, as Larry Horn has pointed out, the fact that *be able* is more prolexic than *can* may also enter the picture, via the maxim of Manner. Later I will discuss examples that are less confounded; for the present purposes *Can you* . . . is at least mnemonically useful.)

For the second point—that some conventional uses are also calculable —Sadock turns to examples of idioms and euphemisms, which become conventionalized by stages; at an intermediate point, he observes, an idiom like *spill the beans* or a euphemism like *go to the bathroom* may be entirely "transparent," in the sense that speakers can work out the implicature that led to its original use, while its idiomaticity is evident, say, in its syntax (Sadock cites *Dean spilled the beans to Congress,* and Jerry Morgan's example, *My dog went to the bathroom on the living room carpet*).

I will not dispute Sadock's observations, except for a few minor quibbles. In defense of pragmatic explanation, however, I want to make two basic points in this chapter. First, there is a difference between being able to assign some rationale to a usage and explaining it pragmatically; the first, but not the second, is consistent with the usage's being conventional. Here I think the vagueness of the term "calculability" has led Sadock astray. Second, and still more important, pragmatic explanations do not determine usage in the same way that competence is supposed to determine performance; in fact, it is in the nature of the phenomenon that they should underdetermine usage grossly. This second point, in turn, will lead us back to the methodological question I raised at the beginning.

2. THE FORM OF A PRAGMATIC EXPLANATION

I want to start by discussing Sadock's second objection—that a use may be calculable and conventional at the same time. His examples involved phrasal idioms and euphemisms (*spill the beans, go to the bathroom*), which are only some of the class uses of expressions that we call "partially motivated." This class also includes various compounds (*breakwater, cold war, underhanded*), words derived in other ways (*distemper, himself, laughable, recall*), as well as the "idiomatic" uses of single morphemes ("*foot* of a mountain," "*dead* battery"). What all of these uses have in common is that we can calculate SOME rationale for them, given the conventions that govern other uses of the items involved, but the rationale is not sufficient to explain the circumstances or frequency of their actual use. In short, we say that a use of an expression is partially motivated when we have a bad pragmatic explanation for it.

A satisfactory pragmatic explanation of a use of an expression has several parts. First, it contains a specification of the conventional use of the expression, and of the use that is to be explained, and a number of relevant features of the "context," broadly construed: all of the information that speaker and hearer can presuppose about one another's intentions, about various kinds of background knowledge, about the physical setting, and so on. Second, it contains a demonstration, usually in the form of a description of a set of inferences, that the use in question is the best way available to the speaker of accomplishing a particular conversational purpose (referring, or communicating a certain proposition, or whatever) in that situation, given only the specifications of conventional use, context, and so on. There are other ways to put this, of course; we can talk about "literal" and "conveyed" meanings instead of uses, for example, and slice up the context in various ways. But the net effect is the same.

An explanation of this form fails when we can't attribute its terms to the speakers who use the expression in question; that is, when we can't assume it provides them with a reason, or enough of a reason, for doing what they do. In the simplest cases, the explanation fails because it involves the assumption of factual presuppositions that do not actually hold in the contexts the expression is used in, assuming that speakers have no ulterior motive for operating against false presuppositions. For example, consider the difference between *country music* and *New Orleans jazz*. The first, we would say, is a stereotyped compound, while the second is fully "compositional." The reason is that in the theory of country music that is popularly presupposed, it is not best identified by its rural origin, or even, nowadays, by its association with the most rural parts of America.

Whereas New Orleans jazz *is* best identified by its provenance; wherever it happens to be played now, it is still identified by reference to certain classic New Orleans exemplars. But even if country music is no longer defined as "the kind of music they used to play in the country," its rural associations are still very much a part of common knowledge. So speakers can come up with AN explanation for the usage, and could even attribute that explanation to the generation of speakers that initiated the expression. But the explanation does not account for present-day usage, so we have to assume that a convention has stepped in. (Other examples of the same process are *nylons* for stockings, or *Russian dressing*.)

But note that the assumption that a phrase like *country music* is conventionalized does not depend simply on the fact that it is not the most rational way of going about identifying country music—that it is not entirely compositional, if you like. We also have to assume that speakers have no ulterior motive for behaving in a way that is irrational from a strictly informational point of view. And speakers frequently abandon strict rationality for what we can think of as affective reasons, when they "violate a maxim" to produce a metaphor, a euphemism, or an ironical or sarcastic utterance. And we understand such utterances only by invoking assumptions about speakers' ulterior motives in conversation—the production of pleasure or pain for either participant, for example—as well as assumptions about the sorts of inhibitions that lead us to dissimulate aggression, and so on. We can think of uses like these as being "affectively determined," as Weber put it; they are much more important than a lot of the literature on pragmatics would have us believe. For instance, Grice's discussion of irony is quite simplistic for ignoring them. He says, roughly, that, as speaker *A* has said something he obviously does not believe, he must mean to get across something else, some obviously related proposition, the most obvious of which is the opposite of the one he has said. But apart from the fact that we can be ironic without saying the opposite of what we mean (consider *Jimmy Carter has such an honest smile*), it is obvious that there are any number of subsidiary conditions that an ironic utterance must satisfy: It has to involve an evaluative judgment, it has to be ultimately directed at the speaker himself (which is one of the things that distinguishes irony from sarcasm), and so on. The point is that we can interpret an utterance as "meaning its opposite" only in the light of assumptions about whatever irrational motives speakers may bring to the context. And the same holds for euphemism, where we require assumptions about what things speakers are willing to go to unreasonable lengths to avoid saying, and why. (A television host can novelly euphemize prostitutes as "street hostesses," for example, but he cannot euphemize airline pilots.) With out-and-out metaphors, the interpretation depends on our ability to see why a speaker should wish to behave as if the world were factually different from how it is. When *cold war* was first coined, for example, it involved reference to an economic and political rivalry as if it were a state of armed belligerancy, and speakers were capable of seeing the polemical reasons for such a usage.

A metaphor does not become conventionalized simply because it gets tired. It is still a purely metaphorical usage when we call someone a tiger or an angel or say that *so-and-so is like a rat in a cage.* (By contrast, simple repetition may be sufficient to deprive a euphemism of its original justification, if the expression becomes increasingly a "standard" way of referring to a certain kind of thing.)[2] Conventionalization comes when the relevant assumptions about speaker intentions and affective purposes no longer justify the use of the expression in all its contexts. This could be the result of a change in purely "factual assumptions," as when theological beliefs change. (So it may be conventional now to say *He's gone to meet his Maker.* And certainly we presuppose less now about bats out of hell than about rats in cages.) Or there may be a change in evaluative presuppositions. As I write in 1979, for example, the spirit of *entente* seems to have robbed *cold war* of its original import, so that we continue to use the expression only because it is in some measure conventional to do so. Or the change may be due to a very amorphous shift in sensibilities. As we have come to eschew sentimentality, phrases like *give one's heart* and *break someone's heart* have moved from metaphors to idioms. (I do not mean to suggest that all idioms start out life as metaphors. I do not see why an expression like *Johnny-on-the-spot* or for that matter *spill the beans* has to have a real story, except that romance would have it that way.)[3]

All of these considerations have to be kept in mind when we try to determine whether a certain use of an expression is conventional, particularly when the use has some notable "usage condition" attached to it— when it is slangy, colloquial, formal, obscene, polite, *etc.*—for these are the bellwethers that tell us that some affective determination is involved.

---

[2] Though a euphemism may remain a euphemism indefinitely, too (cf. *member,* for example, or French borrowings like *fille de joie,* where the expression wears its euphemicity on its sleeve).

[3] Conventionalization is most frequently accomplished, I suspect, when the conventional meaning of the expression itself changes, leaving its pragmatically derived uses stranded. So the loss of certain uses of the English subjunctive facilitated the conventionalization of *God be with you,* and changes in the meanings of *give up* (from "render") and *ghost* (from "spirit") led to the conventionalization of *give up the ghost,* together perhaps with changes in popular theology. In a reverse sort of case, the expression *in the dumps* was originally used literally, and was reanalyzed as an idiom when *dump* acquired its "refuse heap" use.

For example, is it conventional to say *See you later* on parting? Morgan (1978) suggests that it is by way of becoming so, at least for him, since he uses it "even when it is clear to everyone involved that I will not be seeing my interlocutor later." But that isn't a sufficient reason for supposing a convention; what Morgan would really have to show is that he uses the expression even when it would not be APPROPRIATE to express a hope to see the interlocuter later, no matter how obviously insincere that expression might be. (By the same token, it is not conventional to say *Have a nice day* or *Nice to see you* simply because speakers often say these things insincerely.) Or consider the use of "destruction" metaphors to describe intoxication: *wrecked, smashed,* and so on. If these seem less conventional than the corresponding *plastered,* it is because they are justified by current American sensibilities regarding the use of intoxicants, and the attitude with which drunkenness should be regarded; we find it funnier to exaggerate our intoxication than other races do.

Small wonder, then, that there should be no simple practical tests for determining when a use is conventional, given that the determinants are so sensitive. (Sadock's syntactic tests, by the way, are rarely conclusive. I agree with him that *spill the beans* is conventionalized, but the fact that one can say *Dean spilled the beans to Congress* has no bearing on this. The fact is that *spill* itself has a use to mean "divulge," so that we can as easily say *He spilled the plans to the FBI.* And this is only evidence for the conventionalization of the "divulge" use of *spill* if we assume that strict subcategorization is entirely a syntactic matter, which seems to me dubious.[4] In any case, such tests are not often applicable, even if we have an interpretation for them; they are wholly irrelevant to the status of *cold war* or *Have a nice day,* for example.) And the sensitivity of the analysis necessary to produce a pragmatic explanation for a use is only part of the problem. Everything will be worse confounded when we consider how to go about attributing that explanation to a group of speakers, in order to show that it provides THEM with a reason for behaving as they do.

3. ATTRIBUTING THE EXPLANATION TO SPEAKERS

Once we have come up with a plausible-sounding pragmatic explanation for a usage, there are two problems that we have to overcome in attri-

[4] To make this argument, we would have to assume for example that "active" and "middle" uses of verbs like *hit* or *touch* were lexically distinct items, since only the former appear in passives. We would also have to assume that the uses of *show* to mean "appear" and "cause to see" were governed by different conventions. I think there are good arguments against both claims, but the point is not really relevant here; it is enough to point out that the interpretation of this kind of syntactic test is at best highly arguable.

buting it to actual speakers. The first is familiar enough: Here, as any-where else in linguistics, we do not require that our explanations must be "psychologically real" in the crassest sense, models of the processes that every speaker must go through every time he arrives at the right infer-ence.[5] In the first place, there is no way to have direct access to what goes through the speaker's mind, especially if we make the usual assumption that we are at best describing "tacit" knowledge and beliefs, inaccessible to conscious reflection; as a consequence, the best we can say is that the explanations we offer are consistent with the capacities and beliefs of the speakers we are interested in, and that speakers behave as if they had worked them out, if only by a set of approximations. Second, there is no reason at all to suppose that speakers should recalculate implicatures on repeated use of a form in a certain way in the same type of situation, no more than we would expect a poker player to recalculate repeatedly the odds on filling an inside straight in a game of draw. Once made, a single calculation will serve as a basis for a more efficient rule of thumb, what Morgan (1978) calls a "short-circuited implicature." And finally, we can assume that most implicatures are never worked out at all, but rather "in-tuitively grasped," as Grice puts it, whatever the mechanism is. So what our explanations do, in the best of cases, is to provide a justification for the intuitions that speakers act on.

In these cases, however, we assume that all speakers COULD work out the relevant implicature; that it is generally calculable, in some sense, even if it never gets calculated. And even this is too strong an assumption, for it equates a speaker's knowledge that he has a good reason for doing something with his knowledge of what that reason is. If we allow that a speaker can substitute an on-line strategy for the recalculation of an infer-ence that he has already made, it seems a small step to saying that he has equally good grounds for using the strategy when he simply assumes on some authority that some calculation would justify his action. By analogy, no chess player could know all of the justifications for the strategies em-ployed in the standard openings; some of these have to be learned as rules or habits of play. What a player does know is that the moves he makes COULD be justified, or that somebody he trusts has justified them. And where he has equally good or better reason for trusting somebody else's judgement as for trusting his own, we should be willing to say that he has a good reason for playing as he does, and that the inferences that justify his making such-and-such moves—even if he is unaware of them, or inca-pable of being made fully aware of them—would also explain his making those moves. Thus it is not necessary that a pragmatic explanation be

---

[5] This, I assume, is why Grice uses the expression "capable of being worked out," which has little else to recommend it.

even theoretically available to all or most of the speakers whose behavior it explains—I mean, consistent with their beliefs and capacities. They may be entirely incapable of working out the necessary inference, either because it is too complicated, or because it turns on knowledge or assumptions that they cannot presuppose in ordinary discourse. Yet if the explanation is available to some portion of the community, even a small one, whose members can make themselves generally—and, in the privileged sense, commonly—believed by others, then we can still say that the explanation accounts for general conformity to the use in question, since everybody will believe that he has a good reason for conforming.

Really, this is just an extension of what Putnam (1975) calls the "division of linguistic labor." Putnam points out that the use of many "natural-kind" terms, like *gold* and *lemon*, is in large part determined by a small community of experts whose job it is to fix the criteria that define the classes denoted by the terms. Other speakers may in fact be unaware of the actual criteria used, and identify exemplars of gold or lemons solely by consulting "stereotypes"; still, they will abide by expert opinion in settling disputed cases. Or, they may in fact know the relevant criteria— though Putnam does not discuss this possibility—yet have no idea WHY those particular criteria are used: whether, for example, the possession of such-and-such an atomic weight is a necessary property of gold, or merely a useful way of identifying it. We might also point out that the phenomenon has nothing to do with Putnam's philosophical realism, and extends to classes defined by other than physical properties, as noted by Evans (1977). We rely on experts, for example, to define the categories named by such words as *felony, baseball, grade-A prime, sloop, socialism, income*, and *incest*, though authority may be institutionalized to varying degrees. In fact it is only with the simplest and most basic categories that knowledge is evenly distributed throughout the population; relative to a community, we can even discern "experts" on the definition of such categories as we name with *jazz, stew, tabloids, hippies, vanity* and *mauve*. And this gives a further grounds for variation, as speakers may even be ignorant of what KINDS of criteria are relevant to the definition of each class; they may not know, for examples, whether *vegetable* names a natural kind, or whether tabloids are defined by their form or content. Yet their uncertainty is not reflected in the description we give the actual convention governing usage. That is, we can still say that the convention governing the use of the word *felony* ordains its use to refer to such-and-such, giving the technical definition, and that everyone is bound by this convention, and that they try as best they can to conform.

It will be easy enough to extend the division of linguistic labor to the division of pragmatic labor, to move from the role of specialists in determining the content of conventions to their role in determining the explanations that allow nonconventional uses of expressions. The most obvious examples of the process in which a small group is entrusted with justifying usage involve the unequal distribution of factual knowledge—the same inequalities that lead to specialist definitions in the examples we have just discussed. Take the use of phrases like *book price* (of a car), *financial vice-president, Broadway play, reasonable doubt, firing pin,* or *zone defense.* Most nonspecialist speakers learn these as single chunks, and although the explanation for the usage is more-or-less apparent after the fact, few would be capable of evaluating that explanation, or deciding for themselves that this was the very best way of referring to the standard market price of a used car, etc. Yet these phrases do not feel like stereotyped compounds (*country music, sports car, blank cartridge, margin account*), where we assume that meaning is not entirely compositional, that the explanation that we can work out—for even these latter are largely "transparent—is not a sufficiently good one to motivate the usage synchronically. And the only difference between the cases lies in whether we attribute the explanation to authority or not. Thus we assume that *book price* is entirely motivated for a car salesman, or *Broadway play* for a New York drama critic, but that even a gunnery officer would prefer to use some form other than *blank cartridge* if it were not conventional to do so.

The division of pragmatic labor is actually less interesting where factual assumptions are concerned than where it touches on the evaluative and affective presuppositions that we talked about earlier, for these are no more evenly distributed throughout the culture than any others. For one thing, the differences in sensibility that distinguish one social group from another are often the basis for the use of metaphors, speech-formulas, and expressions that are fully justified only when those sensibilities can be presupposed. For example, I have argued elsewhere (Nunberg, 1978) that the use of the word *dope* for marijuana, when it was first introduced, took its effect from the presence of a set of presuppositions about drug use that distinguished a class of "unregenerate" drug users from more apologetic "liberals," and so that it caught on as any vogue joke does, because it was apposite, and not simply because it happened to be arbitrarily adopted by prestige speakers. In fact we can assume that even speakers who were not entirely party to the sensibility that licensed the joke, but who aspired to be, must have realized that hip speakers had good reason for calling marijuana *dope,* so that they themselves had reason for using *dope* in that way, at least in conversations where they could assume that their intention to make a joke could be apprehended. (They would be, in fact, as someone who tells a joke he doesn't quite get.) It was only when speakers continued the usage in the knowledge that the attempt at humor was lost —and not simply worn—that any conventionalization could be assumed. To take another example, consider the use of *too* to mean "extremely," which has sometimes been popular among speakers who aspired to a kind of jaded *mondanité*. I think the use was largely self-explanatory—it pretended to presuppose absolute standards of comparison where none could be reasonably assumed—hence its presumptuousness, which is apparent to most speakers. But if the joke here is easy enough to get, it is in fact appropriate in many fewer contexts than it has been told in; that is, it is less often said because it is arch than because it is supposed to be arch. So here again the values of a small group license the practices of a much larger one.

Another example, of a different sort: Morgan (1978) discusses the pragmatic uses of allusion, such as when someone says *I want to be alone,* or *Am I my brother's keeper?* Here, knowledge of the circumstance of the original utterance contributes to its being cited in circumstances when the speaker wants to recall the original context to the hearer, usually in order to suggest a parallel between the original context and the context of utterance, or some other situation under discussion. Where a quote is commonly associated with a particular speaker and occasion, there is rarely a question of its repeated use being conventional. But there is another sort of allusion, to a familiar situation like a running gag. Morgan calls these "cliches," and gives as an example *I've got a headache,* spoken between spouses at bedtime; similar examples are *We've got to stop meeting like this,* and *No more mister nice guy.* In a way, these are like familiar punch lines, can be treated as particular quotes might be, so long as the associated situation of utterance (that is, the gag-type) is commonly familiar, and the use of the expression is actually restricted to contexts in which the original joke-situation might reasonably be invoked. For examples, if I encounter a friend by chance three days in a row on line at the Motor Vehicle Bureau, I could say "We've got to stop meeting like this," making as if our encounters were prearranged. At a certain point, however, the allusion may fade; association with the original circumstances of use may no longer motivate the allusion. So, for example, the expression *Your place or mine?* may still be recognizable as a punch line, but the associated joke may no longer have any propositional content, as it were. At that point we can no longer appeal to allusion to the original context(s) of utterance to explain the present use.[6]

---

[6] "Quotation" (or "mention") is a notion with a number of heuristically useful applications. For example, we can think of many speech-formulae (like *No more mister nice guy,* or *Hold your horses*) as citations from scenarios that are only partially accessible but

Division of labor enters here in an obvious way. For example, many more speakers are liable to quote *To be or not to be* to a hearer pondering a deep problem than would be able fully to justify their usage; THEY know only that it is a quote from *Hamlet* that is appropriate to those circumstances. But they believe also that an authoritative reading of the play would license their use of the quote, and to the extent that they are right, we can say that the circumstances of the original utterance justify their citation of it, even if they have only a vague idea of what those circumstances are.[7] A more complicated twist would be required to justify the use of an expression like *Break a leg,* which Morgan also discusses. It is my impression that most users of this expression know of its use among theater folk, and of the rationale for using it. Whether or not it is conventional in its restricted theatrical use (see the following), I think that the extended uses to wish someone good luck before a difficult encounter require no additional conventions, so long as the circumstances are those in which it might be appropriate to invoke a "trouper" sensibility. In this case speakers "borrow" the rationale for a practice from the subcommunity that it is commonly attributed to, though they may have only an imprecise idea of why those people have that sensibility in the first place; that is, they may not know why actors would be the sort of people to wish someone good luck by uttering a malediction.

The difficulty in determining whether some of these uses are conventional is only natural, and again let me point out the naïveté of supposing that there can be easy tests to help us along. It is hard enough to validate

---

which we want nonetheless to invoke. And many borrowings can be treated as quotations; when we say *c'est la vie,* for example, we quote a Frenchman to suggest to our listener the attitude of bemused resignation that we associate stereotypically with the French. In irony, we quote a more innocent self; in sarcasm, the voice that we think the other would like to have heard. All of these cases are related to the classic semantic problem of quotation contexts ("Galileo said S") in that all of them involve occasion for dissociating oneself from the content of one's utterance.

[7] This is as good a place as any to make one important equivocation. I have been a little inconsistent up to here, suggesting on the one hand that a practice was pragmatically justified if the community could assign it a rationale, whether collectively or individually, and on the other hand that it was justified for an individual if he believed that it could be assigned a rationale (or more accurately, believed that it could be commonly assigned a rationale). Obviously it is possible in both theory and practice that the two criteria should not converge; that a speaker should be wrong in what he assumes is commonly believed about a certian usage. But I think speakers are in general reasonably skillful at apprehending what is commonly believed about an expression, even if it is different from what they themselves believe, and even when there is a lot of heterogeneity in what is commonly believed—in which case they at least know that there is heterogeneity—and so it does not seem to me too much of a distortion to assume for argument's sake that speakers are always correct in such beliefs.

an explanation when we have only to attribute its terms to a particular context (say when we are dealing with a unique conversational implicature), especially where the "irrational" mechanisms of humor, irony, or persuasion come into play. It is harder still to validate an explanation when we are not sure to which actual contexts we have to be able to attribute its terms; that is, who has enough authority to carry usage along with them. In any event, it should be clear that a speaker's ability to come up with AN explanation for a use is neither a necessary nor sufficient condition for saying that the use is conventional, and so that Sadock's examples of idioms and euphemisms are beside the point. What matters is that we—or the speakers themselves—be able to attribute a SUFFICIENT explanation to the group that uses the expression, seen collectively.

4. WHY PRAGMATIC EXPLANATIONS UNDERDETERMINE USE

The points we have made about the division of pragmatic labor are also relevant to the second of Sadock's objections, that an explanation may underdetermine the usage we actually observe. (This is the *Can you . . .* type of case.) But the point here is easier to make in the light of some general observations about what it means to say that usage is determined collectively.

It would be misleading to interpret all this talk of "experts" too narrowly, as some of the examples we have up to now discussed might lead us to do, and to assume that there are two classes of linguistic practices, those determined collectively by small numbers of people, and those determined individually. EVERY linguistic practice is determined collectively, in the sense that a speaker can never act on an assumption, either about meaning or about the inferences that give rise to implicatures, unless he can attribute it to a common conversational ground, which is to say, unless he can assume that it is acceptable to other speakers as a basis for discussion. When we use a word like *gold,* the ground contains the assumption that gold is that stuff that the experts say it is, plus some rough and ready heuristics for identifying gold in practice ("a soft yellow metal," etc.). But we also noted that there is considerable division of labor in the determination of usage even where no institutionalized expertise is involved. We assume that some speakers are better than others, for example, at identifying examples of the things we call *jazz,* or *vanity,* or *smoothie;* what these speakers can do, in the main, is to articulate theories of musical forms, or the virtues, or social types, that best characterize what other speakers who are in the know about such things are likely to operate on, and that less sophisticated speakers will try to conform to in their usage as best they can. In these cases, it is true, a larger part of the "meaning" of the work is likely to form part of the ground in most contexts, but the difference is only relative. Most speakers do not have very clear ideas of the differencne between jazz and pop, for example, or vanity and narcissism, and they will change their usage according to what more authoritative speakers tell them.

There is some specialization, in fact, even in the determinaton of the meanings of the most common terms. Consider the sentence frame, *A isn't* REALLY————. We could construct as potentially informative a sentence by filling the slot with *red* or *a physical object* as with *gold* or *a felony;* there are very few categories whose criteria are not subject to revision on more expert opinion. It is only when we come to terms that designate logically basic relations, like *whole* or *and*—Putnam's "one criterion words"—that we can expect individual theories to be so manifestly uniform that the collective theory can only duplicate them.[8]

The same holds, naturally, of the explanations we assign to the nonconventional uses of expressions. Alongside *book price,* for example, we could cite phrases like *transistor radio* or *summer print* (dresses); although the assumptions that licence these uses are accessible to a great many more people than truly "specialized" explanations, they are scarcely evenly distributed among members of the community. Where expressions involve irony, sarcasm, or other rhetorical effects, there is a natural differentiation that is best expressed in the old line about jokes: "Some people can tell 'em and some people can't." And here again, not even the simplest inferences are exempt from variation. Consider the use of sentences like *If he's a lawyer then I'm the king of France* to assert "He's not a lawyer." Surely not everybody can grasp the equivalence of *not p* and *if p then q,* for a *q* that is obviously false—nor does everybody have to. All we require is that the equivalence shall be apparent to enough speakers to carry the rest.

What we have shown up to now is that certain practices are justifiable only when we consider the "beliefs"—I am not sure that that is the right word—of the community as a whole. And the explanations of those practices are correctly attributed only to what we can call the "collective representation," where all of the propositions that members of a community are committed to accept, or behave as if they accept, are lodged in an undifferentiated whole. As long as a practice has this collective justifica-

---

[8] Even here, however, there is reason for caution. Whenever an item can change in use, it must be the case that there is at least a possibility that speakers will disagree as to what it means, unless the change is due to purely syntactic or phonological factors. And, as few items are exempt from meaning-change, it is only very rarely that we can ignore the difference between collective and individual determination of meaning.

tion, it need not be mentioned in a description of the collective representation of linguistic conventions themselves, or *langue*. (I should add a note of caution here, because linguists sometimes talk of notions like the *conscience collective* with a note of ontological horror, as if it were a creation of Jung, rather than Durkheim and his predecessors. In fact the ontological status of social facts, like that of "mind," is neither here nor there; both have proven to be durable and useful constructs, and reductionists have not fared very well in getting rid of either, perhaps for the same reasons.)[9]

Now it is usually assumed that there is no empirical difference between a view of language in terms of *langue* and one in terms of idealized competence (see, e.g., Chomsky, 1964). And although there are good a priori grounds for suspecting otherwise (for one thing, there is no reason to suppose that the best representations of social facts need be learnable by any individual speaker), it is true that the difference between the two points of view has never had any real importance to linguistic theory or practice. I think the implicit assumption has always been that competence comes out empirically the same as *langue* under a sufficiently severe idealization; the "ideal speaker in the homogeneous speech community," and so forth.

I won't thrash this out in detail here. Let me simply observe that the assumption is right for syntax and phonology, and wrong for semantics. The trick is that the relevant homogeneity has to extend to the factors that influence performance, as well as to linguistic practices. These factors ARE pretty much uniform so far as formal regularitities are concerned (that is, speakers are RELATIVELY uniform with respect to memory limitation, or articulatory apparatus.)[10] So it is not too severe an idealization to assume that a sentence that is hard to parse for one speaker will be hard to parse for all speakers, or that a word that is hard to pronounce for one speaker will be hard to pronounce for everyone. And consequently, explanation can always be offcred at the individual level; no performance strategy will be justified collectively that is not justified individually. (Thus a community will avoid multiple self-embedding or certain consonant clusters only if the process makses sense to each of its members.)

In semantics, by contrast, the "performance factors" that determine linguistic practices are not uniform for all members of the community; as we have seen, a practice can have a collective rationale that is not evident

---

[9] Cf. Durkheim, *Les règles de la méthode sociologique:* "Traiter des faits d'un certain ordre comme des choses, n'est donc pas les classer dans telle ou telle catégorie du réel; c'est observer vis-à-vis d'elles une certaine attitude mentale."

[10] the order of magnitude of variation in such matters is reflected in Miller's well-known characterization of the number of items that short-term memory will accomodate as "7 ± 2."

to all its members. The net effect is that here *langue* determines *parole* more indirectly than in syntax or phonology, even when we assume in each case a homogeneous representation of linguistic conventions, since in semantics we have to contend with the fact that the conventions themselves, and the strategies whereby they come to be exploited, will be represented only imperfectly in the minds of individual speakers. So where we are forced to take the social point of view—in pragmatics and semantics, that is—our explanations must necessarily be less determinate, and have less predictive value. (When people are not sure why they are doing what they are doing, that is, they do not do it so well.)

Here again, we can refer to Putnam's examples. It is fair to say that the convention governing the English word *gold* allows its use only to refer to gold—I mean, to that particular element and nothing else. And if the stereotype that individual speakers use to identify gold sometimes misses the mark—if they include fool's gold, say, and exclude white gold—that does not mean that they are behaving—or think they are behaving—in accordance with different conventions. They are TRYING to use the word as convention dictates; it is just that they do not have the means, or sometimes the motive, to do so rigorously. Collectively, they approximate the convention as best they can, and to say that the convention actually ordains the use of *gold* to refer only to (real) gold is to describe the limit of that approximation. In exactly the same way, we can abstract over all the uses of a work like *vanity* to arrive at a category in a collective theory of character, and say that this category is what speakers are trying to refer to, after their various fashions. (In the case of *vanity*, of course, there is a lot more variation than with *gold*, even in terms of who the experts are taken to be. So we either assume a very severe idealization to a homogeneous collective representation—the sort that we allow when we talk about, say, "the Renaissance theory of character"—or we restrict ourselves to talking about well-defined subcommunitites.) In either case, a description of the convention itself is not a description of what speakers do, but of what they are trying to do, and as such, it still explains their behavior.

In exactly the same way, pragmatic explanation will specify a class of contexts in which a certain use of an expression is licensed, but speakers who are partially or wholly unaware of the content of the explanation will only be able to approximate these contexts in actual behavior; here as well we can expect them to resort to the use of stereotypes. For example, speakers who are not specialists will use expressions like *reasonable doubt* or *zone defense* inaccurately, because they lack the technical knowledge required to use them correctly; still they will assume that the meanings of the expressions are entirely compositional. The explanation we assign to a slang metaphor like *dope* for marijuana will cover only its use in contexts in which speakers want to indicate a certain kind of specious irony about drug use, but it will account indirectly for the use of the expression in a great many more contexts, when it is used by speakers who know only that the use turns on some sensibility that characterizes the speakers they want to identify with. That is, the explanation justifies its use by initiates in a context-type that noninitiates can identify only by a rough stereotype, THEIR idea of "hip." Or take the *Break a leg* example; the extended use of the expression by theater people—say to wish someone good luck before he undertakes a difficult confrontation—may be imperfectly construed by other speakers, who will use the expression as a general good luck wish, or who may restrict its use to contexts in which they want to invoke their own stereotype of the plucky actor. In either case, the fact that they are at a remove from the community in which at least the extended use of the expression is completely justified will affect the way they use the term, but the explanation of the use by theater people will explain their use too, if indirectly.

This, then, is the first reason why pragmatic explanations underdetermine use: In a heterogeneous community, pragmatic explanations specify only the goal for a set of indifferent individual efforts. There is a second kind of underdetermination, as well, which takes us back to Sadock's objection. An explanation may allow a number of equivalent realizations of a strategy, yet only those who know the explanation will be in a position to choose freely among these. For example, a chess player who has learned the openings by heart is not at liberty to substitute freely variations that are strategically equivalent, even though he may know that such substitutions are theoretically justifiable. And by the same token, only a gifted joke-teller can weave variations on a punch line; other speakers may be aware that such variation is possible (and that the effect of the joke will remain more-or-less the same), but they are best off recounting the story exactly as they heard it. So it is often the case that we find more uniformity in collective linguistic practice than the explanation we offer would seem to require, simply because the strategy involved happens to have become popularized in a single realization, and individual speakers are incapable, like the average joke-teller, of improvising productive variations. For example, Morgan (1978) mentions the use of the sentence *Do I look like a rich man?* as a response to a request for money. Let us assume that the same effect would be achieved by the responses *Do I look like Nelson Rockefeller?* or *Do you take me for a millionaire?* or any number of equivalents, but that speakers actually produce only the first of these. It would be more reasonable to lay their conformity to unimaginativeness than to convention. Or consider another of Morgan's examples, the use of fatuous questions like *Is the Pope Catholic?* or *Does a bear shit in the woods?* to indicate that the interlocutor has asked something whose answer is obvious. Morgan suggests that the fact that most speakers have only a limited number of such answers available indicates that a "convention of usage" determines their choice. I suspect that most of Morgan's conventions of usage are really instances of situations in which one of a number of possible alternatives has been adopted by most speakers, either out of laziness, unimaginativeness, or for another reason, which we will come to shortly.[11]

The reason that such usages SEEM conventional, of course, is precisely that there seems to be no grounds for one alternative being picked over another; the selection is arbitrary. (Or synchronically arbitrary; there may have been a historical reason for one alternative being more salient than another). But this is not sufficient grounds for assuming a convention. If we recall Lewis's (1969) definition, we suppose a convention only when, roughly, there is universal preference for conformity to a given regularity. (In Lewis's terms, R is conventional only if, given general conformity to R, almost everyone prefers that others conform to R; and that if there were general conformity to R', almost everyone would prefer that others conform to R'.) So for example, I prefer that everyone call dogs *dogs* if most people call dogs *dogs*, and that everyone call dogs *cats* if most people call dogs *cats*. But that is because there is no other reason for calling dogs *dogs* in the first place; there will be successful coordination only if (almost) everybody conforms. By contrast, I do not really care whether small chil-

---

[11] I find it difficult to accept Morgan's point that there can be "conventions of usage" that are not linguistic conventions; I suspect that most of his examples involve either "partially motivated" uses, or no conventions at all. It seems to me that there can be only one form of convention governing language use: "Say x in situation S." Morgan gives examples like the following: "When some sneezes, say the German word *Gesundheit*." But this appears equivalent to saying, "When someone sneezes, say *Gesundheit*," with the added proviso that speakers' knowledge that *Gesundheit* is a German word will itself influence its use. This is really like any other case of partial motivation—*kick the bucket*, or example—except that here there is the added fillip that the "motivating" convention holds in another speech community. As for other candidates for "conventions of usage" (such as the use of *Gentlemen, start your engines* to start motor races) if we assume that this usage is conventional— and I think there is enough preference for conformity (to be discussed in what follows) here to say that it is—then it is a linguistic convention *tout court*. This is not to say that participants cannot come up with an explanation for the usage—that they cannot parse the sentence that is conventionally used in this situation, for example, or that this perception does not thereby determine, say, how they pronounce the signal. But their explanation again does not account for the regularity of use, assuming that they know that no variations on the formula are permissable. But Morgan raises a number of challenging points; I do not know what to make of the status of a regularity like *Change the subject by talking about the weather*, for example.

dren call dogs *bow-wows* or *rowfs* or *arf-arfs* or what, and I suspect the children do not care either, since coordination—in this case, under-standing—will not be much affected one way or the other. (Admittedly, there is probably always SOME slight preference for linguistic conformity, even when it serves little purpose; people who say *economics* with a long *e* probably wish everybody else said *economics* with a long *e*, and people who say *It is I* surely wish that everyone else said *It is I*. But there is a corresponding preference for variation, too, where understanding is not affected. And the preference for conformity here is not of the same order as in the cases of true convention, nor does it have the same motivation—in pure game-theoretic terms, it has no motivation at all.)

Now I see no reason why a speaker who always responds to an obvious question with *Is the Pope Catholic?* should have any preference at all as to what expression other speakers should use to the same purpose; if any-thing, we would expect that he would value the speaker who varied his answer. And so there is no grounds for supposing that his own regularity owes anything to convention; certainly he does not conform because he prefers that everybody conform. And I expect we could make the same argument about many other regularities that look like conventions simply because so many obvious alternatives offer themselves. But I should ex-press a couple of reservations here, which complicate the picture. First, there may be a preference for conformity which, although not actually justified by the desire for coordination, is nonetheless based on something stronger than the weak velleity in the *economics* case. For instance, I sus-pect that the standard story on the *break a leg* example—"Theater people believe that if you wish somebody bad luck, your wish won't come true" —is not sufficient to motivate the exclusive use of *break a leg;* one would think that *lay an egg* or *die* would do as well. But it is unlikely that the reason that these alternatives are not exploited is simply that members of the community are unimaginative; it is more reasonable to suppose that *break a leg* is a ritual utterance, that a certain magic is attached to the use of that particular form. In that case, however, there can be no question of the usage being conventional at all: People conform to it not out of an in-terest in uniformity, but because those are the only syllables that God or Thalia will attend. (Analogously, Aladdin says "Open sesame" to the door to the cave because only that expression works for him; he would not care if it should happen that the door opened for others when they said "Open sorghum.")

The *break a leg* example is interesting, but not too important for our purposes. There are other cases, however, that are more vexing, where there may be a pressure for conformity without a preference for it. We have up to now sidestepped the question of how speakers can know that a practice is justified without knowing what that justification is, or even being in a position to have good intuitions on the subject. In general, I think, they rely on a combination of the information that they do have available, and observations of the usage of others. For example, suppose that a noninitiate speaker hears *dope* used once or twice by a speaker he regards as hip, and that he knows enough about the literal meaning of *dope* and the relevant sensibilities to suspect that the usage must be clever, but not enough to figure out if it is licensed by presuppositions that are fairly general in the hip community, or only by presuppositions that hold in a very local context. Then he does not know whether he can get away with trying to make the joke or not—whether he can plausibly pretend that the same presuppositions govern his contexts as govern those of his hip friend. Obviously the knowledge that a number of hip speakers use the term in this way is going to help him to decide, not that the use is in any way conventional, but on the contrary, that the cleverness of it is generally appreciated. In the same way, if someone who knows very little about football hears a particular coach refer to a *zone defense* or an *I-formation*, he may be able to figure out part of the rationale for the usage, but he will not be convinced that it is entirely motivated until he hears the use repeated in other contexts by other speakers. Even where authority is more etiolated, as in the case of answers like *Is the Pope Catholic?* the same situation may occur; a speaker may not be sure that the use is generally regarded as clever until he hears it used by others. So there is some grounds for saying that the currency of a particular expression is a necessary condition for there being a general appreciation of the fact that it has a good rationale. This does not entail, of course, that speakers have a preference that everyone else should conform to such a usage; the conformity matters to them only insofar as it is evidence that they themselves are justified in the usage.

In one sense, this is just a variation of what we said earlier about the incapacity (or timidity) of most speakers when it comes to innovation. But this way of putting it has an interesting consequence when we ask after the nonoccurrence of certain uses in certain communities. For example, Americans and English both use the expression *not much* in an ironic way, to express scepticism about what somebody else has said. But only the English use *not many* (or *not many, Benny*) to indicate scepticism as to an assertion about quantity. And in this case I can see nothing in the different national characters to predict the usage, nor can it be that no American has ever been clever enough to make the obvious extention. So it must be that *not many* was never used ENOUGH among a key group of American speakers to catch on there, for whatever accidental reason. The point is that the ''precedent'' that justifies the assumption that a usage is justified may have to be rather extensive, before it will become a generally adopted move. But let me emphasize again that this is not evidence for saying that the British use of *not many* is conventional. All we can assume is that this particular strategy happens to have had a more salient prece- in Britain than in America. The case is not different in KIND from the dif- ference in salience that makes *To be or not to be* more widely quoted than *Cast thy nighted color off,* or *We've got to stop meeting like this* more often said than *I thought I heard a seal bark.*

This takes us to the last complication I wanted to mention. Even where two realizations of a strategy are equally well motivated at the collective level, there will likely be a difference in implicature at the individual level according to whether a speaker chooses a well-worn path or not. So a speaker who answers a fatuous question, say, with *Is Philip Roth a mi- sogynist?* will achieve a different effect from one who uses the more com- mon *Is the Pope Catholic?* But this difference will be over and above the conversational rationale that is collectively assigned, indifferently, to ei- ther utterance. In either case, that is, the implicature "That was a stupid question" is the same; the first simply gilds the lily a bit. (In which con- nection, we could point to the analogous difference between saying *gild the lily* and the historically correct *paint the lily,* where an added implica- ture of arrogant erudition attaches to the use of the second, but where the conversational purpose of the quote is otherwise the same.)

5. CONCLUSION

I can easily see how many linguists might find these conclusions de- pressing, and how others might see all their worst suspicions about the "sloppiness" of pragmatics confirmed in them. It is not simply that we cannot "test" for conversational implicature in any simple way, nor even that our demonstrations that such-and-such a usage is not conventional are not subject to any sort of empirical confirmation, in the sense of the natural sciences; even when we can assign a pragmatic explanation to a use it has only a limited predictive value. The difficulties vary according to cases, of course—we can deal with the pragmatics of conjunctions with more rigor than with the more descriptive reaches of the lexicon, but even with the pragmatics of a work like *and,* the same problems intrude. The fact is that the empirical study of natural-language semantics simply cannot compare in objective rigor with the study of it syntax or phonol- ogy, and that no increase in technical sophistication is likely to alter the basic picture.

At the same time, all that any of this means is that linguistic semantics is properly included among the "interpretive sciences" (or *Geisteswissenschaften*, if you insist), and that it is responsible to the canons of explanation that hold for THEM. Now there is a considerable literature on this subject, to put it mildly, and this is not the place to go into it. But I should mention one point, which bears directly on Sadock's despair over the possibility of "knowing for sure" if a practice is conventional. The distinction between the interpretive and natural sciences has long been drawn around the crucial role of "understanding" (*Verstehen*, in the jargon) in formulating and validating hypotheses that proceed from assumptions about human beliefs and desires; the idea is that the analyst has to be able to put at least part of his foot into his subject's shoes. And the point has sometimes been made, as well, that understanding may provide a kind of certainty that is not available in the natural sciences, or in those branches of the human sciences (syntax, the psychology of perception) in which it plays little or no role. To take a linguistic example, it may be harder to demonstrate objectively that a certain utterance is ironic or flip than, say, that the operation of verb phrase deletion is subject to considerations of syntactic identity. But we are no less certain of the first claim than the second. In the end, there is more than one kind of "knowledge for sure."

REFERENCES

Chomsky, N. (1964). *Current Issues in Linguistic Theory*. The Hague: Mouton.

Cole, P., and Morgan J. (Eds.), (1975). *Syntax and Semantics: Speech Acts*. New York: Academic Press.

Cole, P. (Ed.), (1978). *Syntax and Semantics 9: Pragmatics*. New York: Academic Press.

Evans, G. (1977). The causal theory of names. In S. Schwartz (Ed.), *Naming, Necessity, and Natural Kinds*. Ithaca: Cornell University Press. Pp, 192–215.

Fodor, J. A., and Katz, J. J. (Eds.), (1964). *The Structure of Language: Readings in the Philosophy of Language*. Englewood Cliffs, N.J.: Prentice-Hall.

Grice, H. P. (1975). Logic and conversation. In P. Cole and J. Morgan (Eds.), *Syntax and Semantics 3: Speech Acts*. Pp. 41–58.

Horn, L. R. (1978). Remarks on neg-raising. In P. Cole (Ed.), *Syntax and Semantics 9: Pragmatics*. New York: Academic Press. Pp. 129–220.

Katz, J. J., and Fodor, J. A. (1964). The structure of a semantic theory. In J. A. Fodor and J. J. Katz (Eds.), *The Structure of Language: Readings in the Philosophy of Language*. Englewood Cliffs, N.J.: Prentice-Hall.

Lewis, D. K. (1969). *Convention: A Philosophical Study*. Cambridge, Mass.: Pp. 479–518. Harvard University Press.

Morgan, J. L. (1978). Two types of convention in indirect speech acts. In P. Cole (Ed.), *Syntax and Semantics 9: Pragmatics*. New York: Academic Press. Pp. 261–280.

Nunberg, G. (1978). Slang, usage-conditions and *l'arbitraire du signe*. In *Parasession on the Lexicon*. Chicago Linguistic Society, Department of Linguistics, University of Chicago. Pp. 301–311.

Nunberg, G. (1979). The non-uniqueness of semantic solutions. *Linguistics and Philosophy,* **3**(2), 143–184.

Putnam, H. (1975). The Meaning of Meaning. In H. Putnam, *Mind, Language and Reality.* Cambridge: Cambridge University Press.

Sadock, J. M. (1978). On testing for conversational implicature. In P. Cole (Ed.), *Syntax and Semantics 9: Pragmatics.* New York: Academic Press. Pp. 281–297.

Toward a Taxonomy of Given–New Information

Ellen F. Prince

1. ON THE CONVEYING OF INFORMATION IN LANGUAGE

It is a truism that, when people use language naturally, they are usually attempting to convey information. Occasionally, the only information conveyed is of a purely social or ritual nature; such is the case in (1), where each speaker is doing little more than informing the other that s/he is aware of the other's presence, is not hostile, and will part ready to come into friendly contact again at some future time:[1]

[1] Erving Goffman has pointed out (personal communication) that other types of information, in addition to ritual information, are conveyed in indirect ways—for example, meta-communication information. Furthermore, what makes ritual information ritual information is not the information itself but the indirect (ritualized) way in which it is presented. That is, if A makes the following utterance to B, A's utterance willl exemplify what I shall call, for lack of a better term, "objective" information:

> [A and B are passing each other on the street]
> A: *I am aware of your presence, I am not hostile, and I shall part ready to come into friendly contact again at some future time.*
> B: *Damn sociolinguists . . .*

The matter is obviously complex but, fortunately, not crucial to the subject of this chapter. See Goffman (1967) for a discussion of different types of information conveyed.

223

(1)   [*A* and *B* are passing each other on the street]
        A: Hi.
        B: Hi.

Utterances that convey only ritual information in the sense used here are
typically short, (virtually) asyntactic, and relatively few in number; with
most utterances, it is impossible for a speaker/writer to avoid conveying,
in addition (or instead), "objective" information, although there is, of
course, nothing to prevent that objective information from being banal or
even silly.[2] Thus (2) conveys, in addition to the ritual information analogous to that conveyed in (1), the objective information that (*A* thinks that)
it is a very hot day:

(2)   [*A* to *B* at bus stop on a summer day]
        What a scorcher!

One presumably universal feature of natural language is that the objective information conveyed is not conveyed on a single plane. That is,
there is an INFORMATIONAL ASYMMETRY in that some units seem to convey or represent "older" information than others. Given–new distinctions can be found on different levels—the sentence, the discourse, the
participants' discourse-models—as will be seen in what follows. On all
levels, however,—and perhaps this is not only universal, but also distinctive of human language—the crucial factor appears to be the tailoring of
an utterance by a sender to meet the particular assumed needs of the intended receiver. That is, information-packaging in natural language re-
flects the sender's hypotheses about the receiver's assumptions and beliefs and strategies.

---

[2] There are some apparent counterexamples to this. One, the monologue, can however be
construed as a sender conveying information to a receiver, the only aberration being that a
single individual is playing both roles. It would be of interest to study naturally occurring
monologues to see just how the information they convey is structured and distributed. Another is the utterance whose utterer believes that there is in fact no receiver, such as a lecture to an obviously distracted audience, a dissertation written for a presumedly uninter-
ested and lazy adviser (see Chomsky, 1975, p. 61 for a poignant description of such an
experience). In such cases, the utterance itself, as an object (e.g., a lecture, a dissertation),
tends to have ritualistic import, which accounts for why the sender bothers to produce it.
And part of the ritual seems to be that the sender acts AS THOUGH there were a receiver.
Other, less interesting, cases are those where the sender believes s/he is conveying information to a receiver but is in fact mistaken (e.g., unbeknownst to the sender, the telephone has
been disconnected or God does not exist or an unopened letter is destroyed in a fire). Such
cases are not relevant here because it is only the sender's assumptions at the time of producing the utterance that are relevant to the structure and distribution of given–new information, as we shall argue in what follows.

In what follows, I shall discuss briefly these three different levels of given–new information and some of the major literature associated with each (Section 2), and then I shall examine more closely one of these levels and propose a provisional txonomy for it (Section 3). Following will be an illustrative analysis of two naturally occurring texts—one an informal oral narrative, the other a formal written didactic piece —and a comparison of the two with respect to the structure and distribution of given–new information in them (Section 4). Finally, I shall suggest further areas of research that seem particularly promising (Section 5).

2. "GIVEN–NEW"

The general notion of given versus new information figures prominently in much linguistic literature, under that name or under one of its aliases: old–new, known–new, presupposition–focus, and so on. It has been invoked both in the explication of many sentence-level phenomena (e.g., Gapping, Dative, Pronominalization, Left and Right Dislocation, sentential subjects, *it*-clefts, *wh*-clefts, Topicalization) and in the explication of how discourses are structure and understood. Bolinger, Chafe, Chomsky, Clark, Horn, Jackendoff, and Kuno are just a few of the linguists who have found the notion relevant to their work.

Unfortunately, however, this intuitively appealing notion has never received a satisfactory characterization that would enable a working linguist to not only invoke it but to actually put it to use. In fact, if one considers the definitions that have been presented, one discovers that there is not one notion involved but (at least) three.[3] Of all the linguists who have used these terms or their synonyms, those that are perhaps the most strongly associated with the notion are Chafe, Clark and Haviland, Halliday, and Kuno. It is rather surprising, then, that, when their discussions on the subject are closely examined and compared, it becomes evident that no two of them mean quite the same thing, and that, in some cases, the differences are quite large. Space does not here permit a thorough investigation of the literature involved, so I shall simply discuss briefly the three levels of givenness that their notions may be thought of as belonging to, in order that the reader may have a clearer idea of what we shall then be examining.

---

[3] As added evidence of the gravity of the situation, let me mention that the Old/New Information Workshop held at Urbana, Summer 1978, was quickly and quite appropriately dubbed the "Mushy Information Workshop."

2.1 Givenness$_p$: Predictability/Recoverability

In speaker–hearer terms, givenness in the sense of predictability/recoverability may be described as in (3).

(3) **Givenness$_p$**: The speaker assumes that the hearer CAN PREDICT OR COULD HAVE PREDICTED that a PARTICULAR LINGUISTIC ITEM will or would occur in a particular position WITHIN A SENTENCE.

This type is represented by what Kuno (1972, 1978, 1979) calls "old–new" information and what Halliday (1967) and Halliday and Hasan (1976) call "given–new" information, although the two notions are defined differently and what is old for Kuno is not necessarily given for Halliday. In particular, Kuno defines old–new information in terms of recoverability: "An element in a sentence represents old, predictable information if it is recoverable from the preceding context; if it is not recoverable, it represents new, unpredictable information [1978, pp. 282–283]." Clearly, recoverability correlates with deletability, but it does not address many other phenomena that are felt to be related to given–new information, for example, the difference in status between a nondeletable pronoun and its antecedent, as in (4).

(4) *Mary paid John$_1$ and he$_1$/*∅ bought himself$_i$ a new coat.*

Compare (4) with (5):

(5) *John$_1$ paid Mary and he$_1$/∅ bought himself$_i$ a new coat.*

If predictability/recoverability were the only criterion by which to judge the newness of an NP, then *he* in (5) would be old whereas *he* in (4) would be new, although, in some sense, they look very much the same age. Thus Kuno (1972) adds a second distinction, that of anaphoric–nonanaphoric, to which we shall return in Section 2.3.

For Halliday (1967), given–new is defined quite differently, in terms of intonation: An intonationally marked or unmarked focus identifies what is new; given is defined as the complement of a marked focus. Thus, in an information-unit with unmarked focus, nothing is given (p. 208). Halliday predicts that what is thus labeled new is "information . . . that the speaker presents . . . as not being recoverable from the preceding discourse [p. 204]." In Halliday and Hasan (1976), new is described as in Halliday (1967), and given is described as "expressing what the speaker is presenting as information that is recoverable from some source or other in the environment—the situation or the preceding text [p. 326]." It is still optional, that is, an information-unit may contain no given information.

Although Halliday's recoverability looks at first blush a good deal like

Kuno's predictability, the two will make different predictions if Halliday's restriction of given to sentences with marked focus is upheld.[4] For example, if (5) were uttered with normal intonation (i.e., unmarked focus), *he* would be old for Kuno and neither given nor new for Halliday.

Halliday's notion does, however, relate directly to a certain class of otherwise mysterious phenomena, illustrated by the famous example in (6a):

(6) a. *John called Mary a Republican and then SHE insulted HIM.*
     b. *John called Mary a Republican and then she insulted him.*

Following Halliday, *SHE* and *HIM* in (6a) would be marked foci (assuming one may have more than one marked focus per information-unit), resulting in the remainder of the unit, *insulted,* being identified as given, that is, recoverable from the preceding context. Now the only way in which it could be recoverable is if it is somehow equivalent to *called a Republican.* Compare with (6b), where no such equivalence is inferred, and (7), where the contrast is even more dramatic than in (6).

(7) a. *John$_i$ called Sam$_j$ a Republican and then HE$_j$ insulted HIM$_i$.*
     b. *John$_i$ called Sam$_j$ a Republican and then he$_i$ insulted him$_j$.*

Here the addition of the marked foci effect two changes: First, because *HE* and *HIM* in (7a) are marked as being new, that is, unrecoverable (in the position which they occupy), they cannot refer to *John* and *Sam,* respectively. Being pronouns, they do, however, refer to some entities already in the discourse-model (about which more will be said), and, in this impoverished discourse-model, the only choices left are *Sam* and *John,* in that order. Thus the marked foci effect a change in coreference. Second, the marked foci cause *insulted* to be identified as given and thus equivalent to *called a Republican,* as in (6a). Therefore, we no longer need say that *called a Republican* in such sentences "presupposes" *insulted* in order to arrived at an account of the understanding this sentence receives. The situation is not quite so simple, of course; consider (8).

(8)   *John called Mary a Republican /and then SAM walked in /and they all started fighting.*

(Slashes indicate information-unit boundaries.) If *SAM* is the marked focus of its information-unit, then *walked in* must be given and should be understood as being equivalent to something in the preceding informa-

---

[4] Halliday, himself, seems not to take the intonation criterion seriously when he remarks that anaphoric items are "inherently 'given' (1967, p. 206)." But perhaps the quotation marks around *given* implicate "not really."

tion-unit, which of course is not the case. Obviously, then, we do not want to say that *walked in* is given, but an analysis that considers only intonation as a primitive cannot distinguish between *walked in* in (8) and *insulted* in (6a) (unless, of course, the stress on *SAM* in (8) is considered to be of an identifiably different type from the stress on *SHE* and *HIM* in (6a)). What is needed is the inclusion of Kuno's predictability as a primitive, along with intonation, perhaps as part of a principle along the lines of (9):

(9)   **Parallelism Principle:** A speaker assumes that the hearer will predict, unless there is evidence to the contrary, that (a proper part of) a new (conjoined?) construction will be parallel/equivalent in some semantic/pragmatic way(s) to the one just processed.[5]

This is obviously a rough and inadequate approximation, but the idea is that, while extra stress always marks its item as new (in the sense of being unpredictable in a particular sentence-position), there are some situations in which the Parallelism Principle can still be invoked (e.g., (6a), (7a)) and others where other factors require its abandonment (e.g., (8)). Perhaps it is only in the former cases that the complement of a marked focus should be labeled as given. (Note that some version of the Parallelism Principle is needed in any event in order to account for the usual understanding of the pronouns in (7b).) Much research, including psycholinguistic experimentation, is required before any contentful version of (9) can be arrived at; what I have tried to do here is simply to isolate the notion of givenness in the sense of predictability/recoverability and to suggest that a consideration of speakers' hypotheses about hearers' beliefs and strategies must be a primitive.

2.2 Givenness$_s$: Saliency

In speaker–hearer terms, givenness in the sense of saliency may be roughly described as follows:

(10)   **Givenness$_s$:** The speaker assumes that the hearer has or could appropriately have some particular thing/entity/ . . . in his/her CONSCIOUSNESS at the time of hearing the utterance.

Chafe's (1976) notion of given–new information falls under this rubric; for Chafe, given information represents "that knowledge which the speaker assumes to be in the consciousness of the addressee at the time of the utterance," and new, "what the speaker assumes he is introducing into the

---

[5] See Kuno (1974) for a discussion of the notion of parallelism.

addressee's consciousness by what he says [p. 30]." He takes it to be a binary distinction; thus known items that are introduced into the discourse for the first time are as new as unknown ones; for example, the bold-faced NPs in (11a) and (11b) are equally new:

(11)   a. *I saw **your father** yesterday.*
       b. *I saw **a two-headed man** yesterday.*

Furthermore, for an NP to qualify as given, its referent must have been explicitly introduced in the discourse or be present in the physical context or be categorized in the same way as a referent previously introduced or physically present (p. 32). Thus an inferentially related NP cannot be given, unless the inference is one of categorization. In the following examples (originally from Haviland and Clark, 1974), Chafe (pp. 41–42) calls *the beer* given in (12a) and new in (12b):

(12)   a. *We got some beer out of the trunk. **The beer** was warm.*
       b. *We got some picnic supplies out of the trunk. **The beer** was warm.*

At the same time, however, Chafe states (p. 31) that only (but not all and only) given items can be pronominalized. Examples like (13) then suggest that inferentially related NPs in general might have to be included as possible given items:

(13)   a. *Pick two numbers, add six to the first number, and then multiply it by the second number.*[6]
       b. *Harry threw up and Sam stepped in it.*[7]
       c. *In New York **they** drive very differently from the way **they** drive in Philadelphia.*

Chafe's notion of givenness is the model for the notion used in Prince 1978a for the analysis of the function of *wh*-clefts, except that it was extended to allow for any inferences so long as they could be deemed situationally appropriate.[8] Thus the bold-faced NP in (14) is given following Prince 1978a, but presumably new following Chafe 1976:

(14)   *If I write loosely of a noun as being in the status GIVEN, **what I really mean** is that the idea which this noun expresses has this status.*   (Chafe, 1976; p. 29.)

---

[6] I thank Bonnie Webber for this example.

[7] See P.R.N. Tic Douloureux (1971).

[8] New$_s$ information is not discussed in Prince 1978a and the question of whether the given$_s$ –new$_s$ distinction is binary is not addressed.

That is, following Prince 1978a, the writer of (14) is purporting to assume that it is appropriate for the reader to have in mind, by the time s/he reaches the comma, that the writer really means something if he writes loosely of a noun as being in the status *given*.

There is of course a difference between the givenness of pronouns like the one in (15) and the givenness of *wh*-clauses like the one in (14):

(15)   [A_i to B_j as C_k passes by, in view and out of earshot]
         How old do you think he_k *is?*

The difference is that, if the utterance is to be felicitous, the sender's assumptions about what is in fact in the receiver's consciousness must be correct in (15) but need not be in (14). That is, some markers of givenness$_s$ (e.g., pronouns) correlate with a loss of explicit information such that understanding is greatly impeded if the item is not actually given$_s$ for the receiver, whereas other markers (e.g., subject clauses) do not correlate with any loss of information and permit senders greater leeway in treating items as given$_s$. Flagrant misuse will indeed make the utterance sound inappropriate or bizarre, as in (16), but not incomprehensible:

(16) a.   [Customer opening service-encounter]
           ?*What my friend bought here* was a beautiful scarf.
      b.   [Newscaster opening evening news]
           ?*That Carter will resign tonight* has just come over the wire.

It seems that those items that must in fact be given$_s$ for an utterance containing them to be felicitous are marked morphologically (pronouns, including deictics) [but cf. (13)], whereas those items that require only that their givenness$_s$ be appropriate are marked syntactically (e.g., subject clauses). (See Horn, 1978 for a discussion of the givenness$_s$ of subject clauses.) As in the case of givenness$_p$, much research is required, including psycholinguistic experimentation, to discover how language users actually go about marking and recognizing linguistic forms as representing given$_s$ and new$_s$ items.

2.3 Givenness$_k$: "Shared Knowledge"

In speaker–hearer terms, givenness in the sense of "shared knowledge" may be described as follows:

(17)   **Givenness$_k$:** The speaker assumes that the hearer "knows," assumes, or can infer a particular thing (but is not necessarily thinking about it).

This type is represented by what Clark and Haviland (1977) call given–

new information: given is "information [the speaker] believes the listener already knows and accepts as true" and new is "information [the speaker] believes the listener does not yet know (p. 4)." Whether the hearer knows the information directly for having been explicitly told it, or indirectly via inferencing ("bridging") is immaterial; thus *the beer* is given$_k$ in both (12a) and (12b) for Clark and Haviland, as would be the bold-faced items in (18) (when uttered felicitously):

(18) a. *Have you heard from **Jane-Carol** recently?*
 b. *We got some beer out of the trunk and **it** was warm.*
 c. *Where were **your grandparents** born?*

Kuno's (1972) notion of anaphoric–nonanaphoric, mentioned earlier, likewise falls under the rubric of givenness$_k$: An NP is anaphoric if "[its] referent . . . has been mentioned in the previous discourse" or is "in the permanent registry (p. 270)," where "the permanent registry" corresponds to what the speaker assumes about the hearer's assumptions. Presumably, Kuno's From-Old-to-New Principle (1979), which is posited in order to account for certain word-order phenomena in flexible word-order languages and for some syntactic constructions in English (Dative, Passive), is sensitive to givenness$_k$. That is, when we say that the fact that (19a) is better than (19b) is related to a tendency to put old information before new information, we are using *old* in the sense of "shared knowledge" (givenness$_k$) and not in the sense of predictability (givenness$_p$) or saliency (givenness$_s$), as *John* and *a boy* are equally unpredictable and unsalient and differ only in that *John* is usually given$_k$ ("in the permanent registry"), whereas *a boy* is new$_k$:

(19) a. ***John** hit **a boy** on the head.*
 b. *?**A boy** was hit on the head by **John**.*[9]

2.4 Relatedness of the Three Types of Givenness

Although different from one another, predictability, saliency, and "shared knowledge" are not mutually independent: If a speaker assumes that the hearer can predict that some particular item or items will occur in some particular position within a sentence, then the speaker must assume that it is appropriate that the hearer have some particular thing in his/her consciousness. And, if the speaker assumes that the hearer has some particular thing in his/her consciousness, then the speaker must assume that the hearer has some assumption or can draw some inference. Further-

[9] These examples are from Kuno (1979, p. 6).

more, all three levels sometimes involve cases where some item is "given" for extralinguistic reasons, showing that all levels must ultimately relate to extralinguistic phenomena, in particular to what the speaker thinks is or should be or could appropriately be in the hearer's mind. For example, consider (20)–(22) in their most usual understandings:

(20) a. ∅ *Wanna fight?*   (Given$_p$)[10]
      b. [Man to woman at ball, with appropriate body language]
          Shall we ∅?   (Given$_p$)

(21) a. [A_i to B_j as C_k walks by, in view and out of earshot]
          ***He**$_k$'s going to Austria.*   (Given$_s$)
      b. [Professor beginning first lecture of term]
          What we're going to look at this semester *is the world's indifference to the Boat People.*   (Given$_s$)

(22) a. *Hi, **I**'m home.*   (Given$_k$)
      b. *Where's **Daddy**?*   (Given$_k$)

Thus, an understanding of givenness in the sense of "shared knowledge," though it reeks of things "nonlinguistic," is germane (and, perhaps, prerequisite) to an understanding of givenness in the other two senses, and I shall now focus exclusively on "shared knowledge," or givenness$_k$.

3. SO-CALLED "SHARED KNOWLEDGE"

3.1 Terminology

As a first step, let us discard the term SHARED KNOWLEDGE once and for all, for it has given rise to great confusion. If one thinks about it for a moment, one sees that all a speaker has to go on when treating something as given$_k$ or "shared" is what s/he assumes the hearer assumes. The view that says that each individual has a belief-set and that, for any two individuals, the belief-sets may be overlapping, the intersection constituting "shared knowledge", is taking the position of an omniscient observer and is not considering what ordinary, nonclairvoyant humans do when they interact verbally.

At the same time, GIVENNESS, with or without a distinguishing subscript, is not a very convenient term either, as evidenced by its confusing

---

[10] Although, in the rest of this chapter, the notion of givenness is reserved for entities (representable by NPs), what seems to be predictable and hence given$_p$ in (20) are not entities (*Do you, dance*).

use in the literature. For lack of something better, I propose the term AS-SUMED FAMILIARITY. At least, it lacks the unhelpful connotations of symmetry and fact and does not sound like anything else (see, however, Christopherson, 1939 and Hawkins, 1978.)

3.2 The Problem

We may now word the basic problem as follows. From the point of view of a speaker/writer, what kinds of assumptions about the hearer/reader have a bearing on the form of the text being produced, where that form is not uniquely determined by the "objective" information that the speaker/writer is attempting to convey? From the point of view of the hearer/reader, what inferences will s/he draw on the basis of the particular form chosen? We are, therefore, NOT concerned with what one individual may know or hypothesize about another individual's belief-state EXCEPT insofar as that knowledge and those hypotheses affect the forms and understanding of LINGUISTIC productions. Thus, although the problem is of general relevance to cognitive psychology in that it touches on matters of reasoning and knowledge, it is first of all a linguistic problem, if a goal of linguistics is to produce a theory of discourse that distinguishes between a random sequence of sentences and something we would intuitively call a "text."

The solution to the problem then may be seen as requiring three parts: (a) a taxonomy of linguistic forms, both morphological and syntactic; (b) a taxonomy of the values of Assumed Familiarity; and (c) an account of the correlation between the two. Structural linguistics and transformational grammar has provided us with the first part, at least for forms that are identifiable on the level of the sentence or less, and this chapter is an attempt to provide the second. Hopefully, once the two taxonomies have been arrived at, further research can determine the correlation.

3.3 The Taxonomy

One question that arises, then, is what the values of Assumed Familiarity are, that is, is it a binary distinction, a continuum, or something else? Consider the sentences in (22):

(22) a. *Pardon, would **you** have change of a quarter?*
      b. ***Noam Chomsky** went to Penn.*
      c. *I got on **a bus** yesterday and **the driver** was drunk.*
      d. ***A guy I work with** says **he** knows your sister.*
      e. *Hey, **one of these eggs** is broken!*

It seems impossible to group the bold-faced NPs in (22) into two homogeneous and discrete sets: *you, Noam Chomsky, the driver, he,* and perhaps
one of these eggs are all somehow felt to be familiar, that is, familiar to
the hearer, yet they are all different. Likewise, *a bus, a guy I work with,*
and perhaps *one of these eggs* are somehow felt to be new, or unfamiliar
to the hearer, yet they are intuitively not the same.

   To get a better idea of what I think is going on, I should like to propose
a not very original analogy. Consider a text to be like a recipe. The goal of
the recipe writer is to instruct the recipe reader on how to produce a particular dish. Two recipes for the same dish may be dramatically different;
compare, for example, *Le Répertoire de la cuisine,* the very slim cookbook that professional French chefs use, where each recipe is just a few
lines long, with a standard fat American cookbook, where major ingredients are listed, much of the equipment specified, and many of the processes spelled out.[11] Even then, however, some things are left unstated;
even *The I Hate to Cook Book* does not tell us where to find boiling water.
Why such differences and apparent inconsistencies? The obvious answer
is that the writer of a recipe has a certain set of assumptions about what

---

[11] Following are two recipes for roast suckling pig, one from Rombauer, I. S., and Becker,
M. R. 1931, *The Joy of Cooking* (p. 408), and the other from Gringoire, Th. and L. Saulnier,
1914, *Le Répertoire de la cuisine* (p. 81). They are cited here in full as a dramatic illustration
of the effect that the sender's hypotheses about the receiver's beliefs has on the form of the
text. First, *The Joy of Cooking:*

   Roast Suckling Pig:

                              10 servings
   Preheat oven to 450°.
   Dress, by drawing, scraping and cleaning:
      A suckling pig
   *Remove eyeballs and lower the lids. The dressed pig should weigh about 12
   pounds. Fill it with:*
      Onion Dressing, page 457, or
      Forcemeat, page 458
   *It takes 2½ quarts of dressing to stuff a pig of this size. Multiply all your ingre-
   dients, but not the seasonings. Use these sparingly until the dressing is combined,
   then taste it and add what is lacking. Sew up the pig. Put a block of wood in its
   mouth to hold it open. Skewer the legs into position, pulling the forelegs forward
   and bending the hindlegs into a crouching stance. Rub the pig with:*
      Oil or soft butter
      (A cut clove of garlic)
   Dredge it with:
      Flour
   *Cover the ears and the tail with aluminum foil. Place the pig in a pan uncovered in
   the oven for 15 minutes. Reduce the heat to 325° and roast until tender, allowing 30
   minutes to the pound. Baste every 15 minutes with:*

the reader knows about ingredients, processes, and equipment, about what equipment the reader has available, and about what staples the reader keeps on the shelf.

Turning back to discourse, let us say that a TEXT is a set of instructions from a speaker to a hearer on how to construct a particular DISCOURSE-MODEL. The model will contain DISCOURSE ENTITIES, ATTRIBUTES, and LINKS between entities. A discourse entity is a discourse-model object, akin to Karttunen's (1971) DISCOURSE REFERENT; it may represent an individual (existent in the real world or not), a class of individuals, an exemplar, a substance, a concept, etc. Following Webber (1978), entities may be thought of as hooks on which to hang attributes. All discourse entities in a discourse-model are represented by NPs in a text, though not all NPs in a text represent discourse entities.

When a speaker first introduces an entity into the discourse, that is, tells the hearer to "put it on the counter," we may say that it is NEW. New discourse entities are of two types, however. In one case, the hearer may have had to CREATE a new entity, akin to going out and buying a suckling pig, in which it is BRAND-NEW. In the other case, the hearer may be assumed to have a corresponding entity in his/her own model and simply has to place it in (or copy it into) the discourse-model, akin to taking some staple off the shelf when its presence is suddenly taken for granted in a recipe (e.g., salt). Call this type UNUSED. In the sentences of (22), assum-

---

About 2 cups boiling stock and the pan drippings
Remove the foil from the ears and tail before serving. Place the pig on a platter.
Remove the wood from the mouth. Replace it with a small:
  Apple, lemon or carrot
Place in the eyes:
  Raisins or cranberries
Drape around the neck a wreath of:
  Small green leaves
or garnish the platter or board with:
  Cinnamon Apples, page 111, Apples Stuffed with Sweet Potatoes, page 111,
  Apples Stuffed with Mincemeat, page 603, Tomatoes Florentine, page 307, etc.
Make:
  Pan Gravy, page 322
To carve, place head to left of carver. Remove forelegs and hams. Divide meat down center of back. Separate the ribs. Serve a section of crackling skin to each person.

Now, compare with the recipe as presented in *Le Répertoire de la cuisine:*

Cochon de Lait Anglaise:
—Farcir farce à l'anglaise. Rôtir. (Translation: *English Suckling Pig:* Stuff with English stuffing. Roast.)

ing each is discourse-initial, *Noam Chomsky* is Unused, that is, assumed
to be in the hearer's model, whereas *a bus* and *a guy I work with* are
Brand-new and must be created by the hearer. Brand-new entities themselves seem to be of two types: ANCHORED and UNANCHORED. A discourse entity is Anchored if the NP representing it is LINKED, by means of
another NP, or "Anchor," properly contained in it, to some other discourse entity. Thus *a bus* in (22c) is Unanchored, or simply Brand-new,
whereas *a guy I work with* in (22d), containing the NP *I*, is Brand-new
Anchored, as the discourse entity the hearer creates for this particular
guy will be immediatly linked to his/her discourse entity for the speaker.
In the data, all Anchored entities contain at least one Anchor that is not
itself Brand-new; that is, we find NPs like (23a) but not like (23b).

(23)   a.   *a guy* ⎧   *I*   ⎫ *work(s) with*
              ⎪   *John*   ⎪
              ⎨ *the plumber* ⎬
              ⎪ *a woman I know* ⎪
       b. *?a guy* ⎩*a woman works with*⎭

We shall return to this in what follows.

Now, if some NP is uttered whose entity is already in the discourse-
model, or "on the counter," it represents an EVOKED entity. There are,
grossly, two ways in which an entity can have come to be Evoked: Either
the hearer had evoked it earlier, on textual grounds, by following instructions from the speaker—that is, it was once New or Inferrable (to be discussed later)—or the hearer knew to evoke it all by himself, for situational
reasons. Call the first type TEXTUALLY EVOKED, or simply EVOKED, and
the second SITUATIONALLY EVOKED. Situationally Evoked entities represent discourse participants and salient features of the extratextual context, which includes the text itself. In (22d), *he* is Textually Evoked,
whereas, in (22a), *you* is Situationally Evoked.

The third and most complex type of discourse entity are the INFER-
ABLES. A discourse entity is Inferrable if the speaker assumes the hearer
can infer it, via logical—or, more commonly, plausible—reasoning, from
discourse entities already Evoked or from other Inferrables. In (22c), *the
driver* is Inferrable from *a bus*, plus assumed knowledge about buses, that
is, *Buses have drivers*. A special subclass of Inferrables are the CON-
TAINING INFERRABLES, where what is inferenced off of is properly contained within the Inferrable NP itself; in 22e, *one of these eggs* is a Containing Inferrable, as it is inferrable, by a set–member inference, from
these eggs, which is contained within the NP and which, in the usual case,
is Situationally Evoked. Perhaps the diagram in (24) will make these distinctions somewhat clearer:

(24)

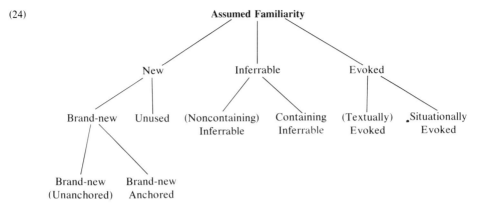

In addition, all seven types may occur with one or more new attributes, as the discourse-initial sentences in (25), (26), and (27) illustrate:

(25) a. *I bought **a beautiful dress**.*   (Brand-new + attribute)
      b. ***A rich guy I know** bought a Cadillac.* (Brand-new Anchored + attribute)
      c. ***Rotten Rizzo** can't have a third term.*   (Unused + attribute)

(26) a. *I went to the post office and **the stupid clerk** couldn't find a stamp.*   (Inferrable + attribute)
      b. *Have you heard **the incredible claim that the devil speaks English backwards?*** (Containing Inferrable + attribute)

(27) a. *Susie went to visit her grandmother and **the sweet lady** was making Peking Duck.*   (Evoked + attribute)
      b. ***Lucky me** just stepped in something.* (Situationally Evoked + attribute)

4. ILLUSTRATION

Now let us consider and compare two naturally occurring texts, representing two different styles, to see how the taxonomy I am proposing works and what, if any, patterns appear. The first text we will look is an informal oral narrative; the speaker is a white, female, middle-aged, middle-class suburban Philadelphia college graduate. She has recently broken some bone in a fall and is wearing a cast. She is at home. The hearer is a friend, of the same sex and background, but with an advanced degree in linguistics and a tape recorder in her handbag. The speaker does not know that she is being taped. First, the text:

(28)   a. *Well, I have a friend of mine called me;*
         b. *a friend of hers who I know —two weeks—well,*
         c. *last week she called and said, "Well, you have*
         d. *company. Jan fell down four flight of steps." They*
         e. *have a house like this, and she was going to a*
         f. *luncheon and the women were honking the horn outside;*
         g. *she heard them, right? And usually she lets the door*
         h. *open but she didn't this time. So she comes*
         i. *running down the steps and she fell down four and*
         j. *landed on her side. Her right side's fractured. She's*
         k. *over at Holy Redeemer. She tried to get up and couldn't*
         l. *so she—and she realized—and they were still honking,*
        m. *see? So then after a while, she thought one of them'll*
         n. *have enough sense to come to the door, ring the bell,*
         o. *right? So she couldn't get up she said, she—it was a—*
         p. *so she crawled to the door and then finally one of the*
         q. *women came and rang the bell and she said to them, "I'm*
         r. *on the floor, I fell and I can't get up." So Nancy said,*
         s. *"Well, open the door," and she said, "I can't reach*
         t. *the knob," she said. "I'm really hurting." She said, "I*
         u. *can't pick myself up." She said, "My God, what did you*
         v. *do?" She said, "I don't know, I fell down the steps."*
         w. *So she said, "Well, can't you roll over on your other side?"*
         x. *and she said, "Honest to goodness, I can't do anything,"*
         y. *she said. "Can't you come in?" She said, "Well, how am I*
         z. *going to get in?" She said, "Well, try the kitchen window,*
        aa. *that—that's open." She said, "Tell Jane," who's a tiny*
        bb. *little thing (she's only about four feet ten), she said,*
        cc. *"Tell—can you hike Jane up and get her—go in the*
        dd. *garage and you'll find a stool or something for her to*
        ee. *get on and then hike her through the kitchen window."*
         ff. *So that's what they did. So she goes through and she says*
        gg. *she landed in the sink. Well, naturally, it's like*
        hh. *our kitchen. So she had taken her shoes off, right?*
         ii. *She had heels on and she took them off when they hoisted*
         jj. *her. She was on a step ladder but then they still*
        kk. *had to give her a little push, right? So she got in, she*
         ll. *said she sat right in the sink. So she had to work*
       mm. *her way out of that and she got in and here she opened*
        nn. *up the front door and it took the four of them to get*
        oo. *her up and she was screaming, she was in such pain.* (Wolf-
             son, 1976, pp. 160–61)

The notation is explained in (29), and the Assumed Familiarity analysis is given in (30):

(29)   *Notation*
        BN: Brand-new
        BN_A [__]: Brand-new Anchored [*Anchor*^{type}]
        U: Unused
        I(__)/__: Inferrable (*entity inferrable from*^{type})/inference-type
        I_C(__)/__: Containing Inferrable (*contained entity inferrable from*^{type})/inference-type
        E: (Textually) Evoked
        E_S: Situationally Evoked
        S.A.: Stereotypic Assumption

(30)   a. I_i: E_S (Discourse-participant = Speaker)
           a friend of mine$_{i_j}$: $BN^A[i^E]$
           me$_i$: E
        b. *a friend of hers*$_j$ *who* I_i *know*$_k$: $BN_A[j^E, i^E]$
        c. *she*$_j$: E
           you$_i$: E
        d. *company*$_k$: ?BN (if in fact entity)
           Jan$_k$: E + A(ttribute)
           four flight of steps: BN + A
           they$_{k+}$: I(k^E)/member–set
        e. *a house like this:* $BN_A[this\ house^{E_S}]$
           she$_k$: E
        f. *a luncheon:* BN
           the women$_l$: I(*luncheon*^{E})/S.A. or frame
           the horn: I(*car*^{l}(*luncheon*^{E})/frame)/S.A. (Luncheon frame; Cars have horns)
        g. *she*$_k$: E
           them$_1$: E
           she$_k$: E
           the door: I(*house*^{E})/S.A. (Houses have doors)
        h. *she*$_k$: E
           she$_k$: E
        i. *the steps:* either I(*house*^{E})/S.A. (Houses have steps)
                        or   E (from capsule statement at beginning)
           she$_k$: E
           four: I(*the steps*^{E})/set–subset

j. *her$_k$ side:* I(k^E)/S.A. (People have sides)
   her$_k$ right side: E + A
   she$_k$: E

k. *Holy Redeemer:* U
   she$_k$: E

l. *she$_k$:* E
   they$_l$: E

m. *she$_k$:* E
   one of them$_{l_m}$: I(l^E)/set–member

n. *the door:* E
   the bell: I(*the door^E*)/S.A. (Doors have bells)

o. *she$_k$:* E
   she$_k$: E

p. *she$_k$:* E
   the door: E
   one of the women$_{l_m}$: E + A

q. *the bell:* E
   she$_k$: E
   them$_l$: E
   I$_k$: E

r. *the floor:* I(*the house^E*)/S.A. (Houses have floors)
   I$_k$: E
   I$_k$: E
   Nancy$_m$: E + A

s. *the door:* E
   she$_k$: E
   I$_k$: E

t. *the knob:* I(*the door^E*)/S.A. (Doors have knobs)
   she$_k$: E
   I$_k$: E
   she$_k$: E
   I$_k$: E

u. *myself$_k$:* E
   she$_m$: E
   you$_k$: E

v. *she$_k$:* E
   I$_k$: E
   I$_k$: E
   the steps: E

w. *she$_m$:* E
   you$_k$: E
   your$_k$ other side: I(k's side^E)/S.A. (People have two sides)

x. *she$_k$:* E
   I$_k$: E

y. *she$_k$:* E
   you$_m$: E
   she$_m$: E
   I$_m$: E

z. *she$_k$:* E
   the kitchen window: I$_C$(*kitchen*^{I}(*house*^{E})/S.A.)/S.A. (Houses have kitchens; Kitchens have windows)

aa. *that:* E
    she$_k$: E
    Jane$_n$: I(l^E)/set–member
    who$_n$: E

bb. *she$_n$:* E
    she$_k$: E

cc. *you$_m$:* E
    Jane$_n$: E
    her$_n$: E

dd. *the garage:* I(*the house*^{E})/S.A. (Houses have garages)
    you$_m$: E
    a stool or something: BN
    her$_n$: E

ee. *her$_n$:* E
    the kitchen window: E

ff. *that:* I(preceding propositions)/propositions = act
    they$_l$: E
    she$_n$: E
    she$_n$: E

gg. *she$_n$:* E
    the sink: I(*the kitchen*^{E})/S.A. (Kitchens have sinks)
    it: E

hh. *our kitchen:* U
    she$_n$: E
    her shoes: I(n^E)/S.A. (People have shoes on)

ii. *she$_n$:* E
    heels: E + A

she_n: E
them: E
$they_l$: E (Actually, *they* $= l - n$)

jj. her_n: E
she_n: E
a little step ladder: either BN $+$ A or E $+$ A (from *a stool or something*)
$they_l$: E (actually $l - n$)

kk. her_n: E
she_n: E
she_n: E

11. she_n: E
the sink: either E (from capsule statement) or I(*the kitchen^E*)/S.A.
she_n: E

mm. *that:* I(preceding propositions)/propositions $=$ situation
she_n: E
she_n: E

nn. *the front door:* E $+$ A
the four of them$_l$: E $+$ A

oo. her_k: E
she_k: E
she_k: E

(Adverbials, expletives, dummies, and idiom-pieces have been omitted.)

Obviously, space does not permit a step-by-step discussion. A few points, however, are worth mentioning. First, nearly all of the subjects are Evoked, whereas less than half of the nonsubjects are. In contrast, one-sixth of the nonsubjects—but none of the subjects—are New. As for the Inferrables, they account for nearly one-third of the nonsubjects but only one-fifteenth of the subjects. The figures are presented in Table 1.

The types of inferences needed for the Inferrables are mostly culture-based, involving the Stereotypic Assumptions discussed in Prince 1978b in relation to existential presupposition (e.g., *Houses have doors, People have sides, Kitchens have sinks*). One set—*luncheon* to *women* to *horn* in (30f)—suggests that the much more complex notion of "frame" may in fact be necessary.

There are also some logical inferences: set to subset, as in *the steps* to *four* in (30i), and set to member, as in *they* to *one of them* in (30l)–(30m).

TABLE 1

**Analysis of Subjects and Nonsubjects in Oral Text
(by Number and Percentage)**

	Subjects (76)		Nonsubjects (43)	
Evoked				
E	66	86.8%	18	41.9%
E_S	1	1.3%	0	0.0%
E + A	4	5.3%	3	7.0%
Total	71	93.4%	21	48.8%
Inferrable				
I	5	6.6%	12	27.9%
I_c	0	0.0%	1	2.3%
Total	5	6.6%	13	30.2%
New				
U	0	0.0%	2	4.7%
BN_A	0	0.0%	3	7.0%
BN	0	0.0%	3	7.0%
BN + A	0	0.0%	1	2.3%
Total	0	0.0%	9	20.9%

One inference is logical—member to set—but also culture-based: *Jan* to *they* in (30d), where the speaker must assume that the hearer assumes that people like Jan are members of some relevant set, presumably a family.

One other point bears mentioning. In Prince 1978b, it was claimed that, in colloquial discourse, unmodified and unexplained proper nouns are not used unless the speaker assumes that the hearer is already familiar with the referent. At first blush, this text seems to falsify that claim, and, in fact, the hearer assured me that she had never heard of Jan, introduced in (30d), or Nancy, introduced in (30r), and could not have been expected to by the speaker. One might discount the case of *Jan* as being part of direct discourse, but no such loophole exists for *Nancy*. Worse yet, other such occurrences appear in other data, none of which can be dismissed as performance errors. However, it turns out that, when whole texts are analyzed, it becomes clear that these putatively deviant proper nouns do NOT in fact represent what I am here calling Unused entities (which do obey the ''constraint'') but represent rather Evoked entities, with the added attribute that the entity has a certain name. For example, by (30p), the hearer has already constructed an entity for the woman who had enough sense to get out of the car and come to the door. All that the NP *Nancy* in (30r) requires, then, is that the hearer assign the name *Nancy* to that entity.[12] In contrast, *Holy Redeemer* in (30k), which cannot be analyzed as Evoked + Attribute, was in fact independently known to the hearer and exemplifies the more obvious use of proper nouns as Unused information that was at issue in Prince 1978b.

An interesting problem that requires more research for its resolution is the status of discourse entities introduced by what is referred to above as a "capsule statement," or "abstract" (Labov and Fanshel, 1977). That is, narratives frequently begin with a statement of the point or justification of the rest of the narrative, in which certain entities are represented. The question for us is whether those entities that are represented in such capsule statements are considered to have been evoked or not. In (30), there are two possible capsule statements:

(31) a. *You have company. Jan fell down four flight of steps.*
      b. *So she goes through and she says she landed in the sink.*

Of the eight NPs in (31), five (*you, Jan, she, she, she*) are already evoked and do not present a problem. One, *company,* does not even clearly represent a discourse entity directly. (It seems to "prepare" the hearer to meet with a new entity; compare with *You're not alone.*) As for the remaining two NPs, *four flight of steps*[13] and *the sink,* the next coreferential NPs (*the steps, the sink,* respectively) are ambiguous as to whether they represent Evoked or Inferrable entities. My own intuition inclines toward treating them as Inferrable, but the decision is not clear. If these next-mentions are in fact Inferrable and not Evoked, then we conclude that, although entities may somehow be "introduced" in capsule statements, they are not, however, actually evoked there. Analogous questions would no doubt arise in the treatment of entities represented by NPs in the titles of written texts, but of course it is quite possible that the two situations will be shown to work differently.[14]

---

[12] Note also that the entity represented by *Jan* in (28d) is originally introduced by a re-paired string (*a friend of hers who I know*), which might have been edited out in a less faithful transcription. This raises important methodological and theoretical questions about the treatment of repairs in linguistic analyses of naturally occurring data.

[13] *Four flight of steps* seems to be an irrelevant and unrepaired performance error; it should be *four steps.*

[14] Gerald Prince has pointed out (personal communication) the problematic situation where some entity in a title (e.g., *A Fight*) may serve as a label for—or be the entity representing—the whole text that follows but does not correspond to any individual entity within that text (e.g., a description of two individuals debating). Titles then may serve not so much for the addition of entities and attributes to a discourse-model as for framing the discourse-model that is about to be constructed. Experiments reported in Bransford and Johnson (1972, 1973), where the presence of a title grossly affected the subjects' processing of a text, support this view of a title (and perhaps a capsule statement) as a metatextual object.

Analyses of this and other naturally occurring texts with respect to Assumed Familiarity reveal a number of patterns or tendencies. First, we find a preferred hierarchy or scale for what type of entity is used, more or less as in (32):

(32)   *Familiarity Scale*

$$\left\{ \begin{matrix} E \\ E^{S} \end{matrix} \right\} > U > I > I^{C} > BN^{A} > BN$$

For example, consider the bold-faced NPs in (33) (in their most usual understandings):

(33)   a. *I bought a Toyota.* (E^{S})
       b. *Ellen bought a Toyota.*   (U)
       c. *One of the people that work at Penn bought a Toyota.* (I^{C})
       d. *A person that works at Penn bought a Toyota.* (BN^{A})
       e. *A person bought a Toyota.*   (BN)

It seems that, if a speaker is in a position to say one of these on basis of his/her hypothesis about what the hearer knows and chooses instead to say one lower on the scale (to refer to the same individual), s/he will be seen, if found out, to have been deviant in some way (e.g., evasive, childish, building suspense as in a mystery novel). Put differently, we may say that the use of an NP representing a certain point on the scale implicates that the speaker could not have felicitously referred to the same entity by another NP higher on the scale. The recognition of such a scale permits this sort of implicature to be subsumed under the Gricean maxim of Quantity.

Note that the use of the scale must be relative to the speaker's hypothesis about the hearer's belief-set and cannot be construed as a statement about the relative probability of a particular type of NP occurring. For example, U is higher on the scale than I in spite of the fact that most texts contain more Inferrable entities than Unused ones. The reason is that most entities discussed are simply not previously assumed to be known to the hearer; for example, if the speaker of (22c) happened to know that the bus driver's name was Jake but assumed that the hearer did not know this, s/he could not substitute *Jake* for *the driver* and still be deemed coherent. If, on the other hand, the speaker thought that the hearer did already have an entity for this individual with the attribute of having the name *Jake* and simply said *the driver*, the hearer, by following the Familiarity Scale, would infer not-Jake and would, if s/he ever found out, feel that the speaker had "withheld information." The Familiarity Scale may fall under a more general Conservation Principle that says that hearers do not like to make new entities when old ones will do and that speakers, if they are cooperative, form their utterances so as to enable the hearer to make maximal use of old entities.[15]

From the analysis of informal conversational texts like the one presented in (28), it seems that the same Familiarity Scale holds for NPs representing anchors, within BN^A entities. That is, the NPs in (34) represent the same scalar inequalities as those in (33), except that (34e) is virtually unacceptable:

(34)   a. *A friend of yours bought a Toyota.*   (E^S)
     b. *A friend of Steve's bought a Toyota.*   (U)
     c. *A friend of my neighbor's bought a Toyota.*   (I)
     d. *A friend of a guy I know bought a Toyota.*   (BN^A)
     e.?*A friend of a guy's bought a Toyota.*   (BN)

In fact, whereas the scale seems relevant in all types of discourse, the use of Brand-new Anchored entities, which is a means of UPGRADING an entity on the scale, seems to be characteristic of informal conversational discourse as in (28).

More special to informal conversational discourse, however, is the tendency to reserve subject position for NPs at the higher end of the scale. In fact, we find a variety of syntactic constructions that appear to be used at times solely in order to enable the speaker to do this, that is, to keep entities low on the scale out of subject position: existential *there,* *it*-clefts, Left Dislocation out of subject position, relative clauses, and a variety of so-called "run-on" sentences, for example

(35)   a. *"I had a little boy, black, about ten years old, HE used to go with me."* —Terkel (1974; p. 132)
     b. *"There's some male beauty shops, THEY deal more in your feminine men and actors."* —Terkel (1974; p. 317)
     c. *"There are some funerals, THEY really affect you."*   (Terkel, 1974, p. 661)[16]

---

[15] Compare Sacerdoti's (1977) principle, "Use existing objects." Stenning (1978) has noted the same phenomenon and points out that traditional mystery novels violate this principle by causing the reader to create an entity for the murderer and for each other character, telling him only at the end to collapse the entity for the murderer with the entity for a particular other character.

[16] Although such constructions usually result in the subject representing an Evoked entity, as in the examples of (35), they sometimes result in the subject being lower than Evoked on the Familiarity Scale. It is always the case, however, that the new subject is higher on the scale than would be the subject of the corresponding simple sentence. In (i), for example, the subject is an Inferrable, in contrast to the corresponding Containing Inferrable of (ii):

(i)   *"I had a pair of shoes, the soles were loose."*   (Terkel, 1974, p. 576.)
(ii)   *The soles of a pair of shoes I had were loose.*

Furthermore, deletion of subject relative markers appears to occur in just such cases, for example, in the first line of the narrative in (28) and in the sentences of (36):

(36) a. *"We got **a lot of fancy Cadillac cars** don't tip."*   (Terkel, 1974, p. 298).
      b. *"I had **a great-great-great-grandfather or something** fought that Revolution."*   (Terkel, 1974, p. 42.)
      c. *"There was a **piece of four-inch bone** never mended."*   (Terkel, 1974, p. 52.)

On this point, Anthony Kroch (personal communication) has noted that, in his large corpus of oral discourse, ALL instances of subject relative marker deletion occur in sentences like those of (36), that is, where the syntactically main clause is informationally weak, having either an Evoked NP subject (usually *I*) or a dummy subject (*it, there*), and a semantically weak verb (e.g., *be, have, know*), and where the syntactically subordinate (i.e., relative) clause is highly informative. Thus it seems that the more formal counterparts to (36) are not (37), as one might think, but (38):

(37) a. *We have a lot of fancy Cadillac cars which/that don't tip.*
      b. *I had a great-great-great-grandfather or something who/that fought that Revolution.*
      c. *There was a piece of four-inch bone which/that never mended.*

(38) a. *A lot of fancy Cadillac cars don't tip.*
      b. *A great-great-great-grandfather or something fought that Revolution.*
      c. *A piece of four-inch bone never mended.*

In summation, it seems that we can distinguish a phenomenon that is perhaps true of discourse in general, the tendency to use an NP that is as high on the Familiarity Scale as felicitously possible, and one related phenomenon that seems especially pertinent to informal conversational discourse, a conspiracy of syntactic constructions resulting in the nonoccurrence of NPs low on the scale in subject position.

Now let us consider another text, the beginning of a chapter in Hymes 1974. Note that, unlike the oral narrative, this text is actually intended for us as receivers, insofar as we are linguists who read English, the group Hymes is presumably addressing. First, consider the written text and the rather crude analysis that follows:

(39) a.   *Linguistic Theory and Functions in Speech*
      b. *The late Uriel Weinreich (1966:399) observed:*

c. *"Whether there is any point to semantic theories which*
d. *are accountable only for special cases of speech—namely*
e. *humorless, prosaic, banal prose—is highly doubtful."*
f. *"The purpose of this chapter is to generalize Weinreich's*
g. *statement, and to remove the qualification: linguistic*
h. *theories accountable only for such cases of speech cannot*
i. *be consistently justified. I shall try to bring out the*
j. *plurality, priority, and problematic (empirical) status*
k. *of functions in speech.*
l. *In speaking of "functions," I do not intend to raise here*
m. *the many issues that attach to the notion of "functionalism"*
n. *in the social sciences, and, more generally, in the philo-*
o. *sophy of the sciences and humanistic disciplines. I*
p. *use the term first of all because its use by the*
q. *Prague School has associated it with the perspective*
r. *developed here, and because it does seem the appropriate*
s. *general term for a necessary idea. In their methodological*
t. *reflections on worlds of human knowledge, scholars such as*
u. *Ernst Cassirer and Kenneth Burke have found the question*
v. *of function, and, in human action, the question of function*
w. *known as purpose, indispensable. That the burden of proof*
x. *lies with the advocate of the relevance of concern with*
y. *such questions in linguistics today, does not reflect the*
z. *nature of language, but the limitations of current linguistics.*
aa. *The burden of proof ought to be, and I believe will come to*
bb. *be, on those who think that linguistics can proceed*
cc. *successfully without explicit attention to its functional*
dd. *foundations.*   (Hymes, 1974, pp. 145–146.)

(40) **Assumed Familiarity Analysis** (TO BE TAKEN WITH LARGE GRAIN OF SALT):

a. *linguistic theory:* U (or U + A)
   functions in speech: U or $I_c(speech^U)$/?
b. *the late uriel Weinreich:* U (or U + A)
c. *whether there is any point to semantic theories which are accountable only for special cases of speech—namely humorless, prosaic, banal prose:* I_c [*(that) there is a point to
   semantic theories which are accountable only for special
   cases of speech—namely humorless, prosaic, banal prose*^{I_c}
   (semantic theories . . . $^{U (or\ I_c \cdots)}$]/theories have a point
   to them)/proposition can be true or false
f. *the purpose of this chapter:* $I_c(this\ chapter^{Es})$/chapters have
   a purpose (or U)

Weinreich's statement: I(preceding propositions)/propositions which someone$_i$ has observed/written/uttered = someone$_i$'s statement

g. *the qualification:* I(preceding propositions)/whether *P* is highly doubtful = qualification
   linguistic theories accountable only for such cases of speech: I(*semantic theories . . . prose*^{E})/particular to general

i. *I:* E$_S$
   the plurality, priority, and problematic (empirical) status of functions in speech: I$_C$(functions$^{U\,(or\,E)}$)/?functions have attributes . . .

l. *"functions":* E
   I: E

m. *the many issues that attach to the notion of "functionalism" in the social sciences, and, more generally, in the philosophy of the sciences and humanistic disciplines:* I$_C$(*notion of functionalism*^{1} (*functionalism*^{1}(*functions . . .* ^{E})/objects to 'ism')/ism = notion)/issues attach to notions + A

o. *I:* E

p. *the term:* I(*functions*^{E})/metalinguistic assumption
   its use by the Prague School: U (or: I$_C$(*Prague School*^{U})/Prague School used/uses terms

q. *it:* E
   the perspective developed here: I$_C$(*here*^{E})/we are developing a perspective here

r. *it:* E
   the appropriate general term for a necessary idea: I$_C$(*an idea*$^{?BN}$ + A)/terms are for ideas + A

s. *their methodological reflections on words of human knowledge:* I$_C$(worlds of human knowledge$^{?U}$)/?people reflect on worlds of human knowledge + A

t. *scholars such as Ernst Cassirer and Kenneth Burke:* I$_C$(*Ernst Cassirer and Kenneth Burke*^{U})/member(s) to set (or: U)

u. *the question of function:* U (or: I$_C$(*function*^{E})/function is a question)

v. *the question of function known as purpose:* I$_C$(*the question of function*^{E})/things are known as other things

w. *that the burden of proof lies with the advocate of the relevance of concern with such questions in linguistics today:* I$_C$(*burden of proof*^{1} (*notion of functionalism*^{E})/notions are such that there is a burden of proving them)/burdens lie with some person(s)

y. *the nature of language:* U (or: I_C(*language*^{U})/things have a nature)

z. *the limitations of current linguistics:* U (or: I_C(*current linguistics*^{U})/current linguistics has limitations)

aa. *the burden of proof:* E
   I: E

bb. *those who think that linguistics can proceed successfully without explicit attention to its functional foundations:* I_C(*that linguistics can proceed . . .* $^{U \; (or: \; I(\; . . .)/ \; . . . \;)}$)/people think such things

Immediately obvious is the decrease in Evoked entities and the increase in complex Inferrable and Containing Inferrable entities, compared with the oral narrative presented earlier. The figures are given in Table 2.

In spite of (and contributing to) the shakiness of the analysis, a number of systematic differences between the two texts is apparent, all of which indicate additional complexity in the written text. First, in contrast to the situation in the oral narrative, we find here a high degree of METALIN-GUISTIC inferencing. Although it may be a straightforward matter to infer that what Weinreich observes, [i.e., the quoted sentence in (39c)–(39e)], constitutes *Weinreich's statement* in (39f)–(39g), it is less obvious that part of that quoted sentence—the *wh*-word and the VP *is doubtful*—constitute *the qualification* in (39g).

TABLE 2

Analysis of Subjects and Nonsubjects in Written Text (by Number)

	Subjects (12)		Nonsubjects (16)	
Evoked				
E:	5	41.7%	2	12.5%
E_S:	1	8.3%	0	0.0%
E + A:	0	0.0%	0	0.0%
Total	6	50.0%	2	12.5%
Inferrable				
I:	1	8.3%	3	18.8%
I_C	4	33.3%	7	43.8%
Total	5	41.7%	10	62.5%
New				
U:	1	8.3%	4	25.0%
BN_A:	0	0.0%	0	0.0%
BN:	0	0.0%	0	0.0%
Total	1	8.3%	4	25.0%

Second, in addition to the metalinguistic problem, a great deal of complexity arises from the extreme ABSTRACTNESS of many of the entities involved. It is one thing to create an entity out of an already expressed proposition or set thereof, as the *that* requires in the oral narrative in (28ff) (*That's what they did*), but quite another to present a proposition as an entity, as is the case with the sentential subject in (39w)–(39y) in the written text.

Third, and more important, correlating with the large increase in the occurrence, in the written text, of Containing Inferrables is A BLURRING BETWEEN WHAT IS UNUSED AND WHAT IS INFERRABLE which does not arise in the oral narrative. There, the entities are all either assumed to be known to the hearer (e.g., *Holy Redeemer*) or not (e.g., *a friend of mine*), or inferrable on the spot (e.g., *one of them*). In contrast, is the reader of the written text assumed to have known, before reading *its use by the Prague School*, that a certain term was/is used by the Prague School, or is s/he assumed to have known simply that there is/was a Prague School and to infer from the NP that the Prague School used the term? Similarly, is the reader expected to have known, before reading *scholars such as Ernst Cassirer and Kenneth Burke*, that there is a class of scholars to which Cassirer and Burke belong, or is s/he expected simply to have known that Cassirer and Burke exist and to infer from the NP that there is a class of scholars of which they are members? Obviously, the answer is that there can be no sharp line in such texts: What is an Unused entity for one intended reader will be a Containing Inferrable for another; the latter reader, however, having fewer "staples" in his "closet," so to speak, will have much more work to do to construct the desired discourse-model.

A fourth difference between the two types of texts concerns the CULTURAL ASSUMPTIONS required for the inferencing. Note that both the oral narrative and the written text require certain assumptions; the two differ, however, in the nature of these required assumptions—for example, *Doors have knobs* versus *Notions are such that there is a burden on someone of proving them*. That is, like the entities themselves, the cultural assumptions required for inferencing in the written text are of a highly complex and abstract nature.

A fifth difference, and perhaps the one causing the greatest difficulty for the linguist analyzing texts like the written one, is not so much the abstractness of the entities or assumptions, per se, as the sheer SIZE OF THE ENTITIES. Many of the entities in the written text, but not in the oral text, are themselves made up of entities and attributes, the composing entities themselves often being complex.

Finally, when we consider the syntactic environments of the entities, still other differences appear. In contrast to the oral narrative, just one half of the subject NPs in the written text represent Evoked entities, and only one-eighth of the nonsubjects do, as shown in Table 2. Further, over two-fifths of the subjects are Inferrables, mostly of the Containing Inferrable type. No Brand-new entities occur at all, but a few Unused ones do, in subject as well as nonsubject position. (As suggested earlier, a more knowledgeable reader than I would of course have more Unused entities and fewer Inferrables.) Note, however, that, in both texts, subjects are more likely to be Evoked than Inferrable and more likely to be Inferrable than New.

5. AREAS FOR FURTHER STUDY

As this chapter is too inconclusive to warrant a conclusion, I shall instead close by outlining what I would like to see it lead to. The first step is obviously to refine/revise/replace the taxonomic model presented here. Although it is fairly adequate in its present form for texts like the oral narrative, it is far too crude for texts like the written one. The large and diverse number of NPs that now may fall under the category *Inferrable* — ordinary NPs, gerunds, *wh*-clauses, *that*-clauses, etc.—can perhaps be broken down into more manageable and meaningful subgroups.

One problem that has been skirted here is whether Assumed Familiarity is binary or, as in the taxonomy presented here, ternary, or something else. Although the data seem to indicate fairly clearly that it is not a continuum, it is not obvious at this point whether a binary or a ternary division is more appropriate. Intuitively, one can think of Inferrables as being classified under New—they were not previously in the discourse-model —and, at the same time, as being classified, along with Evoked, under some category Old—they are made up of old parts. Before we can motivate a decision for one or the other, however, further research is needed, included psycholinguistic research on the processing of discourse.

Once an adequate taxonomy of Assumed Familiarity is arrived at, it can, coupled with already existing taxonomies of linguistic form, lead to a deeper and clearer account of the correlation between form and understanding in natural language. Such an account can aid in several specific areas of research. In particular, it can shed light on questions of FUNCTIONAL SYNTAX by enabling analysts to describe explicitly, precisely, and, hopefully, in universal terms, the salient features of the environments in which different syntactic constructions occur.[17] Certainly, it will

---

[17] It is encouraging that Richard Rhodes reports (personal communication) that the taxonomy of givenness$_k$ presented here holds up nicely for Ojibwa, a language that appears on the surface to have a very different pattern of information distribution from English (see Tomlin and Rhodes (1979).

aid in DISCOURSE ANALYSIS and, whether desired or not, it will force a distinction between different STYLES of discourse, by characterizing the nature and complexity of the entities and inferences involved and the morphology and syntax of the NPs representing those entities.[18] Further, it might prove useful in research on THE DEVELOPMENT OF DISCOURSE COMPETENCE in children (and adults?) and on THE PROCESSING OF DISCOURSE by children and adults. Finally, one would hope that it would help us to arrive at a clearer understanding of the other kinds of givenness, predictability and saliency, discussed earlier.

In a somewhat different vein, an adequate taxonomy of Assumed Familiarity and the subsequent account of the form–understanding correlation will aid in the study of what reading and writing entail beyond decoding and encoding. Contra Olson 1977, where it is claimed that written language is explicit whereas oral language leaves much out, the analyses presented here suggest that just the opposite is the case: The comprehension of formal, literary discourse depends a great deal more on inference, quantitatively and qualitatively, than the processing of informal, colloquial discourse. More generally, such research will have practical relevance wherever the control of linguistic complexity is at issue, wherever it is the case that the sender has less-than-perfect intuitions about the receiver and wants to be understood.

ACKNOWLEDGEMENTS

Parts of this chapter appeared in Prince (1979), and an earlier version was presented at the San Diego State University Linguistics Colloquium, April 24, 1979. I should like to thank Cathy Ball, John Fought, Erving Goffman, Jeff Kaplan, Tony Kroch, Susumu Kuno, Bill Labov, Gerry Prince, and Bonnie Webber for their insightful comments and criticisms.

REFERENCES

Bransford, J. D., and Johnson, M. K. (1972). Contextual prerequisites for understanding: Some investigations of comprehension and recall. *Journal of Verbal Learning and Verbal Behavior,* **11,** 717–726.

Bransford, J. D., and Johnson, M. K. (1973). Considerations of some problems of comprehension. In W. G. Chase (Ed.), *Visual Information Processing.* New York: Academic Press.

Chafe, W. L. (1976). Givenness, contrastiveness, definiteness, subjects, topics, and point of view. In C. Li (Ed.), *Subject and Topic.* New York: Academic Press. Pp. 25–55.

[18] Note, for example, that the sort of "blurring" between Unused and Containing Inferrable entities that arises in the written text seems to covary with a text's having more than one intended receiver and/or a text's sender not knowing the receiver(s) well. See Rubin 1978 for a discussion of these and other parameters along which discourses may differ.

Chomsky, N. (1975). *Reflections on Language.* New York: Pantheon.

Christopherson, P. (1939). *The articles: A Study of Their Theory and Use in English.* Copenhagen: Munksgaard.

Clark, H. and Haviland, S. (1977). Comprehension and the given–new contract. In R. Freedle (Ed.), *Discourse Production and Comprehension.* Hillsdale, N.J.: Lawrence Erlbaum Associates. Pp. 1–40.

Goffman, E. (1967). On face-work. In E. Goffman, *Interaction Ritual.* Garden City, New York: Anchor Books. Pp. 5–46.

Halliday, M. A. K. (1967). Notes on transitivity and theme in English. Part 2. *Journal of Linguistics,* **3,** 199–244.

Halliday, M. A. K., and Hasan, R. (1976). *Cohesion in English.* London: Longman.

Haviland, S. and Clark, H. (1974). What's new? Acquiring new information as a process in comprehension. *Journal of Verbal Learning and Verbal Behavior,* **13,** 512–521.

Hawkins, J. A. (1978). *Definiteness and Indefiniteness.* Atlantic Highlands, N.J.: Humanities Press.

Horn, L. (1978). *Présupposition, thème, et variations.* Unpublished Manuscript.

Hymes, D. (1974). *Foundations in Sociolinguistics: An Ethnographic Approach.* Philadelphia: University of Pennsylvania Press.

Karttunen, L. (1971). Discourse referents. In J. McCawley (Ed.), *Syntax and Semantics 7: Notes from the Linguistic Underground.* New York: Academic Press. Pp. 363–386.

Kuno, S. (1972). Functional sentence perspective. *Linguistic Inquiry,* **3,** 269–320.

Kuno, S. (1974). Lexical and contextual meaning. *Linguistic Inquiry,* **5,** 469–477.

Kuno, S. (1978). Generative discourse analysis in America. In W. Dressler, (Ed.), *Current Trends in Textlinguistics.* Berlin and New York: de Gruyter. Pp. 275–294.

Kuno, S. (1979). *On the Interaction between Syntactic Rules and Discourse Principles.* Unpublished manuscript.

Labov, W., and Fanshel, D. (1977). *Therapeutic Discourse.* New York: Academic Press.

Olson, D. (1977). From utterance to text: The bias of language in speech and writing. *Harvard Educational Review,* **47,** 257–281.

Prince, E. F. (1978a). A comparison of *wh*-clefts and *it*-clefts in discourse. *Language,* **54,** 883–906.

Prince, E. F. (1978b). On the function of existential presupposition in discourse. In D. Farkas, W. Jacobsen, and K. Todrys (Eds.), *Papers from the Fourteenth Regional Meeting of the Chicago Linguistic Society.* Department of Linguistics, University of Chicago. Pp. 362–376.

Prince, E. F. (1979). On the given/new distinction. In W. Hanks, C. Hofbauer, and P. Clyne (Eds.), *Papers from the Fifteenth Regional Meeting of the Chicago Linguistic Society.* Department of Linguistics, University of Chicago. Pp. 267–278.

Rubin, A. D. (1978). *A Theoretical Taxonomy of the Differences between Oral and Written Language* (Technical Report No. 35). Bolt Beranek and Newman, Inc. Cambridge, Mass.

Sacerdoti, E. (1977). *A Structure for Plans and Behavior.* New York: Elsevier–North-Holland.

Stenning, K. (1978). *On why making reference out of sense makes it so hard to make sense out of reference.* Paper presented at the Sloan Workshop on Indefinite Reference, University of Massachusetts, Amherst, December 2.

Terkel, S. (1974). *Working.* New York. Avon Books.

Tic Douloureux, P. R. N. (1971). A note on one's privates. In A. Zwicky *et al.* (Eds.), *Studies Out in Left Field: Defamatory Essays Presented to James D. McCawley on the Occasion of His 33rd or 34th Birthday.* Edmonton and Champaign: Linguistic Research, Inc. Pp. 45–52.

Tomlin, R., and Rhodes, R. (1979). The distribution of information in Ojibwa texts. In W. Hanks, C. Hofbauer, and P. Clyne (Eds.), *Papers from the Fifteenth Regional Meeting of the Chicago Linguistic Society*. Department of Linguistics, University of Chicago. Pp. 307–320.

Webber, B. L. (1978). Jumping ahead of the speaker: On recognition from indefinite descriptions. Paper presented at the Sloan Workshop on Indefinite Reference, University of Massachusetts, Amherst, December 3.

Wolfson, N. (1976). *The Conversational Historical Present in American English Narrative*. Unpublished doctoral dissertation, University of Pennsylvania.

Almost

Jerrold M. Sadock

A sentence of the form *almost P*, in which *almost* is a verb phrase modifier, is used as if it meant, among other things , "not P." For example, someone who says *Sam almost died* would be taken as indicating that Sam didn't die. Other uses of *almost* work the same way. Uttering *Bill has an almost black dog* will convey the impression that Bill's dog is not completely black. But what is the nature of the connection between the English word *almost* and the negative proposition? There are three possibilities:

1. *Almost P* means, among other things, (has as part of its logical form) "not P." In this case, *Sam almost died* is simply false if Sam died.[1]
2. *Almost P* presupposes "not P" and means only the other things alluded to in (1). If this is so, then the sentence *Sam almost died* has no truth-value if Sam did die. Although "not P" is part of the conventional force of *almost p*, it is not part of its semantic content. The fact that *almost P* is related to "not P" is still a grammatical fact under this treatment. Very similar to this theory is one that dispenses with the notion of presupposition in favor of the notion of conventional implicature (Karttunen and Peters, 1975). If *almost P* conventionally implicates "not P," then *Sam almost died* is strictly speaking true, even if Sam actually died,

---

[1] For a radically semantic account of the meaning of *almost* that contrasts sharply with my radically pragmatic account, see Tönisson (ms.).

257

but it is inappropriate in a conversational context where Sam is known
to have died. This is due to a conventional implicature carried by the word
almost and thus is also a matter of linguistic description.

3. *Almost P* conversationally implicates "not *P*." On this theory, *Sam
almost died* is true even if Sam died, but it is uncooperative to use the
sentence if one knows that he did. Here, all that has to be said about the
conventional content of *almost* is the rest of what is said under the
treatments in (1) and (2). This information, coupled with principles of cooperative conversation and, perhaps, facts about the context of the utterance and certain background assumptions, is enough to allow "not *P*" to
be "worked out" on the basis of an instance of the utterance of *almost P*.
Context and background knowledge do not seem to be of much importance in this case, so the implicature would have to be what Grice (1975)
called a generalized conversational implicature.

The third account of the connection between *almost P* and "not P,"
the one I shall argue is correct, differs from the other two in the important
respect that it simplifies the grammar of the language. No independent
statement of the implicature needs to be made in describing English. According to this treatment, accounting for the fact that this implicature is
present is not really within the province of the grammarian or logician at
all, but rather is the job of the psychologist or sociologist. With heavy
doses of Gricean pragmatics, a very great deal of grammar can be completely done away with by making supposedly arbitrary lexical and syntactic facts follow from a few general principles of conversation. As these
psychological or sociological principles are independently required to account for nonlinguistic aspects of human behavior, the result is a genuine
simplification of the total description of the way the forms of a particular
language are used.

Now, to show that "not *P*" can in principle be treated as a conversational implicature of the utterance of *almost P*, it is first necessary to show
that there exists a sequence of quasi-logical steps leading from the latter
to the former, and that they involve conversational principles. In other
words, conversational implicatures must, as Grice argued, be calculable.
The implicature will also depend for its existence on the meaning (in the
strict sense) of *almost*, but in this case, not on the particular circumstances surrounding the utterance of a sentence containing it. At any rate,
it will be necessary to worry about the semantic content of *almost*. I shall
argue that the meaning of *almost* is such as to make a statement of the

---

[2] I lean toward using the term "imaginary world" in the definition of *almost* rather than
the technical term "possible world". The reason for this is that in sentences where *almost*
modifies nondegree predicates, the imaginary world that is conjured up can involve logical
contradictions. Consider (i):

form *almost P* true just in case there is a possible world[2] in which *P* is true that is not very different from the real world. The phrase "not very different" is purposely vague because *almost* is a hedge—in the sense of Lakoff 1972, a fuzzy concept. Rather than being just true or false, *almost P* would seem to be more-or-less true or false, depending on the circumstances, and would thus seem to require a fuzzy logic along the lines of that in Lakoff's work.[3]

To see that this is so, let us consider the family of degree predicates *tall to degree x*. Let us choose a particular degree, say 6 ft., and a particular entity, say my filing cabinet, and predicate almost having height to that degree of it:

(1)   *My filing cabinet is almost 6 ft. tall.*

Presuming that the filing cabinet is less than 6 ft. tall, the truth of (1) would seem to be some function of the ratio of the actual height of this object and 6 ft. Thus, if the cabinet is in fact only 5½ ft. tall, (1) is pretty true. But if the cabinet is just 4 ft. tall, (1) is pretty far from true. Yet (1) is truer if the oaken item is 4 ft. tall than if it is 3 ft. tall [in which case (1) is pretty darn false], and so on. Thus the truth of (1) seems reasonably to be a smoothly varying function of the height of the filing cabinet.

Note, however, that the degree of truth of (1) is not only dependent on the actual height of the object. Consider

(2)   *Arthur is almost 6 ft. tall.*

Under ordinary circumstances (2) would not be judged very true at all if Arthur were only 5′6″ tall. Why is a filing cabinet that is 5½ ft. tall almost 6 ft. tall and a person the same height not? The reason is this: Both (1) and (2) set the high point of the scale of comparison at 6 ft., but the scale is somewhat context dependent. For filing cabinets, the smallest height that

---

(i)   *961 is almost a prime number.*

I believe this sentence might be adjudged true because the only blot on 961's record as a prime number is the sad fact that it is the square of 31. If this one little fact were not true, then 961 would be a prime number. The imaginary world in which 961 is a prime number is not very different from the real world in the nontechnical sense that only one proposition has to be changed to gain access to it, but of course it is VERY different from our world in the technical sense that it is an inconsistent world and lacks mathematics.

[3] Fuzzy logic can be avoided by removing the clause "which is not very different from the real world" from the semantic specification of *almost* and making it a conventional implicature. If this is done, *almost P* would always be true if *P* could possibly be true, but would admit of various degrees of appropriateness, depending on how near the possible world is to the real world, again in a purposely vague sense. The choice between fuzzy logic and fuzzy pragmatics is not very important to the thesis of this chapter, which is concerned with what is conventional and what is conversational in the understanding of *almost,* but it is clearly more in the spirit of the Gricean enterprise to keep the logic two-valued than not to do so.

we can reasonably expect is perhaps 12 in. For adult human beings (one of which I shall assume Arthur is), the smallest reasonable height is somewhere in the vicinity of 5 ft. The height of the filing cabinet in our example is therefore 90% of the context-determined scale, whereas Arthur's is only half of it. Half way to *x* is not almost *x*.

Much the same thing can be seen by comparing the following examples.

(3)   *Almost 1000 demonstrators picketed.*

(4)   *Almost 990 demonstrators picketed.*

Suppose the actual number of demonstrators was 950. Surprisingly, (3) seems truer than (4)—surprisingly because (3) is 5% off the mark whereas (4) is only about 4% off. The trick here seems to be that, in the absence of context, it is only the last nonzero figure that fixes the scale, and not the whole figure.[4]

A second area of vagueness in the use of *almost* has to do with the direction of the scale (see Horn 1976 for other instances of scale reversal). Whereas (5) and (6) set the same value for one endpoint of the scale, that endpoint is in one case the high point, and in the other, the low point.

(5)   *It's almost freezing.*

(6)   *It's almost melting.*

Therefore, (7) can be taken in two ways depending on whether, for example, there has just been a heat wave or a cold snap.

(7)   *It's almost 0° Celsius*

Certain predicates, like *tall* and *short*, are already directed, so *almost* can only be understood as referring to the directed scale determined by the predicate itself. Sentence (8) indicates clearly that John is taller than Bill, and Sentence (9) that John is shorter than Bill, whereas (10) indicates neither.

(8)   *John is almost as short as Bill.*

(9)   *John is almost as tall as Bill.*[5]

(10)   *John is almost the same height as Bill.*

---

[4] The same facts hold for other sorts of approximations as well. Thus *about 1000* is a much coarser guess than, say, *about 990*, and *about 6 ft. tall* is all right for a 5′6″ filing cabinet, but not for a 5′6″ man. For a fuller discussion, see Sadock 1977.

[5] It is possible, in fact desirable, to treat only one of a pair of predicates such as *tall* and *short* as lexically including the direction of the scale. Thus *short* can be treated as meaning something on the order of "having height to an extent that is below the average" while its

Almost can also modify nondegree predicates and when it does, the meaning of *almost P* is less clear. The possible world referred to in the definition of *almost* can differ from the real world in many ways and still not be "very different" from it. Thus *almost a linguist* can be predicated of someone who does linguistics in his spare time but holds no degree, or of someone who holds a degree but does bad work, and so on.

After this brief excursus on the semantic properties of *almost*, I return to the fact that *almost P* conveys "not *P*." As I have said, I believe this is a generalized conversational implicature based in part on the meaning per se of *almost*. The first order of business is therefore to supply the scheme of reasoning that leads from the utterance, the conventional meaning, and conversational principles to the implicature. The existence of such a scheme would make it at least possible that "not *P*" is, in fact, a conversational implicature.

The reasoning scheme I suggest is fairly straightforward and follows closely other less controversial analyses based on Gricean principles, such as Horn's (1973) analysis of the relationship between *some x are P* and "not all *x* are *P*." In a perhaps overly embroidered form, the reasoning might proceed as follows:

1. Speaker *S* has uttered *almost P*.
2. I know, as a speaker of English, that this means that *S* believes that there is a possible world, not too different from the real world, in which *P* is true.

---

apparent partner, *tall*, can be given a less specific meaning on the order of "having height to some extent." The reason that *Arthur is tall* so strongly indicates that Arthur's height is above average would then be traced to a conversational implicature. Saying only that Arthur has height to some extent is not a particularly enlightening contribution. In almost all circumstances, we would be forced to search for a way to make this trivial observation relevant. The relevance cannot be sought in the speaker's desire to convey that Arthur's height is surprisingly small since if that were the case he could (and therefore should) have said *Arthur is short*. So all that remains is the presumption that the speaker meant to convey his feelings that Arthur's height is unusually great.

Note how well this treatment accords with the view that *tall* is the unmarked member of the pair. As such, it is the one that appears in neutral contexts:

(i)   *Arthur is 5 ft. tall.*

(ii)   **Arthur is 5 ft. short.*

Furthermore, the notion that *tall* only conversationally implicates height greater than average whereas *short* says less than average, explains why (iii) does not imply that either Arthur or Bill is tall, but (iv) does imply that both are short.

(iii) *Arthur is as tall as Bill.*

(iv)   *Arthur is as short as Bill.*

3. There is a conversational principle, the maxim of Quantity, that requires speakers to say as much as is required.
4. Because P entails "there is a possible world in which P," but not vice versa, saying P is saying more than saying *almost P*.
5. Speaker S knows that it is of some interest to me whether P is true or not—otherwise, why would he have said *almost P*?
6. I presume that S is obeying the maxim of Quantity.
7. Therefore S cannot believe that P is true.
8. But S must know something about the situation or he would not have said *almost P*.[6]
9. Therefore S must feel that P is false.
10. Furthermore S knows that I am capable of figuring all this out.
11. Therefore, in saying *almost P, S* wished to convey, among other things, "not P."

An important characteristic of this particular exercise in conversational logic is that it refers only to the fact that the utterance was made, the meaning of the uttered expression, and to general principles of conversational behavior, but does not involve any variable facts about the context in which the utterance occurred. The claim is therefore that the success of this implicature does not depend on context, that is, that this is a generalized conversational implicature, and this, as I have already pointed out, is true.

Besides allowing a simplification of the grammar at no additional descriptive cost, the pragmatic account of the relationship between *almost P* and "not P" has certain positive advantages.

First, it explains the nondetachability of the implicatum. All expressions that are even nearly synonymous with *almost* carry with them the same understanding. The following sentences can only be properly used if the speaker believes that Bill did not swim the English Channel.

(11)   *Bill nearly swam the English Channel.*

(12)   *Bill came close to swimming the English Channel.*

(13)   *Bill came within a hair's breadth of swimming the English Channel.*

---

[6] Note that this assumption is not warranted in all situations where *almost P* is properly uttered. Thus consider the following example provided by an unnamed reviewer: *We must be almost over our destination; let's descend below the clouds and see exactly where we are.* Importantly, this example would not ordinarily be heard as amounting to (among other things) "We are not over our destination now." The reason for this would seem to be that assumption (8) and its corollary (9), are not justified. What this example shows, then, is that under special circumstances, the implicature "not P" is cancelable (this will be further discussed in what follows).

(14)   *Bill just about swam the English Channel.*

If "not *P*" were a specific, lexical aspect of the understanding of *almost P*, and independent of the rest of the meaning of the sentence, then one would expect there to be some adverbial expression *A* such that *AP* would have the meaning of *almost P* but not indicate the speaker's belief in the falsity of *P*. But, as we have seen, there is no such adverbial. According to the pragmatic analysis, anything that has the meaning of *almost* should share the implicatures it generates as these implicatures are based on meaning. Thus, under the pragmatic analysis, an otherwise mysterious lexical gap is explained.[7]

A second fact that lends support to the idea that "not *P*" is a conversational implicature is that it can be reinforced—it can be made explicit without producing redundancy. Consider (15) as an answer to the question *Did Bill swim the English Channel?*

(15)   *Almost, but not quite.*

Although *almost* is sometimes defined as "not quite" [e.g., in *The American Heritage Dictionary* (Morris, 1969)], the two expressions are quite distinct, as the lack of redundancy of (15) shows. *Not quite P* MEANS "not *P*"; the proposition is false if *P* is true. This can be seen by comparing (16) and (17):

(16)   *Not only did Bill almost swim the English Channel, in fact he did swim it.*

(17)   **Not only did Bill not quite swim the English Channel, in fact he did swim it.*

Sentence (16) is admittedly a bit odd, a fact that will be discussed later, but (17) is simply nonsense. It involves an outright contradiction.

But *not quite P* is related to *almost P* in a certain way: *Not quite P* presupposes (or has as a conventional implicature) the semantic content of *almost P*. The sentence

(18)   *Bill didn't quite swim the English Channel.*

is not false if Bill did not even come close, but it is inappropriate in just the same way as is any utterance whose presuppositions are not satisfied.

Now, according to the theory I am arguing against, "not *P*" is a presup-

---

[7] As I argue in Sadock 1978, nondetachability is not a sufficient test for conversational implicature, though it is highly suggestive. It is much more satisfying to have an account of a specific case of nondetachability, such as the pragmatic theory offers, than to chalk the facts up to the vagaries of the lexicon. For the claim that a conversatioanl implicature exists to be plausible, however, nondetachability must be backed up by other positive tests, which is what I attempt to do in the rest of this chapter.

position (or conventional implicature) of *almost P,* and therefore, *almost* and *not quite* should be mirror-image words, similar to *criticize* and *blame* on Fillmore's (1971) analysis. Both would involve the same conventional content, but what is asserted by one would be presupposed by the other, and vice versa. But there is a definite asymmetry between *almost* and *not quite,* just as my analysis predicts. Whereas (15) is an impeccable answer to the question of whether Bill swam the Channel, (19) is distinctly strange.

(19)   ?*Not quite, but almost.*

The reason for the oddity of (19) under my analysis is that the second phrase adds nothing. It simply asserts what has already been presupposed. In (15), on the other hand, the second phrase presupposes what has just been asserted—a perfectly normal state of affairs—and, moreover, adds something in that it asserts what is otherwise merely a conversational implicature.

This same assymmetry is to be found in other cases where there is a pair of expressions related to one another in such a way that one asserts *P,* while the second presupposes *P* and asserts *Q.* Thus the conjoined sentence *It rained and John realized that it had* is perfectly normal. But reversing the conjuncts produces an odd redundancy that is reminiscent of the one we find in (19):?*John realized that it had rained and it had.*

Notice further that the conjunction in (15) must be *but.* Cf.

(20)   **Almost, and not quite.*

This is also what we see in clearer cases of the reinforcement of conversational implicature, as the contrast between (21) and (22) shows.

(21)   *Bill ate some, but not all, of the cake.*

(22)   **Bill ate some, and not all, of the cake.*[8]

The main difficulty with the conversational analysis of *almost* is that the implicature is not terribly cancelable. As my claim is that "not P" is not part of the meaning of *almost P,* then it ought to be possible to say *almost P* and at the same time assert, or otherwise indicate, that *P* is true. But (23) is very odd.

(23)   ?*Not only did Bill almost swim the English Channel, he did swim it.*

Though this sentence is strange, it is not as strange as (24), which is contradictory, and (24), I claim, has just the meaning that has been erro-

---

[8] This sentence is (irrelevantly) appropriate as a response to the claim that Bill ate all of the cake.

neously attributed to (23). Sentences of the form *just fail to P* assert the same thing as *almost P* and presuppose, in virtue of the contrastive stress on *just*, "not *P*."

(24)   *Not only did Bill **just** fail to swim the English Channel, he did swim it.

But why, then, is (23) strange at all? Why should it be any stranger than (25)?

(25)   Not only did Bill eat some of the cake, he ate all of it.

I suggest that the context-free implicature in the case of *almost* is so strong that explicit cancellation will always be difficult. It is stronger than the implicature from *some x are P* to "not all *x* are *P*" but this, I think, is because the two cases are not completely parallel. We CAN find a parallel to *almost* in the family of English existential expressions by searching for one that emphasizes how little it takes to satisfy the existential proposition. *A fraction of* is such an expression. Therefore, the implicature from *a fraction of x are P* to "not all *x* are *P*" is harder to cancel than the corresponding implicature from *some x are P*. This is demonstrated clearly by the difference in acceptability between (26) and (27).

(26)   Some, and possibly all, poodles have spots.

(27)   ?A fraction of, and possibly all, poodles have spots.

The conversational implicature associated with (27) is stronger because (27) contains more conventional information than (26) and the failure of the implicature would amount to a more serious violation of the maxim of Quantity. Now *almost* is to *possibly* as *a fraction of* is to *some*. Indeed there is a weak conversational implicature from *possibly P* to "not *P*," but it is weaker than the one arising from *almost* and it is much more easily canceled.

Despite the strength of the implicature that *almost* triggers, one can drum up cases where the implicature does not arise. For example, the phrase *almost black* ordinarily suggests 'not black', as we should by now expect. But suppose the Belchee Seed Company offers a prize to the first person ". . . who breeds an almost black marigold."[9] Let us further sup-

---

[9] In the statement of the contest's rules, the word *almost* should not be read with extra stress. Stressing a word that is instrumental in conveying a conversatioanl implicature can have the effect of emphasizing the implicature and elevating it to something close to semantic content. Thus in response to the question *Did you eat all of the cake?* one may respond with *I ate some of the cake*. In answer to *May I have cake and ice cream?* an appropriate response might be *You may have cake or ice cream*. Similarly, a contest to see who can first breed an ALMOST black marigold is a different contest from the one I am interested in.

pose that Luther Lompoc shows up with a jet black marigold. We may leave aside the question of whether anything can be completely and scientifically black; it is enough for us to assume that the contestant and the judges all assume that the flower is, in fact, black. It seems clear that Lompoc is entitled to the prize. But if *almost black* literally meant 'not black', he should not be. It might be imagined that the reason we feel that the breeder of a truly black marigold should get the award has something to do with our sense of fairness, and nothing directly to do with the use of the word *almost* in the contest rules. But this cannot be the case because our intuitions change when something is substituted for the word *almost.* If the prize were to be awarded to the first person ". . . who breeds a not-quite-black marigold", Lompoc would not win. His flower was, by assumption, black, and that is not "not quite black." Though our sense of fairness might be offended, our intuitions into the language tell us clearly that there is a difference in meaning between *almost* and *not quite,* and that difference is just what I have been arguing it is: *not quite P* means 'not P'; using *almost P* merely suggests 'not P', however strongly.

Although I believe that the simple definition that I have been working with gives a good account of many of the properties of *almost,* a serious deficiency of it is that it does not seem to distinguish *almost* from *about.* Unless something more is said, no differences will be imputed to the understanding of (28) and (29).

(28)   *Bill is almost 6 ft. tall.*

(29)   *Bill is about 6 ft. tall.*

Yet there clearly is a difference. One can infer from (28), but not from (29), that Bill is not 6 ft. tall and in fact is less than 6 ft. tall. It would seem that the definition of *almost* must be more complicated than that of *about,* in order to capture the greater intuitively felt specificity of *almost.* It appears to be the case, that is, that (28) says more than (29). I shall argue, though, that it is actually *about* that is more complicated in sense.[10] I shall argue that a conversational implicature is also responsible for the fact that (28) indicates that Bill is less than 6 ft. tall but that an additional aspect of the meaning of *about* tends to cancel the implicature in (29).

Evidence that *about* is the more complicated of the two from the point of view of lexical content comes from the fact that *about* is much more

---

[10] It is a paradoxical property of radically pragmatic approaches to language description that apparently specific words and phrases can be assigned very nonspecific meanings. Expressions with very general meanings loom large just because they say so little. In an effort to endow these forms with conversational relevance, users of language will treat them AS IF they were quite specific in sense.

restricted in distribution than *almost*. The more complicated, and hence specific, the content of a lexical item is, the fewer are the semantic frames in which it can occur without oddity. Thus *lion* can occur wherever *lioness* can (e.g., *a pregnant* ———), but there are environments where *lioness* is excluded (e.g., *a pride of* ———, or *a* ——— *rampant*). This follows from the fact that *lioness* differs from *lion* only in having an extra component to its meaning. The two words stand in a privative opposition.

The distributional relationship between *almost* and *about* is similar. With the exception of a few idioms such as *about to* and *just about*, *almost* can occur wherever *about* can. But the distributional privileges of *almost* are considerably greater than those of *about*, as (30) and (31) show.

(30)   *Bill almost/*about ran around the block.*

(31)   *Bill is almost/*about a genius.*

In general, *about* is restricted to modification of predicates expressing quantities, whereas *almost* is not. This difference shows up quite clearly in the following examples:

(32)   *Bill is about as tall as Sam.*

(33)   **Bill is about tall.*

Tall does not express a quantity but *as tall as Sam* does. Therefore (32) is grammatical and (33) is not. I suggest that *about* be given the following definition: A sentence of the form *about P* is true just in case *P* is a quantitative proposition and there is a possible world not very different from the real world in which *P* is true. I am suggesting, then, that *about* means something very much like *almost exactly*, a phrase whose form tells us that it is more complex than *almost* alone. Note that *almost exactly* is impossible in (30), (31), and (33), but is fine in (32). The distribution of this phrase precisely matches that of *about*. Note also that *almost exactly* matches *about* in not conveying ''less than.''

I must now show that there is an inverse correlation between the restriction to modification of quantitative predicates and the directedness that is part of the understanding of *almost*. One source of evidence comes from the fact that the requirement of exactitude in the definition of *about* is relaxed for nonquantitative predicates that express completion. *About done, about finished, about ready, about over, ets.*, are all fine. Another nonquantitative predicate that anomalously allows *about* is *dead*, possibly because it describes the completion of life. At any rate, the thing to realize about such expressions with *about* is that they are much closer in effect to the matching expressions with *almost* than the contrast between

(28) and (29) might have led us to believe. *About ready,* to take just one example, indicates "less than ready" just as much as *almost ready* does. It is not just a matter of readiness either being a property of something or not; we can speak of degrees of readiness. And when we do, *about* and *almost* cease to be paraphrases. Thus, (34) indicates that Bill is less ready than Sam, whereas (35) does not.

(34)   *Bill is almost as ready as Sam.*

(35)   *Bill is about as ready as Sam.*

A similar indication of the correlation between the directedness of approximating expressions and their ability to hedge set-membership predicates as well as quantitative predicates is the following. For reasons entirely mysterious to me, *just about* is not restricted to predications of quantity, as shown by the fact that (36) is unremarkable.

(36)   *Bill is just about a genius.*

Now, *just about,* in contrast to *about,* is understood as directed when applied to quantitative predicates. From (37) we understand that Bill is less than 6 ft. tall.[11]

(37)   *Bill is just about 6 ft. tall.*

I believe that the fact that *almost* is understood as indicating a directed scale when it is used as a modifier of quantitative predicates can be explained in the following way.

As we have seen, *almost P* conversationally implicates "not *P*" very strongly. When *P* is a quantitative proposition, *not P* generally conversationally implicates "less than *P*." We understand (38) as indicating not only that Bill is not exactly the same height as Sam, but that he is, in fact, shorter than Sam.

(38)   *Bill is not as tall as Sam.*

The implicature is much stronger for negated propositions than for the corresponding nonnegated ones. (For an extended discussion of the greater power of negatives to trigger pragmatic effects, see Givon, 1976.) Example (39) could easily be used to indicate that Bill is at least as tall as Sam, but it could also be used to mean only what it says, namely that Bill and Sam are the same height.

(39)   *Bill is as tall as Sam.*

The reading for (38) that says only that Bill and Sam are not exactly the

---

[11] Intuitions appear to differ on this.

same height is much harder to get, though it does exist. This difference between negatives and affirmatives can, I believe, also be referred to the maxim of Quantity. Without the implicature, (38) would say only that Bill and Sam are not exactly the same height. This is not an especially interesting fact since two people chosen at random rarely are. Therefore, implicatures are strongly favored with negative statements like (38). Furthermore, it is clear why the implicature of (38) is that Bill is less tall than Sam, rather than vice versa. The sentence is about Bill. It would clearly be saying more about Bill to say that his height was greater than Sam's than to say that it was not greater. So by failing to say that Bill is taller than Sam, the speaker of (38) conveys that Bill is *not* taller, via the maxim of Quantity.

As far as (39) is concerned, however, there is no great difference in informativeness between the understanding with the implicature and the one without it. It is saying quite a bit to say that Sam and Bill are exactly the same height, but saying that Bill is not shorter than Sam can also be pretty informative. For this reason, then, neither understanding of (39) is particularly prominent.

I assume that conversational implicatures are ordinarily transitive; that if *A* conversationally implicates *B*, and *B* conversationally implicates *C*, then *A* conversationally implicates *C* as well.[12] Therefore, as *Bill is almost as tall as Sam* conversationally implicates "Bill is not as tall as Sam" and *Bill is not as tall as Sam* conversationally implicates "Bill is shorter than Sam," then *Bill is almost as tall as Sam* conversationally implicates "Bill is shorter than Sam."

In virtue of the definition I have postulated, *about P* should conversationally implicate "not exactly *P*," which it does. But a sentence of the form of (40) does not implicate that Bill is shorter than Sam and neither does one of the form *about P*.

---

[12] William Lycan (personal communication) has pointed out that there is no particular reason to expect conversational implicatures to be transitive. A conversational implicature, according to Grice, is generated on the basis of the fact that a particular linguistic form, with a particular meaning, is uttered. Since the first-order implicature is not uttered, we should not expect it to produce further conversational implicatures. Yet Grice himself talks at times as if it can. In discussing the effect of an abrupt change of topic in a conversation, following the remark *Mrs. X is an old bag,* Grice writes:

"B has blatantly refused to make what he says relevant to A's preceding remark. He thereby implicates that A's remark should not be discussed and, perhaps more specifically, that A has committed a social gaffe [1975, p. 54]."

Here it is quite reasonable to suppose that the more specific implicature is a result of the conveyance of the more general one. After all, If B had changed the topic by SAYING *That remark should not be discussed,* the more specific implicature would also go through.

(40)   *Bill is not exactly as tall as Sam.*

I have argued that the word *almost,* which seems complicated from the point of view of what it conveys, is actually very simple in terms of its conventional content. Although *Bill is almost as tall as Sam* ordinarily is used to convey, inter alia, that Bill is not as tall as Sam and that he is, in fact, shorter than Sam, I have tried to show that none of this needs to be arbitrarily associated with the definition of *almost.* Rather, I proposed that *almost* has a meaning so general and uninformative that its apparent specific import arises naturally through the mechanism of conversational implicature. My purpose has been to demonstrate that careful attention to the constraints on the use of language can result in a considerable simplification of that collection of arbitrary statements we call the grammar of a language.

ACKNOWLEDGEMENTS

This chapter has benefited greatly from the criticisms of at least the following people: Gerald Gazdar, Laurence Horn, Lauri Karttunen, William Lycan, James McCawley, Jerry Morgan, Stanley Peters, and Ivar Tönisson. I apologize to those whom I should have mentioned and absolve those whom I have mentioned from blame for errors which remain in the chapter. Two anonymous reviewers of an earlier draft of this work did perhaps more than anyone else to help me make sense of what I was trying to say.

REFERENCES

Cogen, C., Thompson, H., Thurgood, G., Whistler, K., and Wright, J. (Eds.), (1975). *Proceedings of the First Annual Meeting of the Berkeley Linguistics Society.* Department of Linguistics, University of California, Berkeley.
Cole, P., and Morgan, J. (Eds.), (1975). *Syntax and Semantics 3: Speech Acts.* New York: Academic Press.
Corum, C., Smith-Stark, T. C., and Weiser, A. (Eds.), (1973). *Papers from the Ninth Regional Meeting of the Chicago Linguistic Society.* Department of Linguistics, University of Chicago.
Fillmore, C. J. (1971). Verbs of judging: An exercise in semantic description. In C. J. Fillmore and D. T. Langendoen (Eds.), *Studies in Linguistic Semantics.* New York: Holt, Rinehart and Winston.
Fillmore, C. J., and Langendoen, D. T. (Eds.), (1971). *Studies in Linguistic Semantics.* New York: Holt, Rinehart and Winston.
Givón, T. (1976). *Negation in language: Pragmatics, function, ontology.* Unpublished Manuscript, University of California, Los Angeles.
Grice, H. P. (1975). Logic and Conversation. In P. Cole and J. Morgan (Eds.), *Syntax and Semantics 9: Pragmatics.* New York: Academic Press. Pp. 113–127.
Horn, L. R. (1973). Greek Grice: A brief survey of proto-conversational rules in the history

of logic. In Corum *et al.* (Eds.), *Papers from the Ninth Regional Meeting of the Chicago Linguistic Society.* Department of Linguistics, University of Chicago.

Horn, L. R. (1976). *On the Semantic Properties of Logical Operators in English.* Doctoral dissertation, University of California, Los Angeles (reproduced by the Indiana University Linguistics Club, Bloomington).

Karttunen, L., and Peters, S. (1975). Conventional implicature in Montague grammar. In Cogen *et al.* (Eds.), *Proceedings of the First Annual Meeting of the Berkeley Linguistics Society.* Department of Linguistics, University of California, Berkeley.

Lakoff, G. (1972). Hedges: A study in meaning criteria and the logic of fuzzy concepts. In Peranteau *et al.* (Eds.), *Papers from the Eighth Regional Meeting of the Chicago Linguistics Society.* Department of Linguistics, University of Chicago.

Morris, W., (Ed.), (1969). *The American Heritage Dictionary of the English Language.* Boston: Houghton Mifflin.

Peranteau, P. M., Levi, J. N., and Phares, G. C. (Eds.), (1972). *Papers from the Eighth Regional Meeting of the Chicago Linguistic Society.* Department of Linguistics, University of Chicago.

Sadock, J. M. (1977). Truth and approximations. In K. Whistler, R. D. Van Valin Jr., C. Chiarello, J. J. Jaeger, M. Petruck, H. Thompson, R. Javkin, and A. Woodbury (Eds.), *Proceedings of the Third Annual Meeting of the Berkeley Linguistics Society.* Department of Linguistics, University of California, Berkeley.

Sadock, J. M. (1978). On testing for conversational implicature. In P. Cole (Ed.), *Syntax and Semantics 9: Pragmatics.* New York: Academic Press.

Tönisson, I. J. "A Semantics for *Almost.*" Unpublished manuscript, Stanford University.

Formal Semantics and Extralinguistic Context

Ivan A. Sag

1. INTRODUCTION

Indexical elements, by which I mean such English expressions as *I*, *you*, *here*, *now*, *then*, *that*, *that woman*, *etc.*, pose intriguing problems for theories of natural language semantics in general, and for model-theoretic approaches to semantics in particular. Expressions like these raise difficult questions about the role of extralinguistic context in a theory of (literal) meaning.

A particularly intuitive approach to this problem has been developed by David Kaplan (1978). In "The Logic of Demonstratives," Kaplan attempts to extend the standard techniques of model-theoretic semantics to deal with a logical language containing indexical expressions like the ones just listed. As will become obvious shortly, I will draw extensively from Kaplan's research in the discussion that follows.[1]

---

[1] The basic idea of introducing contextual features into a formal semantics can be found at least as early as Montague (1968, 1970). Montague proposes to extend Scott's notion of POINT OF REFERENCE, or indices, to include the aspects of context which are to be found in the later work of Kaplan. The distinction between Kaplan's theory and Montague's is discussed below (see Sections 4, 5, and 6).

273

One can easily distinguish two extreme positions vis à vis the role extralinguistic context plays in the enterprise of formal linguistic semantics, by which I mean the enterprise of providing a precise characterization of truth, logical consequence, argument validity, paraphrase, contradiction, logical truth, and the like for natural languages. On the first view, one provides a recursive definition of truth and denotation for a natural language (and a concommitant account of other traditional semantic phenomena) with no appeal to extralinguistic context, not even time. This extreme position, which involves a model theory much like that standardly assumed in a system of predicate or modal logic, appears to be falsified by the mere existence of sentences containing tense morphemes or other indexical expressions.

On the other exterme, one might take the position that natural language semantics is not at all compositional in the same way as the semantics of logical languages. On this view, truth and denotation, as well as all semantic concerns, can be analyzed only by extensive appeal to some characterization of extralinguistic context, including, so it would appear, speaker's intention. Meaning, on this view, is determined in some fashion (I am not sure which) as a consequence of dependencies that hold between sentences, contexts of utterances, and speakers' intentions; "meanings of wholes" are not functions of "meanings of parts."

Why is this an extreme view?—For the obvious reason that in a vast number of reasonably clear cases, meaning, truth and denotation all depend on certain general principles of semantic composition. There are no cogent arguments that have been offered for accepting a semantic theory that states otherwise. To abandon semantic compositionality is to abandon semantics as a research area.

But if neither of these extreme positions is tenable, what, then, is the middle ground? The problem, as I see it, is to develop a model-theoretic semantics for natural language that admits contextual determination of meaning in just those cases where aspects of context play a role, but that allows principles of semantic composition to function in a familiar fashion. The purpose of this chapter is to explore several ways in which this might be done.

Note that there are two very different ways in which—or so it has been supposed—context affects the intended interpretation of an utterance. Indexical expressions, such as *I* or *you,* must be evaluated in a context of utterance in order for any literal meaning at all to be associated with an utterance that contains such expressions. Context must thus in some cases be consulted in order to establish propositional content, that is, prior to the determination of truth conditions.

On the other hand, once this propositional content of an utterance (i.e., its literal meaning) is established, context may play a role in the determination of a particular (indirect) utterance meaning. This is, of course, the familiar device of Gricean conversational implicature, the nature of which requires that literal meaning be established prior to contextual considerations. There are thus two distinct ways—one strictly semantic, the other strictly pragmatic—in which context has been assumed to play a role in the interpretation of utterances.

Now consider an example like (1), (due to Nunberg, 1977), which is typical of the class of examples I will be considering in this chapter.

(1)   *The ham sandwich is getting restless.*

As Nunberg observes, with respect to certain contexts—for example if (1) is uttered by a waitress to another waitress—the subject NP of (1) can be assumed to denote, not a ham sandwich, but rather a contextually determined individual who is in a certain relation to a ham sandwich, say an individual who, in the relevant restaurant context, orderd a ham sandwich.[2]

What is the role of context in examples like (1)? Is this a case of an absurd literal meaning (an attribution of restlessness to a culinary object) rescued from pragmatic absurdity by the Cooperative Principle augmented by some ancillary principle which guides Gricean inferencing? Or is the shift from ham sandwich to ham sandwich orderer somehow more directly involved in the semantics of such utterances? Perhaps the shift from ham sandwich to individual who is in some relation to a ham sandwich (possibly different from context to context) is like the shift in denotation that accompanies indexical expressions as they are uttered in various contexts.

The question I am raising is a difficult one to answer, and I certainly do not intend to settle the matter here. Nonetheless, because, as Nunberg and others have shown, this kind of contextual alteration of meaning is far more pervasive in English than might have been thought, it may well be the case that in providing formal semantic analyses, the model-theoretic

---

[2] I will return to example (1) later. If the reader finds it peculiar or thinks it atypical, I refer her/him to Nunberg's dissertation and to Nunberg (1979), where a plethora of such examples, all plausibly viewed as part of everyday conversational language, are considered. The following are typical:

(i)   *New York won, 21–17.*
(ii)   *There was a rush on IBM.*
(iii)   *Queen-six bets.*
(iv)   *He hit a home run two games ago.*
(v)   *He's one of the most creative DJ's in radio.*
(vi)   *Please take those forms over to Philosophy.*

apparatus should be modified so as to allow transfers of reference (or of sense) in various contexts. This approach, rather than one of the first kind, where all examples like (1) are pushed off to pragmatic theory and are abstracted away from in semantic analysis, is intuitive on the grounds that these transfers seem very different in kind from the kind of inferential operations that lead one from *It's hot in here* to the sense of "Please open the window," which clearly deserve treatment of the first type.

Furthermore, as we shall see, there are related problems—for example, the contextually variable interpretation of noun–noun compounds such as *finger cup* and *patio pencil*, which appear not to lend themselves to an analysis of the first type. This is so for the simple reason that such expressions have no clear literal meanings which can be assigned to them prior to Gricean inferencing. I return to this matter in Section 5.

With the idea in mind, then, that a modification of the formal semantics may be the appropriate approach to the problem at hand, I set as my task in this chapter to explore various ways in which such modifications might be carried out. Once one shifts to providing semantic analysis with respect to contexts, instead of possible worlds (though possible worlds are still essentially involved), the modifications one needs to make in order to handle the contextual dependence of examples like (1)—and many others in the literature, as we will see—are not nearly as drastic as one might think. The question I wish to pose here, put most generally, is HOW CONTEXT DEPENDENT IS NATURAL LANGUAGE SEMANTICS? I will attempt to establish a hierarchy of the various possible approaches to this problem.

My purpose here is to outline these approaches in the most general terms possible. Hence I will not be concerned with certain issues that arise in the analysis of English. I will in fact couch my discussion in terms of a logical language (L) in terms of which I assume English, or another natural language may be analyzed (that is, I assume a translation procedure from a natural language into L). L will be a version of standard predicate calculus. The points I take up with respect to the semantics of this language will carry over, I believe, to other logical languages commonly used in semantic analysis, in particular to the kind of typed languages utilized by Montague and others, which allow an analysis of complex functor expressions which appear to be pervasive in natural languages.

The essential point I hope to demonstrate here is that, whatever techniques are employed to analyze expressions whose sense varies from context to context, those techniques need not abandon or violate the principle of compositionality for semantics. In addition to showing that this is the case, I will sketch various ways in which these examples can be analyzed by techniques of formal semantics. The role of context may be pervasive in natural language, yet semantics, I will suggest, should remain discrete and autonomous.

2. STRICT CONTEXT-INDEPENDENT SEMANTICS

If all sentences of a natural language could be assigned a literal meaning without regard for any aspects of the extralinguistic context in which they were uttered (I mean to include here time of utterance), then one could provide a simple, intensional model-theoretic semantics for L. A model structure of L might be a triple, as in (2).

(2) $M = \langle U, W, I \rangle$

Here U is a nonempty set, the universe of individuals or entities; W is a nonempty set of possible worlds; and I is an assignment function which assigns appropriate INTENSIONS to each basic expression of L.

The intensions assigned by I may be simply functions from possible worlds to the appropriate denotational domain. Thus, if L contains two-place predicates like **love,** the intension of **love** assigned by I (written I_{love}) is a function from possible worlds to sets of ordered pairs of individuals from U, that is, $I_{love} \in (\mathscr{P}(U \times U))^W$.[3] Similarly, if L contains a constant term **Richard Nixon,** $I_{Richard\ Nixon}$ is a function from possible worlds to U ($\in U^W$), a constant function if one accepts Kripke's theory of rigid designators.

Truth in a strict context-independent semantic frame work is relative to possible worlds only, and is given by rules such as (3).

(3)   If P is a two-place predicate and c_1 and c_2 are constant terms, then "P(c_1,c_2)" is true in w, where $w \in W$, iff
        $\langle I_{c_1}(w), I_{c_2}(w) \rangle \in I_P(w)$.

For example, *Richard Nixon loves Checkers,* which we shall assume translates into L as **love (Richard Nixon, Checkers),** is true in a world w just in case the ordered pair whose first member is the denotation of **Richard Nixon** in w (which is found by applying $I_{Richard\ Nixon}$ to w) and whose second member is the denotation of **Checkers** in w [$I_{Checkers}$ (w)] is an element of the denotation of **love** in w, which is the set of pairs of individuals whose first member loves the second in w (arrived at by applying I_{love} to w).

This kind of semantics takes no account of time or of contextual factors of any sort. There is no provision for interpretations changing with respect to time. Such a system is thus not sufficiently rich to accommodate

---

[3] I employ the following standard notations: A^B designates the set of all functions from B to A; $\mathscr{P}(A)$ designates the power set of A; $A \times B$ designates the set of all ordered pairs whose first member is an element of A and whose second member is an element of B, that is, the cartesian product of A and B (where A and B are any sets).

the trivial observation that the truth conditions of a sentence like (4), suitably translated into L, make reference to previous events.

(4)   *Richard Nixon resigned.*

Similarly, specifying the truth conditions for sentences involving aspectual operators, such as

(5)   *Richard Nixon had been campaigning.*

presumably requires appeal to some temporal information not found in models like (2).

All such appeals to time may be thought of as appeals to extralinguistic context. Sentences such as (4) and (5) may be evaluated for truth only with respect to a time of utterance.[4] No strict context independent semantics of the sort just considered can attain truth conditional adequacy for a language that contains sentences like (4) or (5), as presumably all natural languages do. Hence one need not even consider sentences containing indexical terms to reject strict context-independent models as a basis for the semantic analysis of natural languages.

3. TEMPORAL CONTEXT-INDEPENDENT SEMANTICS

The defects of strict context-independent semantic systems just mentioned appear to be eliminated in systems where the truth of sentences is evaluated with respect to indices, or "points of reference",[5] which for the moment will be regarded as world–time pairs. A model for such a system, which is close to that of Montague (1968, 1970), is as in (6), where T is a nonempty, linearly ordered set of times, which are assumed to be common to all possible worlds.

(6) $M = \langle U, W, T, I \rangle$

As before, U is the universe of individuals and W a nonempty set of possible worlds. The assignment function I, however, here assigns to each basic expression of L an intension which is a function from indices to the appropriate denotational domain. For example, in such a system I_{love} is a function from world–time pairs to sets of ordered pairs of individuals from U ($I_{\text{love}} \in (\mathscr{P}(U \times U))^{W \times T}$). Similarly, I_{walk} is a function from indices to the power set of U ($I_{\text{walk}} \in (\mathscr{P}(U))^{W \times T}$), and the intension assigned

---

[4] Sentences need not be uttered, of course, to be true or false at a given time. The intended sense is that a sentence is true with respect to a time of utterance if it would be true if uttered at that time.

[5] I use this notion in the sense of Scott 1970 and Montague 1973.

to individual constants is a function from indices to individuals (e.g., $I_{\text{Richard Nixon}} \in U^{W \times T}$).

A recursive definition of truth and denotation is provided in such a system by rules of a sort we will turn to in a moment. Crucially, the addition to L of tense operators (e.g., H for the past tense operator), and truth rules such as (7) allows the problem of providing truth conditions for sentences such as (4) and (5) (suitably translated into L) to be addressed.

(7)   If ϕ is any sentence of L, $H[\phi]$ is true at (w,t) iff there is some time t′ such that t′ < t and ϕ is true at (w,t′).

Denotation of nonindexical expression receives a straightforward account in temporal context-independent semantic systems. Constant terms (which serve as the translations into L of proper names) and basic predicate expressions are assigned denotation by a rule such as (8), and the denotation of complex terms (e.g., definite descriptions) may be assigned by rules such as (9). [Here $|\alpha|_{\text{wt}}$ designates the denotation of α (α is an expression of L) at (w,t).]

(8)   If α is a basic expression of L,
        $|\alpha|_{\text{wt}} = I_\alpha(\text{w,t})$.

(9) $|(\imath x{:}\phi)|_{\text{wt}}$ = the unique individual i who satisfies ϕ at (w,t) if there is one, and † otherwise.[6]

Given rules like these which define denotations for the expressions of L, one can define truth for simple sentences in terms of these denotations; (10) is a formulation of such a rule.

(10)   If P is an n-place predicate, and $t_1 \ldots t_n$ are term expressions, then "$P(t_1, \ldots ,t_n)$" is true at (w,t) iff $\langle |t_1|_{wt}, \ldots ,|t_n|_{\text{wt}}\rangle \in |P|_{\text{wt}}$.

Denotation, and hence truth, are determined by appeal to the intensions assigned to basic expressions by the assignment function I. Thus these notions are characterized in those cases where the relevant expressions of L have intensions that specify unique denotations (extensions) for each

---

[6] In a sharper formulation, truth and denotation would be defined with respect to a variable assignment as well. Thus Rule (8) would be revised as in (i).

(i) $|\alpha|_{wtf} = I_\alpha(w,t)$

A more precise formulation of Rule (9) would be (ii).

(ii) $|(\imath x{:} \phi)|_{wtf}$ = the unique individual i such that ϕ is true at (w,t) with respect to the variable assignment just like f except that the value of x is i (written $\models_{wtf} \phi$), if there is such, and † otherwise († is an element not contained in U, W, or T, which renders sentences either truth value-less or false).

index. But this is precisely what indexical expressions such as *I* or *you* lack. At any given index, there is no unique denotation for such an expression. The denotation of *I* or *you* (more precisely of their translation into *L*) can be determined only once further extralinguistic information is known, specifically, who has uttered the sentence in question to whom. Thus even temporal context-independent semantic systems are not rich enough to provide an adequate basis for the semantic analysis of natural languages, all of which (to my knowledge) contain such indexical expressions.

4. STRICT CONTEXT-DEPENDENT SEMANTICS

As noted in the introduction, certain techniques for overcoming the defects of context-independent semantics have been developed by Kaplan (ms.). A fundamental innovation in Kaplan's system is that truth and denotation are defined recursively, not only with respect to an index, but also with respect to a CONTEXT. Kaplan-contexts include a specification of such extralinguistic factors as an agent (roughly, who is speaking), an audience, a time of utterance, a place of utterance, and a world of utterance. Following Kaplan, we define a context as a five-tuple, employing the notation in (11).

(11)   If c is a context, $c = \langle c_{ag}, c_{aud}, c_T, c_p, c_w \rangle$

where c_{ag} = the agent of c
c_{aud} = the audience of c
c_T = the time of c
c_p = the place of c
c_w = the world of c

Models now become six-tuples, as in (12).

(12) $M = \langle C, U, W, T, P, I \rangle$

Here *C* is the set of contexts of the form given in (11), *P* is the set of places, and *U, W, T,* and *I* are as before. Certain other conditions on contexts must be met, which need not concern us here (see Kaplan (ms.) for further details). I will refer to any system of this sort as a *strict context-dependent semantic system* if it utilizes only those features of context that can be specified independently of the beliefs and other attitudes of the speaker (the agent).

For nonindexical expressions, denotation is defined as before, but always with respect to a context. I follow Kaplan's notation in the statement of Rule (13) [$|\alpha|_{cwt}$ is read: "the denotation of α at (w,t) when taken in the context c].

(13)   If α is a nonidexical expression,
$$|\alpha|_{cwt} = I_\alpha(w,t)$$

The denotation of indexical expressions is given by rules such as (14) and (15). (I use **I** and **you** as the translation into L of the English words I and you respectively).[7]

(14) $|\mathbf{I}|_{cwt} = c_{ag}$

(15) $|\mathbf{you}|_{cwt} = c_{aud}$

Once L is extended to include idexical expressions and the semantics of L is extended to include rules for their denotation, one need make only a trivial modification of the truth rule given in (10) for simple sentences, namely (16):

(16)   If P is an n-place predicate, and $t_1 \ldots t_n$ are term expressions, then "P $(t_1, \ldots, t_n)$" is true at (w,t) when taken in the context c [written $\models_{cwt} P(t_1,\ldots, t_n)$] iff $\langle |t_1|_{cwt}, \ldots |t_n|_{cwt} \rangle \in |P|_{cwt}$.

The techniques sketched here can be extended to variants of L which include other expressions, such as *now* (whose analysis involves c_T), *here* (involving c_p), *yesterday*, and the like.

Context-dependent semantic systems provide a powerful basis for the analysis of truth and denotation in natural languages. However, strict context-dependent systems of the sort just sketched are still not rich enough to accommodate certain phenomena that are pervasive in natural languages, for example, demonstrative reference. The truth or falsity of the sentences in (17) cannot be ascertained simply by consulting the contextual information in Kaplan-contexts like (11).

(17)   a. *Checkers likes **that**.*
        b. ***This** dog walks.*
        c. ***She** is intelligent.*
        d. *Nixon objected to **those**.*
        e. *Checkers is **this** tall.*

Calculating the denotation of the bold-faced expressions in the sen-

---

[7] As is well known, certain natural languages have rather complex systems of person deixis. The many interesting problems that arise in this area can, I believe, be dealt with by defining denotation rules in terms of appropriate set-theoretical operations on the various elements specified in Kaplan-contexts. In the analysis of English, such an approach might be utilized to distinguish audience from addressee.

tences of (17) requires an appear to further contextual information, such as what is being pointed to, or indicated in some other fashion, by the agent of the context. In the next section, I will explore various ways in which the notion of context can be modified to provide an analysis of these and various other examples that appear in the linguistic literature.

5. EXTENDED CONTEXT-DEPENDENT SEMANTICS

Montague (1968) suggests that sentences like (17a) can be dealt with simply by expanding the notion of index to include a specification of, say, what a speaker is pointing to. This is equivalent to expanding a Kaplan-context in the same way. However, adding a single such specification is insufficient, if sentences containing more than one demonstrative term are considered, for example:

(18)   *This is bigger than **that**.*

A natural language sentence may contain any number of demonstrative terms. Thus, minimally, an adequate extension of a Kaplan-context would have to include a specification of a reference for each such demonstrative, as noted by Lewis (1972, 213ff).

This could be effected by augmenting contexts with an assignment function (c_f) which assigns a denotation to each demonstrative term of L which translates the corresponding natural language demonstrative. Let *Dem* be the set of all such demonstrative expressions (***this***$_1$, . . . ***this***$_n$, . . . ; ***that***$_1$, . . . , ***that***$_n$ . . . ; *etc*). Then each c_f is an element of the set of functions from *Dem* to the universe of individuals ($c_f \in U^{Dem}$). This allows the denotation of simple individual-denoting demonstrative terms to be assigned by the following denotation rule.

(19)   If α is a demonstrative term of L, then $|\alpha|_{cwt} = c_f(\alpha)$

The definition of truth and denotation otherwise proceeds as in a strict context-dependent system.

I refer to any system of this sort as an EXTENDED CONTEXT-DEPENDENT SEMANTIC SYSTEM if it utilizes features of context that may not be specifiable independently of the intentions and beliefs of the speaker (the agent). I take demonstrative reference to involve specifications of this sort.

Some would no doubt disagree with this view, arguing (with Kaplan) that demonstrata are determined independently of the speaker's beliefs or intentions. But consider examples like (20), whose content cannot be ascertained without appeal to the speaker's intention.

(20)   *That is green.*   [pointing from across the room at a huge mural which contains intricate detail in many colors]

Surely the truth or falsehood of (20) depends crucially on what part of the mural the speaker intended to refer to. Because of cases like this, I believe that even the speaker intended to refer to. Because of cases like this, I believe that even simple demonstrative reference is different in kind from the kind of example mentioned earlier, which can be dealt with in a strict context-dependent semantic system.

Demonstrative reference has further interesting properties which indicate the inadequacy of strict context-dependent systems. As Nunberg (1977) shows, the demonstrated object (the *demonstratum*) is not necessarily the same as the intended referent, as for instance in the following cases.

(21)   a. *Hearst brought* ***that.***   [pointing at a copy of the *New York Times*]
       b. ***This*** *might have been prevented.*   [pointing at picture of disheveled person]

In (21a) it is possible to construe the reference of *that* as the *New York Times* COMPANY, and in (21b) *this* may refer to the event (presumably an assault) which brought about the situation depicted in the picture. This is an attested example, cited by Nunberg.

Such cases of demonstration–reference mismatch pose an interesting problem for the formal semantic analysis of natural language. As Nunberg shows, which transfers of reference are possible is not arbitrary. Language users are guided by shared cultural assumptions and mutual knowledge in assigning reference to demonstrative expressions. And this is an important observation which a linguistic theory must take account of.

Reference transfer of this sort could be handled in a number of ways in a context-dependent semantic system. One possibility is the following: The c_fs could do all the work—specifying in some contexts transferred referents for demonstrative terms, and in other contexts, nontransferred referents. Pragmatic theory of course includes the theory of contexts and would have as its task the clarification of which c_fs are possible and which are not. Presumably this clarification would involve notions of shared cultural assumptions and mutual knowledge.

Alternatively, Kaplan-contexts could be augmented with reference transfer functions (for which I will use the notation c_{RT}) which map demonstrated entities to entities referred to ($c_{RT} \in U^U$). Demonstrative term denotation could then be given by the following rule.

(22)   If α is a demonstrative term of L, then $|\alpha|_{\text{cwt}} = c_{RT}(c_f(\alpha))$

c_{RT} would include the identity mapping for cases of nontransferred demonstrative reference. Which c_{RT}s are possible and which are not would be explicated within pragmatic theory.

A third alternative, much like the second, is to introduce a demonstrative operator into L (call it R), which functions syntactically to make new demonstrative terms from demonstrative terms (if α is a basic demonstrative term of L, $[R\alpha]$ is also). Natural language demonstrative pronouns then translate into L either as a basic demonstrative term or else as a term constructed with the R-operator. For example, *this* would translate either as **this**$_n$ or [R **this**$_n$], for some n. Reference transfer is associated with the presence of the R-operator in the L-translation of the given demonstrative expression, and the denotation of demonstrative terms is given by rule (23).

(23)   If α is a basic demonstrative term of L, then
    a. $|\alpha|_{\text{cwt}} = c_f(\alpha)$
    b. $|[R\alpha]|_{\text{cwt}} = c_{RT}(|\alpha|_{\text{cwt}})$

under either of the last two proposals, c_{RT} could map a copy of the *New York Times* into the *New York Times* Company and/or a picture of a person in a disheveled state into the event that brought that state about, thus accounting for the reference transfers in examples like (20) and (21).[8]

Let us now return to example (1) on its Nunbergian interpretation.

(1)   *The ham sandwich is getting restless.*

Examples of this sort might be viewed as another case of reference transfer (though this matter is open to dispute, as we will see shortly). The mechanism we have developed so far is easily extended to handle such cases. We need only allow c_{RT} to play a role in determining the denotation of definite NPs as well as demonstratives.

Again, this could be done in more than one way. One way would be to allow the R-operator to create new terms from definite descriptions—if $(ıx: \phi)$ is a term of L, so is $[R(ıx: \phi)]$. The denotation rule in (23b) remains unchanged, and such denotations as the man who ordered a ham sandwich (in the context at hand) are arrived at by application of a c_{RT} to the

---

[8] It is possible to modify this account to allow complex reference and referent is mediated by another object (or more than one), and more than one reference transfer function. Indeed, Nunberg suggests that (21) is such a case.

One modification which would accomplish this is to allow R to make demonstrative terms from any demonstrative term, including one already constructed by means of R. The denotation of $[R\alpha]$ would be computed by applying c_{RT} to $|\alpha|_{\text{ctw}}$, and that of $[R[R\alpha]]$ by applying c_{RT} to $c_{RT}(|\alpha|_{\text{ctw}})$, and so forth. I am indebted to Jon Barwise for this suggestion.

denotation of the definite NP, in this case, the ham sandwich. Pragmatic theory places (perhaps drastic) constraints on which c_{RT}s are possible, but once the transferred denotations are fixed, the compositional semantic machinery proceeds as usual.

This account formalizes Nunberg's approach to the problem at hand; yet I think there is some reason to doubt whether it is the appropriate analysis of the *ham sandwich* examples. Note that examples like the following also allow Nunbergian interpretations.

(24)   a. *There are five ham sandwiches sitting at table 9.*
      b. *Every ham sandwich at that table is a woman.*

That is, (24a) and (24b) may be interpreted as paraphrases of *There are five ham sandwich orderers sitting at table 9* and *Every ham sandwich orderer at that table is a woman,* respectively.

Now it seems clear that the words *five* and *every* here are functioning semantically as they usually do. What is altered is the sense of the head noun *ham sandwich* which expresses here a property of beings, not one of culinary objects. Once this is observed, it is easy to see that the same is true of Nunberg's original example [(1)]. *The* performs its normal semantic function. Only the nature of the description, that is, the sense of the common noun, is altered.

Perhaps, then, a more perspicuous way of handling these examples within an extended context-dependent semantic system is to introduce contextually based sense transfers. This could be done by augmenting Kaplan-contexts with a sense-transfer function (c_{ST}) which, for these cases, maps one-place predicate senses to one-place predicate senses, as indicated in (25).

(25) $$c_{ST} \in (\mathscr{P}(U)^{W \times T})^{(\mathscr{P}(U)^{W \times T})}$$

A c_{ST} could map the sense of ham sandwich onto the sense of ham sandwich orderer (that is, map the function picking out the ham sandwich orders at each index).

Again, we may add a new operator to L, call it S, which forms one-place predicates from one-place predicates (for any one-place predicate P of L, $[SP]$ is also a one-place predicate). The denotation rule in (26) effects the desired sense-transfers, once we have c_{ST}s within Kaplan-contexts.

(26) $\|[SP]\|_{cwt} = [c_{ST}(I_P)]\,(w,t)$
      (where I_P designates the intension of P, as earlier)

By applying c_{ST} to the intension of the predicate P, we obtain the new intension, which when applied to an index $[(w,t)]$ gives the transferred denotation of the expression $[SP]$.

The translation procedure from English into L would allow a common noun, like *ham sandwich,* to translate either as a basic expression of L (**ham-sandwich**) or else as a predicate constructed with the S-operator ([S **ham-sandwich**]). The noun phrase *the ham sandwich* would then be rendered into L as either (27) or (28).

(27)   ($\imath x$: **ham-sandwich** (x))

(28)   ($\imath x$: [S **ham-sandwich**] (x))

The denotation of (27) will be a ham sandwich, that of (28), will be a ham sandwich orderer, presuming c_{ST} performs the appropriate transfer of sense. Here *the* plays its ordinary semantic role as would *five* and *every* in a similar analysis of examples (24a) and (24b).

Which sense-transfers can be effected by c_{ST}s is again to be explicated by pragmatic theory. Once we have an explication of that, the problem of where such transfers can occur reduces to the problem of how we translate a natural language into L—specifically, where in the translation procedure we allow the S-operator to be introduced.[9]

There are in fact other linguistic studies that provide evidence for contextually based sense-transfers of just this sort, namely those of Clark and Clark (1979) and Kay and Zimmer (1976). I cannot explore here all the alternatives available for analyzing their examples within an extended context-dependent semantic system, but I will indicate at least one or two ways their data could be accommodated.

Clark and Clark show that English nouns can be turned into verbs freely, that the interpretation of such denominal verbs may vary from context to context, and that such pragmatic factors as mutual knowledge play a significant role in determining which interpretation a given denominal verb will take on in a given context. This is not to say that all denominal verbs are semantically free in this way (some denominal verb meanings are surely conventionalized), but only that in a vast number of cases, such as the following, the sense of the verb may vary with the context.

(29)   a. *He **porched** the newspaper.*
       b. *My sister **Houdini'd** her way out of the locked closet.*
       c. *We all **Wayned** and **Cagneyed**.*

[9] There remain several questions of detail which I will not explore here. For example, the S-operator could be eliminated, allowing c_{ST} to be involved in the denotation rule for all one-place predicates (c_{ST} would then have to include the identity mapping for cases lacking sense-transfer). Also, there is the question of whether multiple sense transfers should be effected by iterated S operators. I leave these problems for future investigation.

   d. *We were **stoned** and **bottled** by the spectators as we marched
      down the street.*

Even coinages that appear at first blush to be totally uninterpretable become totally transparent in context. Furthermore, such coinages are extremely common in everyday colloquial usage. For example, *to teapot* is
fully interpretable in a context like the following (Clark and Clark, 1979,
p. 786).

(30)   [Imagine that Ed and Joe have an odd mutual acquaintance, Max,
        who occasionally sneaks up and strokes the back of people's legs
        with a teapot. One day Ed tells Joe . . .] *Well, this time Max
        has gone too far. He tried to **teapot** a policeman.*

Here it is clear that the sense of *to teapot* is "to rub the back of the leg
of _____, with a teapot." The sense of *to teapot* will vary from context to
context, as will the sense of, say, *to Houdini,* in examples like those in
(31).

(31)   a. *I would love to **Houdini** those ESP experiments.*
        b. *Joe got **Houdini'd** in the stomach.*

Which interpretation is assigned to this verb depends on what the inter-
locutors might know about Harry Houdini—that he was an escape artist
[hence the sense "to escape (from)" in (29b)], an exposer of mediums
[hence the sense "to expose as fraudulent by careful analysis" in (31a)],
etc.

   These examples are prime candidates for a transfer of sense analysis of
the sort I suggest for the *ham sandwich* case. One proposal would go
roughly as follows. Assume that there is a lexical rule that creates transitive verbs from nouns both common and proper. Assuming that common
nouns normally translate into L as one-place predicates, proper nouns as
constant terms, and transitive verbs as two-place predicates, the translation process associated with the lexical rule could be as formulated in
(32).

(32)   If a is a noun with L-translation α then a is also a transitive verb
        with L-translation $[S\alpha]$.

Under this proposal, the examples in (33), to pick slightly simpler
cases, would have roughly the expressions of (34) as their respective L-
translations.[10]

_____
[10] The syntax of L must of course be altered slightly to allow the S-operator to form two-
place predicates from one-place predicates and from constant terms.

(33) a. *Sandy porched Kim.*
      b. *Sandy Houdini'd Kim.*

(34) a. [*S porch*] (*Sandy, Kim*)
      b. [*S Houdini*] (*Sandy, Kim*)

The predicates in (34) are evaluated in terms of c_{ST}, as in (26), the only difference being that c_{ST} must be allowed to map one-place predicate intensions and term intensions to two-place predicate intensions. Thus the set of c_{ST}s is greatly expanded. Given what I have said so far, the set of c_{ST}s is as indicated in (35).

(35) $c_{ST} \in (\mathscr{P}(U)^{W \times T} \cup \mathscr{P}(U \times U)^{W \times T})^{(\mathscr{P}(U)^{W \times T})} \cup (\mathscr{P}(U \times U)^{W \times T})^{(U^{W \times T})}$

It is essential that some constraints be placed on the set of possible c_{ST}s.

The analysis of (34a) would then proceed as follows. As **porch** is a one-place predicate, the sense of **porch** (I_{porch}), is a function from indices to subsets of U ($\mathscr{P}(U)^{W \times T}$)—that is, a function from indices to the set of porches at each index. A c_{ST} maps the sense of **porch** onto roughly the sense of "throw onto a porch ," more precisely onto that function which gives for each index the set of pairs of entities the first of which throws the second onto a porch at that index. This intension is an element of $(\mathscr{P}(U \times U))^{W \times T}$.

We evaluate [*S* **porch**] in (34a) in accordance with our earlier rule as in (36).

(36) $\|[S \ \textbf{porch}]\|_{\text{cwt}} = [c_{ST}(I_{\text{porch}})] \ (w,t)$

A c_{ST} applied to I_{porch} gives us the desired transferred intension which when applied to (w,t) gives us the set of pairs of individuals the first of whom throws the second onto a porch at (w,t). The evaluation of the truth of (34b) then proceeds as before, that is, according to Rule (16).

Some account along these lines I believe accurately formalizes the ideas developed informally by Clark and Clark. Further variations are possible. It is crucial to all such proposals that a theory of pragmatics clarify which c_{ST}s are possible, and under what conditions these c_{ST}s are arrived at. The observations of the Clarks about the importance of mutual knowledge, as well as further observations of Nunberg's, thus play an essential role in the pragmatic theory that must accompany a semantic analysis of the sort I have sketched here.

A very similar phenomenon is the interpretation of compound nouns, is discussed by Kay and Zimmer (1976). They show that the sense of a given common noun may vary with the context of use. Again, some compound nouns have conventional interpretations (e.g., *finger bowl, waste basket, red cap, manpower*), yet noun–noun compounding in English is a productive process and the semantic interpretation of coined compounds is not fixed in the way that word sense is generally fixed. They cite as an example the compound *finger cup*, which, they argue, can have any of the following interpretations:

(37)   "cup held between the tips of the fingers"
        "cup with incised indentations for the fingers in lieu of handle"
        "cup that holds one finger of whiskey"
        "cup that holds two fingers of whiskey"
        "cup for washing one's fingers in"
        "cup that is shaped like a finger," and so on.

A crucial feature of these compounds, as Kay and Zimmer note (p. 32) is that the modifying noun (i.e., the first noun) is used to narrow the sense (and hence the reference) of the head noun. Building on this insight, we can provide an account of these contextually based sense-transfers within an extended context-sensitive semantic framework in much the same way as the Clark and Clark examples were dealt with. The modification that must be made is further expansion of the class of c_{ST}s.

Suppose we include among c_{ST}s functions from one-place predicate intensions (all members of $\mathcal{P}(U)^{W \times T}$) to intentions of functions from one-place predicate denotations to one-place predicate denotations—that is, to functions that are members of $(\mathcal{P}(U)^{\mathcal{P}(U)})^{W \times T}$. The lexical rule that forms compound nouns, with the associated translation process, is the following:

(38)   If a and b are common nouns whose respective L-translations are α and β, then $a\widehat{\ }b$ is a (compound) common noun with the L-translation: $[[S\alpha]\beta]$ ($a\widehat{\ }b$ designates the concatenation of a and b).

The transfer of sense will be effected by our earlier rule for evaluating expressions containing the S-operator, although $[S\alpha]$ is here a modifier of the one-place predicate β. The resulting function (the denotation of $[S\alpha]$) is then applied to the denotation of β to give the denotation of the complex one-place predicate $[[S\alpha]\beta]$. This account presumes the denotation rule for predicate modifiers given in (39) and is illustrated for the case of *finger cup* in (40).

(39)   If γ is a one-place predicate of L and δ is a (possibly complex) functor expression which makes one-place predicates from one-place predicates, then $|[\delta\gamma]|_{\text{cwt}} = |\delta|_{\text{cwt}} (|\gamma|_{\text{cwt}})$

(40)   a. *finger cup* translates into L as $[[S \textbf{ finger}] \textbf{ cup}]$, which is a one-place predicate
        b. $|[S \textbf{ finger}]|_{\text{cwt}} = [c_{ST}(I_{\textbf{finger}})](w,t)$, which is a function from sets to

sets whose members are for washing ones fingers in, or are
shaped like a finger, *etc*. [by Rule (26) and the appropriate c_{ST}s]
  c. $|[[S \text{ finger}] \text{ cup}]|_{cwt} = |[S \text{ finger}]|_{cwt}(|\text{cup}|_{cwt}) = [[c_{ST}(I_{\text{finger}})] (w,t)]$
     $(I_{\text{cup}}(w,t))$,

which gives the set of cups whose members are for washing one's fingers
in, or are shaped like a finger, *etc*. [by (b) and Rule (39)].

Once we have the appropriate c_{ST}s specified by the theory of pragmatics, it is clear that the sense of compound nouns can be accounted for by
the same mechanism we used for the sense transfers of denominal verbs,
as I have indicated. A similar analysis is possible for the case of genitive
modifiers, also discussed by Kay and Zimmer, and for certain other examples like (41), which perhaps would require c_{ST} to map intensions of names
of propositions to individuals.

(41)   *Here comes old "I am not a crook" again.*

I will not explore the details of such analyses here.

It is important to note that the examples considered in this section provide strong evidence against developing a purely pragmatic (i.e., Gricean)
analysis of the sort mentioned in Section 1. Denominal verbs and noun–
noun compounds have no appropriate literal meanings independent of
context. Hence any attempt to account for their contextually variable interpretation by standard Gricean inferencing encounters the formidable
difficulty of there being no input for the Gricean machinery to operate on.
These examples thus provide strong support for developing extensions of
the model-theoretic apparatus of the sort I have been considering.

The techniques developed in this section are quite general and exces-
sively powerful. Yet they provide a basis for analyzing the various
puzzling and recalcitrant examples discussed in the literature that show
the effect of context on meaning. In context-dependent semantic systems,
however, a sharp distinction is maintained between those elements whose
semantic analysis involves contextually based sense or reference transfer,
and those whose semantic analysis does not. This seems to be an intuitively
satisfactory distinction to make, yet the matter is no doubt controversial.
In the next section, I explore briefly a kind of analysis where no such
distinction is made formally.

6. CONTEXT-SATURATED SEMANTICS

A crucial aspect of context-dependent semantic systems, all of which
are essentially modifications of the basic approach outlined by Kaplan, is
the distinction between CHARACTER and CONTENT (these terms are also

due to Kaplan). The character of an expression is that function which gives for each context the sense (intension) of the expression in that context. The content of an expression (in a particular context) is that sense defined by its character.

Context-dependent systems associate with each expression of L both a character and a set of contents. This is an intuitive and appealing way of characterizing the notion "what is said" on a given occasion of utterance and at the same time allowing for cases where "what is said" may vary from context to context, as we have seen.

A somewhat different approach to the problem of indexicals was suggested by Montague (1968, 1970). Montague's proposal was to add essentially the same information specified in Kaplan-contexts directly to indices. An index would then be a specification of, not only a world and a time, but also an agent, an audience, a place, a demonstrated object, or, following any of the suggestions made in the previous section, a sense transfer-function, a reference transfer-function, *etc.* Meanings on this view remain as functions from indices to the appropriate denotational domain. The notion of content, essential to Kaplan's account of meaning, is lacking in Montague's. I will refer to any such theory which blurs the distinction between character and content, and hence the distinction between indexical expressions (those with nonconstant character) and nonindexical expressions (those with constant character) as a context-saturated semantic system.

I believe that if indices are augmented in the same fashion that Kaplan-contexts were in the preceding section, then a very similar account can be given of the various examples that I have discussed. At least the recursive definition of truth and denotation can proceed roughly as before with only trivial modification of our earlier rules. In fact, much the same options are open within a context-saturated semantic analysis, including the possibility of augmenting L with one or more logical operators (R,S).

So, if each index i specifies a time (i_T), a world (i_W), a place (i_P), an agent (i_{ag}), an audience (i_{aud}), an assignment function for demonstratives (i_f), a reference transfer function (i_{RT}), and a sense-transfer function (i_{ST}), denotation rules will look like (42) for simple cases.

(42)   If α is a basic expression of L, and i is an index, $|\alpha|_i = I_\alpha(i)$.

If as before, the R-operator is used for reference transfer and the S-operator for sense transfer, their proper functioning is guaranteed by denotation rules like the following.

(43) $|[R\alpha]|_i = i_{RT}(|\alpha|_i)$

(44) $|[S\alpha]|_i = [i_{ST}(I\alpha)](i)$

There is exactly the same reliance on pragmatic theory, and exactly the same urgent need to constrain the class of reference- and sense-transfer functions.

Indexicality of the sort I have discussed in this chapter is thus not likely to settle the matter of which kind of system, context-dependent or context-saturated, is more appropriate for the semantic analysis of natural language. Rather, that question will be settled by considerations of the sort suggested by Kaplan—for example, the question of whether the notion of content must be embodied within a semantic theory, or the matter of whether sentences such as (45) should be regarded as necessary truths, as it appears they must in a context-saturated theory.

(45)   *I am here now.*

The problems I have raised here appear to be completely independent of the Kaplan–Montague controversy.

7. CONCLUSION

In this chapter I have explored some of the consequences of various context-dependent linguistic phenomena for the formal semantic analysis of natural language. Accepting that the various examples I have take from the linguistic literature are to be analyzed in terms of contextually variable propositional content, I have tried to classify the semantic systems that are capable of dealing with them. Such systems are seen to very most significantly with regard to what kind of contextual information is represented, and how it is accessed. I have treated the various cases discussed by Nunberg, Clark and Clark, and Kay and Zimmer in terms of an extension of the kind of apparatus proposed by Kaplan for the formal semantic analysis of indexicals.

The skeptical reader has by now surely asked her/himself: "What CAN'T you do with devices as powerful as those introduced in Sag's paper?" This skepticism, I feel, is appropriate, but only to a point. Indeed, one must develop a theory of contexts, a theory of reference transfer and a theory of sense transfer. I have here only sketched general frameworks.

Yet the various scholars whose work I have cited (most notably Nunberg and the Clarks) have begun to develop such theories. Their taxonomies and demonstration of the need to consider shared cultural assumptions and mutual knowledge are directly to the point. It is clear that the nature of the required theory is pragmatic, and not semantic, and progress in the theory of meaning can only come by carefully distinguishing between the two.

It is true that the approaches suggested here shift much of the burden of the analysis of meaning to the theory of pragmatics, but the semantic theories that remain have substantial content. The central point I have tried to make here, which is quite independent of the problem of articulating an interesting and constrained theory of contextual influence on the interpretation of sentence parts, is that meanings of wholes must still be calculated as a function of meanings of parts. Pragmatic factors may be pervasive in determining the interpretation of terms, common nouns, denominal verbs, noun–noun compounds and the like, but semantics remains compositional. That is, if a theory of meaning is to give a precise characterization of truth, contradiction, and logical consequence for natural language—as it must—then there must still be principles of semantic composition, principles that are part of a semantic system that remains discrete and autonomous, even in the face of examples like those I have considered here.

ACKNOWLEDGEMENTS

The research reported in this chapter was conducted during 1978–1979, while I was an Andrew Mellon fellow at Stanford University. The ideas presented here were developed through interaction with members of the Bay Area Pragmatics and Semantics Discussion Group which included Dwight Bolinger, Eve and Herb Clark, Chuck Fillmore, Georgia Green, Jerry Hobbs, Paul Kay, Beatriz Lavandera, Jerry Morgan, Geoff Nunberg, Chiahua Pan, Bob Stalnaker, Henry Thompson, Elizabeth Traugott, Tom Wasow, and Steve Weisler. I am especially indebted to Bob Stalnaker for extensive discussions, insightful suggestions, and an abundance of patience. In addition, I would like to thank Jon Barwise, Barbara Partee, and John Perry for valuable suggestions. At the risk of being repetitive, let me thank Herb Clark, Paul Kay, Geoff Nunberg, John Perry, Martha Pollack, Bob Stalnaker, and Steve Weisler for commenting on an earlier draft of this chapter. Finally, let me thank Joseph Stern, many of whose detailed and helpful comments on this paper were received too late to be incorporated into the final version. Ideas similar to those discussed here are developed in Stern (1979).

REFERENCES

Clark, E. V., and Clark, H. H. (1979). When nouns surface as verbs. *Language*, **55**, 767–811.

Kaplan, D. (1978). DTHAT. In P. Cole (Ed.), *Syntax and Semantics 9: Pragmatics*. New York: Academic Press. Pp. 221–243.

Kaplan, D. The logic of demonstratives. Unpublished manuscript, Department of Philosophy, University of California, Los Angeles.

Kay, P., and Zimmer, K. (1976). On the semantics of compounds and genitives in English. *Sixth California Linguistics Association Conference Proceedings.*

Lewis, D. (1972). General Semantics. In D. Davidson and G. Harman (Eds.), *Semantics of Natural Language.* Dordrecht Reidel. Pp. 169–218.

Montague, R. (1968). Pragmatics. In R. Klibansky (Ed.), *Contemporary Philosophy: A Survey.* Florence: La Nuova Italia Editrice. (Reprinted in Montague 1974.)

Montague, R. (1970). Pragmatics and intensional logic. *Synthese,* **22,** 68–94. (Reprinted in Montague 1974.)

Montague, R. (1973). On the proper treatment of quantification in Ordinary English. In J. Hintikka *et al.* (Eds.), *Approaches to Natural Language.* Dordrecht: Reidel. (Reprinted in Montague 1974.)

Montague, R. (1974). *Formal Philosophy.* New Haven: Yale University Press.

Nunberg, G. (1977). *The Pragmatics of Reference.* Unpublished doctoral dissertation. C. U. N. Y. Graduate Center, New York. (Reprinted by Indiana University Linguistics Club, 1978).

Nunberg, G. (1979). The Non-Uniqueness of Semantic Solutions: Polysemy. *Linguistics and Philosophy,* **3.2,** 143–184.

Scott, D. (1970). Advice on modal logic. In K. Lambert (Ed.), *Philosophical Problems in Logic,* Dordrecht: Reidel.

Stern, J. (1979). *Metaphor as demonstrative: a formal semantics for demonstratives and metaphors.* Unpublished doctoral dissertation, Columbia University.

Irony and
the Use—Mention
Distinction[1]

Dan Sperber and Deirdre Wilson

1. INTRODUCTION

An ironical utterance is traditionally analyzed as literally saying one
thing and figuratively meaning the opposite. Thus the ironical remark
What lovely weather would have the figurative meaning ``What awful
weather,'' and so on.[2] An explicit semantic theory designed to incorpo-
rate such an account would have to provide, first, a definition of figurative
meaning; second, a mechanism for deriving the figurative meaning of a
sentence; and third, some basis for explaining why figurative utterances
exist: why a speaker should prefer the ironical utterance *What lovely
weather* to its literal counterpart *What awful weather* which, on this analysis, means exactly the same thing. It is because they provide no answers
to such questions that traditional semantic accounts of irony ultimately
fail.

[1] A shorter version of this chapter appeared in French in *Poétique, 36,* 399–412. We
would like to thank Diane Brockway, Robyn Carston, and Julius Moravcsik for a number of
helpful suggestions.
  [2] For example, Quintilian defines irony in terms of the fact that ``we understand something
which is the opposite of what is actually said [Quintilian IX. II, p. 44].'' See also Turner,
1973, p. 216.

RADICAL PRAGMATICS

At first sight, Grice's (1975, 1978) pragmatic approach to irony looks more promising than the traditional semantic approach. Grice attempts to reanalyze the notion of figurative meaning in terms of his independently motivated category of conversational implicature. Thus, for Grice, ironical utterances would conversationally implicate, rather than figuratively mean, the opposite of what they literally say: *What lovely weather* would have no figurative meaning, but would conversationally implicate that the weather was awful. Grice's proposal would relieve semantic theory of the problems of defining figurative meaning and deriving the figurative meaning of an utterance. However, these problems are not solved simply by transferring them from the semantic to the pragmatic domain. It still has to be shown how the interpretation of ironical utterances can be successfully integrated into Grice's pragmatic framework. In this chapter we shall argue that it can not, and that existing pragmatic accounts of irony are as seriously defective as earlier semantic accounts.

Grice's departure from the traditional account of irony is not a radical one. It is based on the same assumption—the assumption that what the speaker of an ironical utterance intends to get across is the opposite of what he has literally said. In fact the only disagreement between Grice and more traditional theorists is over whether the substitution mechanisms involved are semantic or pragmatic. Grice's account, like the traditional one, fails to explain why an ironical utterance should ever be preferred to its literal counterpart: why someone should choose to say *What lovely weather* rather than the more transparent *What awful weather*. As will be seen, it also fails to make explicit exactly how the move from literal meaning to conversational implicature is made in the case of irony. Finally, it fails to show that the "conversational implicatures" involved in irony are of the same type as the more standard cases of conversational implicature to which they are supposed to be assimilated. For these reasons, Grice's purely pragmatic account of irony also fails.

In this chapter, we offer an account of irony that goes some way toward solving the problem raised by both traditional semantic and pragmatic approaches. In particular, it explains why ironical utterances are made, and why they occasionally (but not always) implicate the opposite of what they literally say. Unlike the traditional theory, it makes no reference to the notion of figurative meaning. Unlike both the traditional theory and Grice's account, it involves no substitution mechanism, whether semantic or pragmatic. Unlike Grice's theory, it assumes that there is a necessary (though not sufficient) semantic condition for an utterance to be ironical. Furthermore, the crucial fact that ironical utterances convey not only propositions (which can be accounted for in terms of meaning and implicature), but also vaguer suggestions of images and attitudes, finds a natural description in the framework we propose.

2. SOME METHODOLOGICAL PRELIMINARIES

There are a number of obvious similarities between linguistics and the study of rhetoric. Rhetorical judgments, like linguistic judgments, are ultimately based on intuition; rhetoric, like linguistics, is a branch of cognitive psychology. It is well known that linguistic judgments may be affected by explicit teaching or conscious theorizing; the same is true of rhetorical judgements, only much more so, because many rhetorical categories such as "metaphor," "figurative," or "irony" are part of everyday speech. Because of this, informant work in rhetoric must be approached with a certain amount of methodological caution.

For example, suppose we ask an informant whether (1) or (2) could be ironical when said by someone caught in a downpour:

(1)   *What lovely weather.*

(2)   *It seems to be raining.*

Anyone who has been taught the traditional definition of irony, that ironical utterances say one thing and mean the opposite, will naturally say that (1), but not (2), is ironical. He will say this even though he may notice that both (1) and (2) could be said in the same (wry) tone of voice which a naive informant would precisely call ironical. Given enough responses of this type, we might well take the traditional definition of irony as being strongly confirmed; however, this would be a mistake, since it is the definition itself that is directly responsible for the judgments which "confirm" it.

The best way of avoiding these pitfalls is to ask questions that have no stereotyped response. The ultimate goal is to find intuitive relationships among the data, intuitive ways of grouping them, which do not simply reflect conscious, explicitly defined categories. This is not because stereotyped responses or conscious categories are uninteresting, but because they only provide insight into cultural peculiarities or idiosyncrasies. A GENERAL theory of rhetoric should be concerned with basic psychological and interpretative mechanisms which remain invariant from culture to culture.

There is another, closely related point. The traditional study of rhetoric, which dates back 2000 years, offers a rich and subtle set of analytical concepts. These concepts are interesting in themselves; it is possible that some of them will have a necessary role to play in any future theory of rhetoric. However, it would be a mistake to prejudge the issue. It should not be taken for granted that even the major rhetorical categories, such as alliteration, ellipsis, hyperbole, metaphor, metonymy, irony, and so on, correspond to genuine natural classes of facts, playing clearly defined and distinguishable roles in speech production and perception. It is possible that the whole idea of tropes and their classification is destined to go the same way as the notion of humors in medicine; it is possible that verbal irony and its associated attitude have about as much claim on our attention as black bile and the atrabilious temperament.

The notion of irony is an abstract one, based on a rather arbitrary range of examples which have themselves been rather inadequately described. Because of this, it seems to us to be a mistake to take IRONY itself as the object of investigation, and to limit one's attention to its more standard cases. There is a whole range of utterance-types that can be more or less loosely called ironical. The basic facts to be accounted for are the particular effects produced by particular utterances, and the perceived similarities among them. We should be looking for psychological mechanisms that can account for these effects and their interrelationships. When we have found some, it might be interesting to make some comparisons between the resulting (provisional) conceptual scheme and the framework of classical rhetoric, to see which notion of irony emerges, if any; but the existence of a unified category of irony should not be taken for granted.

Quite independently of the existence of irony, there are already strong grounds for rejecting the notion of figurative meaning itself. For example, consider the treatment of disambiguation, which is a major problem for any pragmatic theory. Every hearer (or reader) almost instantaneously disambiguates each of the utterances he hears. Even if we ignore figurative meanings, and consider only the literal senses of an utterance, narrowly defined, almost every utterance is ambiguous. In fact, almost every utterance is multiply ambiguous, with possible semantic interactions among its individual ambiguous constructions. Most utterances also contain referential expressions which may have a wide range of possible referents, even when the shared knowledge of speaker and hearer is taken into account. It is thus quite typical for an utterance to have dozens, or even hundreds, of possible propositional interpretations. However, speaker and hearer are normally able to select a single one of these interpretations without even realizing that they have made a choice. It is generally agreed that this choice is a function of the context; but to define the function, as opposed to simply claiming that it exists, is no easy task.

As long as we only have to choose among the literal senses of an utterance, the task is still an approachable one; the set of possible interpretations remains finite, and will be specifiable on the basis of a fairly restricted range of semantic and referential variables. One can think of several types of explicit procedures that could be used to eliminate all but one of the possible interpretations. The difficulty lies not so much in conceiving of such a procedure in principle, as in choosing and justifying the right one. On the other hand, suppose that we have to take into account not only the literal senses of an utterance, but also the whole range of figurative senses that are loosely based on them via relations of resemblance, contiguity, inclusion or inversion; in this case, the set of possible interpretations becomes to all intents and purposes nonenumerable. And if this is so, it is hard to see how one could even set about giving an account of disambiguation, which is not, we repeat, a rare and marginal phenomenon, but a basic factor in the interpretation of every utterance.

Thus the notion of figurative meaning, whatever its value for the analysis of figures of speech, becomes a real source of difficulty as soon as we look at other aspects of the interpretation of utterances. The question is whether these difficulties are caused by the complexity of the data—which cannot be ignored—or whether they result from some inadequacy in the concepts being used to analyze them.

Obviously, a speaker may sometimes intend to convey something other than one of the literal senses of his utterance. When he wants to convey something IN ADDITION TO one of the literal senses, the notion of conversational implicature is relevant. This presents no problem for a theory of disambiguation; on the contrary, it has a role to play in such a theory. If figurative meaning could be analyzed in terms of conversational implicature, as Grice has proposed, disambiguation would be fairly straightforward. However, in the case of figurative language, the speaker normally intends to convey something INSTEAD OF one of the literal senses of his utterance; the implicature has to be seen as SUBSTITUTING FOR the literal sense. The idea that an implicature could actually contradict the literal sense of an utterance—as it would in the case of irony—does not square with Grice's central claim that implicatures act as premises in an argument designed to establish that the speaker has observed the maxims of conversation in saying what he said. It follows that the interpretation of ironical utterances cannot be reduced to the search for conversational implicatures without grossly distorting the notion of implicature itself. Grice does not succeed in integrating figurative interpretations into his overall pragmatic theory.[3]

---

[3] For more detailed discussion of Grice's treatment of figurative language, see Wilson and Sperber (forthcoming).

This being so, if the substitution theory of irony is correct, some notion of figurative meaning seems called for, and the problems it gives rise to seem to be forced on us by the data themselves. However, if it were possible to give just as good an account of the data, but without any appeal to the notion of figurative meaning, and using only independently motivated concepts (literal sense, implicature, *etc.*), it is clear that this would be preferable to the traditional account. An approach along these lines has already been suggested for the cases of metaphor, synecdoche and metonymy in Sperber 1975b; in this chapter we attempt to extend the analysis to irony. The problem will be taken up in more detail in Sperber and Wilson (forthcoming).

3. SOME BASIC DATA

Consider the utterances in (1) and (2) (repeated here for convenience) and (3)–(8), exchanged between two people caught in a downpour in circumstances that are otherwise normal:

(1)   *What lovely weather.*

(2)   *It seems to be raining.*

(3)   *I'm glad we didn't bother to bring an umbrella.*

(4)   *Did you remember to water the flowers?*

(5)   *What awful weather.*

(6)   *It seems to be thundering.*

(7)   *I'm sorry we didn't bother to bring an umbrella.*

(8)   *Did you remember to bring in the washing?*

There are two obvious ways of grouping these examples. First, there are close syntactic and lexical parallels between (1) and (5), (2) and (6), (3) and (7), and (4) and (8). Second, in a less straightforwardly definable way, (1)–(4) have something in common which distinguishes them from (5)–(8). Consider (1)–(4) in turn.

What lovely weather. In the circumstances described, it is inconceivable that the speaker meant to get across the literal meaning of his utterance. In fact, it is certain that he believes the opposite of what he has said. However, it is not so obvious that it was this belief that he primarily intended to get across, as would be claimed by both the semantic and pragmatic accounts of irony referred to above. In the first place, suppose this

WAS his primary intention: How would it be recognized? Ironical utterances are not always distinguishable by intonation from their literal counterparts. When there is no distinctive intonation, it is clear that the choice between literal and ironical interpretation must be based on information external to the utterance—contextual knowledge and other background assumptions—rather than the form or content of the utterance itself. Where such external information is lacking—for example where (1) is said in the course of a long distance telephone call—then the utterance would certainly be taken as literal. In other words, knowing the speaker's beliefs about the weather is a precondition for, rather than a consequence of, recognizing that his utterance was ironical. The standard approach to irony, which claims that the main point of an ironical utterance is to convey the opposite of what is said, would thus make every ironical utterance uninformative, both on the level of what is said and on the level of what is implicated. The speaker would be intending to communicate a certain belief, but, in the absence of any special intonation, his intention would only be recognized by someone who already knew that he held that belief.

We have already mentioned another problem with this account. If the speaker of (1) meant to indicate that he thought the weather was awful, why not say so directly? What is the point of the indirect approach? What difference is there between saying *What lovely weather* ironically, and *What awful weather* literally? On both standard semantic and pragmatic accounts, there is nothing to choose between these two remarks, and therefore no particular reason for ever being ironical.[4] This is clearly not right. Moreover, the data do not entirely support the standard description of ironical utterances.

The only clear intuition is that the speaker of (1) does not mean what he has literally said, and lets it be understood that what he has literally said is the opposite of what he really believes. Obviously, his real beliefs can be deduced from this, but we cannot necessarily conclude that his main intention—or even a subsidiary intention—was to get these beliefs across. He might instead have been trying to express an opinion, not about the weather, but about the content of (1) itself—to indicate, for example, that it had been ridiculous to hope that the weather would be lovely.

It seems to be raining. This clearly does not express the opposite of what the speaker thinks; it just expresses LESS than what he thinks. Whereas (1) was odd because the speaker did not believe what he said, (2) is odd because its truth is so patently obvious. Although it might have been relevant or informative as the first few drops of rain were falling, in the middle of a downpour it could never be seriously made except by

---

[4] A similar point is made in Harnish 1976.

someone with incredibly slow reactions. The speaker is not trying to pretend that he is such a person; nor is he parodying anyone in particular. What he is trying to do is to bring to mind just this exaggerated slowness of reaction which would itself be worth remarking on in the circumstances. For an utterance to have this effect, it must be obvious that the speaker is drawing attention to its content, while at the same time dissociating himself from it. What is important is the content of the utterance, rather than what it is about.

I'm glad we didn't bother to bring an umbrella. Like (1), this is a case where the utterance does not directly reflect the speaker's views; where in fact he believes the opposite of what he says. One could imagine (3) being used to echo an earlier remark made to, or by, the speaker or hearer before setting off: *Don't bother to take an umbrella,* or *Let's not bother to take an umbrella,* for example. By repeating this advice in the pouring rain, the speaker of (3) underlines its futility.

Clearly someone who asks *Did you remember to water the flowers?* cannot mean the opposite of what he says. Indeed it is hard to see what would BE the opposite of (4), or of most other ironical questions. This is a further argument against both standard semantic and pragmatic accounts of irony. The question in (4) is odd because, like (2), it is so obviously irrelevant in the circumstances. The speaker is not interested in the answer; he is much more likely to have asked the question precisely to highlight its irrelevance and the pointlessness of asking or answering it in the circumstances. If we also suppose that the hearer is fanatical about keeping his flowers watered, (3) will have the further implication that the question is USUALLY pointless, and that the hearer's obsession is ridiculous. Thus, what the speaker actually communicates is not question (4) itself, but an attitude to it and to the state of mind that might give rise to it.

Although incomplete and imprecise, these observations about (1)–(4) do at least make clear what these utterances have in common that distinguishes them from (5)–(8). Someone who utters (1)–(4) cannot but dissociate himself from the content of his utterance, either because it is clearly false, as in (1) and (3), or because it is clearly irrelevant, as in (2) and (4). The only way to understand him is to assume that he is expressing a belief ABOUT his utterance, rather than BY MEANS OF it. What (1)–(4) express is an attitude of the speaker to his utterance, whereas what (5)–(8) express is an attitude of the speaker to what his utterance is about: the weather, the rain, and the appropriate steps for dealing with them. This distinction between two basic types of utterance is entirely missed by both standard semantic and pragmatic accounts of irony. On both standard accounts, the ironical utterance of (1) is about the weather, and is thus indistinguishable from the literal utterance *What awful weather.* On our account, there is a crucial difference between the two utterances, because one expresses an attitude to the content of an utterance, whereas the other expresses an attitude to the weather.

4. THE USE–MENTION DISTINCTION

The intuitive distinction we have just illustrated using (1)–(4) and (5)–(8) as examples is closely related to the distinction drawn in philosophy between the USE and MENTION of an expression. USE of an expression involves reference to what the expression refers to; MENTION of an expression involves reference to the expression itself. Thus *marginal* is used in (9) to refer to the doubtful grammatical status of certain examples:

(9) *These examples are rare and marginal.*

It is mentioned in (10a) and (10b), where reference is made to the word *marginal* itself:

(10) a. *"Marginal" is a technical term.*
      b. *Who had the nerve to call my examples marginal?*

When the expression mentioned is a complete sentence, it does not have the illocutionary force it would standardly have in a context where it was used. Thus, the remark in (11a) is uttered in (11b) without actually being made, the question in (12a) is uttered in (12b) without actually being asked, and the order in (13a) is uttered in (13b) without actually being given:

(11) a. *What a shame!*
      b. *Don't just say "What a shame"; do something.*

(12) a. *What is irony?*
      b. *"What is irony?" is the wrong question.*

(13) a. *Be quiet!*
      c. *"Be quiet! Be quiet!" And suppose I feel like talking?*

This may be used as a test for distinguishing between use and mention of sentences.

The use–mention distinction is a logical one. In formal languages, mention is distinguished from use in a conventional way, and there can be no question about whether a formula contains a mention, nor about what is being mentioned. In natural languages, mentions take a variety of forms, some of which might seem to be intermediate cases, falling somewhere between use and mention. Moreover, cases of mention in natural languages are not usually studied in their own right, but only for the role they play within the frameworks of either "reported speech" or "opaque contexts." Both frameworks are inappropriate for the study of mention; they are too broad in some respects and too narrow in others.

The reported speech framework is too broad because there are standard cases of indirect speech such as (14), where the indirectly reported proposition (15) is part of a larger proposition, and there is no demarcation line, explicit or implicit, to set it off as a case of mention:

(14)   *They say that it is going to rain.*

(15)   *It is going to rain.*

The reported speech framework is also too narrow, because a number of clear cases of mention do not involve any report of speech, even in the very loose usual acceptation. Sentences (16) and (17) are examples:

(16)   *A yellow flag means "stay away."*

(17)   *"Stay away" is a grammatical sentence.*

The opaque context framework is too broad because it covers cases of indirect speech such as (14), (18) and (19), which clearly fall outside the scope of any notion of mention, however extended:

(18)   *Oedipus wanted to marry Jocasta.*

(19)   *Oedipus wanted to marry his mother.*

The contexts in (18) and (19) are opaque, since the substitution of the coreferential expressions *Jocasta* and *his mother* is not truth-preserving. However, we would not want to say that these expressions are mentioned. The notion of opaque context, as usually understood, is also too narrow, because it does not account for cases such as (13b) (where *"Be quiet! Be quiet!"* is certainly mentioned, but where no opaque context is involved; see also (27)–(30) in what follows). One could of course say that the null context is opaque under certain conditions, but the conditions would have to be defined.

There is a real need for a comprehensive account of mention in natural language, which would cover not only mention of an expression, as in (11)–(13), but also mention of a proposition, as in what is usually referred to as "free indirect style."[5] In free indirect style, an independent proposition is reported with an optional comment in a parenthetical phrase, as in (20):

---

[5] For recent work on free indirect style, see Banfield 1973 and McHale 1978.

(20)   *He will come at five, he says.*

It seems clear that (20) is equivalent in logical structure to (21) rather than (22), and is therefore a genuine case of mention:

(21)   *"I will come at five," he says.*

(22)   *He says that he will come at five.*

There are thus two properties that may be used to distinguish various types of mention in natural language; looking at these, one can see why it is sometimes felt that there are intermediate cases between the poles of pure use and pure mention. On the one hand, we can contrast explicit mention, as in (23) and (25), with implicit mention, as in (24) and (26). On the other hand, we can contrast the two different types of object that may be mentioned: linguistic expressions, as in (23) and (24), and propositions, as in (25) and (26):

(23)   *The master began to understand and to share the intense disgust which the archdeacon always expressed when Mrs Proudie's name was mentioned. "What am I to do with such a woman as this?" he asked himself.*

(24)   *The master began to understand and to share the intense disgust which the archdeacon always expressed when Mrs Proudie's name was mentioned. "What am I to do with such a woman as this?"*

(25)   *The master began to understand and to share the intense disgust which the archdeacon always expressed when Mrs Proudie's name was mentioned. What was he to do with such a woman as this, he asked himself.*

(26)   *The master began to understand and to share the intense disgust which the archdeacon always expressed when Mrs Proudie's name was mentioned. What was he to do with such a woman as this?*

[Trollope, *Barchester Towers*]

In formal language, only the explicit mention of an expression is possible; this is illustrated in (23). However, implicit mention of an expression, as in (24), explicit mention of a proposition, as in (25), and implicit mention of a proposition, as in (26), are equally clear cases of mention from a logical point of view, unless the concept of mention is arbitrarily restricted to mention of expressions. It is from a linguistic point of view that mention of a proposition is harder to identify than mention of an expression, and implicit mention harder to identify than explicit mention; hence the impression that there are mixed forms. The most difficult cases to identify are those where a proposition is implicitly mentioned. When the context gives no indication that the free indirect style is being used for reporting speech—as in (26), for example,—it is often possible to process an utterance quite satisfactorily without consciously noticing that it is an utterance of a particular logical type, closely related to quotation. When the mention does not involve reported speech proper, it is less easily identifiable still, and it would not be too much of a surprise to come across whole classes of implicit mention of propositions that have so far been overlooked or misinterpreted. Ironical utterances are a case in point.

5. IRONY AS ECHOIC MENTION

Consider the following exchanges:

(27) a. *I've got a toothache.*
      b. *Oh, you've got a toothache. Open your mouth, and let's have a look.*

(28) a. *Where can I buy pretzels at this time of night?*
      b. *Where can you buy pretzels? At this time of night? At Barney's, of course.*

(29) a. *I'm tired.*
      b. *You're tired. And what do you think I am?*

(30) a. Doolittle: *Listen here, Governor. You and me is men of the world, ain't we?*
      b. Higgins: *Oh! Men of the world, are we? You'd better go, Mrs Pearce.*

[G. B. Shaw, *Pygmalion*]

In these examples, the propositions used in (a) are implicitly mentioned in the responses in (b). These cases of mention are clearly not reported speech, in the sense that they are not intended to inform anyone of the content of a preceding utterance (such an intention would be pointless, since the utterance has only just occurred). Rather, they are meant to indicate that the preceding utterance has been heard and understood, and to express the hearer's immediate reaction to it. Apart from this instant echoing of a preceding utterance, there are also cases of echoic mention that are less directly related to what has gone before—for instance, where the proposition mentioned is not the one just uttered but what the hearer takes to be one of its pragmatic implications:

(31) a. *I'm a reasonable man.*
      b. *Whereas I'm not (is what you're implying).*

There are cases where what is echoed is not an immediately preceding utterance, but one that occurred some time ago:

(32) *It absolutely poured. I know, it was going to rain (you told me so). I should listen to you more often.*

There are cases of echoing where the sources are very distant indeed:

(33) *Jack elbowed Bill, and Bill punched him on the nose. He should have turned the other cheek (as it says in the Bible). Maybe that would have been the best thing to do.*

There are also what one might call anticipatory echoes:

(34) *You're going to do something silly. You're free to do what you want (you'll tell me). Maybe so. But you still ought to listen to me.*

Such cases of echoic mention are extremely common in ordinary conversation, and considerably more varied than we have time to show here. In each case, the speaker's choice of words, his tone (doubtful, questioning, scornful, contemptuous, approving, and so on), and the immediate context, all play a part in indicating his own attitude to the proposition mentioned. In particular, the speaker may echo a remark in such a way as to suggest that he finds it untrue, inappropriate, or irrelevant:

(35) *'You take an eager interest in that gentleman's concerns', said Darcy in a less tranquil tone, and with a heightened colour.*
      'Who that knows what his misfortunes have been, can help feeling an interest in him?'
      'His misfortunes! repeated Darcy contemptuously, 'yes, his misfortunes have been great indeed.'
      [Jane Austen; *Pride and Prejudice*]

(36) *'Now just attend to me for a bit, Mr. Pitch, or Witch, or Stitch, or whatever your name is.'*
      'My name is Pinch', observed Tom. 'Have the goodness to call me by it.'
      'What! You mustn't ever be called out of your name, mustn't you?' cried Jonas. 'Pauper 'prentices are looking up, I think. Ecod, we manage 'em a little better in the city!'
      [Charles Dickens, *Martin Chuzzlewit*]

There are also cases where what is echoed is not a proposition expressed by an utterance, but a thought imputed by the speaker to the hearer:

(37)   *Elinor looked at him with greater astonishment than ever. She begant to think he must be in liquor; . . . and with this impression she immediately rose, saying,*

'Mr Willoughby, I advise you at present to return to Combe—I am not at leisure to remain with you longer.—Whatever your business may be with me, it will be better recollected and explained tomorrow.'

'I understand you,' he replied, with an expressive smile, and a voice perfectly calm, 'yes, I am very drunk.—A pint of porter with my cold beef at Marlborough was enough to over-set me.'

[Jane Austen, *Sense and Sensibility*]

We have presented examples (35)–(37) as cases of echoic mention; we could equally well have presented them as cases of irony. The utterances in question are patently ironical: The speaker mentions a proposition in such a way as to make clear that he rejects it as ludicrously false, inappropriate, or irrelevant. For the hearer, understanding such an utterance involves both realizing that it is a case of mention rather than use, and also recognizing the speaker's attitude to the proposition mentioned. The whole interpretation depends on this double recognition. Recovery of the implicatures (38) for (35), (39) for (36) and (40) for (37) will follow automatically:

(38)   *He has not been the victim of misfortunes.*

(39)   *You have no right to demand that I call you by your proper name.*

(40)   *I am not drunk.*

Not only it is unnecessary to appeal to the notion of figurative meaning in dealing with the interpretation of (35)–(37) [and their implicatures (38)–(40)], any account in terms of figurative meaning will actually be incomplete. Suppose we treat (38)–(40) along traditional lines, as figurative senses rather than implicatures of (35)–(37). Then either the proposition that constitutes the figurative meaning must be understood as USED, and the status of the utterance as echoic mention will disappear; or it will be understood as MENTIONED, and since it is not patently false, inappropriate or irrelevant, there will be no way of explaining the speaker's attitude of mockery or disapproval. Either way, an account in terms of figurative meaning will necessarily overlook a central and obvious aspect of the interpretation of the utterance.

The analysis we are proposing, although it involves implicatures, differs from Grice's in at least two important respects. Grice sees violation of the maxim of truthfulness as both a necessary and a sufficient condition for ironical interpretation. When an utterance is patently false, he argues, the hearer interprets it as implicating the contradictory of what was literally said. We have already mentioned one problem with this account: Unlike standard implicatures, the "implicature" carried by an ironical utterance must be substituted for, rather than added to, what was literally said, because otherwise the total message conveyed would be a contradiction. A more general problem is that violation of the maxim of truthfulness is in fact neither necessary nor sufficient for ironical interpretation. It is not necessary because of the existence of ironical questions, ironical understatements, and ironical references to the inappropriateness or irrelevance of an utterance rather than to the fact that it is false. Numerous illustrations have been given earlier in the chapter. Furthermore, as Grice himself points out (1978), patent falsehood or irrelevance is not a sufficient condition for irony—not every false or irrelevant utterance can be interpreted as ironical. What is missing from Grice's account is precisely the fact that ironical utterances are cases of mention, and that the propositions mentioned are ones that have been, or might have been, actually entertained by someone.

On our analysis, recognition of an ironical utterance as a case of mention is crucial to its interpretation. Once the hearer has recognized this, and has seen the speaker's attitude to the proposition mentioned, the implicatures in (38)–(40) follow by standard reasoning processes. They are typical cases of conversational implicature, and not problematic in any way. Our account of irony thus fits more naturally into Grice's overall framework than the account he himself proposes.

It might be suggested that there are two distinct types of irony: "echoic" irony, as illustrated earlier, whose interpretation involves a recognition of its status as mention, and "standard" irony, whose interpretations involves a recovery of its figurative meaning.[6] The problem with this suggestion is that there is a whole range of intermediate cases between the clear cases of echoic irony and the "standard" cases (see below). If there were two totally distinct processes, one based on mention and the other on figurative meaning, each resulting in a different type of irony, such intermediate cases should not exist.

It seems more accurate to say that all examples of irony are interpreted as echoic mentions, but that there are echoic mentions of many different degrees and types. Some are immediate echoes, and others delayed; some

---

[6] See for example Cutler (1974), who distinguishes between "spontaneous" (standard) and "provoked" (echoic) irony.

have their source in actual utterances, others in thoughts or opinions; some have a real source, others an imagined one; some are traceable back to a particular individual, whereas others have a vaguer origin. When the echoic character of the utterance is not immediately obvious, it is nevertheless suggested. Within this framework, we return to our original examples of irony, Sentences (1)–(4).

What lovely weather. Suppose that, as we were deciding to set off on our walk, someone told us that the weather was going to be lovely. It is quite clear that (1) is an ironical echo of this remark. Or suppose we have spent a rainy winter talking about the walks we will have in the summer sun. The echoic quality of (1), though its source is more distant, is nonetheless clear. Even when there is no prior utterance some vague echoing is still involved. One normally sets off for a walk in the hope or expectation of good weather: *What lovely weather* may simply echo these earlier high hopes. In all these cases the remark in (1) is interpreted along exactly the same lines. There is no question of a move from one figure of speech to another, or one type of irony to another, with quite different interpretation processes being involved; the only move is from obvious cases of echoic mention to much vaguer (and duller) varieties of the same thing.

It seems to be raining. Suppose someone had originally made this remark just as the rain was starting. By repeating it in the middle of a downpour, the speaker of (2) shows how laughable it was, in retrospect, to be in any doubt about whether it was really raining. Even when there is no prior utterance, (2) would have a similar effect: By pretending a degree of hesitancy which is completely inappropriate in the circumstances, it conjures up a picture of a quite ludicrous degree of inattention or failure to react.

It should be obvious without further contextualisation that (3) (*I'm glad we didn't bother to bring an umbrella*) and (4) (*Did you remember to water the flowers?*) are naturally interpreted as ironical echoes of advice on the one hand, and obsession on the other, which are both totally irrelevant in the circumstances. Whether the advice was actually given or not, whether the obsession was put into words or not, does not affect the status of the utterance as echoic mention, but only its degree of pointedness.

What we are claiming is that all standard cases of irony, and many that are nonstandard from the traditional point of view, involve (generally implicit) mention of a proposition. These cases of mention are interpreted as echoing a remark or opinion that the speaker wants to characterize as ludicrously inappropriate or irrelevant. This account makes it possible to give a more detailed description of a much wider range of examples of irony than the traditional approach can handle. In particular, it provides a unified treatment of ironical antiphrasis and meiosis, which are traditionally regarded as two quite different things. Moreover, it makes no appeal to the notion of figurative meaning, nor to any other notion not fully justified on independent grounds.[7]

6. SOME FURTHER ASPECTS OF IRONY

Our analysis sheds some light on a number of further problems with the treatment of irony. We shall mention five of them here. Four we shall deal with rather briefly: the relation between irony and parody, the "ironical tone of voice," the shifts in style or register that often occur in ironical utterances, and the moralistic overtones that they sometimes have. The last problem, which we shall look at in more detail, has to do with the fact that ironical utterances often seem to be aimed at a particular target or victim.

1. According to the traditional analysis, irony and parody involve quite different production and interpretation processes: Irony involves change of meaning, whereas parody involves imitation. There is no necessary relation between the two, and any similarities that exist must result from similarities in the attitudes of ironist and parodist. If irony is a type of mention, however, it is easy to account for the similarities and differences between irony and parody, and for the fact that intermediate cases exist. Both irony and parody are types of mention: Irony involves mention of propositions; parody involves mention of linguistic expressions. In other words, parody is related to direct discourse as irony is to free indirect discourse.

2. Within the traditional framework, the existence of an "ironical tone of voice" is rather puzzling. Why not also a "metaphorical tone of voice," a "synecdochical tone of voice," and so on? When irony is seen as a type of mention, the ironical tone of voice falls quite naturally into place: It is merely one of the variety of tones (doubtful, approving, contemptuous, and so on) that the speaker may use to indicate his attitude to the utterance or opinion mentioned.

3. It is well known that ironical utterances often involve a switch in style or register. For example, it is quite common to show that one's utterance is ironical by changing to a more formal or pompous style:

---

[7] It is widely accepted, though not entirely uncontroversial, that free indirect speech may be used to ironic effect (see McHale 1978, p. 275–276 and references therein). What is lacking in the extensive literature on this subject is any attempt, on the one hand, to explain why this connection should exist, and on the other hand, to construct a unified theoretical account of irony around it. In this article, we hope to have shown that such an attempt is worth making.

(41)   *That's done it—you've broken the vase. I hope you're satisfied, my lady.*

There is nothing in the traditional account of irony that would lead one to expect such shifts. However, they can be quite easily explained on the assumption that irony involves echoic mention of a real or imagined utterance or opinion. [In (41) the speaker is echoing the sort of deferential remark that he implies the hearer is expecting.] As in free indirect discourse, the implicit mention of a proposition sometimes involves mention of an expression.

4. From the point of view of the traditional theory, there is a strange asymmetry in the uses of irony. One is much more likely to say *How clever* to imply "How stupid," or *How graceful* to imply "How clumsy," than the other way round. This connection of irony with implications of failure to reach a certain standard has often been noted. There is no explanation for it in terms of the traditional process of meaning-inversion, which should be able to work just as well in one direction as in the other. However, on our account there is a straightforward explanation. Standards or rules of behavior are culturally defined, commonly known, and frequently invoked; they are thus always available for echoic mention. On the other hand, critical judgements are particular to a given individual or occasion, and are thus only occasionally available for mention. Hence, it is always possible to say ironically of a failure *That was a great success,* since it is normal to hope for the success of a given course of action. However, to say of a success *That was a failure* without the irony falling flat, the speaker must be able to refer back to prior doubts or fears, which he can then echo ironically. In the face of an imperfect reality, it is always possible to make ironical mention of the norm. In the face of a perfect reality, there must be past doubts or fears to echo if the mention of a critical judgment is to count as ironical.

5. The claim that ironical utterances are aimed at a particular target or victim is based on a variety of intuitions, sometimes clear-cut, sometimes less so. Within the traditional framework, there are two quite separate processes that might account for this aspect of irony.

On the one hand, every utterance whose literal sense would carry overtones of approval will have a corresponding figurative sense with critical overtones. The intended victim, on this account, would be the object of the criticism. For example, if (42) has the figurative meaning (43), then Fitzgerald would be the victim of the irony in (42):

(42)   *Fitzgerald plays by the rules.*

(43)   *Fitzgerald cheats.*

On the other hand, the person to whom the ironical utterance was apparently addressed may fail to detect its figurative meaning. The immediate result will be that any third parties present (who immediately detect the figurative meaning and are thus revealed as the true addressees of the irony) will feel drawn into a conspiracy with the speaker, at the expense of the person to whom the remark was overtly made. For example, if (44) has the figurative meaning (45), and if Billy fails to notice this, then on this account Billy becomes the intended victim of the irony in (44):

(44)   *Go on, Billy, you're nearly there!*

(45)   *Go on, Billy, you're nowhere near!*

These two processes may on occasion select the same victim. This would happen, for example, if (46) has the figurative meaning (47), and Jeremy fails to detect it:

(46)   *Go on, Jeremy, your story's really interesting.*

(47)   *Don't go on, Jeremy. Your story's really boring.*

Someone who restricts himself to examples of this last type, as happens rather too often, would get the misleading impression that the traditional theory can provide a unified account of how an ironical utterance chooses its victim. However, anyone who looks at the differences between examples like (42) and (44) will immediately see that two quite different processes are involved, and that they are not necessarily related at all.

Moreover, it is easy to think of quite ordinary examples that are not accounted for in terms of either process. Suppose the following remark is made ironically to someone who dislikes classical music:

(48)   *Of course all classical music sounds the same!*

On the one hand, the figurative meaning of this remark has no critical content; on the other hand, in normal circumstances the hearer is unlikely to mistake the speaker's intentions. In this case, neither process will apply, and there is no immediate explanation within the traditional framework for the clear intuition that the hearer of (48) is also its intended victim.

Within our framework it would be possible to define two processes that would correspond closely to those used in the traditional account. Instead of figurative meanings, there would be pragmatic implications or implicatures which might carry critical overtones; instead of a failure to distinguish literal from figurative meanings there would be a failure to distinguish use from mention. The framework we are proposing is thus at least as explanatory in this respect as the traditional framework.

However, the analysis of irony as a type of mention does involve a quite central claim which has no equivalent in the traditional framework, and which by itself provides a more satisfactory explanation for a much wider range of intuitions. Within our framework, an ironical remark will have as natural target the originators, real or imagined, of the utterances or opinions being echoed. If the remark also carries critical overtones, or if the hearer fails to detect the speaker's ironical intent, the ironical effect may of course be reinforced, but it may equally well be achieved when neither of these conditions is present.

In example (46) the victim is Jeremy, because the utterance echoes an opinion of himself that he expects to hear. In (44) the target is Billy, because the utterance echoes an opinion imputed to him, that he is nearly there. In (42) the victims are all those who think or claim that Fitzgerald plays by the rules: Fitzgerald himself, and in certain circumstances the hearer too, will be a victim in virtue of this. In (48), it is the hearer who is the victim, because the utterance echoes an opinion he is believed to hold. In (1), if the weather forecast has predicted good weather, it is this forecast that is echoed in the remark "*What lovely weather*"; on the other hand, if no one in particular has actually made such a prediction, our account correctly predicts that the irony is not aimed at any particular victim.

The analysis of irony as a type of mention thus makes it possible to predict which ironical utterances will have a particular victim, and who that victim will be. When the utterance or opinion echoed has no specific originator, there will be no victim; when there is a specific, recognizable originator, he will be the victim. Thus, when the speaker echoes himself, the irony will be self-directed; when he echoes his hearer, the result will be sarcasm. In the traditional framework, the ad hominem character of irony is a function of the propositional content of the utterance; in our framework, it is a function of the ease with which some originator of the opinion echoed can be recognized. The many cases where these two accounts make different predictions, as in (48), should make it possible to choose between them.

7. A FINAL EXAMPLE

In Shakespeare's *Julius Caesar,* Act 3, Scene 2, Mark Antony says six times that Brutus is an honorable man. This is frequently cited as an example of irony, but on closer examination it raises a number of problems for the traditional theory. The first time Mark Antony says "Brutus is an honorable man,'' there is no perceptible irony; the inclination is to take it as a propitiatory remark, suitable to an occasion where Mark Antony is about to give Caesar's funeral oration with Brutus's permission. It is not until he says it for the third time that the ironical interpretation is really forced on us, and from then on it increases in intensity. In the traditional framework, we would have to say that at the second or third repetition the literal meaning is replaced by the opposite figurative meaning—there can be no intermediate stage between literal and figurative interpretation.

In our framework, Mark Antony has to be seen from the very first as MENTIONING the proposition that Brutus is an honorable man. He first mentions it in a conciliatory tone of voice. No doubt it is not his own most personal opinion, but he is prepared to put it forward in a spirit of appeasement, echoing the sentiments of Brutus's supporters. Then, each time he repeats it, he mentions it in the context of further facts which make it clear that he is dissociating himself from it, more strongly each time: The irony is first hinted at, then strengthened, then forced home. Mark Antony carries his audience with him, through a series of successively more hostile attitudes to a proposition which itself remains unchanged from start to finish. At every stage the proposition is mentioned, and not used.

This example brings us back to our preliminary remark that the concept of irony itself is open to reconsideration, not just in its intension but also in its extension. In classical terms an utterance either is ironical or it is not. The picture we are suggesting is different: Although an utterance either is or is not a mention, a mention may be more or less ironical, with many intermediary and complex shades between stereotypical cases of irony and other kinds of echoic mention.

8. CONCLUSION

As an undersized boy trips over his own feet while coming in last in the school sports, one spectator turns to another and remarks:

(49)   *It's a bird—it's a plane—it's Superman.*

This remark is clearly ironical. Because it is an actual quotation, it fits quite straightforwardly into our framework as a case of echoic mention; however, it poses considerable problems for both standard semantic and pragmatic accounts of irony. Within these frameworks, it would have to be analyzed as carrying the figurative meaning or conversational implicature in (50):

(50)   *It's not a bird, it's not a plane, it's not Superman.*

But if (49) figuratively means or conversationally implicates (50)—which is literally true—it is hard to see why it would also be taken as a joke. There is a further problem for Grice's approach, since the implicature in (50) is completely uninformative in the context, and would itself violate the maxims of conversation. Our proposed analysis, by virtue of its ability to handle (49) and similar examples, proves both more explanatory and more general than either of the traditional alternatives.

Compared with traditional semantic approaches, Grice's approach to irony is radically pragmatic: The proper interpretation of an ironical utterance is assumed to consist solely of conversational implicatures, logically derived according to pragmatic patterns of inference. If what we have been arguing in this chapter is correct, then Grice's and other similar approaches to irony (and more generally to figures of speech) are too "radical" in one respect, and not "radical" enough in another.

In the first place, ironical utterances do have one essential semantic property: They are cases of mention, and are thus semantically distinguishable from cases where the same proposition is used in order to make an assertion, ask a question, and so on. As has been seen, this semantic distinction is crucial to the explanation of how ironical utterances are interpreted, and indeed why they exist. Without this distinction the echoic character of irony will be overlooked, and it will thus be impossible to make the correct prediction that where no echoing is discernible, an utterance, however false, uninformative or irrelevant, will never be ironical. In this respect, then, a purely logical-pragmatic approach to irony is too radical.

In a second respect, though, a logical-pragmatic approach to irony remains too close to a semantic one. In both cases it is assumed that the interpretation of an ironical utterance consists solely of propositions (whether entailments or implicatures) intended by the speaker and recoverable by the hearer. Now it has long been recognized that the understanding of figures of speech, and of irony in particular, has nonpropositional, nondeductive aspects. An ironical utterance carries suggestions of attitude—and sometimes, as in (49), of images—which cannot be made entirely explicit in propositional form. In this respect a logical-pragmatic model does not provide a better description—let alone a better explanation—than a semantic model. On the other hand, our analysis of irony as a case of echoic mention crucially involves the evocation of an attitude—that of the speaker to the proposition mentioned. This attitude may imply a number of propositions, but it is not reducible to a set of propositions. Our analysis thus suggests that a logical-pragmatic theory dealing with the interpretation of utterances as an inferential process must be supplemented by what could be called a "rhetorical-pragmatic," or "rhetorical" theory dealing with evocation.[8]

To conclude: The value of current pragmatic theory, as inspired by Grice's work, lies mainly in the fact that it relieves semantics of a number of problems for which it can provide a more general and explanatory treatment. However, in the case of figurative utterances, the move from semantics to logical pragmatics merely creates a number of new problems, without providing solutions to many of the problems raised by the traditional semantic approach. Taking irony as an example, we have tried to show that, given an adequate semantic analysis of ironical utterances as echoic mentions, the problems with both the traditional semantic account and Grice's pragmatic account dissolve away. A number of problems still remain; what we are suggesting is that logical pragmatics must in turn be relieved of these problems, which can be given a more general and explanatory treatment within the rhetorical component of a radically extended pragmatic theory.

REFERENCES

Banfield, A. (1973). Narrative style and the grammar of direct and indirect speech. *Foundations of Language,* **10**, 1–39.

Bever, T., Katz, J. J., and Langendoen, D. T. (Eds.). (1976). *An Integrated Theory of Linguistic Abilities.* New York: Crowell.

Cole, P. (Ed.). (1978). *Syntax and Semantics 9: Pragmatics.* New York: Academic Press.

Cole, P., and Morgan, J. (Eds.). (1975). *Syntax and Semantics 3: Speech Acts.* New York: Academic Press.

Cutler, A. (1974). On saying what you mean without meaning what you say. In *Papers from the Tenth Regional Meeting of the Chicago Linguistics Society.* Department of Linguistics, University of Chicago. Pp. 117–127.

Grice, H. P. (1975). Logic and conversation. In P. Cole and J. Morgan (Eds.), *Syntax and Semantics 3: Speech Acts.* New York: Academic Press. Pp. 41–58.

Grice, H. P. (1978). Further notes on logic and conversation. In P. Cole (Ed.), *Syntax and Semantics 9: Pragmatics.* New York: Academic Press. Pp. 113–127.

Harnish, R. M. (1976). Logical form and implicature. In T. Bever, J. J. Katz, and D. T. Langendoen (Eds.), *An Integrated Theory of Linguistic Abilities.* New York: Crowell. Pp. 313–391.

McHale, B. (1978). Free indirect discourse: A survey of recent accounts. *PTL: A Journal for Descriptive Poetics and the Theory of Literature,* **3**, 249–287.

Quintilian. (1966). [*Institutio Oratoria*] (H. E. Butler, Trans.). Loeb Classical Library. London: Heinemann.

---

[8] The psychological basis of this rhetorical theory is discussed in Sperber (1975a), and Sperber and Wilson (forthcoming).

Sperber, D. (1975a). *Rethinking Symbolism*. Cambridge: Cambridge University Press.

Sperber, D. (1975b). Rudiments de rhétorique cognitive, *Poétique, 23*, 389–415.

Sperber, D., and Wilson, D. (Forthcoming). *Foundations of Rhetorical Theory*.

Turner, G. W. (1973). *Stylistics*. London: Penguin Books.

Wilson, D., and Sperber, D. (1979 and forthcoming). On Grice's theory of conversation. (French version in *Communications, 30*, 80–94. English version to appear in P. Werth (Ed.) *Conversation, Speech and Discourse*. London: Croom Helm.)

Index